I0833963

HOTSPUR.

A Tale

OF THE

OLD DUTCH MANOR.

BY

MANSFIELD T. WALWORTH,

AUTHOR OF "LULU."

New-York:

CARLETON, PUBLISHER, 413 *BROADWAY.*

M DCCC LXIV.

A TALE

OF THE

OLD DUTCH MANOR.

CHAPTER I.

The distant, tinkling bell of memory recalls the town of C——. The noble old State of New York boasts of no fairer garden spot within its broad limits. The elms love to adorn the streets of C——. There their graceful branches droop lower, their symmetrical trunks shoot higher, and their foliage wears in summer a more emerald lustre than in any other portion of the State. Like faithful sentinels they guard the many aristocratic mansions of the wealthy, and the neat white cottages of the middling classes. They bear themselves as if they were proud of their character of protectors against the fierce rays of the summer sun. Noble, old trees—many a bright intellect has studied and blessed your beauty; many a lovely eye detected through your branches the silver stars of God.

A blue lake lies not far from the fair town of C——. And a range of forest covered hills stretches away in the distance to teach the inhabitants variety of thought and grandeur of purpose. The town is the paradise of fruit trees which wave to the passing breeze their luscious burdens of blushing peaches and golden apples.

One dreary winter within the memory of many now living a strange family arrived in the town of C——, and purchased a furnished mansion of large proportion and surrounded by a large and highly cultivated garden, which in summer bloomed with roses and teemed with clusters of ripening grapes and rarest fruit. The white haired father of this new family was a calm, dignified gentleman of sixty who bore the quiet and euphonious name of Grayson. Rumor gave him the reputation of being a retired merchant from the metropolis, comfortable in circumstances, and generous and hospitable in his style of living. Shortly after his arrival, he presented to the clergyman of the Episcopalian church of C——, a letter from the bishop of the diocese, commending him to the good will and charity of all good churchmen. On the ensuing Sunday he appeared among the quiet and solemn worshipers at the beautiful and Gothic chapel of St. Paul, attended by his son and daughter, both apparently between the ages of twenty and twenty-five, and remarkably elegant and stylish in appearance and dress. This cultivated and agreeable trio gradually and naturally became acquainted with and became a part of the society of C——. Their cultivated intellects, their familiarity with European capitals, their gentle manners, and their generous hospitality gave them ready access to the hearts of their fellow churchmen. Their connection with the chapel of St. Paul, however, was no recommendation for them to the large and gloomy congregation of the Presbyterian church of C——. By this Calvinistic society they were soon rated as follows: "*high church; wordly; wine bibbers.*"

The chariot wheels of Time ploughed heavily through the snow drifts of a long winter; but emerged at last into the warm sunshine of an unusually lovely spring. The venerable dress-maker, dame nature, was already fitting her delicate green mantles to the elms of C——, and displaying her delicate patterns upon the lilac bushes. While from the swinging branches of the trees, the happy birds trilled love notes or warbled hymns of praise to God. Soon all was hushed before the queenly tread of evening; and the western clouds grew sombre; and then the holy stars came out to watch while Nature slept.

Come with me now, kind reader, for the solemn clock of C—— is striking slowly out, on the still air, the hour of twelve; the hour of silence and of dreams. Tread with me softly up the graveled walk to the proud mansion's door. Fear not at this late hour to try the ivory knob upon the door. Come in—I hold the key of memory.

The inmates of the mansion sleep; and our soft footfall on the carpet will awaken none. The dim hall lamp now guides us past the drawing-room and the wide dining-hall to a far room, where a lone watcher still remains awake, and dressed and thoughtful. Enter we then with cautions step, this boudoir of this fair and gentle maiden, and seek a spot behind yon drooping curtain of crimson silk, where we may witness unsuspected and respectful her movements in her privacy. The kneeling figure at that small table of carved oak, over which a plain white cloth is spread, and on which rest two lights in polished silver candlesticks, is the figure of the fair and graceful lily who revels in the name, Blonde Grayson. Aye! in her infancy so fair was she, so gentle was her light blue eye, so soft her golden hair, they named her "Blonde." And when the young girl reached maturity, and the rich blood of sweet sixteen mantled her cheek, and the snowy whiteness would not leave her polished brow, or her thin Grecian nose, or her smooth dimpled chin; and her soft, gleaming hair waved back in little ripples from her brow, and then fell mantle-like in golden showers about her form, they still would call her "Blonde." And now, when twenty-four summers have ripened her beauty, and the gathering wisdom of experience in the world's ways, and the light of many books have set the seal of earnest thought upon her brow, how worthy she appears to bear the gentle title "Blonde." She is above the medium height of women; but her graceful figure bears it well, and every movement is a charm. She will never, if she lives to the full age of sixty, make one movement that shall not seem consonant with poetry and music. Her style is almost slender; and her face quite oval; and her fingers tapering to the pink nails; and her feet dainty. She has contrived to gather her wonderful luxuriance of hair in some modern braids upon the back of her classic head, but the ripples of gold she cannot straighten out, as they commence at the part of her hair, and assert their rights even to the very end of the luxuriant mass. Her eyebrows are very faintly traced, but the eyelashes deepen in color till they seem at times to cast weird shadows upon the large blue eyes so full, at times, of sweetness or of mystery. Her lips are not the full voluptuous lips of Venus; but thin and white and spiritual, like Psyche. But the smile which reveals the small pearl teeth is radiant, and small dimples come and go with it. But she is kneeling now before the Eternal; and the open book, upon the oaken stand between the silver candlesticks, holds her eyes captive as she prays. God bless her, for she loves her faith, and oft times yearns for Heaven. Study her dress while yet she is absorbed, for when she rises again and turns, you will no longer remember it in the more powerful attraction of her face and witching eyes. Her slate-colored merino is belted at her slender waist with a silken ribbon of the same mild hue, secured by a gold buckle. The dress is high necked, and the sleeves full from the shoulders to the wrist, where they become quite small to fit tightly and accurately to her arm. The sleeves are slashed, too, and through the openings gleam the snow-white muslin under-sleeves. A standing collar of gathered muslin circles her white throat, and is secured by a small white lava breast-pin on which two doves are delicately carved. A row of slate-colored buttons extends from her breast-pin to her waist-buckle, and similar buttons circle her sleeves at the wrists. Then from her slender waist, the full, slate-colored merino sweeps to the floor most gracefully as she kneels.

Her arms rest upon the oaken table on either side of her book of devotion, and she moves her lips in prayerful whispers. Some good priest had told her many years ago in her childhood that God loves not a sleepy prayer. That he demands of his children to seek his throne of grace in the full possession of all their faculties, and to employ their last sleepy moments in their own worldly affairs. Thus she always finished her devotions in good time, and employed her last conscious moments in arranging her room or reading her correspondence. Who shall dispute God's right to the attentive and recollected prayer of full consciousness?

Retire a trifle further, gentle reader, behind this crimson silk curtain; for Blonde Grayson rises from her prayers, and moves toward the black marble centre-table, whereon a shaded lamp is shedding its mellow rays. Here, in the full blaze of light, is her work basket, through which a narrow blue ribbon is woven, and in which may be seen her work and scissors and bodkin, with two unopened letters which she has yet to read. Seating herself beside this black marble table and reclining comfortably against the padded back of her cosy rocking chair, she draws her work basket towards her, and studies the address on the first letter. Ah! She recognizes the writer in the clean, running handwriting of her distant female friend. You may know it is a woman's letter as she spreads it open before her by those wonderful crossed lines, which the weary, sleepy eye must separate and decipher. Perdiction seize the damsel who first invented the crossing of lines in a letter. As Blonde peruses the mysterious contents of her friend's letter, her varying emotions flutter across her lovely features, and now and then the cunning dimples steal out in her cheek, the constant attendants of her smiles. And now the mysterious interlacing of crossed lines being all satisfactorily interpreted, she turns to the remaining letter in her basket.

"Who can *this* be from?" she exclaims, glancing at the

modest white envelope which bears the well known post mark of the town of C——. An unknown hand, and a gentleman's. The drowsy god who taps so gently on her eyelids, vanishes from her room in an instant. Mystery and midnight! Something very interesting gleams out from those bold, manly tracings of the pen. She bows her golden hair nearer and nearer to the paper, and surprise flashes across her face, and then a blush, deepening every instant as she reads. There is a fluttering, nervous manner in her movements now, so unlike the calm composure of the last half hour, as she bends her head still lower in the interest of this strange and unexpected letter. At last she places the finished letter upon the black marble table, and then quickly presses her fair white hands upon her closed eyes, as if to isolate the exciting thought from all external objects.

"How strange; how strange!" she murmurs to herself, at length, dropping her fair hands into her lap, "I never even *dreamed* of this."

She raised the letter from the table again, and once more carefully studied its contents. Then as she replaced it in its envelope, and deposited it in her work basket, she smiled one of her dimpled, pleased smiles, and murmured softly,

"That gifted, earnest soul *loves* me, and I never thought of love. I cannot but admire him; he is talented, handsome, noble and generous—excellent family position; wealthy—but only think—he is younger than me—yes!—one—two—*three* years younger than me. Oh! what shall I say to him. If I encourage him in my answer, he says he will come bounding to my side like a lion. But if I chill him in my note, what will he do? I must have time to reflect—I cannot wound him, he has been so kind to me—but then he is so young—and his family, what will they say?—they are as blue and intolerant toward churchmen as sin—indeed, indeed it is none of my doing. And he prefers me to all those pretty young girls he is with so much."

Blonde glanced quickly into the long mirror opposite her chair, and smiled as she studied herself in the glass.

"I thought I was growing old—what does this young man find in me to admire, I wonder. He must be twenty-one and I am twenty-four last month. Oh! he is so ardent—his words fairly burn. But what did I hear?—they say he is a little wild—in college he did something or other which gave his father much trouble. But then young men will be young men the world over, and I do despise these tame young saints.

Three admirers have I had and not one who seemed as desperate as this young man. His language thrills me—he declares that God has given me the destiny of his soul. That is wrong, but he meant no harm. How graceful his figure is: and he is the best waltzing partner I ever knew. But then—but then I must have some one older than myself that I can look up to and respect. I know he will make his way in the world—every one calls him bright, and his eye flashes like an eagle. Intellect is hereditary in that family."

Blonde Grayson studied long and intensely, resting her cheek upon her closed hand. She was ambitious of position and affluence in life: but with her dreams mingled earnest desires and sighs for true and constant affection. Without the last she feared to embark upon the sea of matrimonial life. Her friends had formed alliances to secure wealth and distinction; and for a time all was clear sailing and a calm sky. But alas! her memory pointed too faithfnlly to uncongenial matches, indifference, desertion, lonely agony, contempt, and lingering death. The spectre, experience, ever arose before her, shaking his bony finger and solemnly muttering *beware! beware!* The friend of her girlish days, the pride and beauty of her neighborhood, had fled in horror from the demoniac vices and the ruffian hate of "a most excellent and wealthy match." The great world's opinion was a fool's opinion, and her poor, gentle, lonely friend was slumbering beneath the sods of the valley, and the eye of God blazed vengeance over the grave of His persecuted and heart broken angel. No wonder, that every breath of love which floated to the ear of Blonde Grayson met the cold surface of the shield, caution. No wonder that her dreams of wealth and power were sometimes traversed by a shudder.

Again and again had she refused the ardent suitors who were attracted by her rare charms and her sparkling intellect, because she had discovered, or fancied she had discovered, some overweening passion or selfishness which might render her married life only an existence of misery and disappointment. But with all this experience, and with all this timidity of approaching the matrimonial altar, she nevertheless was conscious of a nature which waits to find a worthy object about which to cling, and on which to place the priceless offerings, unbounded confidence and love. Thus every offer which came to her made her expectant heart to vibrate; and from its hidden casket in her soul stole forth the patient elfin, Hope, to watch the movements of the new suitor. But the triple ideal which haunted her dreams—wealth, and rank and heart—seemed never to approach her; and she turned away to maidenhood again, lonely, dejected, and weary of the search. But now this beautiful dreamer, with her mature judgment and her angel beauty, rising from her bowed attitude of prayer, discovered in her little work-basket all she had wished for—rank, and wealth, and heart. His family was of the noblest in the State, his claim to wealth undoubted, and his heart was in his eyes. His generous impulses, his warm, self-sacrificing friendships, and his ardent reverence for woman were known to all. If man could ever love, he could and would. It was the surprise of this offer, when she had expected to watch in some one gradual and dawning love; it was the youthful character of this suitor, when she had expected to look up to mature age, and not down to ardent youth, which perplexed her. For three years of seniority in a gifted woman are often a gulf of separation from a young man of twenty-one. When he was a schoolboy of fourteen, she was a belle in society, with her circle of admirers. Now he had grown tall, and brilliant, and eagle-eyed, and her eyes looked up to his when his strong arm whirled her in the dance; but she felt older, and she knew more of the world; the arts of concealment, and prudence, and caution, were hers, not his.

Other thoughts, too, possessed her; other apprehensions were vexing her brain. A girl of twenty-four knows much, hears much, of young men in her own circle of society. He was a dare-devil. He knew not the precise limit between discretion and fear. He seemed to despise both words as synonymous; and she knew of occasions when this mistake had brought him into trouble. Could she curb his impetuous nature without offending him? Would his fire burn low till it was wanted for serviceable purposes? Was there no danger that his ardent and generous impulses might lead him, where so many lovely natures fall, into the whirlpool dissipation. Blonde Grayson sat long and late in he comfortable seat, with the mellow lamp light illumining her soft, white hands and her blue eyes so thoughtful and so puzzled. Once she took her heart in her hand, as she reached forward for her pen. But the precious pearl, slid quickly back into her bosom, at the beckoning of caution.

"Oh!—if I could play him on my hook as I have others, till I know him better and have proved him: but I feel that he is not one to be trifled with. He has come to me like a meteor: so will he go—I feel it—I know it. Brief as my acquaintance has been I know he is not like most men; a slight goes to his heart like a dagger.

"How quietly he came here, last Sunday, and asked to accompany me to St. Paul's. He smiled when he said his family would 'shake him,' for daring to attend my church. He said he feared nobody in religion. I know he would go to St. Paul's —*that* matter would never be in the way. I always knew he *liked* me: but I surely never dreamed that he would write me such a note."

At last, Blonde Grayson arose from her seat and sought her writing desk, in an adjoining room. She brought it quickly in, and placed it on the black marble table in the mellow lamp light; and opening it, she took out delicate note paper and a pen. Then, seating herself once more, she bowed her golden hair, and wrote these lines.

Past midnight.

MR. HENRY LANSING:—Your surprise letter is open before me. I am as one who walks in dreams. The unexpected language of your letter thrills me. The burning words reveal the sincerity and earnestness of your story. They seem to convey that most profound and touching sentiment of manly love which the expectant heart of a true woman craves from one who has her secret thoughts. You bear in the world the reputation of a noble and generous nature; and the affection which you have a right to claim from woman, by virtue of that nature, must be utterly devoid of selfishness, and, like your own love, spontaneous and self existent. If I were to accept this unexpected and honorable offer of your hand, I tell you, in sincerity of heart, what I would be doing. I would be accepting your hand, not from any love which ever existed in my heart for you, (for I never even *dreamed* of such a thing) but simply because you are a noble, high-toned gentleman, combining in your worldly position all those gifts which tend to make a woman happy and satisfied in life. Is this the love you would have? My estimate of you tells me *no!* If I have read you aright, during the happy but brief acquaintance of three months, you would not have a love which sprang from such selfish motives. I never thought of love, during our brief acquaintance. Can you then understand my surprise when a letter came from you bearing the fresh, dewy flower of the heart? I am bewildered as one to whom a priceless treasure is offered which I feel I have no right to accept. Oh! had I known you longer, God only can tell what might have sprung up in my heart. To me you have been a new acquaintance in a strange town; your courtesy winning my regard; your noble traits of character developing day by day. I appeal to your generous nature to bear me witness, that I have never in our intercourse employed words, or glances, or manner, that could be construed into dawning evidences of love.

Your words of fire rêveal to me that you and I worship the same high ideal. Love with us must be inferior only to the love we owe our Eternal Father—it must reach beyond this fleeting life, to a life hereafter—it must be the love which glows through eternity, under the protecting hand of God. Time, and change, and death, cannot dissever it. Be this ideal of the heart right or be it wrong, neither you nor I can cease to believe it, for it is the dream of our natures. Would you have me then deceive you by accepting your offer, which comes to my heart like a gentle shower upon an unprepared garden. I know you would not. You will respect me—will you not—for the truth which flows from my pen? You will remember me kindly—will you not—for the candor which dictates these lines? May the angels of God brighten your pathway ever.

BLONDE GRAYSON.

CHAPTER II.

BLONDE GRAYSON slept long and heavily, a leaden, dreamless sleep or stupor. The unusually late sitting of the past night so wearied her, that when the maid came to awaken her in the morning at eight, she requested not to be disturbed, as she was too unwell to attend at breakfast. That morning her alarm clock on the mantle marked the hour of ten before she arose. Then as the last chains of sleep fell suddenly off her, she arose and opened her window upon an elm-guarded street, and breathed the balmy air of the hastening spring. The draught seemed to revive her, for a dull sense of headache had arisen from the bed with her, and she now wrapped a blue merino robe about her, and sank into her easy chair for reflection or reverie. She had shaken out her golden wavy hair, so that now it fell around her on every side like a mantle, loosely, carelessly, as one would fancy an angel's style to be. No roses flushed her cheek now, and her luminous blue eyes looked sad; and in them reigned troubled thoughts, loneliness, and something like regret. A warm, enthusiastic heart, in all probability fluttering with the timidity and freshness of a first love, had opened itself to her gaze, and in all its earnestness and abandonment of pride had said to her, "Take me and love me, or I die." It was a manly heart, she felt assured; and yet it was gentle in its newly found passion, and it had freely given all to her. Though the excitement and interest of a marriage offer were not new to her; still there was kindness enough in her nature to make her feel sympathy for this brilliant young man who had sent his heart—through his letter, fluttering to her feet. She had frankly answered him—"I never thought of love." This she knew would pierce his eager, expectant heart like a dagger. It seemed to her, as she sat so carelessly and languidly in her chair with her golden hair falling upon her blue robe, and straying away over her pale cheeks, that fate had forced her to commit a cruel deed. She never could exult, as many girls have done, that her beauty had given her another heart to string upon her chain of conquests. She only felt that her letter would estrange in all probabiiity, from her society, one who had welcomed her to a strange town, with all those delicate words and attentions which stamp themselves indelibly on the memory of every true heart.

A true woman appreciates a friend: and Blonde had been conscious of more sympathy of mind and heart with Henry Lansing, than with any one of her new acquaintances in C——, save only her bosom friend, Clara Peyton. And now she anticipated that she was about to lose his genial companionship, and the stirring melody of his ringing laugh, because he had learned to love her too much. It was barely possible, that, like other temperaments which had fallen under her notice, his disposition might lead him to find more of hope than despair in her carefully worded reply. For had she not written, "Oh! had I known you longer, God only can tell what might have sprung up in my heart." But she feared otherwise; she feared that the high and delicious hopes which dictated his offer would fall at once, and gloomily into the deepest despair; and complete isolation from her society would ensue.

She was perfectly conscious that her reply had been dictated by principle and duty; but might she not have infused into the refusal of his offer, something more of hope for the future; something that would retain him in her presence, and give her opportunity to know him better, and also to test the dormant feelings of her own heart. She was more perplexed now in the bright spring morning as to her own purposes in his regard than she had been at the lone, thoughtful hour of midnight—for some wonderful chords in the human heart vibrate when we learn that we are loved. The beautiful tendril, gratitude, reaches forth its tiny hands to grasp the being who loves us, and bright eyed pride rejoices. She was already curious to know the effect of her letter upon him; and she feared, hoped, doubted in rapid succession. Then she stood up before her mirror, and commenced to run her comb slowly and thoughtfully through her beautiful mantle of hair.

A clear, sweet, youthful voice suddenly echoed along the great hall of the mansion, as if a bird had entered for an informal call; up, up the staircase it came nearer and nearer, caroling its high notes like the tree songsters, harmonious and happy.

"Jewels of pearly dew
Glitter upon my breast;
And my hair is decked
With the new blown flower
Away! from thy dreamy rest."

Then a heavy sigh and an exclamation at the interminable length of the stairs was heard—then quickly beating footsteps along the upper hall—and then Blonde heard her bed-room door burst open behind her. Turning, she beheld her bosom friend, Clara Peyton. Bounding, rather than walking, she crossed the floor, and flung her arms about Blonde, and kissed her warmly on each cheek.

"Past ten o'clock and uncombed. I declare, just as I expected. Your habits are getting no better very fast since you came to this fair town. You are pale—are you sick? Here—sit down. I will comb out that golden mesh. You beautiful, indolent, darling Blonde, I came for you to walk with me—the air is lovely, and the grass is so velvety, and the birds are whirling over the meadows half crazy with delight. I want to take you to see old Rosy's garden and conservatory. The good old soul will be delighted to see us. It's one of my favorite rambles. Lean your head against the chair if it aches—I can comb just as well. The walk through the fields will do you good—beautiful meadows, running brooks and everything—trees and everything. You wicked child, you have been reading late at night again—I warned you—do you remember? You old blue stocking! do you notice my new muslin?—isn't it sweet? Do you see the little pale violets all over it. And my new flat; do you like it?—don't say, no or you'll break my heart. How quick I jerked the white feather out of it. That stupid woman can't understand my taste. This band of strawberry leaves woven with strawberries I did myself. This flat is the softest, whitest straw I ever saw; just put your hand on it. Oh! where did you get that pearl ring? One, two, three, *four* pearls. Oh! Blonde, you've got a beau, and you are keeping it from me; from ME, your own, own Clara. Tell me now, that's a darling, who is he?"

The fair-cheeked, violet-eyed girl of seventeen, the rampant impersonation of the bloom and freshness of spring, ceased combing back the long tresses of her friend, and planting a fresh dewy kiss upon Blonde's lips, said, "Tell me, sweetheart, who is he? My ears are the grave, you know—nothing goes there but remains in there till the resurrection."

"Oh! you vivid imagination," said Blonde, still resting her pale cheek upon the blue chintz back of her chair, "my brother gave me that ring Christmas. How far is it to the old what's her name's garden? A walk will revive me, I know; pull that bell rope in the corner. I want a glass of cold milk for my breakfast, and some bread, then I'll go with you; what shall I wear?"

Clara Peyton bounded away to the bell rope, and gave it a jerk that made the bell below ring furiously. Then, while the servant was running up the stairs to answer the call, she stood by the door, patting it nervously with her soft white hand, and said "Blonde, we are going to have a new clergyman at St. Paul's. I heard father say so. He is young and unmarried, won't the girls have an excitement? He comes from a church in New York, and they say he is very high church—'way up.' What makes you so listless this morning? There, you sit right down again. I'm not going to allow you to do a thing this morning, until you feel better. I'll search your wardrobe, and find something appropriate for you to wear, and fix you all up. Ah! here's Mary. Mary, you bring a glass of right cold milk and a plate of thin white bread for Miss Blonde; she'll be ready for it in about ten minutes."

Then Clara removed her flat with its graceful wreath of straw berry leaves from her dark curls, and placing it with the respect due to a new hat on Blonde's bed, she said, "Where is your gold comb? I'll make your charms affective this morning, see if I don't." Then as she moved about her lovely friend, arranging her luxuriant hair, she sang in a low, musical murmur from the German of Heine

"And yonder sits a maiden
The fairest of the fair;
With gold is her garment glittering,
And she combs her golden hair.
With a golden comb she combs it;
And a wild song singeth she,
That melts the heart with wondrous
And powerful melody."

At length she succeeded in gathering Blonde's tresses into such a mass of golden braids upon the crown of her head, that the gold comb appeared to sustain the luxuriant mass by its own strength; and from the comb also, fell upon her neck and shoulders, heavy loops of golden braids. From the part of her hair on the forehead, the wavy, misty, puffed lines of gold, passed downward almost to the corner of her eye, and then swept gracefully backward, concealing entirely her ear, and leaving only visible the pendant ear-rings, which were plain gold hoops. Clara looked at her handiwork for a moment in admiration, and then said, "Now stand up, and inspect yourself. It's a full dress—party style, I know; but it looks splendid—and you must wear it to please old Rosy—she has good taste, and I want my friend to be presented in her best looks. You are wonderfully indifferent and listless, this morning. I hope nothing is on your mind. There, you are smiling at my freak about arranging your hair so. No one will think it inappropriate for a walk, after I put on your straw flat, with broad cherry-red streamers; nothing will show under that, except the wavy puffs in front, and a few of the drooping braids. Now for the dress—leave it to my taste—put yourself in my hands for once. Here comes your breakfast. Devote yourself to that, while I overhaul your wardrobe."

Blonde laughed in spite of her depression of mind and body as she slowly made way with her simple morning repast to hear her friend's comments, as she opened and closed the wardrobe doors, and drew out the drawers of the black walnut bureau.

"You extravagant child—you've dresses enough here for the entire congregation of St. Paul's—and such under clothes. that embroidery is exquisite: and here I declare is a skirt the same. What in the name of goodness possessed you to put so much work on that—it's your own work, too—I know the stitch right well. Oh! what a beautiful handkerchief—it's good enough for an angel's nose—where DID you get that lace—did you embroider *that*, too—what quantities of summer silks and muslins—oh ! here's a love of a party dress—golden satin, with point lace undersleeves, and here's a collar to match—what do you wear *that* with. Oh ! Blonde, here's a miniature—may I open it ? I'll bring it to you—the case is beautiful—all covered with little doves ; making love to each other, I suppose."

Blonde opened the miniature case and handed the picture to Clara for her inspection.

"Oh ! Oh !—you black-muzzled being, with your staring black eyes," she exclaimed—"did HE presume to address you ? What did you tell him ? Where does he live ? I wish you would sit down some day and tell me all about your love affairs before you came to C——. I see a color that will match the cherry ribbons on your flat, I believe," she continued, diving her arm into the depths of an immense drawer and drawing out a new cherry red merino with a row of large black velvet buttons extending from the neck of the dress to the bottom of the skirt.

"Now you will create a sensation along the streets of C——. Come, on with it—and we will be off for the green meadows—oh ! you darling !—it fits your figure to a charm—now for some kind of a collar."

Thus she rattled away, not giving her friend an opportunity to reply, and all the while arraying Blonde in her elegant walking apparel, hunting her gloves, diving into her bureau drawers for handkerchief, undersleeves and breastpin. Finally, she placed in Blonde's hand her fringed parasol, and taking up and replacing on her own dark curls, her new flat, she said, "I don't know which to admire most—your flat or mine. Come along, fairy, we'll trip the sunny fields in style this morning. What are you dreaming about. Were you ever in love, Blonde ?"

"No ! indeed," replied she, abstractedly, as she threw an embroidered white silk mantle over her shoulders, and then followed Clara slowly towards the door, drawing on, at the same time, her small, tapering gloves. "My head aches this morning—but I am so glad you came and forced me out into the fresh air—it will cure me, and save me the horrors of a blue day in my room."

The mansion appeared to be deserted as the two walked slowly down stairs to the street door, but on the piazza outside they found the tidy looking maid with her broom, who said, quietly, "Miss Grayson, your father said he would return for his dinner at four o'clock, precisely."

"Very well," replied Blonde, pausing a moment to reflect, "I will be at home before that hour. Anything else, Mary?"

"No! Miss," replied the girl hesitatingly, but she added quickly, "Only, I meant to tell you that while you were dressing to go out, a young gentleman rode up to the gate and got off of his horse and fastened him. Then he walked up as far as the violet bed there, but he didn't seem to know whether to come in or not; he stopped a minute and then he turned right back, and walked as fast as he could back to his horse, and away he went galloping down the street as fast as he could go; he was pale as death. I think it was Mr. Lansing, but I am not certain—he had on one of those black felt hats—and it was pulled down so low over his eyes that I couldn't tell if it was him. Any orders for me, Miss Grayson, this morning?"

Blonde's pale face was clouded for a moment by a passing thought, and then she answered, composedly, "Nothing to-day, Mary. Who carried the letters from the hall table to the post-office this morning?"

"Your brother, miss," replied the girl. "He walked out very early, before breakfast, this morning—earlier than usual."

"Come, Clara," said Blonde, "I'm ready now—how charmingly the birds are singing."

They walked out under the branches of the sheltering elms which gently quivered in the breeze. The air was laden with the breath of lilacs and apple-blossoms, and the orchestra of the singing birds was full. They passed a garden where a large crab-apple tree appeared so full of white blossoms as to convey the idea of an immense ball of snow; and upon the fragrant mass of white, two scarlet birds were perched, known by the familiar name of "fire birds." The two friends walked silently side by side for a few moments, until Clara, whose violet eyes wore a puzzled expression since the housemaid's remarks on the strange horseman, said quietly, with her eyes fixed on Blonde's calm features:

"I like Henry Lansing: don't you, Blonde? Why didn't he call, after he had come so far in the yard?"

The features of the fair girl changed not in expression as she replied calmly—

"It may not have been him; some stranger, probably, who mistook the house, and turned back when he was near enough to see that he had made a mistake. I have seen such things before. You ask if I like Mr. Lansing—I do think him very agreeable. He has certainly been very civil to us since we came here to live; but his sister, Mrs. Bounce, for some unknown reason, has taken a dislike to me, I understand, little as she is acquainted with me. We have exchanged calls once, and that is about the limit of our acquaintance. But I believe she does not fancy our church. Indeed, I have heard that she ridicules Episcopacy on all occasions. I was informed, too, that she had remarked upon the fact that we were in the habit of giving gentlemen wine at our parties. It is a custom we always observed in the city—but here in C——, it appears to be unusual—that is, among those who attend the other houses; but I think our church people, generally, here, observe that custom of giving wine to guests, do they not?"

"Certainly," said Clara, "with one or two exceptions—but has she really commenced her tirades upon you? She is a very bitter woman towards all who presume to differ from her in anything. I wouldn't notice any of her remarks, Blonde, for she is notorious for abusing us all. She made some shockingly uncharitable comments on mother's dancing party, a few years ago; and said we had no right to entice her brother away from his church principles to attend worldly amusements. The thing is perfectly absurd, for her brother belongs to no church; and he said that if he ever joined a Christian church, it would be St. Paul's. He is a right, liberal gentleman, and I suspect he must have a great deal of trouble with her. Indeed, I have heard that she gave him a violent lecture for going with you Sunday to our church. You must have exerted your beauty, Blonde, in a most powerful manner, when you made him brave that storm in order to attend St. Paul's. If I were a gentleman, you could lead me, like a child, with your eyes and hair."

She looked up in her friend's face with such an earnest expression of admiration and affection, that Blonde smiled one of her own peculiarly sweet smiles, and then said,

"Your true, warm heart leads you to say extravagant things to me, I am sure. Oh! what would I have done in this strange town without your friendship to sustain me, and your fearless tongue to defend me? You flew to my arms almost the very week I arrived here. God must have sent you, for you have been so careless of self when I have been concerned. I never can repay you, but I will give you all that I possess—my heart and my confidence."

Clara looked up gratefully, and her violet eyes glistened at these sudden and impulsive words as she replied—

"That is the treasure I covet—your heart and your unbounded faith in me. Perhaps, some day I may learn another kind of love, for they tell us it is the fate of woman; but never, never, can any idol in my heart, be cherished with a purer and more ardent affection than you have contrived to weave about my young heart, since the happy, happy day you first trusted me. Here, Blonde, turn down this street; this will lead us to the green fields through which the path runs—the road you see curving over those rocks, goes by old Rosy's garden, too, but this is our shortest route."

Thus bound in the common chain of sympathy, these two hearts wandered off in conversation upon their mutual hopes and fears of the coming years. One was the impersonation of hope, and vivacity and enjoyment, drinking in the balmy air of Spring, like nectar handed by an angel, unsuspecting of the thorn beneath all pleasure, willing to believe this earth a paradise, and still unconscious of that inevitable hour in Time, when the soul reaches forth to the blue sky its weary, weary wings and begs of the good God for rest and peace eternal. The other was an older star, across whose face the dark and shadowy clouds of change had often passed; but when the drifting veil had gone, there was the star, purer and holier than before. In her heart, faith burned brighter, and imagination dimmer as the years flew by. The night winds as they passed, brought to her memory sighs and moans from the valley of life. They bore upon their rushing wings, words of cruelty, and desolation, and disappointment. They murmured of selfishness, avarice, sin; and though they ceased at times to chill and blow, and light came with the calm, yet her heart remembered them, and whispered thankfully—"Oh, Father of Life, thou hast kindly warned me of the world."

They were indeed friends, though of a recent date. That subtile and sympathetic fire which sometimes warms the hearts of two girls, and at which the ruffian, called the world, is wont to sneer, burned on a constant altar. They were a living refutation of that calumny which so many women freely and boldly pronounce upon their own sex; that no woman who is much admired by gentlemen can have friends, true, earnest friends among women. Clara Peyton and her friend were beautiful, and society acknowledged the fact. Gentlemen were but too happy to follow in the train of either. Contact with the mind of either, developed the electric flash of wit, or the higher charm, intellectual beauty. Both sang as the angels sing—thoughtfully, earnestly. Both were conscious of the many eyes that lighted at their approach, and both were sensitive. Still were they friends, and unselfish friends. Many a time when the dizzy whirl of the violin and the harp sounded below, had one with disheveled hair and a dressing-gown, labored to arrange the other's hair gracefully in the chamber above; fixing and tediously unfixing wreaths of flowers, looping up skirts, stitching flounces, arranging head-dresses only to have them disarranged again to try another effect, and wholly forgetful of the time which yet remained for making one's own toilet. And then the flashing queen of beauty had been dismissed to the festive hall, with the peremptory remark, "Never mind *me*. I am so happy to see you beautifully dressed, it is no matter if I don't be ready to-night." They who have seen this devotion amid the excitement and the absorbing interest of a great ball, are not apt to give full credence to the sweeping assertion that all women are jealous of belles. What! woman! the graceful creation of God's second and more beautiful thought; capable of the highest and holiest devotion—for the honor and love of her Heavenly Father kneeling in the foul air of the lazaretto, and ministering to fearful humanity. Woman! capable of following her loved tyrant of a husband through reproach, and abuse, and insult to a forgotten grave. Woman! for the love of the blue-eyed babe that clings to her sacrificing health, and beauty, and reputation, and hunger-worn and exhausted, capable of bending, in her last gasp, over her child's gentle face, in utter forgetfulness of self. Woman! capable of giving the manly idols of her household, to the chance of battle, that her country's liberties may live. Is she, with the wreaths of love and honor which centuries have flung around her name, incapable of loving, with unselfish love, her beautiful friend who seems to sweep admirers before her at every graceful step, with ease? Perish the thought from the pages of romance, and the lips of woman. She, the self-sacrificing and the noble, is capable of every virtue, equal to every position where greatness of character are demanded. There are many such women, and Blonde Grayson and her friend were of that type.

As they walked at length beyond the limits of C——, and entered the narrow path which wound through the broad meadows, Blonde seemed to regain her vivacity of spirits, and talked eagerly of her love of the beautiful in nature. Her secret, she guarded carefully from her companion, whose curiosity about Henry Lansing she had completely baffled by her indifferent and quiet remarks. She felt that this revelation to her of his secret thoughts, was a sacred deposit which she had no right to disclose, even to her friend. His earnestness had touched her heart, and her feeling was that of intense sympathy and respect.

A walk of a mile through soft green fields and across rippling brooks, and under broad elms, is soon passed by youthful feet in the mild atmosphere of spring. Soon the white rows of apple trees in blossom skirting the garden of old Rosy, arose from the velvety green of the fields; then appeared the glass roof of the conservatory, flashing in the sunlight, and then the white cottage with its low eaves and green blinds, surrounded by young maple trees.

As the two friends reached the stile of the garden, they discovered the old woman seated on her front door step, and weeping bitterly.

CHAPTER III.

The two friends paused for a few moments at the stile, undecided whether to approach the owner of the garden while she appeared so absorbed and distressed with her unknown troubles. At length, they concluded to wander away through the garden quietly, so as not to attract her attention, while the violence of her grief continued, intending to return to her cottage door when she should have become calmer. She did not observe them, as they turned down a labyrinthine path bordered with fresh green privet hedges, and they wandered slowly along, inhaling with the balmy air, odors of apple blossoms, and lilacs, on every side. Early spring flowers were visible in some of the neatly-arranged beds; and occasionally Clara would stoop to gather the modest lily of the valley, or the white flower of the myrtle, with which she was arranging a bouquet for her companion. The distant, forest-crowned, range of hills appeared faintly and blue in the warm, misty atmosphere; and the dark shadows of the drooping elms in the meadows about the garden slept quietly upon the emerald bosom of the young, velvety grass. The busy hum of the honey bees sounded dreamily on every side, as they gathered their small, but luscious stores, from the abundant apple blossoms; and occasionally a robin, in the fullness of his joy, burst forth into song from his high branch. As the two friends passed slowly along the ever-varying paths, they conversed in subdued tones, of the beauties about them, and the correct tastes of old Rosy in the arrangement of her borders. In one walk, she had planted the crab-apple trees in such a perfect manner, that now, on either side of the path, arose snowy masses of white blossoms, which united overhead, and formed a dense and wonderful arch of beauty, for several rods' distance. Then the path led under arbors of grape vines, yet in the bud ; and then under a long arch of wires over which the Michigan roses were trained, waiting for the developing sun and rain. Then Clara, from her recollections of the place, led the way into a small side path, where the dark cedars excluded the sun, and near the end of which a cold spring played, and murmured mysteriously to the protecting shadows of the trees. This secluded spring was in a corner of old Rosy's garden, and once had been the landmark by which this corner of her property could be ascertained before it was carefully surveyed and fenced. The rays of the sun never fell upon this ever living fountain ; and its crystal waters were ever cold and refreshing to those who chose, in the warmest days of summer, to wander to this retired locality. Adjoining this corner of the garden, was a dense wood, belonging to the neighboring proprietor, and some of its stately maple trees extended their sheltering branches far over old Rosy's spring. A narrow gate, through the garden fence, opened into the gloomy wood, and disclosed a narrow, tortuous path, leading far away under the low hanging branches. Blonde and her companion pushed open the gate and gazed along this path under the gloomy trees, which, though yet covered with only a light green mantle, were solemn and chilling.

"Let us walk along this fence, back to Rosy's cottage," said Clara Peyton, "those woods have a forbidding look, and frighten me."

Before they could close the gate, however, voices suddenly broke out from the thicket, a few rods, apparently, away, under the maples. They were angry voices, too ; and then a low curse succeeded, as if muttered savagely, between closed teeth. Then an agonized cry, such a cry as once heard, never fails to haunt the memory : "Murder ! murder ! Oh ! God ! don't kill me ! Murder !" A terrific struggle ensued ; the bushes swayed violently, and the dry twigs crackled and crushed under their feet, as they tramped back and forth in the death struggle. Then a heavy, sullen blow was heard, and all was still again, as death. In a moment, however, a sound was heard, as of a person flying away through the yielding bushes and making for the more remote portions of the forest. The footsteps seemed to the ear to bound rather than walk, and, at last, they died away entirely in the distance.

Clara was trembling and ashy pale, clinging to the gate, where her hand was resting when the struggle commenced. She was perfectly unnerved, and helpless, and her white lips were parted in trembling horror. There was only a paleness, however, on Blonde's face; and her expression was wonderfully composed, during this rapidly enacted horror. She was following with her eyes the evident route of the escaping murderer, where the tops of the bushes, quivering or bending, gave indication of his passage. And only when his footsteps died away in the distance did she turn her eyes on her trembling companion and whisper, "Something must be done at once. If I were a man I would follow that wretch until I knew who he was. Run to the cottage, Clara, and bring the old woman, and any one you can find. I am going right in there, to that murdered man. Oh, God!" she exclaimed, raising her blue eyes to her Father's serene sky, "sanctify us and save us from sin. Don't be so frightened, Clara, it's all over. There is suffering or death under those trees, and I must go at once—but you run away for help—there, hurry, now."

She pushed her friend gently away by the arm, towards the cottage, and Clara then bounded away, as if eager to escape from that dreadful neighborhood. In her fright, the shrubbery brushing her dress, made her fancy some one was trying to grasp her from behind, and this fear made her fly still faster.

And Blonde, the gentle, helpless woman, what were her thoughts, standing alone, and facing that dense thicket, and those solemn trees, where something was surely lying stretched on the ground. She paused one moment, and peered, with dilating eyes, into that silent, gloomy darkness of the unknown thicket. Then she braced herself to her accustomed bearing and whispering to herself, "God protect me, and guide me," she glided away, down the strange path to the supposed scene of the tragedy. The bushes caught her red merino on either side of the path, or swept their stinging branches across her face, and tangled in her drooping braids of golden hair. Onward she pushed her way, in spite of every obstacle, for a short distance farther, and there she found him, oh! horror! not lying on the ground but sitting against a great maple, and looking at her with his black, staring eyes, as she approached. A great gash appeared on the side of his head, and his arms hung loosely and helplessly by his side. His life was fast ebbing away in the crimson stream which trickled through his hair, down upon his heavy, black beard. Horror flitted across her face, but she walked steadily on, and knelt down beside him, glancing first upon the awful fracture in his skull to convince herself that hope was forever gone. Alas, it was a giant's blow.

His eyes were fast taking on the hazy film of death, but he could whisper faintly, "Can you forgive me, Blonde Grayson, now that I am dying?"

She answered in astonishment, "I have nothing to forgive you, Mr. Hartwell—you never injured me or mine."

Again he whispered, "I did, I did seek to wrong you—but God prevented me—will you forgive me, now, when I'm dying?"

"Oh, earnestly, heartily will I forgive you whatever you have done," she answered, striving, at the same time, to raise his head and shoulders more comfortably against the tree.

A soothed expression settled upon his eyes and features, at her reply, and then his head fell away from the kind supporting grasp of her hands. He was dead. Calmly she composed his head and limbs, as best she could, upon the soft, dry bed of leaves, and then looked away toward the gate into old Rosy's garden: no one yet appeared in that direction, and she looked once more upon the face of the dead, standing erect, with her hands clasped in front of her. She experienced no sense of fear, in this fearful solitude, with a murdered man, prostrate before her. The shock to her woman's delicate nature had given place to another sensation, a woman's profound sympathy. She thought of his mother, his sisters, his friends, and their coming agony. She remembered too, that he had loved her in a distant city, and though she had refused his proffered hand; they had agreed to remain outwardly friends; and his miniature was in her possession; the same that Clara Peyton had found in her bureau drawer that morning. She remembered not, in the engrossing contemplation of his ghastly features and the recollection of his family, that here was the highest, most fearful crime known to human laws, and that the murderer was unknown and rapidly making his escape. But after a few moments of watching and waiting for her friend's return, she laid one of her fair hands upon the tree which marked the fatal spot, and leaned forward again over the dead. Then her eyes wandered over his stiffening limbs, and she detected this time a small black object clenched tightly in one of his hands. It appeared to be a narrow strip of black cloth, two or three inches in length. She stooped down and disengaged it from the firm grasp of the dead hand, and then raised it to the light. Ah! she turned deathly pale and her eyes were riveted upon the cloth. A dreadful fascination seemed to hold her trembling; she who had been so wonderfully calm and self-possessed while her companion nearly fainted from the shock of the death struggle now trembled like the aspen leaf. The dreadful evidence and clue of the murderer was in her hand. It was a piece of the assassin's neck-tie, which the victim's hand had torn away in the desperation of the last, muscular struggle, and she recognized it. It was embroidered with black silk thread at the end, and her own hand had done the work. In the caprice of a girl's idle hour, and in answer to a half serious request of a gentleman, she had worked the flower on the end of his neck-tie, and in his presence, and the presence of a party of ladies and gentlemen. And there it was, torn away from his neck, by the dying, violent effort of the victim to save himself. Blonde Grayson, the gentle, timid girl, held the sole and terrible clue of the murderer in her hand. She, alone, of the whole world, knew the guilty wretch. She alone, of all who would gather in horror about the corpse, would be able to identify the assassin by this embroidered flower upon his neck-tie.

Her self-possession deserted her, and the fearful responsibility of her situation overwhelmed her with anguish. Her evidence would entail disgrace upon one of the best and noblest families in the State; a family without a stain of reproach, high toned, generous, universally beloved, and respected. She would be forced by the law to return constant kindness only by delivering up the unfortunate man to the gallows; and other terrible reflections crowded upon her. The isolation of heart which was to come, the loved ties which were to be violently rent asunder rushed gloomily before her vision, and she hesitated. To make the dreadful disclosure would be the work of a moment only; and yet that moment held a human life, dangling in the air, strangling by a hard rope, in cruel agony, passing to the presence of an offended God. Who had the right and the power to turn her innocent spring morning ramble into an irreparable injury to herself and her happiness in life? What was this paramount necessity that demanded of her to open her lips to take away human life. A low, mournful whisper in her ear answered, "God." The thoughtless birds flew joyfully above her head, and twittered gaily from the maples as the warm sun's rays forced themselves among the forest shadows; but in her soul was darkness and gloom impenetrable. Affections of the heart, natural and engrossing, had come violently in conflict with duties. Which must she—which would she surrender? She clasped her hands before her again, and looked once more upon the white face of the murdered man, and shuddered. But the cloth, the fragment fluttered between her clasped fingers, and she could not divert her eyes from it long. They would return to it and stare at it till it seemed to be endowed with a mocking life to torture her earnest soul. But the time for her decision was flying, for loud voices were heard calling to her, and the tramping feet of the hurrying and excited neighbors were sounding under the trees. They were coming nearer and nearer, and her time was short. Only a moment now for decision; only a moment to shield a human life from Eternity. Blonde looked up for an instant through the trees to God; then she started at the wild shouts so fearfully near: then convulsively she thrust the fluttering piece of cloth into her bosom and the murderer was safe; the clue had vanished.

"Oh! here she is," exclaimed a familiar voice at her side, as the bushes were violently parted, and a powerful man appeared with an axe on his shoulder. "You are a brave girl, Miss Grayson, to enter such a gloomy thicket as this to face a murderer. O! God! it is too true," he groaned, as he dropped his axe on seeing the prostrate form on the leaves. Awe-struck and reverently he kneeled over the corpse, and studied the features; but no sign of recognition escaped him, for the murdered man was an utter stranger to the inhabitants of C——. A muttered malediction parted his lips, however, when he saw the fearful opening in the stranger's skull.

"A fearful deed this, Miss Grayson, and done by an arm of iron. See how the bone is fractured. Is there no clue to the villain—or the way he escaped? We might, some of us, overtake him yet; a few moments only have passed since Miss Peyton called to us in the field. Could you see him or hear him leaving? Can't you give us some idea as to who he is, or the way he went, by the sound of his footsteps?"

The honest face of the farmer was turned upward to her in enquiry, and she experienced a feeling as if the blood was all flowing away from her head, back to her heart. "That way he went, beating down the bushes so fast—but I could not see him—only I saw the bushes occasionally shake and bend as he forced his way through. I heard him several minutes, crashing away in that direction." Blonde pointed away, with her tapering finger, into the deeper recesses of the wood. Then, as the indignant woodman arose to his feet, and grasped his axe, looking away under the trees as if he was about to follow the fugitive, she detained him nervously to gain time by saying—"I know this poor victim—his name is Hartwell, and he lives in Hudson—his family are most respectable—how he happened to be here in C——, I cannot conceive;—he called me by name, and asked me to forgive him before he died—and he never treated me with else than kindness; and then he died without a word about his murderer—all was over so quick after I came up."

The woodman paused a moment to reflect, and was immediately joined by two other men of the neighborhood, who dashed through the bushes, excited and eager. Glancing hurriedly upon Blonde, who was standing guard over the body, and then upon the face of the dead, they exclaimed—"a stranger and foully murdered—let's follow the scoundrel—Roy, lead on again—we're no use here, we have no time to lose, either." The individual with the axe at once indicated their respective routes of pursuit, and after a brief whisper with one of the new comers which occasioned a sudden glance into Blonde's face, the woodman plunged into the forest still deeper, and the other two went off by more circuitous paths, intending to meet again at a familiar ravine.

Blonde listened awhile to their receding footsteps, and then as the sounds at last died away in the distance, she looked again upon the corpse of Hartwell and shuddered at the lonely horror of the scene.

But the voices of her friend, Clara Peyton and old Rosy and others, now echoed under the trees, and in a few seconds this new party were standing in astonishment and horror beside the dead—the women trembling, or some of them kneeling down and adjusting more carefully the poor, stiffening limbs of the unfortunate stranger; and the men standing irresolutely at one side discussing the mysterious affair. They had searched the pockets of the murdered man, and found his watch and purse unmolested, and knew then that the deed was not committed for the sake of money. Finally, the four men and a boy, who had come up with the women, raised the corpse upon their shoulders, and bore it away toward old Rosy's cottage in the garden. The females who had gradually regained their ordinary composure, followed slowly, and talked earnestly over the few facts in the possession of Blonde and her friend. Suddenly, however, a robust and red featured girl of eighteen, who had been carefully studying every word that was uttered, stopped in her walk, and exclaimed, abruptly, "Rosy, didn't I see Mr. Henry Lansing leave your door just before this happened, and hurry off down this way? I am sure it was him, though he looked so pale and excited, and acted so queerly that I hardly knew him at first; and then I saw you from our window wiping your eyes on your apron. I know I did."

The whole party of females who were following the corpse, turned interested glances upon the countenance of the old woman addressed, who seemed considerably fluttered by this sudden questioning. She replied, however, at once, in indignant tones—

"Do you mean to throw suspicion upon that young gentleman who left my door a short time before this dreadful affair happened? Shame on you! Mr. Henry Lansing is above such a deed as murder. Nobody in C—— will believe such a thing for an instant. He is too good-hearted, and every body knows it. He did bid me good-bye, and then come this way. He often has done the same thing before. And then he is going away to Europe to-day to travel. He came to say a kind word at parting from his old friend and his mother's friend. And don't you see this man is a stranger, except to Miss Grayson? I believe that was the name you were called, by Miss Peyton," she added, dropping a courtesy to Blonde, who was walking with the rest but entirely absorbed in her own painful reflections, until Henry Lansing's name was mentioned in such a suspicious manner. This name, however, aroused her in an instant, and she fixed her calm blue eyes on the strange girl in deep interest, to hear her reply to the young man's defender. The girl whose remarks had occasioned such profound interest, looked boldly at old Rosy, and there was an air of defiance in her manner as she answered—

"I don't mean to accuse any body, but after such a deed as this, every one will be criticised who was known to be in this garden and the neighborhood—that you can rely on, be he high or be he low—I only know *he* came down the garden in this direction, just before the alarm was raised. He is awful high strung, and every body in C—— knows it. I have known him strike a man quicker than a flash for a matter of words. He may know nothing about this murder, only I say it is strange; he happened to come this way just about the time the thing must have occurred."

Suspicion is easily aroused among disinterested persons by the most trivial circumstances; and the girl's words evidently were turning the attention of her neighbors upon young Henry Lansing's mysterious disappearance in the direction of the forest path, under the gloomy maples. Blonde, confident in her possession of the dreadful clue, retained consummate guard over her emotions; but she was careful to appear interested in the girl's words, maintaining all the while the silence natural to her being a stranger to the party. The three or four women who had been called to the spot by Clara Peyton's alarm, joined in with the accuser of Henry Lansing in magnifying the fact of his presence in the garden a short time before. But Blonde's friend, whose character always shone forth brighter amid adversity and reproach, interrupted them indignantly. Her beautiful mouth curled in scorn and contempt as she broke forth:

"I am just astonished at all you women, trying to throw suspicion on Mr. Lansing, one of the most perfect gentlemen in C——. He never did a mean thing, and you all know it; every one of you. Mary Cowen! who jumped into the lake, under the ice, and dragged your drowning brother out three years ago? And you, too, Mrs. Hazelit, who came and nursed you every night, when you were lying at death's door with that fever, but Henry Lansing's own excellent mother—and she so delicate she ought to have been in bed herself? I am surprised that *you* have nothing to say in favor of her own son; you all know better—how dare you talk in this suspicious way about him? I know he is ignorant of this murder even being committed. It will turn out as I say, when he makes his appearance. He, indeed! murder a man in a retired place, and then run like a thief. It is no more like him, than darkness is like light. He is open and manly in what he does. If you ever know of him killing a man, it will be in the public street of C——, and he won't run after it, either."

Her violet eyes snapped under the new, strawberry-wreathed flat, and her manner, as well as her vigorous defence, turned, for a time, the tide of opinion against the red-featured accuser. And then old Rosy brought her potent tongue to the rescue of her young favorite's character.

"I'll never hear him abused," she said, resolutely. "I know he is quick tempered as well as any body knows it. Didn't he, one afternoon last summer when old Scroon and his son were trying to cheat me by putting their fence posts over the lawful line of my garden—didn't he jerk up one of the chestnut posts, and chase both of them, the cowards. And it turned out he was right, after all. He never committed no murder, that you can rely on. Why, he is the best hearted boy these ten years back you ever knew. He would come flying down the road on his black horse like he was mad, till he reached my gate, and then one quick word to his horse, and over the gate into my door-yard he would leap ; 'for,' says he 'what do Black Hawk and I care for fences ?' And then he would work to help me set out my plants when the storm was coming up, just like he was a common laborer, and he the richest young man in the county. You never saw such a good kind friend as he is to a poor old soul like me that lives lonely, and has hard scratching for a living ; but he's gone now hundreds, and, for all I know, thousands of miles away, and I feel desolate like ; for he used to fling himself on my lounge in the cottage, and sleep for hours, with the flowers nodding over his dark curly hair from my flower stand ; and he said he loved me and tresh flowers better than the whole town of C—— put together. I am sad enough, I can tell you, now he is gone."

The old woman raised her apron to her face, and burst again violently into tears. The discussion ceased at once, and they followed the party who bore the murdered man in silence, until they reached the cottage door. Then old Rosy showed the men a small room where the corpse might await the arrival of the coroner of C——.

CHAPTER IV.

The quiet town of C—— had received a violent shock. A thrill of horror flashed along its elm-guarded streets ; and the excitement grew each moment wilder. Citizens gathered in little groups on the street corners, or before the hotels, discussing the mysterious rumors concerning the murder. Then, as the afternoon wore away, it was discovered that something practical was occuring to remove the reproach and stigma which all felt had fallen upon the town, from the bloody death of an innocent stranger who had trustingly entered its limits. An inquest was then proceeding, under the direction and superintendence of the coroner, at the cottage in old Rosy's garden ; and streams of people were passing over the green meadows towards the scene of the murder, and thence finding their way to the cottage, and the presence of the unknown dead. The official to whom was assigned the solemn duty of examining and reporting upon cases of mysterious and sudden deaths, had proved himself a prompt and efficient servant of the public. In a few hours he had summoned his jury from the neighborhood; sworn them to a faithful performance of their duty; issued his subpœnas for the attendance of witnesses from different parts of the town, and from the neighborhood of the murder; secured the attendance of the first physician of C—— promptly at the side of the corpse; and while waiting for all the witnesses to arrive had marched his jury, under the lead of Blonde Grayson and her friend, to the fatal foot of the maple, under which the stranger had fallen; and had there carefully inspected the ground, the trampled leaves, the blood, the bent bushes and twigs, looking in vain for some weapon which might have given the death stroke. At length the witnesses were all present, under the young trees about the cottage door, and the jury were seated in silence about the body, which had been placed upon a lounge in the middle of the largest room which old Rosy could claim as her property.

Chairs had been placed under the trees for Blonde and her friend, and they sat close together there, with their arms about each other, waiting to be summoned to testify before the jury in the cottage. The father, Mr. Grayson, who had been summoned at the instance of his daughter, to identify the body of Hartwell, stood erect and dignified behind them, looking calmly around upon the crowd, which had gathered about the door. The two friends were conversing earnestly and in a low tone concerning the disposition manifested around them by many to cast suspicion upon Henry Lansing. Clara appeared vehement in his defence, but Blonde was reserved in her expressions, and finally ceased talking, but listened attentively.

At length, Clara was summoned before the jury, and she walked timidly and slowly into the house, leaving Blonde with her father, who immediately occupied the vacant chair. They sat in perfect silence for a few minutes; but the crowd pressed closer around the door in their eagerness to see and hear what was transpiring within the cottage, and left the father and daughter comparatively isolated and under the trees.

"Tell me, father," said Blonde, "exactly what I swear to when I take an oath in there, by the corpse. What are the words the law requires me to promise?"

"It is this, substantially," he replied, "that you swear that the evidence you shall give concerning this murder, shall be the truth; the whole truth, and nothing but the truth, so help you God."

She repeated the words, slowly and solemnly, after him. "The truth, the *whole* truth, and nothing but the truth." Then an expression of anxiety swept across her sweet face, and for a few moments, she appeared to study profoundly, looking down upon the soft, waving grass at her feet, and with her hands clasped in her lap. Her father was too absorbed in his own reflections, gazing away over the meadows and the garden at the distant blue mountains, to notice her anxiety in her meditations.

These were her thoughts as her blue, mysterious eyes veiled themselves, deeper and deeper, under her drooping eyelashes.

"What is the *whole* truth? All that I know?—all that I may suspect? And what right have I to suspect? Is that piece of silk," (here she looked cautiously around upon the crowd, and seeing no one observe her, she thrust her hand into her bosom and felt the concealed fragment of the necktie, and gave it a further shove under her dress,) "is that piece of silk destined to take away a human life, possibly to be the means of destroying a soul, forever in perdition? That is no good evidence of guilt, surely. Some one may have stolen that necktie, and had it on during the murder. How can I tell who was wearing it? Have I a right to throw suspicion upon a respectable gentleman by producing it? It may condemn him, and he still be innocent. Then his blood surely will be on my soul. But if it should really be him—oh! what will become of my hopes—my happiness? But it may not be him at all, and then I may be destroying the only clue which might lead to the detection of the real murderer. But how did it happen to be clenched so tightly in Mr. Hartwell's hand? It *must* have come from the murderer's neck. I fear it did. Yes, I am sure it did. Some one else may have stolen it, and worn it—it is possible. But ought I to tell the jury who it belonged to?—They may not ask me. But suppose they *do* ask me if I have any clue. What shall I say? I swear to tell the *whole* truth. Does that mean to tell every fact, or every impression, or every suspicion, on that dreadful spot, whether they ask me or not? But this gentleman is a noble character; above doing such a deed—why must I mention him and his necktie? Suspicion will surely alight upon him if I do, and I have no right to make him suspicious to these people, without other evidence than this fragment of silk. It surely cannot be right or me so to do. They will perhaps hang him on my evidence. This murder is not committed from mercenary motives—that is clear enough. They will look for a higher motive, and will naturally suspect some one who is above want. I am afraid of this pervading and infernal democracy, which so often in these days, gives a gentleman no chance for his life, unless he buys it with gold. They love to suspect some man a little above them of everything that is bad. I must not furnish a victim to suspect. But the blood of Hartwell cries to God. I dare not conceal a murder. My soul yearns for eternal life, and I shall lose it, I know, if I conceal this dreadful sin. But, *he* never could have done it—never, never. There can be no motive—he even, I firmly believe, never heard of such a man as Hartwell. There is no earthly reason to think so. I will not injure him, unjustly, cruelly injure him, simply because a thought flashed through my mind when I found the fragment of silk. But if they ask me if I know of any clue, what shall I say? They may not ask me *that*—then all will be well. But if they *do*, what then? Alas! the *whole* truth. I cannot deny that there is a clue. I will not perjure my soul; oh! no! oh! my God! don't let them ask me that question—prevent it, by Thine almighty power."

The longer she considered the fearful secret which was thrust into her bosom just under the neck of her merino dress, the more undecided did she become. Conscience, hopes, affections, fears, duties, all respectively rushed through her brain asserting their claims, and she wished herself a thousand miles away from the dreadful neighborhood, and dreadful responsibility. Her reverie was abruptly closed. She started like a guilty being at a sudden voice behind her.

"Your turn has arrived, young lady. The jury await your presence." It was an officer of the law who summoned her. There was no escape, and she followed him as he forced a way for her through the dense throng about the door. A murmur of admiration at her rare beauty passed around, as the crowd discovered at last who was following the officer, and they moved respectfully aside for her to pass. With her eyes bent modestly upon the ground, she passed amid the excited throng, and was ushered into the jury-room and the presence of the dead.

The physician who had been summoned to examine the wound, was the intimate and loved medical adviser of her family. He stepped at once toward her and said, "You are agitated, Blonde, at this dreadful scene, and this solemn assembly. The jury will permit you to lean on my arm during the examination." She passed her arm gratefully through his, and accompanied him to the head of the murdered Hartwell. The oath was administered to her, and then she was directed to look upon the face of the dead, and inform the jury if she was able to identify his person. She quietly stated, without a minute's hesitation, and in her clear, musical tones, the name, residence and former occupation of him who had gone to his final account, accompanying her statement of his identity with a few remarks regarding his former intimacy at her father's house, before she had moved to the town of C——. The condensed and explicit nature of her remarks, so unlike the rambling statements of most females on the witnesses' stand, evidently produced a favorable impression upon the coroner, who bowed respectfully at the conclusion of her answer, and said, slowly and distinctly:

"Now please tell us, Miss Grayson, carefully and accurately as you can, how you happened to be in this garden at the hour of the day, in which you came; what o'clock it was, when you came; who was with you; and what happened here, in connection with this dead man: tell us all you can, about this murder, and leave us to judge as to the materiality of everything you saw, did or heard. Commence with stating the hour, as nearly as you are able, of leaving your home to walk; give us an idea of how long you were in reaching the garden, and then more accurately everything you did, saw, or heard, in relation to this murder."

The word "*saw*" made her feel faint; but she nerved herself for the statement of facts, and reflecting a few moments to satisfy herself concerning the hour of her leaving home, she commenced, slowly and cautiously, to give in her evidence, which was carefully written down. When she came to the death struggle, and the silence which followed, and then the flying footsteps, which bounded off through the forest, she noticed that every juryman of the ten who had answered the coroner's summons was gazing directly into her face, which was partly concealed by her drooping flat. She paused in embarrassment; but the coroner encouraged her, and the physician drew her arm closer to his side, to sustain her, and she continued. She described the manner in which she had sent away her companion for assistance, and then her own tramp through the bushes to the presence of the dying man. Then she related the few words he had whispered to her, and her own replies, and then his falling away from her supporting arms, dead.

She paused, and pressed one of her fair hands tightly over her eyes, and stood thus for a moment, in silence, and studying inwardly what she should say next.

The coroner, supposing she had finished, said, seriously, "Your story is carefully and properly told, Miss Grayson; listen to me now while I ask you only one more question, and then you can retire."

Blonde experienced a secret satisfaction at this remark, and her hand dropped from her eyes. What was her surprise and horror, when the coroner, after reflecting an instant only, looked directly into her eyes, and asked, solemnly, "Have you any clue?"

An iron hand grasped her heart and she turned deathly pale, almost as ghastly as the face of the dead beside whom she stood. The physician felt her weight like lead upon his arm, but she trembled not; she was as motionless as the marble statue. Alas! there was no escape now. The solemn officer of the law concluded his sentence: "Have you any clue, or reason, slight as may be, to suspect that this murder was committed by "—he paused an instant, again fixing his bright, searching, gray eyes upon her countenance, to read her soul. Then he pronounced the name: "Henry Lansing."

An electric flash of joy swept the iron hand from her heart. She said boldly and truthfully, "No! thank God! Not the slightest."

The voice of truth is often trumpet toned, and irresistible to the listener. So it was then in the ear of the honest coroner. He said at once, "You may retire, now, Miss Grayson; your testimony is perfectly satisfactory. I only regret, that yon are not able to aid us in unraveling this fearful mystery. You may go."

She turned gladly away from the inquest, and walked out of the cottage, leaning on the arm of her physician, and with the murderer's clue nestling in her bosom. Under the trees, she was allowed once more to rejoin her friend, Clara Peyton; and, escorted by the physician, the two friends walked to the gate, opening into the highway. There they found Mr. Peyton's carriage waiting for them; and, thanking the doctor for his attentions, they were soon rolling away toward the drooping elms of C——.

While the two friends were riding toward home with a sense of great relief at escaping from the crowd, and the ex citement of the inquest, and were relating to each other their respective statements before the coroner's jury, the sun was fast declining toward the Western horizon.

But a far different scene was being enacted, at the same hour, about a mile and a half north of the town, and in the opposite direction from old Rosy's garden. The same sun which poured its slanting rays over the two friends in the carriage, there fell upon high and bare rocks, with smooth round tops, which were twenty or thirty feet above the level of the highway. The road wound irregularly through these bare and singularly isolated rocks, but was gradually rising toward the still more lofty forest which crowned the mountain just above them. One would hardly realize how much he was ascending in leaving the town by this rocky highway, until he had mounted to the top of one of these isolated rocks, and then looked back over the route he had come. Then he would see far, far, below him, and nearly two miles away, the town of C—, almost entirely buried under its luxuriance of drooping elm branches. Then, casting his eyes still further up the winding highway, toward the forest above him, he would realize that he stood about midway between the houses of C— and the top of a gradually ascending mountain, and that the streets of the town had been marked out just at the point where the mountain softened away into a great plain. From these rocks, too, he would see a broad lake, beyond the limits of the town, glistening in the rays of the setting sun, and girdled by a forest of its own. On either side of this gradually ascending mountain, and about a mile distant from the lofty rocks, and parallel with the general direction of this rising rocky highway, might be seen the the dusty lines of two other roads, making their way to the northward. From the summit of one of these isolated rocks, the eye commanded the entire line of these three roads, from the points where they emerged from under the elms of C——, away to the points where all three buried themselves again in the northern forest. It was a beautiful and exciting view, and motionless on the summit of one of the highest and most smoothly rounded rocks, stood a youthful form leaning on the muzzle of his gun, and quietly enjoying the scene. He was a slim, graceful boy; thirteen summers might have passed over his head, and his eye rivaled the exquisite blue of the sky above him. His physical development indicated more of activity than muscular strength; but the breadth of his shoulders suggested that in a few years he might develop manly powers equal to most men. At his feet lay the trophies of his day's hunt, and his fox hound was standing beside him, snuffing the gentle breeze which began to whisper its evening notes over the mountain side. The boy's eye now and then dilated with interest as it moved over the landscape, and detected some new object of wonder or beauty in the distance. It was one of those mysterious blue eyes which, in the slightest shadow, deepens in lustre, and expands its pupil till it almost seems a flashing black eye. Young as he appeared, the poetic nature was rapidly developing in him, and familiarity with wild scenery, and leaping water-falls, and whispering woods, was daily maturing that nature, till already the subtile music of the winds, and trees, and waters, detained him in long reveries and gentle dreams. Ah! dream on, gentle boy, while yet thou hast the opportunity, for bye-and-bye the great practical world will laugh to scorn thy fancies, will despise thee for the angel chord which God has fastened in thy heart, and which they never can comprehend this side of death; and will sting thee with reproaches, because thou art a dreamer, and hast a calm and dignified contempt of lucre, and this world's gains. They will labor to bring thee down to their own level, far down below the worship of the beautiful, the heroic, the sublime, the generous, the self-sacrificing; down, down, to the earth wisdom, which binds a life time to the car of glittering gold. Dreams, and poetry, and music, and devotion, and enthusiasm, are thy birth right. A gentle mother, whose eyes are twins of thine eyes, and whose soul communes closely with God, will guard and guide, and encourage thy poetic nature while she lives, and seek to render it serviceable to the cause of Heaven. Thy fiery brother, with his flashing eyes, so radiantly black and genius marked, will twine his kindred nature about thine own, to foster it, till it is ready to suffer persecution from the world unflinchingly, and in its trial hours thrill forth its sweetest music. But these may pass away in death, and thou be left alone. Start then, with God. Looking up trustingly into His serene sky, devote thy heart to Him in thy Spring time; and the music of Nature will breathe more sweetly to thine ear, thine aspirations, thy enthusiasm, thy ambition, thy contempt of meanness, and deceit, and selfishness, will enrich the soil about the roots of thy tree of Life until its branches bend with fruit for suffering humanity. Poetic and refined natures have their mission from the Eternal. By their flowing words, their celestial imagery, their exultant, elevating music, their cultivation of the beautiful and refined in sentiment, and the noble and pure in purpose, they are called upon to lead humanity to the contemplation of lofty models, in order that humanity may learn thus to look away from gold mines up to stars, from the material up to the spiritual, from self to God, the centre of Light in Eternity. Their mission is to better the condition of weak, erring, wandering, suffering men, and make goodness more attractive than vice, that men may enter the spiritual life at last prepared. Dream on, fair hunter boy, upon thy native mountain side, respectful to the will of God.

The reverie of this solitary appreciative youth was suddenly broken. The rapid beat upon the rocky highway of horse's hoofs sounded distinctly on his right, and he turned quickly to discover the stranger. A powerful black horse already streaked with foam on his broad chest and sides from violent flight along the highway was coming up the mountain road bearing a pale but fearless rider. It was a fugitive seeking to bury himself from the gaze of his fellow men. It was Henry Lansing. His black felt hat drooped gracefully, but carelessly over his face, and under its shading rim black eyes glittered, roving and beautiful. His thin, pale lips were compressed, hiding his flashing white teeth, so regular and perfect when his smile chose to reveal them. His chin was small and singularly pointed, his nose straight and thin, and his complexion dark. His face was thin, and his features all regular and artistically beautiful, save only his pointed chin, which curled out from his under lip more prominently than is usual. He was closely shaved, and his chin smooth as a young girl's. His raven black hair, curling naturally, was cut short and brushed forward, covering his ears entirely from sight. He was apparently five feet and eleven inches in height, and gracefully moulded in form and limb as the mythical Adonis. As if the spirit of mystery had suddenly possessed him, he was clothed entirely in black. His narrow, rolling collar, of the finest white linen, was circled by a black silk neckcloth, with long, flowing ends. The collar was the only white object visible upon him, as he rode along the highway on his raven black favorite, with the low crowned, soft black felt hat drooping over his face. He looked every inch of him, as he bounded along, what the town of C—— named him, "a handsome, graceful daredevil."

As he dashed in his headlong pace by the high rock on which the boy was leaning on his gun, a sharp, shrill, familiar whistle met his ear, and he suddenly reined in his flying steed, and stood in the highway, motionless. Another similar whistle met his ear, and looking up, he beheld his brother. He evidently had calculated upon meeting him some where in the neighborhood, for he immediately beckoned to him to leave the rock, and come to the highway. The boy gathered up his birds, and, throwing his fowling piece over his shoulder, turned to descend the shelving back of the rock up which he had come. His eye chanced, however, to roam backward and downward towards the town of C—— for an instant, before he left the summit of the rock, and in that glance he discovered two horsemen coming up the rise of the mountain at breakneck speed. An exclamation escaped him, as he descended the rock, and he muttered to himself, " There seems to be no mercy for horse flesh to-day, for some reason or other. Harry is riding like a madman, and so are the other two." A minute more, and he was standing beside his brother's horse. Henry Lansing dismounted, and, holding his watch and heavy gold chain out to his brother, said, with quivering lip, " Keep this to remember your only brother by—for you will see him no more. I am in great trouble, Gurty, and I am going off alone, by myself, into the world. I wish to leave no trace—do not you breathe to mortal that you have seen me. I know you love me, and will think of me very, very, often. Be kind to mother, for she is an angel. I leave you this charge to keep till my return—conceal my words and my route to-day from every one. No one knows which road I leave by, and it is best." He shoved the watch nervously into the boy's hand, as he stood looking in his brother's face in wonder at this singular proceeding, and unable to utter a word in reply. Henry Lansing threw his arm around Gurty, and pressed him to his breast; then, in the twinkling of an eye, he sprang upon his horse. Before he could leave, however, the boy, who had regained his wits, exclaimed, " How can I conceal your route, when two men are close behind you, urging their horses up the mountain as fast as they can. I saw them from that high place there."

" Impossible !" was the reply, " who has any concern in following me ? Are you certain, Gurty, that they were following ?"

" Certain ?" exclaimed the boy, " Why, they are tearing along up this road, and will be here before two minutes."

The rider muttered something inaudibly, turned and gazed an instant back the way he had come, then, reining his horse's head towards the mountain summit, said, quickly, " Hide yourself, Gurty, to save questions. Black Hawk was never overtaken yet."

The next instant, he was flying up the mountain road like the wind.

* * * * * * *

The abdicating monarch, Day, folded his golden robes about him, and retired calmly and solemnly, down the horizon of the West. The last gleam of his sceptre crimsoned the lake, gilded the mountain top, tinted the gathering clouds; then vanished. But a mighty monarch strode upon the scene to contest the empire of the earth with Night. It was the King of Storms. From the northward hurried the rumbling thunder wheels of his gathering forces, and the gloomy front of the threatening clouds, his advance guard, moved solemnly into view. The wind moaned, and rushed, and shrieked, before his advance, and the helpless mountain trees flung their arms to heaven for help. The young, springing grass, trembled and sighed; the shrinking forms of the half clad bushes uttered plaintive cries of terror, and the forest howled and roared in agony. Upward and onward from the East moved Night with her opposing forces, and her gloomy line of battle swept away the lingering light of evening, and then closed sternly with the howling spirits of the storm. Confusion and horror and impenetrable darkness clung together about the mountain top. Yet in despite of all, and with the unflinching tenacity of purpose which sustains man when acting from a sense of duty, two awe struck horsemen clung to the mountain side and slowly struggled up the rocky path against the storm. They sought to overtake the raven colored steed and its pale rider whose mysterious forms had moved vaguely once or twice before their vision just before the heavy pall of impenetrable darkness settled upon the mountain. The rocky road was growing every instant, as they toiled upward, still more arduous: but they knew the summit was at hand, with its comparatively level forest road. Ah! how little did they know the speed of that graceful, powerful beast whose clattering hoofs had sounded occasionally to their ears, apparently just ahead of them. That mocking dare-devil of a rider had lingered now and then; merely, to whet their eagerness of pursuit, knowing far better than they the tortuous peculiarities of the forest road upon the summit, and that when once among the gloomy trees, Black Hawk would leave them like the wind. A mighty, overpowering rush of the wind down the mountain, met the pursuing horsemen, and they paused in the profound darkness, unable, for an instant, to proceed. A dazzling flash from the Storm King pierced suddenly the gloomy darkness of the night, and the exceeding brightness of the bolt gave them a full view of the object of their pursuit. Motionless upon the summit of the mountain, and only a stone's throw from them, stood the black horse, and the erect, graceful rider, a tableau party given by the lightning. That dark, handsome face, under the drooping hat, was turned directly towards his pursuers; a gleam of triumph was on the features, almost a smile. Night dropped the veil, and the tableau vanished. It was the last view they ever had of Henry Lansing.

CHAPTER V.

THE inquisition of the coroner's jury, which was finally returned to the criminal court of the county in which the town of C—— was located, certified, substantially, that—Benjamin Hartwell, a resident of a neighboring city, who chanced to be a few hours in C——, through which town he was passing on a journey to the Western States, had left his hotel in the morning for a stroll about the town. He had stated to the landlord of the hotel that he had never before seen the place, and that he felt inclined to view the town and its environs while waiting for the stage which was to convey him on his journey to the West. That he disappeared from the hotel at an early hour of the morning, had been met by several persons about the streets, and that the last information which was given concerning him came from a gentleman who had seen him walking quietly across the meadows toward old Rosy's garden. His identity had been established by the positive statements of Miss Grayson and her father, and also her brother Carl. Miss Grayson and her friend had overheard a loud and angry altercation in the wood, and had heard a desperate struggle, and then the flying footsteps, through the bushes, of the supposed murderer. They had recognized neither of the voices, but Miss Grayson had entered the thicket and discovered the dying man, who recognized her, uttered a few words in no way connected with the manner of his death, and then quickly expired. Three of the neighbors had, under her directions, followed closely upon the retreating fugitive, but had returned baffled, and utterly unable to say who the murderer was. A young girl residing in the neighborhood, had seen Mr. Henry Lansing part with old Rosy, and disappear in the direction of the scene of the murder, only about half an hour before it occurred ; and her testimony was corroborated by the old woman herself, to whom the young man had stated that he was in trouble, which he would not reveal, and that he was certainly going away that day to Europe, to travel. None of his family knew of such a purpose on his part ; and the old woman appeared to be his only confidante in the matter. About ten o'clock on the fatal morning Henry Lansing had been seen to ride rapidly toward the residence of Mr. Grayson, dismount, walk towards the mansion, pause in the garden, reverse his course unaccountably, and dash away on his well known horse, Black Hawk. He had left his horse in the stable about an hour before the murder occurred and had taken him out again about an hour after Miss Grayson had found the murdered Hartwell. No one could testify that he had been seen after taking out his horse the second time, until the two pursuers sent by the coroner, had discovered him at dusk, ascending the mountain on Black Hawk. The last view that they had of him he was standing motionless on the crest of the mountain, revealed for an instant by the flash of lightning. They had slowly traversed the woody road on the ridge of the mountain for miles, amid the rain and the roaring of the wind tossed branches of the trees, but morning had found them in the forest, without the slighest evidence of the fugitive's whereabouts.

No motive could be surmised why he should commit such a fearful crime ; not the slightest evidence existed that he had ever seen such a man as Hartwell. Yet the jury pronounced his actions and presence in the garden on the fatal day in connection with his mysterious flight as very suspicious, and that he ought immediately to be overtaken and arrested, as being either a principal or at least a witness of the murder. But their verdict proved of no avail, for the handsome, gifted, reckless dare-devil, Henry Lansing, could not be tracked. He had gone with the wild flash of lightning on the mountain summit ; and the place of his disappearance became a centre for the speculations of the lovers of the marvelous. It was gradually whispered among a select circle of the saints of C—— that the arch enemy had beckoned for him, horse and all. Public opinion, that most sage counselor and judge, pronounced him guilty of the murder.

But many refused to yield to this decision, and said, fearlessly, that it was a shame to suppose that he knew anything at all of the affair. That he was an honest hearted gentleman, wearing slowly out the garment of high living and dissipation which had clothed his collegiate life; and that a few years would find him one of the best and noblest lights of the community. But where and why had he gone? No one could give a satisfactory answer to this enigma. No one among his friends could tell. Only one individual in the whole town of C—— divined his real motive; and she was a golden-haired girl whose face had been brushed by an angel's wing. She knew of his mother's agony at his mysterious disappearance, the mortification of his whole family at the serious charges brought against him, and which they indignantly denied. And yet she remained perfectly silent in regard to the clue which she possessed of the real criminal. There was not the slightest intention in her mind to allow Henry Lansing to be sacrificed to the malice of his enemies in the net of circumstantial evidence which might enclose him, in case he should be found and arrested. In that event, she would step forward and save him at every sacrifice. But she hoped that contingency would not for a long time occur; and in the meantime she would endeavor to persuade herself as to what steps God, in whom she trusted for direction and guidance, would have her take in this perplexing affair. But three days had elapsed since the dreadful occurrence, and in that brief period of time, she had experienced more distress of mind and of conscience, than in her whole life before. She had placed the little piece of the silk neck-tie carefully in the secret drawer of her toilet box, where she deposited her more valuable jewelry; but she could not resist the impulse to take it out and ponder over it; and she had even laid it upon her prayer-book at night at her devotions, and invoked the direction of Heaven as to what course to pursue in regard to it. No urgent, stimulating voice in her heart or in her understanding, appeared to result from her prayers, and so she waited, and reflected, and became more uneasy and disturbed in her purpose every day. Occasionally a pleasant gleam of light fluttered across her reverie, and that gleam arose from the thought that the brightest and most eligible young man of C—— loved her; loved her so passionately, that her refusal had spirited him away to some remote corner of the earth, where he might escape the burden and distress of her presence. Blonde felt instinctively that this mysterious disappearance was due to her letter, and she was surprised to discover, springing up in her daily meditations, a deepening interest in his fate. The violence with which he had rent their intercourse, was in keeping with her idea of his character, and still she had not expected such an abrupt departure from her society. Her decision, as expressed in her refusal of his hand, she had not intended to be necessarily a final and irrevocable one. But he was gone, nevertheless, and might never return. He might find solace from his disappointment in something more desperate still. And this reflection left a serious expression, for a moment, on that calm, beautiful face of hers. His earnest, burning letter, had failed to move her heart towards him; and yet the startling occurrences in which he had since become involved, arising almost entirely from her rejection of his hand, and his consequent frantic movements, had aided in the concentration of her thoughts upon him. He was indeed gone; gone into the unknown world of Europe, without question, desolate, disappointed and desperate. There was no one beyond that broad ocean to welcome him, none to address words of sympathy and greeting to him. He had left all that makes life dear to the heart, far behind him, and it was all for her. He had laid his pride and his secret together at her feet, only to result in his bitter humiliation. He had resumed his pride again, and either it or his judgment had carried him off. He had fled from her; doubts on the subject were faint, indeed, in her mind.

On the evening of the third day after his singular disappearance, Blonde sat at the open window of her bed room, in the full rays of the rising moon. Her lamp had been placed in a closet, that its rays might not disturb the sleeper who occupied her snow-white bed. She had drawn a low ottoman to the window, and near the head of the bed, and she had been seated there a long time, conversing with her friend, Clara Peyton, who had come to sleep with her. The young girl had finally given way to fatigue, and dropped asleep holding her friend's hand. Her soft white cheek pressed the pillow, and the moonbeams fell upon her face revealing the dark, folded beauty of her long eye-lashes, and the well-defined arch of her jet eye brows. A smile lingered upon her pure lips, which were full and dewy red. One arm strayed away over the coverlet of the bed, where Blonde had placed it after she had relinquished her hand; the other had buried itself beneath her pillow. But Blonde could not sleep. Her tender conscience was at work. Clara had no care; but Blonde was holding the bloody clue of a murder. The thought haunted her; it was leaving its deep mark on her countenance day after day; her blue eyes were daily growing darker, and retiring further back under her brows. Her eyes seemed ever to be studying deeply, and Clara had remarked frequently upon her occasional paleness. A terrible engrossing reality had taken possession of her intellect; something occupied her now besides a girl's dreams or studies, or household duties. Her religion came thundering at the door of her soul, demanding her secret. Justice whispered solemnly in her ears: "He that striketh a man with a will to kill him, shall be put to death." And yet the louder the stern voices of duty and principle called to her, the closer did she clutch the fragment of the neck tie, and hide it tremblingly away. Some fearfully profound emotion of her heart, was the lion in the path of her duty. When she reflected upon the possible consequences of exposing this clue to the public mind, she trembled, and sometimes great burning tears of agony stood in her eyes, and her lips murmured their trembling entreaty—"Oh! God, spare me this, spare me this."

It was one of those fearful secrets which must be openly confessed to the world, or buried solitary and alone in one's own bosom. If it was right, and just, and proper to save an innocent man from suspicion by concealing the clue in her possession, then it was right to share the secret with no human being. If the man was really guilty, then she became the companion of crime. But exposure would be like guiding to her heart the iron hand which would tear away by the bleeding roots, affections which had become a part of her nature. Aye! strong ardent affections, which had woven their many tendrils about her heart, till she had learned to think of death, as only the dreadful time when those tendrils would be broken. Oh! no, oh! no! she could not betray *him* to death.

The moonbeams, pale and beautiful, came wandering in at her window, and the voices of the earth were growing still with the advancing night. The tops of the elm trees faintly fluttered in the silver radiance, and through their interlacing branches, her eye was watching the cloudless sky. She seemed to seek there in its broad expanse, a nearer view of God, of Him who had given all for her, and in return laid claim to all. And as she gazed upward, her tortured soul seemed to sail away to the celestial city, to the feet of her Father, and there to whisper, "Thy will be done. I will do all—deny all, sacrifice all for Thee. Give me Thy peace once more." She arose from her seat, for a sudden purpose possessed her, and her tall, slim figure in its white robe of muslin, stood, graceful and spiritual-like, in the flooding moonlight, at the open window. She turned slowly from the window and her eye fell upon her sleeping friend, over whose calm features the moonbeams now were gliding with more powerful light, and whose expression was as gentle as the sleeping infant, to whom the guardian angel whispers. Oh! what a true, earnest friend, that sleeping girl had proved herself. With all the warmth of her young, ardent nature, she cherished Blonde; and that first winter of their acquaintance, which had just gone, was full of deeds of kindness and devotion to her graceful lily friend. Blonde loved her dearly, and seating herself upon the side of the bed, she gazed long and earnestly upon her calm, gentle face. Then she seemed to brace herself for some great effort, and reluctantly, lingeringly turned away from the bed, and walked to her toilet table, where rested on its white mat, the small box, the secret drawer of which contained the fragment of silk torn from the murderer's throat. She took from her pocket a bunch of small keys and opened the box. A secret spring inside opened at the pressure of her finger a concealed drawer, and from it she removed the fragment of the necktie, and laid it on her dressing table. Then she changed her dress throughout, disguising herself for a street walk. A long, dark cloak of thin spring cloth, extended almost to the floor, concealing the outline of her figure; and she wrapped a black veil about her head so that the mass of her golden hair and her upper face were effectually disguised, and the ends of this covering she tied under her chin. No one would recognize her unless by her height and walk. Then she placed the mysterious fragment of the necktie in her bosom once more, and stealthily sought the door of her room. The hazard of her solitary night excursion flitted across her brain, and she paused irresolutely at the door. Other emotions passed over her face and her pearl teeth pressed tightly upon her lip. The uncertainty of purpose was returning upon her again. Her secret night walk might render her miserable for the remainder of her life. Why might she not wait for a more auspicious opportunity, when daylight was abroad, and when she might act more naturally in carrying out her purpose? This night expedition might be the very act which would entail suspicion of something wrong, if she should be recognized by any one on the street. A voice whispered in her conscience, "Go now, while the desire to please God is urgent, and He will protect you; to-morrow may see your self-denial gone—your firmness overwhelmed by self!"

She turned back a moment to the bedside. Her muffled figure bent over the sleeping girl, in the attitude of unutterable affection and tenderness. She could not endure the thought of leaving her alone. But the desire of throwing off the heavy burden of her secret, and of gaining peace of mind once more, drew her away from the side of her sleeping friend, and she moved slowly and cautiously out of the room, closing the door quietly behind her ; for the other inmates of the house were awake, and she heard her father's voice in conversation below. Noiselessly she glided down the stairs and passed out through a back door, near the room where first she was presented to the reader. She entered at once the moonlit garden, and passed slowly through the shrubbery to a gate opening into a quiet lane. The moon was lighting every thing, and the lane was clearly defined before her on in the direction of the great avenue of C——, where the mass of elm branches appeared in the distance like a dense forest gently undulating in the silver moonlight. All was remarkably silent in the neighborhood, but she knew she would meet stragglers when she emerged from the lane into the avenue. At length she reached the termination of the lane, and paused a moment before exposing herself on the broad street. She stood in the shadow of a stately mansion listening for footsteps, but none appeared to be passing just then. Suddenly her dress was seized from behind, and a cold shudder of fear stupefied her.

She was followed. Turning quickly, with a feeling that her strength was oozing away, she discovered a large dark object holding her dress tightly in the shadow. Another glimpse revealed the absurdity of her terror. It was her brother's immense black Newfoundland dog. He had followed her in his affection and faithfulness from the moment she had left the garden, and now seized her dress to intimate that she had gone far enough for a young unprotected female, without some further recognition and consultation with the canine portion of her family. She stooped down and passed her arm caressingly about the faithful creature, and he manifested his joy by a slow and dignified wave of his tail, and fixing his great luminous eyes upon her muffled countenance. Here was an unexpected difficulty. If persons should fail to recognize her in her walk under the elms, they would certainly know her brother's famous dog. There was but one course to dispose of the difficulty. The dog must go back to his kennel. She spoke in low tones, but sternly—" Go back, sir, I don't want you ; there, that way ; go right back." The dog looked reproachfully at her, but immediately walked away in the direction he had come. She followed him with her eyes, but presently he seemed to consider her order sufficiently obeyed, and laid himself slowly down in the middle of the lane, and fixed his eyes on her to watch her movements. He was evidently in a similar condition with his beautiful mistress. His sense of duty was also in conflict with his affections. He understood that he must obey orders, but the task was exceedingly repugnant to his feelings. But, unlike her, his affections made short pause at duty, for when she moved on in her walk and passed along under the drooping elms of the avenue, he arose to his feet with dignity, and followed her at a distance. He had discovered a conflict of duties, and determined to follow the most agreeable, namely, to protect her in her night ramble. She did not observe her distant guardian, however, for she was absorbed in the thought of how she should proceed most successfully along in the shadows to escape recognition. The solemn clock from the church tower mournfully and slowly marked the hour of eleven. And as she counted the dismal strokes, she realized how lonely and exposed she was in the broad street of a large town, at that ill-omened hour of night. But as she advanced further on her way, she discovered that her nerves were becoming more steady, and the long trailing shadows of the elms grew less gloomy and suspicious to her eyes. She experienced the truth that God smooths the way for those who earnestly desire to please Him. She passed several dark objects of men, walking along under the trees; but no one offered to molest her, even if they were so disposed: for the majestic figure of the dog was ever looming up near her, whenever the approaching footsteps sounded. And one glance sufficed to show that he was an ugly customer to have a difficulty with on the young woman's account. At length she had traversed considerably more than a mile of the length of C——. The place of her destination was at hand. She paused at the gate of a mansion, glistening in the full moon light, with the whiteness of marble. Tall columns of the Corinthian order supported the roof of the broad front piazza, and a marble fountain was flinging showers of diamonds into the moonlight. The inmates of the mansion were evidently asleep, for no light gleamed at the front windows. But Blonde advanced to a wing on the north side of the building, and there she found, as she had suspected, a brilliant light streaming from the windows. It was a lawyer's office, plainly enough, for through the low sash doors of this wing, could be seen distinctly, regular rows of new looking law books in their yellow covers, revealed to the outsider by the clear light of a lamp swinging by its chain in mid-air. She could distinguish, also, through the glass, the lawyer himself, diligently writing at his table; a noble looking individual with a broad white forehead, and thin grey hair. He looked so calmly, and thoughtfully dignified, that one might easily imagine him what he really was, the Chief Justice of the Supreme Court of his State. Had not the discreet, graceful lily, Blonde Grayson, chosen well the exalted personage, to whom her dreadful secret might be confided? Had she not, with rare judgment selected one who would solve her doubts, aid her judgment, and enable her, by his calm counsels and nature experience, to see the path clearly of her moral and legal duties in the matter of the murder?

She advanced again, to one of the sash doors, and ascending the little flight of wooden steps, rapped gently upon the glass. The judge looked up in surprise, but came at once to admit his nocturnal visitor. As he opened the sash door, Blonde removed her veil from her head, and he recognized her at once.

"I am very much honored by your presence, Miss Grayson," he said, in his bland tones, "but are you alone, entirely alone?"

She advanced further into the lamp light of the room before she replied, and glancing nervously around, she said—

"Judge, I want you to draw those curtains over the doors—I do not wish to be seen from the street—the nature of my errand requires the utmost secrecy and dispatch, or I should not have dared to come in this unprotected way."

The individual addressed, at once quietly and calmly drew the curtains over the doors, while she seated herself by the table, and loosened and threw back her cloth cloak. Then he seated himself near her, and resting his elbow on the table, while his hand shielded his large gray eyes from the light, he said—

"I am now at your service, Miss Grayson; please proceed with your communication. I shall endeavor to render you all the assistance or advice in my power."

The conversation was a long and intensely interesting one, and before everything had been satisfactorily arranged in regard to the future course of action to be pursued by each, the solemn clock of C—— startled the two into recollection. It was the hour of midnight. Profound secrecy had been decided upon for the present, at least. There was sufficient reason why the two should part at once. Blonde had been weeping bitterly, but now almost in possession of her usual calmness, she arose from her seat, and drew on her cloak, and wrapped the veil again over her head, concealing her face. The judge informed her that it was best for him not to be seen with her, but that he would follow her at a distance on her way home, near enough to protect her from harm. He pressed her hand warmly as she passed out through the door into the calm moonlight, and said, with a tremor in his voice, "God bless you, gentle girl; God bless you."

In a few moments more, three isolated figures were moving along under the drooping elms. A tall muffled figure of a woman glided far ahead. Several rods behind her, moved the judge, calmly and solemnly under the trees; and on the opposite side of the street, unnoticed by either, walked the watchful dog.

The beautiful night wanderer regained her father's residence in safety, and her key, which she produced from her pocket, gave her admittance to the hall, unnoticed. She turned at once into her boudoir on the first floor, and lighting the candles in her silver candlesticks, opened her book of prayer, and kneeling calmly, returned her God earnest thanks for His protecting care in her night walk, and for that peace of mind and conscience, which had returned to her once more. Then seeking her bed room on the upper floor, she found her friend still peacefully sleeping as when she left her, with the moonbeams straying away over the snowy whiteness of her bed. She was soon sleeping beside Clara Peyton, the calm, sweet sleep of innocence. She had transferred, in part, her burden to the calm, dignified Chief Justice of the Court. She no longer held the mysterious fragment of the necktie. She had left *that* with him.

CHAPTER VI.

ON the morning after Blonde Grayson's secret consultation with the Chief Justice, she was seated in her private room, on the first floor of her father's residence, engaged in conversation with her friend Clara. The two were working industriously upon a large quilt, which was being heavily embroidered for a fair soon to open for the benefit of the chapel of Saint Paul. The ladies of that congregation, designed raising, in that way, a sufficient sum of money to purchase a new and larger organ for their church. The two friends were endeavoring to present to this approaching fair, a valuable specimen of needle-work, which should astonish the congregation, and secure to themselves the palm for industry and zeal in the cause of religion. The animated discussion of the tragedy which occupied all minds in the town of C——, was suddenly, about the hour of noon, interrupted by the ringing of the front door bell. After a short pause, the servant announced to Blonde, the presence of visitors in the parlor,—" Mrs. Lansing and her son have called."

Blonde remarked to her friend that the lady who was announced, had never entered the house before. Ill health had prevented Mrs. Lansing calling with her daughter, Mrs. Bounce, when that lady came to visit the Graysons, shortly after their arrival in C——. Blonde had returned the call, but failed to meet Mrs. Lansing, who was confined to her room by her delicate state of health. This solitary exchange of calls had been the extent of the intimacy of the two families, except that Henry Lansing had called several times after meeting the new family at a party, to the manifest displeasure of his sister, Mrs. Bounce, who desired him to form his intimacies exclusively within the society of her own church. It had thus happened that Henry Lansing's mother and Blonde had never met. It was, therefore, with mingled sensations of curiosity and sympathy towards the lady whose son had fallen into such bad repute within the past three days, that the fair mistress of the mansion, completed her toilet in her bed room above stairs, and descended alone to the parlor. The vehement nature of Mrs. Bounce's orthodoxy in her church had been the means of conveying to the community, or rather to the congregation of the rival church of Saint Paul, the impression that the whole Lansing family, were equally firm, uncompromising and constant in bold declaration of the Calvinistic faith with herself. They were supposed to hold as determinedly and vehemently as herself, that Episcopacy was little better than a weak dilution of the forms and ceremonies of the Church of Rome; and that it engendered worldliness, frivolity and everything else than a spirit consonant with the principles of the gospel. A bold and constant member of a family, often represents to the world, erroneous ideas of the individual characters in that family. He becomes, as it were, the mouthpiece of the family, and the peculiar views of its other members, do not appear, from their inherent gentleness and indisposition to assertions and dogmatic declarations. Thus had the vehement Mrs. Bounce, overshadowed the Lansing family. As Blonde proceeded slowly down stairs, she thought to herself: "This lady, too, cherishes these false notions in regard to us all; why has she called now? Is it her strict sense of etiquette? Is it her condition of mind regarding the charges against her son? Is it the unaccountable pause in this garden of Henry Lansing, which the town is so mystified about? Well! she shall know that I am a lady, if I am a high church woman."

Thus on her guard, with a certain amount of antagonism, social and religious, she quietly opened the parlor door, and swept her tall, graceful figure, into the presence of the strangers. What was her surprise to behold rising, calmly and with the sweetest dignity, from the sofa, where a slim, graceful boy was standing beside her, a lady arrayed in deepest mourning, with a fair, but emaciated countenance, and with exquisitely shaded, dark blue eyes, lustrous with intellect, and gazing into Blonde's eyes with gentle and unmistakable interest. They were eyes, versatile with every emotion, and yet the longer one looked into them, the deeper did the well of the soul which supplied them expression, appear to be. Love from those eyes must be a priceless inheritance. Prayer from those eyes must bring a speedy answer from the Eternal Throne; and as they studied the delicately chiseled features of Blonde, the stranger, appreciation of her beauty lighted them and the emotion which had brought them to that mansion, softened them, before the gentle musical voice had uttered that emotion.

Extending her small gloved hand to Blonde, she said, tremulously—

"I regret so much that I have not been able to know you before, Miss Grayson; and that same ill health which has detained me so long from meeting you, would still have separated us, had it not been that you had touched my heart, oh! so deeply, by your earnest vindication of my noble son, Henry, in this mysterious affair. His honor and his character are dearer to my heart than life. He has gone; God only knows where—but he is no criminal. Your earnest and noble remarks before the coroner's jury, were brought directly to me. And I have almost crawled from my sick room to thank you. Doctor Crammer told me the very words you said, leaning on his arm, in that dreadful room; and that, notwithstanding what you had heard that very afternoon concerning my son's presence in that neighborhood; and notwithstanding the suspicions uttered on every side of you by those unfeeling women, you still pronounced so emphatically, that Harry was, in your belief, entirely innocent. May God bless you—I am your friend from this day."

The mother's pale, thin lips quivered. She could say no more; and Blonde led her to the sofa, where, for a moment, she indulged her over-excited heart in a flood of tears. At length regaining control of herself, and extending her hand to the graceful boy, who was standing with his small gray cap in his hand, at the end of the sofa, and studying all the while this scene was occurring, the beautiful face of Blonde, with the appreciating eye of an artist, she said, kindly—

"Come here, Gurty, this is Miss Grayson—I know you will love any one who defends Harry."

The boy advanced with the easy step and bearing of a prince, extended his sun-browned little hand to Blonde, and said, with his blue eyes fixed in undisguised admiration on her face,

"I never saw a real lady yet, who didn't defend Harry. I think mother minds too much what the other kind say; this town isn't much, any way."

He said this in a quick, spirited way, and with a nonchalant air, which reminded Blonde instantly of his brother. Then he added, with more interest in his tone—

"Miss Grayson, will you allow me to draw back that window curtain a little more? There is a painting, in that corner, of the sea, which I should like very much to have more light on."

"Certainly," replied Blonde. "I shall be happy if you will examine, at your ease, all the paintings. They were purchased by father when we were in Paris; and though not by any great master, you will find, if your taste runs in that way, decided beauties in some of them. If you really take an interest in such matters, I will show you into my brother's studio—it is just across the hall."

The boy's blue eye lighted with interest at once, as he replied, "Indeed, I love pictures—if I could learn to paint I think I should be very happy. Oh! this is the real sea, I am sure, though I never had even a glimpse of the ocean; tell me, Miss Grayson, is that the real color of the sea. I have always supposed it was blue, but this is an angry green."

"Oh, yes," she answered, "it is often that color, seen from the land; but on the broad ocean, you find the real blue tint; but I have been on the sea in all kinds of weather, and I have seen it assume a dozen colors. But come with me, across the hall; this is not the hour of the day when these pictures appear to advantage. My brother will enjoy having you in his room, for he loves an appreciative eye. One moment, Mrs. Lansing, and I will return to you. Come this way, sir, if you please."

She led the way to the opposite side of the hall, and rapped gently at a door. In a moment, a gentleman opened the door, and thrust out his face, to see who was there. He had blue eyes, like Blonde, his sister, but his hair was much darker, and a heavy beard concealed his lower face and throat.

"This is my brother, Mr. Lansing. I have promised this young gentleman, Carl, to show him the pictures in your studio. He loves such things, and he is a brother of Mr. Henry Lansing, whom you like so much."

"Come in, come in," said her brother, extending his hand to the boy, "you are welcome indeed, if you are Henry Lansing's brother; come in, and do just as you like. I am sketching just now, but in a few minutes I will attend to you. Put your cap on that table, and then walk about at your leisure. You are very unlike your brother. How I would like to put your blue eyes into a female face I am painting."

His welcome was so cordial that Gurty's heart was won at once, and he walked quietly into the studio and seated himself, while Carl went back to his easel.

Blonde closed the door upon them, and went back to Mrs. Lansing. She seated herself beside her on the sofa and said,

"The part I have borne in this dreadful tragedy, Mrs. Lansing, has occasioned me more distress than ever I knew: and since you have so kindly ascribed to me merit for doing what was only natural and impulsive before the coroner's jury, I will express to you my horror at finding that in the town of C— family, and standing, and character are no protection against any whim the community may take up with. Your son happened to be somewhere in the neighborhood of the murder half an hour before it was committed, and that fact, in connection with his leaving the town, which any gentleman of legal age may do at any time, fixes the suspicion of the whole town upon him. Why, in that half hour he might have been two miles away from that garden. He is a very rapid walker, I know. See how unreasonable people are in such a time as this. The only person known to be in that neighborhood, who was acquainted with Mr. Hartwell, was myself. There is more reason to suspect me of the act than any other being in this whole town. The finding of the watch and purse unmolested proves that robbery had nothing to do with it. It must have been, therefore, revenge or jealousy; or, as father suggests, it may have been to destroy an heir to an estate, or anything of that nature, and it must consequently be the act of some one who knew Mr. Hartwell, or knew something about him. And not a soul here knew him but our family; not a soul here ever heard of him. And then to think of a jury of men publicly holding up to suspicion your son, one of the finest young men of C——, who had no motive to murder an utter stranger, and concerning whom not a being here has even attempted to surmise a motive."

Mrs. Lansing was charmed. Her mother's heart was gratified at these warm, sensible words, and she said, "If all were as sensible as you, Miss Grayson, many heartaches would be avoided in this world. It is needless for me to say that I am surprised at this dreadful opinion about Henry. I am stunned. In my own church, are persons who have professed for me many years the most ardent affection; and this affection they have assured me extended to my whole family. They have declared to me that they hoped to see the time when they could manifest the sincerity of that affection. And now they have abandoned me as the mother of a murderer. Not one of them has the nerve to step forward to my side and say, 'This is the falsest, most atrocious calumny upon a respectable family that ever was heard of. There is one, whose name was rendered vile by an envious tongue. She was declared unfit for decent women to associate with, and a committee of ladies in my church went from house to house instructing and warning all to shun her society; they came to me, and I told them that if they shunned her, they should shun me also, for she was an innocent woman, and I would stand by her and vindicate her character till my death. The storm passed; time broke the force of the slander, and she stands among the first in the church. I know she would have been hunted away from the church and from the town, but for my interposition. And now she has not one word for my poor boy. If there is one pang more bitter to me than another, it is ingratitude, and I fear I must have committed some fearful act of ingratitude to my God, to have this dreadful judgment come upon me, when I am so weak and weary and faint from sickness. I know I shall linger here on the earth only a short time, at the best, but it seems so lonely and desolate to me, to have all desert me, on account of my boy. And yet when my adorable Lord bowed his head

3*

on the cross it was his bosom friends that left him alone to die Now I can feel his agony, alone. Oh! my God, alone."

Poor weary soul! her life had been a life for others: seeking to assimilate her life to the life of the lowly Nazarene, she lived only that the poor might smile at her footfall in the freezing blast, that the sick might feel a supporting and gentle hand, that the orphan child might look up to a mother's beaming eye once more, that the outcast and the abandoned might hear once more the gentle music of innocence and peace, as she came, angel shod with words of hope and courage, fresh from communion with her Lord in prayer. The great lights of her church neglected her, the force of public opinion swept off her friends, and she trembled in her weakness of body, and her loneliness of heart. The weak and the wicked always bow to storms, and they had left her with her mother's instincts grappling alone with the hurricane. And she so firm in defence of her friends, so constant, so fearless, amid all storms, because her anchor was fastened in the truth, was yet on this account more sensitive at the fact of her loneliness. She knew her child was innocent, and she felt that she was at least entitled to the mere declaration of that fact, from her professed friends. She could have abundance of such sympathy as this: "Oh! Mrs. Lansing, God has cast a great calamity upon your family, but you must try to bear up under it." And then she would exclaim fiercely: "It is false—there is no calamity but lying tongues—he is innocent. How dare you call innocence calamity." They who thought to have her admit the disgrace of her children waked the lioness. Of such material are noble Christian mothers made. She knew her boys had been educated in principles, taught at her knee to be open and straight-forward, and that no meanness, undue advantage, treachery or secret murder was in their natures. This consciousness braced her against the world, and yet, because she was human, she craved support, and she came, trembling and emaciated, from her sick room, to thank Blonde, the stranger, and to bless her.

As she appeared thus constant and almost alone in defence of her child, with a mother's yearning tenderness glistening in her lustrous blue eyes, Blonde experienced a feeling of compunction. How quickly could she raise that burden of distress and mortification from that gentle mother's life; how easily would one word from her lips expose the guilty and sweep the cloud from the character of the innocent. This consciousness rendered her for the instant speechless, and she sat silently beside the mother contemplating her gentle, refined features and studying over again all the doubts and anxieties of the past night, which she had hoped were flown forever. But though she was filled with admiration and respect for this new acquaintance, who clung so earnestly, so tenaciously, to her friends, when they were persecuted, yet the reflection that she herself was bound to her own friends by equally firm and unyielding ties, that she, herself, was bound by all the holy promises of the past to defend and maintain those who relied upon her, checked the words that would otherwise have flown from her lips. She had firmly resolved, if Heaven would allow it, to retain her secret, in company with the judge whom she had consulted. Their mutual promises covered the present time at least. They were not yet to betray the owner of the mysterious necktie, to death. Another emotion was present to her. She believed Henry Lansing had fled in distress of mind at her refusal of his hand; and there before her sat his mother. How little was she dreaming of Blonde's act, being the cause of his singular disappearance. And this reflection, this belief, prevented her lingering upon the cause of his sudden departure. She avoided that subject and diverted the conversation which soon sprang up into other channels.

Mrs. Lansing, in the fullness of her heart and in the relief which Blonde's presence and championship for her child afforded, wandered off into a long account of the life and endearing qualities of her son. Her maternal prejudice gave a fair coloring to every act of his life; and her listener, with her quick perceptions, gained a wonderful insight into the real excellencies of his character, and discerned with ready tact the weaknesses also. She began to realize that she had lost indeed one who was capable of rendering her happy in life. Perhaps he had gone forever. Her interest deepened in the mother. As the conversation turned, naturally enough for two beings who recognized the protecting and loving power of a God, to the subject of religion and its consolations, she discovered that the exquisitely beautiful and motive principle of Mrs. Lansing's life was love—love for the Divine Creator and Ruler of all things. It appeared to be an utterly absorbing and vivifying principle of her existence. She never approached the subject of dogma or of sect. She seemed to realize the Divine presence, and to love it with all the warmth of a high-toned intellect and a beautiful nature. Not a flower or a leaf or a human face passed across her vision that did not speak to her heart of Him. The bright sun that gladdened the morning, said to her heart, "another day to serve Him," another day to cast a flower of charity in the path of His poor, another day to revel in the luxury of music, that the voice might praise Him better, and that the soul might be prepared for another and celestial music beyond the grave. It was enough for her that the beautiful girl, whose fair face and golden hair glimmered before her with the sweetness of a dream, loved Him. They were both children of His own creation; they were both looking heavenward; they both desired to become pure and holy that they might win the eternal refuge of His arms. The fair mistress of the mansion was becoming charmed with her strange guest, and with her stranger language. She had not expected this from a member of the rival church of C——. So womanly, so high-toned in defence of her children and their reputation, so independent of storms, and yet so ardent in her love of God, and all who loved Him. This was indeed a friend worth securing. For such a friend one could well afford to bear the criticism of those who guard church lines, and seek to separate congenial souls by pointing to the barrier, doctrine.

At length Gurty made his appearance at the parlor door, and waited a moment for an opportunity to speak. His blue eyes were radiant with pleasure, and it was evident something in the painter's studio had secured his youthful admiration. Blonde saw him, after a little, standing gracefully and patiently in the door, and said, while her eye noted several resemblances in the boy's manner to the absent brother,

"I hope you have enjoyed yourself in the studio. We have been so engrossed with each other, that I fear you have been neglected."

"Oh, you needn't trouble yourself about that, Miss Grayson—pictures never tire me, and your brother is going to teach me to be an artist. He says I am to come here often, and he is to instruct me. He thinks I have an eye for a painter, and I am delighted. But I came for mother. There is a picture which your brother brought from Florence that will please *her*, I know; do come right now, for he says this is the very best light in the whole day for his studio."

"Dear boy! he is ever thinking of something to please me," said Mrs. Lansing. "I wonder what enthusiasm possesses him now—some girl's face, I'll venture. He tells me every night about some pretty face that has struck his fancy—and he notices every thing about them, too, in a wonderful manner.—Shall we go with him, Miss Grayson? I have prolonged my call already, but your interest in my son Henry encouraged my poor heart so much."

They arose and followed Gurty into the studio. As the mother entered the apartment, her eye lighted for a moment upon the figure of Carl Grayson, seated at his easel, and too absorbed in his art to be disturbed. Then her eye sought Gurty. He was standing at one side of an oval centre-table, with one hand resting lightly upon it. The other was pointing at a small painting in a heavy frame of elaborate gilding. His blue eyes, radiant and triumphant, were on his mother's countenance to watch the effect. It was a painting, delineating a scene in the world's history which had never before been represented to her eye on canvas or in an engraving. She had indeed imagined to a certain extent this sad spectacle; but reared as she had been in the stern principles of Calvinism, this melancholy picture had never chanced to meet her eye. The effect was wonderful. The image which was ever present to her heart, her life, her actions, was before her. It was the sad mockery of the Son of God; the touching, the eloquent, heart-rending "Ecce Homo." The crown of thorns pressed his divine brow, and the trickling blood revealed his anguish. The kingly robe of brilliant hue fell from his shoulders, and his weary hand grasped the reed, the emblem of his sceptre. But oh! the face—the sweet, holy, suffering face of Jesus; in the intensity of his suffering, beautiful and loving still, and looking heavenward for mercy, not for himself, but for those who mocked him in his agony. The awe-struck mother advanced a step nearer, as if bewildered by the strange spectacle; her deep blue eye dilated in horror as the fearful descriptive power of the artist was manifest. But this emotion fluttered away from her features, and in another instant she was kneeling before the painting, convulsively sobbing, "My Lord and my God!"

The boy's expression of triumph vanished in an instant; he looked uneasily for a moment upon her kneeling, trembling figure, and then turned respectfully away and passed behind the screen which concealed the form of Carl Grayson. But Blonde's eyes blazed with the fire of enthusiasm. Her golden hair glittered in the full, mellow light of the sun, with the glory of an angel. She passed rapidly to the side of the kneeling mother, sank upon her knees, and throwing her arm around her shoulders, drew the trembling mother's head to her breast and gazed with her devoutly upon the holy countenance of the Divine Master.

Silence held his gentle sceptre over the painter's studio, and the mellow sunlight pouring in at the windows revealed the first and exquisite union of two hearts in the bonds of that affection which derives its power from mutual devotion to the sufferings and martyrdom of Jesus. And from that hour, when either knelt in prayer before the throne of God, a new name was whispered in that circle of dear ones who are nightly remembered as especial objects of mercy and blessings.

But the fiery and impetuous being who loved them both was wandering far away from that studio, a pale, weary exile, seeking for rest.

CHAPTER VII.

Again the moon lighted the streets of C——. It was the hour of early evening, and many couples were promenading under the elms. The day had been warm and sultry, and when the cool breeze came after the sun had gone down, many were glad to escape from the houses and wander under the trees. The foliage was rapidly developing, and already the sidewalks began to resemble long vistas overarched with leaves. The moonbeams already found much difficulty in lighting the walks, and great, solemn shadows of the branches lay along the pavements. Beyond the limits of the town, in the broad meadows, the dew upon the grass sparkled, and the running brooks flashed in the unveiled power of the moon, which sailed away upward in its silver splendor. Beyond the meadows the dark outline of the forest trees was revealed against the calm and serene background of the cloudless sky. But into the depths of the wild wood the moonbeams struggled faintly, and the shadows held almost undivided sway. Occasionally the trunk of a lofty pine was bathed in silver light, and the rays penetrated even to the dry leaves which lay beneath the low and matted undergrowth. But these ambitious moonbeams only served to render more conspicuous the forbidding gloom and loneliness of the forest. Surely no one would leave the graceful drooping elms of the town, or the glistening beauties of the broad meadows on such a night to wander in the dense and lonely wood so far away. Yet under the solemn maples and amid the tangled bushes in this distant wood, a figure of a human being was cautiously treading, pushing away slowly and stealthily with either arm the impeding branches of the undergrowth, and at intervals pausing and listening attentively. He seemed to fear pursuit, or else was listening for expected footsteps. Sometimes he would peer eagerly into the immense and fearful shadows, which might easily conceal any imaginable horror. Then he would advance slowly again with cautious steps, seeking to avoid the dead branches on the ground which cracked so sharply beneath his feet, pushing away with his arms slowly and steadily the tedious bushes, that their rustling might be more muffled from any lurking ear. At last he had made his way slowly and stealthily to an opening or clearing in the wood, and here again he paused for several minutes, looking suspiciously and carefully at every object about him. The moon for the first time shed its full rays upon his figure, and it was evident that his garments were all of the deepest black. Even the broad felt hat that shaded his face was black as ink. He was robust and tall, and appeared eminently capable of defending himself against an ordinary man by means of a heavy hard wood cane or stick which he carried in his right hand, grasping it about the middle. He seemed to be satisfied, at last, that he was alone in the wood, and again he moved slowly forward, passing the moonlit clearing and entering the dense thicket beyond it, He moved again in the same mysterious manner through the bushes, and past the trunks of the maples and the still darker trunks of the pine, till an unexpected opening in the tree-tops enabled him to see a little, but well-beaten path. The moonbeams lighted it for a few feet distinctly, so that he could trace its direction, and he immediately stepped into it, and advanced more rapidly than before. A few rods further on he paused at the foot of a maple, and stooping down, appeared to search for something at its roots. But the darkness of the place was too great, and he arose, drew from his vest pocket a match, and lighted it against the tree. He held this brief taper low down toward the base of the tree, and in another instant he started so suddenly that the match was extinguished. The bark of the maple was flecked with blood. Here had the unfortunate Hartwell fallen and died. The mysterious stranger in the black garb stood upright and motionless for a moment and listened once more. Not a sound disturbed the silence of the woods, save the faintest whisper of the young leaves. He then very coolly moved out of this little path, and pushed his way toward an enormous pine several rods away, on which the moonbeams chanced to fall with startling distinctness. He soon reached the foot of the pine, and found that he stood in the broad glare of the moonlight. The rough and broken-looking bark of the tree was plainly revealed, and he glanced up its enormous height to the branches at least seventy feet above him. Soon, however, he stooped to the ground, and by the moonlight discovered an opening in the bark or trunk of the tree which he appeared to be familiar with, for he at once thrust his arm up this hole in the trunk, seeking for something. He appeared unable to reach what he was after, for he withdrew his arm from the aperture, and placing his cane upon the ground, rolled up his coat sleeve toward the elbow, and then kneeling upon the leaves, thrust his arm once more and further up the hole. An exclamation escaped him in terror. "Good God! it is gone!" He stood a few moments under the tree completely stupefied with astonishment. The moonbeams fell full upon the arm on which the sleeve was rolled up, and it was plainly to be seen that his shirt sleeve beneath was clean and beautifully white, and the wristband was clasped together by gold buttons, which flashed in the light. There was no remedy for his disappointment, for he smoothed down his sleeve again, took up his cane, and groped his way back to the narrow path. He walked along it in the same cautious manner as before until he reached the gate which opened into old Rosy's garden. He passed into the garden, but kept away from the walks which led toward the old woman's cottage, and followed the direction of one of her fences until he reached the meadows stretching away in the broad glare of the moonlight towards the town. He slowly mounted her fence and let himself cautiously down into the adjoining field. Then he kept as much as possible along under the shadows of the fences until he reached one of the shaded streets of C——. Being then within reasonable bounds for a walk at that hour of the evening, he raised the rim of his hat so that his features could be seen, dropped the point of his cane to the sidewalk, and sauntered slowly along under the elms, careless as to whether he might now be recognized by the passers on the street.

But all the devices and secret movements of men may be thwarted if Heaven so wills it, and by the humblest of instruments and intellects. At the very moment this stranger was kneeling by the pine and thrusting his arm up the hollow of the tree, he was observed, and by the quickest pair of eyes in the town of C——. His exclamation was heard also, and when he turned away down the path toward the garden, two great dilating eyes were watching his course, and waiting for the proper moment to steal away after him. When the gate of old Rosy's garden squeaked slightly to the passing stranger, that sound was heard, and was the signal for pursuit. The dense branches of a maple tree near to the enormous pine were violently agitated. Then a dark figure slid quietly down the trunk to the ground with the easy motions and rapidity of a cat, and stole away under the bushes after the receding footsteps. Arriving at the garden gate, the pursuer flung himself flat on the ground, and held his ear to the earth to listen. A low, chuckling laugh ensued, and the figure, springing to his feet again, turned to look along one of the garden walks, when the moonlight flashed full upon his face. It was as black as a Congo birth could make it. It was a negro boy of seventeen, with a pair of eyes flashing with cunning and intense interest. He wore nothing but a blue checked shirt and a rusty pair of pants. He was bare-footed, and his brown straw hat had evidently once possessed a rim. His whole soul appeared to be in this pursuit, and a wild gleam of joy was ever coming to his eyes. Then he would look serious again, and listen for the stranger's footsteps. Then slowly and deliberately he followed, him, skulking along under the fence, and sometimes lying down flat in the grass of the meadow. His frame was slight, and his height about five feet and four inches, so that he concealed himself readily along the fences, and when the stranger entered the town he was close behind him, a pursuing, skulking shadow. At last the stranger paused before one of the stateliest mansions of the town, stood for a few moments with his eyes raised thoughtfully towards the moon, then quietly ascended the front steps, opened the door, and disappeared inside. The negro boy was close behind him when he paused, and immediately slunk behind one of the great elms. But when he entered the mansion, the boy uttered a low whistle of surprise. His surmises were correct. He recognized the man in the black garb beyond all question. The confirmation of his suspicions appeared to paralyze him, for he stood a long time motionless in the shadow of the tree. At length approaching footsteps recalled him to consciousness again, and he came out from the elm and walked rapidly homeward. He carried with him a secret which would have agitated the honest heart of the coroner of C——, and lifted, in a measure, the burden of suspicion from the absent Henry Lansing.

CHAPTER VIII.

On the ensuing morning, as Blonde Grayson stood at the window of her brother's studio looking out into the garden, she discovered a new laborer at work among the shrubbery.

"Who is that negro boy in the garden, Carl? His face looks familiar to me."

Her brother, without raising his eyes from his easel, replied, "That is one of Mr. Lansing's servants. Father found him early this morning on the streets, and brought him here to work. It appears he had been discharged by the Lansings."

This latter name appeared to interest her, for she said, after a minute's pause, "It is strange they should part with him at this late day. I think Clara told me he had been in the service of the family ever since he was a child; and his father was an old family servant of theirs before him. It is rather hazardous for father to take up with discharged servants without knowing something about them."

"I know nothing about the matter," he replied; "only father told me who he was as I came in from my walk."

Blonde took up her flat with the red streamers from the table and left the studio, walking out through the main hall into the garden. As the boy saw her approaching, he ceased work, and leaning on his rake with one of his glistening black hands, raised the other to his rimless hat in a respectful salute, bowing at the same time with remarkable grace of manner.

"Why! he is a polished gentleman. Few men in this town can beat that," she thought to herself.

She approached close to the boy and stopped in the walk.

"Good morning, sir. You are a strange face. Where did my father find you?"

The boy studied her appearance with his quick, bright eye from head to foot as he replied, quietly and with scarcely a remnant of the Ethiopian accent,

"Good morning, Miss Grayson. He found me at the market, where I was trying to find work. I have left Mr. Lansing's."

"How did it happen," she asked, "that you gave up such a

good place? They are one of the best families here, I should think, to live with."

The boy evidently studied in his mind before he gave his answer. At length he said, "I didn't want to leave. I have grown up with that family, but Mrs. Bounce don't seem to like me since she come."

"Then you left the Lansings' on your own motion—they didn't send you off, did they?"

"Oh! yes, Miss Grayson. I was sent away by Mrs. Lansing. She told me I must go, but she didn't like to say it to me—for she don't believe any of the stories, I know. But Mrs. Bounce, ever since she came, has been trying to get me away—and Mrs. Lansing is so quiet like, she don't like to have trouble with her. She's an excellent lady to work for, and all the servants likes her; but Mrs. Bounce is very different, Miss Grayson—yes! very different."

"But what are the stories?" said Blonde. "They would hardly send you away without some reason for it."

The dark, shining visage looked puzzled for a moment, and then he raised his keen eyes to her countenance as if to take in the calibre of her mind or prejudices, before he committed himself further. Her expression seemed to encourage him, for he said, bluntly:

"Some of the stories is true, and some of the stories is not a bit true, Miss. I own up that I used to go in the saloon, when the folks was gone to church, and play on the piano. They didn't allow that, but I couldn't help that; indeed I couldn't, Miss Grayson. I just love music, and it comes to me natural. I can play on any thing easy. I promised I wouldn't do it, but it was so lonely waiting for them to come from church, I just thought it wouldn't be noticed; but Mrs. Bounce heard of it, some way, and there was trouble right off. She's awful particular about Sunday She's got some verse in the Bible about things playing on Sunday, and she even went and turned off the fountain, 'cause, she said, it wasn't right for it to play on that day. That's about all that's true against me. But Mrs. Bounce says I stole, and that ain't true. I never did steal. I wouldn't no more steal from Mrs. Lansing's family, than I would jump right in the fire. She's a good woman, Mrs. Lansing is, and she's brought me up different from that. If I needed any thing, I'd only to ask her, and she'd git it for me. I'd be ashamed to steal. I would."

He had an honest looking face, indeed; and that went a long way with the lady he was addressing. But she was curious enough to hear further about this family which had come so prominently into public notice, within the past four days; so she enquired of him, the precise words Mrs. Lansing had used in dismissing him from her service.

"She said just this, Miss Grayson, as true as I'm standing here: 'Norman, you've lived with me all your life, and you haven't got many faults; but my daughter don't like you, and when I'm so sick she has to tend to every thing, and it's proper and right for her to have something to say about the servants. I never believed one word about your stealing—but I think you had better go and find a place. If you need a recommend, come back to me, and I'll write one for you. Just so long as you are a good boy, I will remember you, and you shall never want for bread. But it is best you should go; perhaps it will all blow over after a while. But I am too sick to direct you now, myself. Be true to what I have taught you, and I shan't forget you.' And that's just the way we parted, Miss Grayson. That same afternoon, Mr. Henry went off. It was lucky, too, for there ain't a man in this town can come near Black Hawk but Mr. Henry and me. He'd kill any other person what tried to ride him. Mr. Lansing rides wild horses, too, but he can't begin to ride Black Hawk; only Mr. Henry and me. Mr. Henry's a prince, Miss Grayson, a regular prince."

As he uttered this terrible name of the suspected individual, he gazed with his searching eyes at her, curious to detect her bias on the subject of the murder. His mind was soon relieved, for she said, quietly stooping down to gather some violets—

"He is certainly a very excellent gentleman, I am sure. It is very cruel for people to connect him with that dreadful matter; but do you know why he went off so mysteriously? That is what has made the real mischief in the minds of most people. Of course it was purely accidental, and no one has a right to accuse him for that. I know he wouldn't commit such a deed, as I know my own brother would not."

The countenance of the servant beamed with joy, to hear a defence of his young master, whom he had worshiped with all the energy of his faithful heart. Henry Lansing had been to him, the best of friends, and his very ideal of manly perfection. Then a tear slowly gathered in his eye, as he said—

"Oh! Miss Grayson, that is the best word I have heard since I lost my place. They've abused Mr. Henry dreadfully for the past three days, and many has turned against him that ought to be ashamed of themselves. I suspect the reason why Mr. Henry went off so—it wouldn't be right for me to tell why, but Mr. Henry was very unhappy in his mind, that I know. I brought him a letter from the post office the very morning of that day, and when he took it out of my hand, he went down through the garden to read it. In about five minutes, out he come from the garden looking pale as a ghost, and says he—

"'Norman, bring Black Hawk around to the door, right away.'

"I never saw Mr. Henry so troubled before. I've seen him so mad sometimes that he was right white; but this time he looked all broken down. It distressed me dreadful to see him so. When he used to get so mad sometimes, I had to laugh to see him scatter things. But this time he looked like he hadn't a friend in the world. When I brought the horse to the door, there he stood all dressed in black, and I thought likely he was going to call some place. He didn't say one word to me, but mounted his horse, as pale as he was before, and down the street he dashed, and that is the last I ever saw of him. He came back to the stable once, but I didn't see him. I believe he's the best gentleman in the world—and I believe I'd most be willing to die for him. Most people don't seem to understand him, but he's the most reasonable gentleman that ever was."

Blonde was disposed to continue this discussion, not observing that the boy was studying her attentively while he was speaking of the latter. But before she could reply, a little boy on the street ran up to the paling of the garden and cried out,

"Come here, Norman Prince; they've caught Black Hawk, and they're bringing him down this street."

The words seemed to electrify the negro; his keen eyes flashed with excitement, and Blonde's serene face lighted with interest. They both made for the front fence, and looking down the street, beheld a motley crowd of men and boys approaching. The street and the sidewalks were filled with them, and a confusion of loud and excited voices was heard under the elms. In a few moments the head of the procession passed the house, and then appeared in the midst of the excited throng the absorbing object of interest. Henry Lansing's powerful and magnificent charger was tied, by a rope passed through his bridle, to the rear end of a large farmer's wagon which was slowly being drawn down the street by two jaded looking bays. No one in the crowd dared to ride him or lead him, and he had thus been secured to prevent his doing mischief. One of the men seated in the wagon had his head bound up with a white cloth, as if he had been tampering with Black Hawk's heels. The horse was saddled and bridled, and was as clean and glittering in his glossy black coat of hair as if he had been rubbed down for the day. His long black tail swept the ground, and his beautiful head was tossing impatiently at this unusual restraint He did not appear the least humiliated, but stepped forward as proudly as ever. As the wagon passed the gate where Blonde was standing, a low, whistling call sounded under the trees, and the horse attempted to stop, in an instant; but the rope strained on his bridle. He gave one frantic bound toward the sidewalk, and the strands of the rope parted suddenly, and away he dashed along the avenue, free once more. The crowd scattered in every direction to avoid him, and he flew down the road like the wind. Another similar whistling call, trembled mysteriously on the air, and he stopped instantly, then turned back and dashed toward the Grayson mansion again. He trotted close along the garden fence, till his eye caught the figure of Norman Prince. Then he walked quietly up to him and rubbed his nose affectionately against the negro's shoulder. The boy mounted the low fence, and, catching the bridle, sprang to his back. The moment the horse felt his weight, he bounded off with him, leaving the crowd gaping in wonder at the negro's control of the fiery beast. Norman Prince gave one of his graceful, parting bows to Blonde Grayson, and then, throwing out his black chin, in the supercilious style of Henry Lansing, whose manner he imitated to perfection, he flew away with an air of most cool and sovereign disregard of the procession whose centre piece he had so unceremoniously appropriated.

Shouts of derisive laughter broke from the crowd, and an old man exclaimed, " The ghost of young Lansing has entered the nigger. There's style for you."

Blonde endeavored to ascertain, from some of the crowd about the gate, where the horse had been found; but could only learn that it was many miles away to the northward, with no further knowledge of Henry Lansing, connected with the finding of his favorite. The crowd rapidly dispersed, and she turned to walk the garden paths alone, deeply meditating on the boy's communication regarding the letter. Her suspicions concerning the cause of the mysterious flight seemed to be wholly confirmed by the boy's observations ; and as she slowly paced the garden she was whispering to herself, with a bright flush on her downcast face, "He does love me indeed, and he must be very miserable."

Her interest in him was evidently deepening, and she pondered the subject long, pacing back and forth through the shrubbery, until she heard the closing of the gate behind her, and turning beheld Clara Peyton. The young girl was much agitated, and she said at once,

"Oh! Blonde, I have dreadful news—dreadful indeed!—What do you think they have found? A party of schoolboys last evening were wandering about the place where he was murdered, and there they found in a hollow tree, Henry Lansing's fishing spear all covered with blood. Isn't it dreadful? And the doctor says it might make just such a hole in Mr. Hartwell's skull if a strong man had used it. Henry Lansing never did it—never—but this thing makes it look so bad for him that it makes me tremble for him. Every body is talking about it, and most people seem to be glad it is found. But he never did it—I'll say it with my last breath, he never did it."

Here was a complication of circumstances, unfavorable indeed to the absent young man. He was in the neighborhood probably at the time the deed was committed, his own fishing-spear was found concealed close by the fatal maple, covered with blood, and he had fled without apprising any one. To Clara Peyton these three facts appeared abundantly suspicious—but she nevertheless yielded not to the pressure of public opinion, relying on the strength of her ideas of his character to clear him at last of all complicity in the matter. But to Blonde, who knew now why he had fled, and who suspected strongly that she had discovered the real murderer, these three facts amounted to nothing. The discovery of the fishing spear puzzled her indeed. But the other two facts were in their nature such, that she could not explain them to her friend. She could only say,

"Clara, Henry Lansing never committed this murder, even if the fatal weapon did belong to him."

While the two friends wandered among the shrubbery in earnest conversation, Norman Prince re-appeared. He had taken the horse to Mrs. Lansing, and informed her of his new occupation, and where he could be found after Black Hawk should have kicked out the brains of the new coachman who had superseded him in the charge of Mr. Lansing's stables. He had said to her at parting,

"Mrs. Lansing, there isn't a man in this town can manage that horse; and you'll have to send for me—if you'll only let me come back and sleep in the stable on the hay, I'll never come near the house, but jest take care of Black Hawk, and I'll find some place where I can git my meals. I know you'll have to do it if you keep that horse."

Mrs. Lansing would have employed him on the spot, had not the presence of her daughter, Mrs. Bounce, restrained her. She well knew that the return of the negro would be the signal for a scene, and she felt too unwell and feeble to pass through it. She knew how much her son Henry was attached to the boy, and how much confidence he had reposed in him as the custodian of Black Hawk; and her mother's heart yearned toward this only token, the beautiful steed, which Henry had left. The negro, as he rode up the avenue of C——, had passed his hand caressingly over the long dark mane of the horse, and his fingers had met a small string amid the hairs, to which a small note was attached. The note had worked itself out of sight in the thick mane, but Norman Prince had discovered it and given it to the mother. It was addressed to Mrs. Lansing, and only said, "Good bye, dear mother; pray for me, and love Black Hawk for my sake.—Henry."

The mother only said that she would remember the negro boy's offer, and with a heavy and desolate heart had sought the privacy of her room.

Norman Prince related these facts to Blonde and her friend upon his return, and then said,

"I will go back to my work in the garden now. I am very sorry that I had to leave my work, Miss Grayson; but I could not bear to see Black Hawk in the hands of those men. I'll never leave my work again."

He touched his rimless straw hat once more, and bowed his graceful bow, looking alternately at Blonde and her friend, and then turned away towards his work. But a sudden reflection crossed her mind, and she recalled him to her side:

"Norman, it is very clear to my mind that you are to be trusted. I see some things very quickly, and by intuition. You will work for us until Mrs. Lansing may want your services again. Then you are at liberty to go back to her, for she is your friend; I see it. Did my father make any fixed agreement with you, as to your time or wages?"

"No, Miss; he only told me to go to work with these paths, until I saw you, and you would settle everything for him. He said he was too busy to look after me." As he uttered these words, he removed his ragged straw hat, and stood with it under his arm.

"Well, then," she said, "you are to hold the same position here as you did there; and I will give you the same wages as Mrs. Lansing gave you. I will see her, and ask her all about you, and what you received; and you shall have the same here. Is that satisfactory to you?"

The boy choked with emotion. He felt lonely enough, thrown out on the world for the first time from a family with which his whole life was identified. He could scarcely speak, at kind words of confidence so freely offered to him, a stranger, and at the prospect of a home and shelter once more. At length, he said, with the tears slowly rolling down his sable cheeks,

"You are very kind to a poor boy, Miss Grayson. I will try to please you, if Mrs. Lansing lets me stay here; and I think she'll be afraid to take me back, while Mrs. Bounce stays there."

"I want to say one word more to you, Norman, and then you may return to your work. You are attached to Mr. Henry Lansing, and you probably have reason to be so. There is great excitement in this town, about that murder; and some persons are determined that everybody shall take sides against Mr. Henry Lansing. All of this family are pledged to stand by him, and his mother, to the last. This young lady is Miss Peyton, who has known him longer than any of us. She declares that she will assert his innocence in spite of everything, and so will her father. Old Rosy, at the garden in the meadows, is furious on his side; and the Presbyterian clergyman also speaks very decidedly in his favor. Almost everybody else, that I have heard of, is against him. But we are not afraid, and are determined to vindicate his character. Well, then, we rely upon your prudence to assist us. You are expected to trust every one I have mentioned, and no one else, with what you may see or hear on the subject of this dreadful murder Tell no one what you hear any of us say; but tell us everything you hear his enemies say; and we may be able to be of service to Mr. Henry's mother. Will you promise this?"

The boy's countenance expressed the most intense satisfaction, as she proceeded with her noble purpose in regard to his beloved master; but when she disclosed the names of the circle upon whom he was to bestow his confidence, his wary, keen expression returned to his eyes, and he looked thoughtfully down upon the graveled walk. As she concluded, he raised his eyes seriously to her countenance, and, fixing them steadily upon her eyes, until she thought she discovered some mysterious secret in their expression, the boy said, slowly,

"Mr. Henry always said it was a bad plan to trust many people. Have few friends, and trust them, says he to his mother, many a time; and I heard him. I think, Miss Grayson, it will do—I mean, I would rather tell you everything, and let you direct me what to do."

Blonde laughed merrily, at this dignified reserve of the negro, but she said, "That is right, Norman, make your new mistress your sole confidante, and we shall get along very well. You may go to your work now."

He delivered one of his remarkable bows, and withdrew, leaving the friends alone in the walk.

Clara Peyton then informed Blonde of the object of her visit. It was to invite her to meet some friends that evening, at her father's residence; acquaintances, she said, from a neighboring city, and then she added, "There is a gentleman with the party, Blonde, who will surrender to you at first sight; he says he is a monomaniac on the subject of blue eyes and golden hair."

Her friend smiled, but only remarked, "You are the only admirer I care for, Clara. There is your father and the carriage at the gate."

A stylish barouche, drawn by a spirited pair of grays, was dashing up to the mansion, and in it was seated Judge Peyton, who was Clara's father and Blonde's confidante, to whom she had entrusted the secret of the neck-tie, in her stolen night interview; and upon whose legal judgment and experience she relied, to aid her in performing her duty properly toward the outraged community, in the matter of the murder. As Blonde accompanied her friend to the carriage, the judge raised his hat politely to her, and said, "I hope you have accepted my daughter's invitation for this evening."

"Oh, yes," she replied, "it is these trying tea-parties of six or seven that develope our inherent generosity. Clara and I have sworn never to desert each other. You may always rely on me."

The judge laughed his hearty, genial laugh, and the carriage whirled away.

Blonde returned to the walk where Norman Prince was at work, to give him some directions in regard to her flowers, and found him idly leaning on his rake, and apparently studying the details of the Grayson mansion. His back was towards her; but at her footstep he turned quickly, and then she discovered that his face was troubled. The boy glanced cautiously over the garden to see that they were entirely alone, and, finding no one near, said, thoughtfully :

" I might as well tell you now, Miss Grayson, as any time, that I have a dreadful secret. I think I know who killed Mr. Hartwell."

His tones were so calm and earnest that Blonde started.

" I wouldn't tell any one but you, because you are so kind to me, and because you like Mr. Henry. I wouldn't tell you, but I think you will advise me ; and I am so anxious about Mr. Henry that I don't want to do anything too quick."

There was a quiet consciousness of depth and prudence in the boy's manner, at times, which astonished Blonde ; and now she discovered that he had indeed some communication of importance : she said at once, " That is a dreadful secret, indeed ; but you can trust me to act prudently in the matter. If you see fit to entrust the matter to me I shall speak of your communication to no one that can injure you in consequence of the disclosure."

This was all the boy desired, and he stepped quickly to her side, and removing his straw hat, respectfully said, " Miss Grayson, let me whisper the name in your ear."

The fair girl bowed her golden hair, and the negro pronounced in her ear, in a most solemn and mysterious manner, the name of the person whom he had seen on the previous night, at the scene of the murder, searching for something concealed in the hollow pine. Then he withdrew his lips from her ear, and stood erect, gazing at her with his keen penetrating eyes ; she started at the name, but, checking the exclamation which arose to her lips, she slowly raised her eyes to the boy's face, and with a look of real horror in her countenance, she said,

" It is dreadful to mention *that* name. Why do you think so, Norman ?"

He then related to the motionless girl, who veiled her blue eyes with her long lashes, and looked down, during the entire narration, the moonlight scene, and singular movements recorded in the preceding chapter. When he had concluded, she said, " What do you think he could have been hunting for, in the hollow tree."

The boy shook his head, and said, " Perhaps it was the club, or something like that."

Blonde studied in her mind for a few minutes, the boy

keeping his eyes upon her all the while, in intense interest. At last, she said:

"Had Mr. Henry a fishing spear?"

"Why, yes, Miss Grayson, he did have one, and he always used to walk in the woods with it," replied the boy, wholly at a loss to comprehend the connection of her enquiry with the previous conversation.

"How long was it, Norman?"

The boy spread out his arms, as wide as he could, on either side, and said, "About so long, I believe it is."

Then she told him what Clara had said of the discovery of Henry Lansing's fishing spear, covered with blood.

A quick flash lighted his eyes again, and he exclaimed, "He was hunting it up that tree, where he hid it, and I believe he meant to put it where some one would find it, so as to make them suspect Mr. Henry of doing it."

Blonde saw that the boy possessed a clue, almost as important as her own, and that no time was to be lost in informing the judge of this additional link in the chain of circumstances, which was to relieve the absent Henry Lansing of the odium of the dreadful crime. She knew that the negro, also, must not be allowed to disclose, at present, his secret, and she hastened to close his mouth by these words: "You have been of the greatest service to Mr. Henry, by your faithfulness in keeping an eye on that dreadful neighborhood. Your cunning in keeping watch there three nights has been unexpectedly rewarded, and you will save Mr. Henry, all in good time. But you must be as still as the grave—tell no one; but wait till I expose what *I* know. Mr. Henry is safe already, with what I know and with what you know. Leave the management of our evidence to me, and all will be well. Will you do this?"

"Oh! certain, Miss Grayson. I'm mum till you say the word," replied the boy, delighted to hear that his master was secure, even now, from danger.

"Well then," she said, "the first thing for you to do is to get the carriage for me at six o'clock, and drive me over to Judge Peyton's. The man at the stables is going to leave soon, and he will give you the key, and show you every thing. I am going over there to tea. After you have left me there, put up the horses, and then come to Judge Peyton's, and wait for me on the doorstep of his library; it is in the wing of his house. I will walk home with you, for it is bright moonlight until late in the evening."

The boy looked puzzled, and confused, for a moment, but

that expression, so habitual to his eyes, keenness, returned, and he bowed with the utmost formality, as she moved away down the garden walk. He saw that she possessed a greater secret than himself, and that he must be very vigilant in watching her, in order to find it out. And she, as her steps slowly brought her to the door of house, was realizing what a mountain of difficulty was rearing itself before her, in the secret with which the boy had entrusted her. Her thoughts were so serious and engrossing that she failed to recognize the salutations and voices of the beautiful spring, which sounded around her. She only heard the solemn clock of C—— strike one.

CHAPTER IX.

PUNCTUALLY at the hour of six o'clock, Norman Prince drove up to the entrance of the Grayson mansion with the spirited team of bays, which had now become his especial charge. The boy had undergone a wonderful transformation. The rusty pants, and the blue checked shirt, and the ragged and rimless straw hat had disappeared. He had visited his lodging house of the previous night, in the interim, and now was arrayed in a clean suit of a dark yellowish hue, with rows of glistening brass buttons extending down the front of his long and tightly buttoned coat, and around its turned up cuffs. The coat had a narrow cape, and fitted his figure to a charm; and a low crowned hat of the same yellowish hue, was placed upon his short crisp curls. He wore white topped boots, and sat jantily on his high seat, handling his reins with the importance of an emperor.

At length the mistress of the mansion, appeared at the front door, escorted by her brother, Carl. He glanced quickly at the waiting carriage, and then said, as they descended the steps toward the gate—

"Do you notice that you are to flourish along the streets under the auspices of the Lansing livery?"

She looked up in amazement, and said at once, with some chagrin:

"What does this garb mean, Norman? You are no longer expected to wear the livery of the Lansing family."

The boy, as he removed his hat in a graceful bow, and opened the carriage door for her, said,

"It is the only decent suit I had, Miss Grayson, and the clothes of that other man in the stables, wouldn't fit me—I did the best I could."

"I shall have you measured for a new suit to-morrow—you must not wear that dress any more," she said, as she entered the carriage, and the door closed with a snap behind her.

The vehicle rolled rapidly down the street, and curious eyes from the sidewalks followed its course, and wondered and speculated what event had transpired to bring so closely in contact the high church Blonde Grayson, and the livery of the orthodox Lansing family. The maw of public curiosity thus received a large and stimulating morsel, which was soon distributed for more perfect digestion to the inner and more hidden parts of society, denominated tea parties, and sewing societies for the poor. Slightly mortified to find herself, by the lateness of the hour, obliged to hasten to the social gathering at Judge Peyton's, with this livery of the Lansings, seated upon her carriage box, Blonde drew her veil further over her face to conceal her features from the passers on the streets. There were other and more profound matters of interest working in her brain, however, as she rolled rapidly along, and she soon forgot everything in her meditations on the mysterious communication of her new servant. He appeared to have been absolutely positive as to the identity of the person he had watched so carefully about the fatal maple; and this new discovery entailed upon her further and urgent duties in regard to the unaccountable crime, which had so agitated the town. The distinguished judge must also be informed on the subject, and she had provided herself with a means of communicating the facts to him on that very evening, provided she might be prevented, in the presence of the company, from having an oral communication with him. A short condensed statement of the negro's secret, was contained in a note which she clenched tightly in her gloved hand, and which she would not have dropped or lost for any human consideration The urgency of her communicating with the judge at once, was but too evident to her mind; and she felt assured the new partner in the secret would require to be most powerfully and attentively guarded and guided by herself and the judge, to prevent his prematurely disclosing the affair to the public. His faithful heart yearned after his absent master and favorite, and his zeal to clear up the name and reputation of "Mr. Henry" might break through the barriers of caution and the instructions of prudence, which she might rear about his actions, and might lead to the entire ruin of her plans.

Engrossed in these reflections, she reached, at length, the entrance to Judge Peyton's residence, and alighting, was met at the gate by her friend Clara.

"Oh! darling, I am so glad you have come. They are all on the back piazza, and I stole away from them when I heard your carriage wheels. You have got on that dotted muslin that I admire so much. Now I will show them what kind of friends I claim for myself. I can't see your hair, but come right up in my room—I'm crazy to inspect your appearance." Thus she conducted her fair friend up the walk to the main hall, and thence to the second story of the mansion, where she ushered her into her own beautiful and inviting boudoir and bed room.

"Why, Clara," she exclaimed, on entering the room, and removing her bonnet and veil; "you have been changing your room. I never was in this room before, certainly."

Her friend replied, as she took the bonnet and veil to her white polished wardrobe: "This is the room my dear mother occupied before she died. Father would never sleep in it afterwards, and it has been locked up until this Spring. But it is the pleasantest summer room in the house. Those windows admit the south wind, and that door opposite gives a cool breeze through the room on the warmest days. Father will not listen a minute to my request that he should re-occupy it—so I have concluded to keep it myself. I have had it thoroughly cleaned and renovated lately, but I restored the furniture and pictures to the same places they occupied before mother's death—the arrangement of every thing is hers. See how sweet and appropriate was her selection of colors. The embroidery on those white silk curtains at the windows was all done by her own hand, and so was the work on the drapery about her dressing table. Notice this white velvet mat on which she kept her prayer book. This heavy cross on it is made entirely of gold cord. She was very skillful in such work. The prayer book was given to her when she was abroad by an English bishop. Father says I have inherited my taste for embroidery from her."

It was, indeed, an inviting and tasteful apartment for sleeping. The bed was very low, and the the snow white counterpane swept entirely to the floor. A large gilded ring, secured in the ceiling, sustained the gathered ends of the bed curtains, which were of gauzy, misty looking muslin and drooped on either side of the bed gracefully to the floor. The carpet that covered the broad apartment was a pure white tapestry, relieved only by golden lilies. The bureau and chairs, the wardrobe with a full length mirror in each of its doors, the marble top wash stand and table were of polished white, and dotted occasionally with a small golden leaf, recalling the yellow glory of the autumn time. The wash bowl and pitcher, and the porcelain bottles of the dressing table were circled by small golden wreaths of flowers, and the white silk window curtains were looped back with heavy gold cord and tassels. At one side of the centre table, and near enough to receive the yellow rays of the carcel lamp, which was wont to burn there at night, was a kneeling bench of wood, painted to match the furniture, and with white silk kneeling cushion and top cushion, on which rested the mat and the prayer book of the departed mother.

And as Blonde stood before one of the long mirrors, while her friend arranged, for her, the slightly disordered braids of her glorious hair, she seemed in her simple, low necked and short sleeved dress of white dotted muslin, and her drooping wreaths of golden hair, in happy accord and keeping with the two prevailing colors of the room ; and more naturally would be recognized as the graceful spirit of the place than the fair girl who stood beside her with dark, clustering curls and a blue silk dress, contrasting with her plump white neck and shoulders. Alas ! these two lovely girls were both deprived of the society and guardianship of a mother. Mrs. Grayson had died many years before, and Clara's mother breathed her last only one year before Blonde's arrival in C———. Possibly this mutual deprivation made the friends cling more ardently to each other, in their new found friendship and affection.

Blonde's eyes were roving about the apartment and an exclamation of pleasure escaped her as she discovered Clara's portrait against the white and gold dotted wall paper of the room.

" Why, you never told me of that picture of yourself, and it's just you as you are now at seventeen—when did you have that taken ?"

" Oh ! my dear child," she replied, " that is the portrait of my own mother, taken when she was exactly my age ; she was married at sixteen, and that was painted just one year after—wait till I drop the curtains and light my lamp. . I will place the light exactly under the picture, and the effect is wonderful. Father thinks I am very much like her, and I never let him see me with my riding habit on ; but I always steal out the back way to my horse. He seems completely unnerved and wretched when he sees me on horseback; so I always avoid him. He was devoted to my mother with all the intensity of his noble heart. I hope I shall be loved as well some day."

The sun had long since disappeared in the west, and the faint light of the evening was rapidly waning, as Clara drew the curtains and lighted her lamp. When she placed the light in a chair beneath the portrait in such a manner that a broad glare of mellow rays was flung full upon the face of the picture, Blonde was entranced. The general resemblance to the daughter was evident enough. The same luxuriance of dark, clustering curls, the same large, violet eyes, the same soft, white cheek, and dark, penciled eyebrows, and the same plump bust and arms as her friend. But the portrait lacked that power and force of will which lingered about the daughter's dewy lips, and which she had derived, evidently, from her father, the judge. That expression was supplanted in the portrait by one of extreme gentleness and pathos. The mother's lips and eyes betokened the possibility of ardent affection, and sufferings meekly borne for one she might love. Her lustrous, violet eyes were pleading in their depth and tenderness, but she evidently had lacked the determined will which so often forces protection for the loved ones, and which quality was so strongly manifested in Clara's character and lips. It was the young wife, in her happiness and gentleness of emotion, across whose young existence a year of married life had swept its train of tender and fluctuating thoughts, and brought its lamp, experience, for her to swing before her into the dim shadows of the future. Her curls were pressed by a small green velvet cap, with a black feather passing around the front and drooping over her left shoulder. A dark riding habit with small jet buttons revealed the plumpness of her form, and she held in her hand her young husband's new gift, the riding whip with its red coral handle.

Blonde could have lingered before that face for a long time, and her eyes were full of tears from some unfathomable emotion which pressed upon their source, her heart. But it was high time the two friends were making their way to the company below stairs; and she reluctantly followed Clara to the drawing-room, where the strange guests had betaken themselves, when the gathering darkness rendered the back piazza no longer agreeable.

As the two entered the brilliantly-lighted and luxurious apartment, they discovered several ladies and gentlemen sitting at ease on the sofa or lounging about the parlor, examining and commenting on the paintings or turning over the portfolios of elegant engravings at a side-table. The judge was walking about with his calm, dignified manner, and easy conversational tone, making every one happy and entertained, and forgetful of the temporary absence of the young hostess, his daughter. The two came in so quietly that their first announcement was the sound of their new voices engaging in conversation with the two ladies to whom Clara introduced her friend. All eyes were fixed at once and in evident admiration upon the fair and delicate countenance of Blonde. Her charms were always recognized by strangers at the very first glance. No woman dared dispute their ascendancy, and their rare development and magic influence thrilled the hearts of young men at once, and attracted to her the evident and more flattering admiration of older and more cultivated tastes. Superiority of mind and beauty revealed itself at a glance, though the new observer never could conceive the greater excellence of both which was yet to flash forth when her intellect and her eyes were aroused from their calm, lady-like repose. Her salutation to the first two ladies who were presented was winning and gratifying. She could not but exhibit her interest in her friend's guests, Mrs. Ruggles and her daughter, who were distant relatives of Judge Peyton. Her graceful lily hand was extended to them respectively as she expressed quietly her pleasure that they had come, for the first time, to test the hospitality of the citizens of C——. Then she passed with Clara to the sofa, and was presented to two old maids, both prepossessing in expression and extremely well dressed; and then was introduced to the two young gentlemen who had been devoting themselves to the two old maids, standing beside the sofa. One gentleman was apparently thirty; the other scarcely twenty-one. They were brothers, and the Miss Ruggles was their sister, plainly, from family resemblance, instantly detected by Blonde's quick eye. An animated conversation at once arose between Blonde and the parties at the sofa, and Clara turned away to a gentleman and his sister who were engaged in an equally animated discourse with Judge Peyton over some rare engravings, intending to introduce Blonde when a more favorable opportunity should arise. The group about the sofa were all cultivated and agreeable. Foreign travel, a common religious sympathy, and cultivated tastes, introduced speedily topics of conversation, which made the next quarter of an hour fly happily, and brought the sunlight of Blonde's beauty, radiant thought, to her eyes, expanding her blue orbs and revealing their changeful witchery to all. At length, a voice, manly but modulated with the unerring eleganco of a real gentleman, pronounced, unexpectedly at her side, these greeting words,

"I declare, Miss Grayson, you are all so interested in each other, I fear you have forgotten, in the charm of new acquaintances, that some other friends of older date are in existence. I have been looking full ten minutes in the hope of seeing those blue eyes turn their irresistible light on me."

Blonde turned at once and beheld Judge Peyton at her side. She extended her hand cordially, and made some gay reply; but the words were scarcely clear of her lips when a shudder passed over her, and she turned pale as a corpse. Where, in the name of all that is horrible and startling, *was her note?* —that dreadful note, with its ominous secret, which she had carried so carefully and tightly in her hand? It was gone; and she had no more idea of when it left her clenched fingers than the interested faces about her. Gone! oh, merciful God! Where was it gone? Her eyes gathered a hazy film; that iron hand of the coroner's inquest once more grasped her heart in its suffocating power, and she felt that she was falling, fainting. No! her strength flashed back to her frame, and hope to her heart. It must be on the floor of Clara's room. But there was not an instant to lose. No chance hand must find that dreadful note. It must be either in her possession or in the possession of the judge, her counselor, at once. Fly! fly at once to that unlucky bedroom, regardless of forms and the demands of etiquette. There was death for some one glimmering out from the pages of that note. God grant no servant's hand had yet found it on the floor.

Her weakness was only for an instant; her tact and her reason came as quickly to her relief. No one must surmise that she was pale and trembling except from sudden illness. And no one but the Judge was to be trusted in searching for the lost note. If she went to the bedroom, Clara would inevitably insist on going with her. That fact was as clear as an axiom. Her fright, instead of obscuring her sense, now perfected and made it clearer.

"Oh! my dear Judge, I am very faint. Take me to the open air of the garden—quick!—don't any of you come. A quick walk in the garden will restore me."

She placed her arm in that of Judge Peyton, and declining all tenders of other assistance, with an air of command which was innate to her, turned out through the door of the drawing-room on to the piazza in the rear of the house. Seeing that she was followed in kindly interest, she said to the Judge,

"I am used to these attacks of dizziness. Now walk me as fast as you can through the garden, and I shall be over it in a few minutes."

He followed her directions, and they were soon hurrying down to the foot of the garden, and there was no one pursuing, fortunately for her plan. When she discovered that her kind pursuers had followed no further than the piazza, and that she was alone with the Judge, she said to him with a suddenness and earnestness that startled him,

"I had a note to give you, relating to further evidence I have discovered on that dreadful subject, but I have dropped it somewhere between the carriage and Clara's room up stairs. There is no time to lose. No one must see that note but you. Take me the shortest way around to the front door, and while I look in Clara's room, do you look carefully from the gate up the walk to the front door. There is death in that note. Now we must hurry around through this shrubbery, and hunt for it before we are noticed. If Clara does not take it into her head to come after me, all will be well; but I shudder to think it may have fallen into the hands of one of the servants. We have no time for further words till that note is found—come."

Her eagerness admitted of no parley, and the Judge hurried her around by a circular walk to the front door, and she walked instantly up the stairs, scanning each step as she ascended for the lost note. Then she dashed into Clara's bedroom, where she really expected to find it, looked carefully over the floor and the dressing table with a quickly beating heart, and found to her horror that her search was utterly fruitless. A bright light revealed every thing in the room distinctly, but the fatal note was not there. She swept quickly down the stairs again to the Judge at the front entrance, and learned that his search had been equally unsuccessful on the moonlit walk. She pressed her hand to her forehead in anguish, and for a moment seemed hopelessly stupefied. Then seizing the Judge nervously by his arm, she hurried him down the walk out of hearing of the house, and detailed to him clearly the contents of the lost note. It was substantially Norman Prince's experience at the fatal maple.

The usually serene manner of the Judge was startled into nervous activity by her recital. He said hurriedly,

"This is dreadful indeed. That note must be found instanter. But the boy—the negro boy—where is he? I must see him, and teach him to keep his mouth closed without delay."

Blonde exclaimed, "Alas! if we don't find the note the boy's silence will amount to nothing. It's all in the note, every word of it; and if it is found, the town is so excited and on the alert, the arrest will be made to-morrow. How could I be so insane and stupid as to write that note at all? I told Norman to return and wait at your library door. Come—he may possibly be there already."

Pale and trembling with her excitement and apprehension, she followed Judge Peyton around to the wing of the mansion. There they found the faithful negro sitting quietly as he had been directed at the library door, with the full moonlight revealing his sable countenance resting on his clenched hand, and evidently buried in earnest thought. The silver rays of the moon flashed upon the metallic buttons of his Lansing livery, and the gilt band of his low-crowned hat, as he studied earnestly, with his eyes turned upward to the moon. He was so absorbed in his reflections that he had not discovered, even with his quick ear, the approach of footsteps; and at Blonde's exclamation on finding him there, he sprang to his feet in utter surprise. It was an event in his sable experience to be approached so closely and so suddenly without detecting the approaching footsteps. He quickly recovered, however, from his evident surprise, and removed his hat, bowing with his genteel air, as usual. His eyes glittered in the moonlight as he fixed them first on the Judge, and then on the pale face of his mistress. He advanced quickly to Blonde's side, and presented to her a small white object, which she grasped in an instant, and glancing over it, said,

"Where did this come from, Norman?"

"I just found it at the gate, Miss Grayson, as I came in."

"Oh, you blessed boy! I am so glad!" she ejaculated earnestly, relieved of her anxiety in an instant. Then realizing the necessity of taking advantage of the position immediately, she continued, "Go at once into the library with the Judge—he is Mr. Henry Lansing's friend, and what you do for him, you do for me and Mr. Henry; the Judge is safe, true as steel, and will do everything right for Mr. Henry. Go now; God has given us this opportunity. I will hurry back through the garden to the back piazza, and rejoin the company at once."

Seeing the boy hesitated, as if reluctant to be forced thus suddenly into confidence with the Judge, a stranger, she said, "Go at once, as I direct you, with the Judge, and he will tell you what I know myself about this murder. Trust me, Norman—you will be gratified when you hear some things that I have entrusted to the Judge to tell you."

The boy appeared satisfied, for he followed the Judge into the library, and the door closed behind them. Blonde made her way rapidly into the mansion, and not to the company, as she had said, and ascending the front stairs unnoticed, entered her friend's bedroom once more, and immediately pulled the bell-rope for a servant. Her summons was answered by a maid, whom she directed to inform Miss Clara Peyton in the drawing-room, that she was lying down in her room, and not to be concerned for her, as she would return to the company after a few minutes.

While her servant was absent with this message, Blonde threw herself on the bed, and burying her face in the pillow, sobbed and wept like a child. But they were tears of joy and gratitude, for she whispered once through her tears, "Oh, my Heavenly Father! I thank thy Adorable Goodness that every thing—every act of mine in this dreadful affair, is so plainly guided and protected by thy care. The note—the note is safe. I thank thee, Oh God!"

Then rising from her prostrate position, she dried her tears, and re-arranged her beautiful hair before the mirror; not however until the note was burned by her hand, holding it over Clara's carcel lamp, which still remained beneath the portrait. The face of the dead mother looked calmly down upon the fair girl, and Blonde's eyes rested for a moment upon the picture in tenderest interest. This was the beautiful being who had given to life her own darling, constant, idolized friend, Clara. There was an irresistible spell to her eyes, in the touching beauty and pathos in the mother's gentle face; and as she gazed upon it, the tears welled again to her blue eyes from some profound and hidden sympathy. While yet she stood before the portrait, the sound of Clara's anxious and nimble footsteps was heard, as she sprang up two steps at a time, and came tearing into the apartment. Her faithful heart was soon relieved of its anxiety for her friend, and in a few minutes the two returned once more to the drawing-room.

CHAPTER X.

Clara conducted her friend at once to the small table where the gentleman and lady were seated whose acquaintance Blonde had not yet made. During her absence in the garden with the judge, coffee and cake and biscuits had been passed to the company by two neatly dressed girls of Clara's household and now the guests were seated at small tables scattered through the saloon, busily occupied in discussing their supper. The young lady was presented to Blonde, under the title of Miss Seymour; and the gentleman as her brother, the Reverend Marcus Seymour. The clergyman arose, and gave his seat to Blonde, and sought another chair for himself, which he drew up to the table, and discontinued his meal, until the attentive servants had brought Blonde her tiny cup ot coffee, and offered her a plate, and supplied her with refreshments. In the mean time Blonde had an opportunity to scan the features and dress of her new acquaintances. Miss Seymour was decidedly a lady, a short, delicate looking, little personage, with auburn hair and small hazel eyes, which constantly twinkled with interest and enjoyment. Everything appeared to receive a share of her attention, and she entered at once into conversation with the attractive and beautiful Blonde. Her brother was apparently about the age of thirty, of medium height, and lightly, but gracefully moulded. Unlike his sister, his eyes were large, and of a very deep shade of brown. They were marvelously brilliant and beautiful, and in connection with his refined and delicate face attracted the attention of his new acquaintance at once; she discovered with her quick eye that his hair was the same shade of auburn as his sister's, and his profile resembled her also. But he was evidently her superior in every thing, mental and physical, and his character of refinement, sincerity and cultivation was written upon his manly face with unquestionable accuracy. He wore an entire suit of black, and his long and closely buttoned coat was cut in single breasted clerical style, and exhibited his fine form to great advantage. Blonde surmised, at once, that Mr. Seymour must be the identical new clergyman who was expected by the congregation of St. Paul's to occupy the place of their retiring rector. Clara had informed her friend of his arrival in C——, and cautioned her to be on her guard, as the young rector was an unusally attractive and gifted personage, who would be likely to create a sensation among the unmarried ladies of St. Paul's chapel. A genial smile was on his delicately cut lips, as he said to Blonde, with evident admiration of her beauty, as his eyes were fixed so earnestly upon her face, "I am very happy indeed to meet you, Miss Grayson, for I hear you are a very earnest churchwoman, and I expect soon to have the honor of calling you one of my parishioners."

He was very closely shaved, wearing no beard; and as he spoke, cunning dimples showed themselves about his small mouth, and his voice was clear and musical as a silver bell. His small white hand played carelessly with his teaspoon on the little table, and his style was decidedly gentlemanly and prepossessing. Clara had predicted truthfully that the reverend stranger would prove a sensation to the quiet society of the town.

Blonde answered him in her quiet tones, "I am sure your welcome to St. Paul's will be most cordial. We are not a large church, but we are united and harmonious, and have the reputation with the Bishop of having fewer whims and dissensions among ourselves than any other church in the diocese. But I have not as full authority to speak on these matters as others, for I am myself a new-comer in C——. Only a few months ago, in the winter, my father removed to this place, and I have not experienced the genuine home feeling here yet."

He replied in his soft, musical tones, "You have at least one of the delightful associations which cluster about that dearest of names, home, in the person of Judge Peyton's daughter, if I am informed correctly."

"Oh! yes," she said with warmth, "Clara's friendship is indeed almost a home in itself. While God spares me *that* gift I shall indeed, confess that I have an indulgent Father, beyond the clouds. I have had many friends among ladies, before my arrival in C——, but none who come so accurately up to my standard of female friendship as she does. You must pardon my enthusiasm on that subject—but that is a subject which lies very near my heart."

Mr. Seymour laughed his easy, genial laugh, as he said,

"I wish you would be kind enough to inform me what your standard of female friendship is? I love high standards in every thing; and friendship is so interesting a thought to mankind generally, that you should enlighten me—or rather allow me to correct myself and say, I *think* you should."

Blonde could not but detect the spirit of raillery in his words so quietly uttered; and she observed his merry eyes twinkling with the fun he vainly strove to conceal. But she replied, not in the least disconcerted by his manner:

"I see that you are one of that unfortunate class of gentlemen, whose ideas of the friendship of two girls, are based upon very barren facts, and very brief experience in the matter. It has almost grown into a proverb with a dash of a sneer in it, the remark, 'short lived as school girls' friendships,' and you would appear to have adopted that proverb, as the standard by which you estimate *all* female friendship. Know then, that an undying and unselfish friendship is a possibility among women. Clara Peyton is my standard of a friend. She has nothing to gain from me by her friendship. Every luxury and comfort she has from a most generous and indulgent father. Girls nearer her own age than myself, have sought an intimacy with her, and they have offered by their companionship to her greater facilities, for the full enjoyments of her various tastes, than I could possibly do. Their fathers have finer residences, more spacious lawns, more beautiful sail boats on the lake, more gentle and beautiful horses, finer paintings, more princely walks, and fountains, and woods, than my own father would ever dream of owning. She worships music like a devotee; and only by a particular intimacy with these young ladies that I have spoken of, can one gain admittance to their limited and privileged matinèes. And yet for my sake, and to be often near me, she has to forego most of these opportunities of satisfying her tastes. Is not this pure and disinterested friendship? I cannot conceive of one advantage she can gain by association with me, that she cannot have in greater perfection from the society of either one of these ladies. She can have my society and my sympathy always, it is true, but this she can have from many others; and, moreover, she has secured for herself, reproach, even from her relatives, because she prefers my society to others. My standard of female friendship, is Clara Peyton's disinterested words, acts, and constancy for me. No one dare even speak a disagreeable *truth* concerning me, in her presence, let alone a malicious slander. She never startles and pains me by telling me what disagreeable remarks have been made about me, when there is no earthly way for me to relieve or better my condition. She knows it is cruel to tell a friend of slander, which does not demand prompt and immediate action on the part of that friend. When once she has warned me of a particular person, she deems that enough—without torturing my pride and my heart, by daily recitations of the mean things that are said about me. She realizes how cruel it is to tell me satirical and disagreeable remarks, and so she avoids doing it, preferring to see me with a happy expression on my face, and with a kind feeling in my heart toward every one in this town. And I love her for it; for thus she exhibits a desire to make my life seem to me a pleasant one. I do not like to hear disagreeable remarks of myself, and she spares me that infliction. I desire to have as much of the happiness of life as I can, consistently with my religious duties; and she is careful that I shall not see any more of the thorns than are necessary for me. What would you think of the mother who should be daily repeating to her daughter, every unkind remark that might be made of that daughter's complexion, or walk, or peculiarity of accent, or behavior in the society of gentlemen? Would not that mother be deemed unnatural, thus to discourage and torment her young life? And it appears to me that equal consideration is due to the friend who shares one's confidence and affection. Have I said enough yet, or are you unable to discover as much as I do, in these evidences of purity in friendship?"

Mr. Seymour bowed slightly towards her, as was his wont in addressing ladies, and said, a little touched by her sincerity and enthusiasm:

"You have referred to the consideration for your feelings on the part of your friend, in a manner rather novel to me. I have often observed chosen friends indulge in the habit of disclosing to each other, the respective slanders about themselves; and I must confess I never could see the kindness of it. I most assuredly admire the height of your standard in this respect. Most ladies with whom I have the honor of an acquaintance, never have alluded to this delicate consideration—this gentle kindness of holding one's tongue. I am disposed to think that in many ladies, exists a morbid desire to hear every thing that may be said concerning themselves. I have wondered at it often. You have so enlightened me on the subject of real friendship, that I am curious to hear from you what you consider the highest and best quality of friendship in a lady friend. Is it constancy in defending you, when you are in trouble or maligned? Is it truthfulness and candor in pointing out to you your weaknesses or your faults, and kindly counseling you to reform in that respect, notwithstanding your self-love may suffer a pang by it? Is it a gentle and delicate remembrance of your smallest wish at all times? Or is it all these combined, so that you cannot discriminate and elevate one quality or manifestation of friendship above another in your mind?"

Miss Seymour interrupted, "Why, brother, you cannot analyze a lady's idea of friendship so closely as that. Miss Grayson surely cannot answer that question. We know we love, but it is difficult always to define why we love."

Blonde's blue eyes lighted with enthusiasm as she said, "I am not so confident of that, Miss Seymour. When I love, it is an emotion which possesses my whole being. I cannot but think of it, and dwell on the reasons in my mind why I love any person. Love is so precious to me that I wish to understand it, and I do try often to analyze it,"—then, after a brief moment of reflection she continued, stealing at the same time a glance into the clergyman's interested and beaming eyes, "I will tell you, Mr. Seymour, what I deem the highest and best quality of friendship—it is *earnestness.* I care not how that earnestness may manifest itself, whether in rebuke, in flattery, in defence of my actions, or in a quiet manifestation of satisfaction at being in my company. Only let my judgment say to me, 'She means what she says. She means to give me her affections and some of her confidence, and she means never to cease to love me.' Then I am satisfied. A friend may falter in times of great trouble, that is, may not find adequate words to defend me against the storm of stronger intellects, and yet have the determination in her heart, 'I will never harm her. I know she is loveable. I know she is not what they would represent her to be, and at the first moment when I can go to her assistance, I *will* go, and she shall acknowledge that I love her.' When I feel that this is in the heart of my friend, I am willing to wait for her silent tongue to unloose and tell me all, explain to me all. I am not impatient. I can wait months. I know it will all be right at last. I know she will convey to me at last evidences of her love and full explanations of her conduct in the past. I assure you, sir, that no ordinary person can secure that unlimited confidence from me. But let me once receive any person under that shield, my friendship, and from that moment they own me. I trust them to the last. I know they are *earnest. Earnest*—that is enough for me. I am willing to wait their slow movements. They will say nothing, do nothing, really against me. They will turn out, as the expression is, 'all right.' *Earnestness* of heart, sir, is the highest quality of friendship. Earnest friends may sometimes be very unreasonable, and very singular, and very weak, but when once that earnest heart is mine, I can bear a great deal of singularity from it, for I know it cherishes me in its secret depths. Surface is very beautiful sometimes, I know, but give me depth. If you will allow me, I will give an explanation of my meaning, which is a strong one. I have seen a young lady really and sincerely love a gentleman, and treat him for many months with apparent indifference, going with others, and apparently regardless of his society, restrained from motives of secret pride or coquetry, or from an indescribable motive from letting that gentleman know what he is most anxious to know, and yet her love was as deep and unchanging as the bed of the sea. It was a love worth possessing, and yet there were no external manifestations of it. So may there be friendship existing a long time without words, without zealous defence, without personal contact. My standard of friendship is a high one, but it is a real one. I have loved a friend without approaching her for months. When she wanted me, she sent for me; and she never complained that I was intimate with others to her exclusion. She knew I loved her, and she waited for me. She knew when I was ready, I would come to her, and that I loved and appreciated her above every human being that I associated with so constantly. Would my friendship have really been any stronger if I had visited her daily or weekly? I assure you, sir, that there may be the deepest friendship, and yet the world not realize it. For this reason I say *earnestness* of heart is the highest quality of friendship, and not outward manifestations. And," she added, laughing and looking quizzically into his beautiful eyes, "remember what I told you by way of illustration about the young lady's love which she concealed; and never allow yourself to be discouraged if the lady of your pursuit does not exhibit her feelings; they may be all the deeper for that."

Her raillery was all the more unexpected, coming so abruptly after her enthusiasm, and he was obliged to confess that she was able to return a dart of satire in its proper time, and more delicately than himself. He smiled as he replied,

"I would not fancy proceeding in my suit upon such principles as you suggest. I fear my heart would break from long waiting, and then, perhaps, she might not love me after all."

Blonde answered quietly and without raising her eyes from her little coffee-cup, "Very likely."

At that moment Judge Peyton's foot sounded in the hall, and as he entered the drawing-room Blonde discovered the faintest trace of anxiety in his usually calm and composed countenance. She knew that the negro boy had been disclosing to him the name of a prominent citizen of C—— in connection with the moonlight visit to the fatal scene of the murder. However, his familiarity with crime in high life had been great during the many years of his professional career, and as Blonde stole occasional glances at his face during the next half hour, she discovered that the troubled expression was rapidly disappearing under the influence of genial companionship and conversation. Finally he approached Miss Seymour, and solicited from her a song which had been a favorite of his in early life. She complied with the request with the ease and promptness of good breeding which suggests ready acquiescence in displaying those powers which are cultivated in part for society. She accompanied the judge to the piano, and soon song after song was warbled forth at his request, for he was an excellent musical critic, and her voice, though rather feeble, was exceedingly sweet and agreeable to him. After listening to her for a while, the company concluded to leave her voice under the sole supervision of the judge, who stood beside her, turning over her music for her, and conversing with her during the intervals of song in his low, fascinating tones and elegant language. A whist-table was formed, and Clara Peyton was conversing earnestly with one of the young gentlemen who bore the name of Ruggles, while Miss Ruggles looked over the whist-table as a spectator.

Thus Blonde and the clergyman were left for a long time by themselves at the little table from which the servants had removed everything. Mr. Seymour had brought one of the engravings which had attracted his notice earlier in the evening to the little table for his companion's inspection, and the two were conversing upon the subject suggested by the touching scene. It was the representation of the "Last Prayer" of the murdered king of England, Charles the First. The fair girl was bending over the picture in deep interest, and Mr. Seymour was standing behind her chair. While she studied the engraving, he studied her. Her fair neck and shoulders, and her misty, wavy, golden hair, her slight figure in its robe of dotted muslin, and her delicate, graceful hand resting on the table, revealed to his eyes a style of beauty unfamiliar and enchanting. His admiration was engrossing evidently, though he imagined his countenance must possess its ordinary calm expression of enjoyment and ease. A pair of violet eyes, however, across the room, in their occasional wanderings, discovered more of absorption in his looks than he dreamed of as possible, and before Blonde left the house she was informed in a low whisper how carefully she had been studied behind her back by the coming rector of Saint Paul's.

At length a pair of blue eyes looked up to the clergyman's countenance, and a gentle voice said,

" I wish you could see the painting of Charles, by Velasquez, the great Spanish painter. It is now on exhibition in this country. It was painted when he was a young man, in the ardent flush and enjoyment of youth; when life before him was golden tipped, and care and sorrow were only myths. The noble impress and consciousness of dignity are powerfully delineated on his features. He looks the king, every inch of him. There is a naturalness of color in his large blue eyes which is really wonderful. Approach those eyes with the strongest magnifying glass, and as closely as you please, and instead of finding the natural defects in the paint and in the canvas increase, you discover that it is a real human eye of the richest blue, looking directly at you, and the illusion is upon you that it moves and lives. It is the perfection of art. As I gazed upon it, my sympathies were strongly enlisted for the monarch who, at length, was taken in the toils of the Roundheads, and against the acknowledged principles of the law of the land, condemned to die. When I read of the cruelty and inhuman barbarity of his successor, the cold-blooded hypocrite Cromwell, towards the unfortunate Irish who were massacred without pity, I turn with relief to the character of the murdered king. I can discover enough of the unfairness and intolerant spirit of those in this country who claim to possess the principles of the usurper to satisfy me that their representations of the Cavalier King are not safe standards by which to estimate his character. I wouldn't trust the characters of even the ladies of my neighborhood to their tender judgments here in this town. Distortion of character is so clearly to my mind the forte of some of the Roundheads of the present day, that I leave a large margin for improvement in regard to the real character of the English king in history. But I sincerely wish you could look upon that wonderful portrait by Velasquez."

There is a contagious influence in beauty and enthusiasm—and her reverend auditor was not insensible to its influence, for he said, seating himself again beside her,

" History is yet to be rewritten. The independent mind of

this century will not always consent to adopt as truth, the historical records of the past, simply because they are styled 'standard authorities.' Old records and official documents are yearly being dragged forth from the dust of centuries, and made to bear their appropriate part in diffusing light. The ring of the geologist's hammer is heard in the wild wood, and science is daily stalking forth from the rocky defile with her hands filled with the precious records of the past ages. Habits of thought, founded on the dictum of mere human authority, are reeling away stunned by the hammer of truth ; and I firmly believe persistency of research will in time enable us to see more clearly the real motives or the sinister influences which prompted the actions of Charles the First in those instances where his enemies find their evidences of the weaknesses and duplicity of his character. I know it is a dreadful position for any man to be placed in, to be a sworn protector of the laws and the Constitution, and at the same time to be faced by a stern necessity, backed by armies. Those who boast much of firmness and Spartan obstinacy generally in my experience wilt like the flower when the trial comes. The chief of the Apostles was chosen for his firmness, but his decision of character oozed away under the voice of a woman. Charity for human nature is urgently demanded in behalf of those unfortunates, from Charles down to this day, who fall under the tender mercies and tongues of Roundheads. But I should indeed enjoy a look at the work of Velasquez. It is a source of regret to me, that with my excessive love of art I am denied opportunities for its enjoyment. But I shall, on visiting the city, endeavor to see this wonderful portrait which moves you so powerfully. Ah ! the music is over, and they are coming for your contribution to the divine muse. Do you sing, Miss Grayson ?"

"Oh yes, Mr. Seymour, every lady in C——, nearly, is a musician or a singer. You will be surprised, on extending your acquaintance, to find how many cultivated voices there are here among the young ladies. My friend Clara must sing for you when a good opportunity occurs."

Before she had concluded, she was interrupted by Judge Peyton who had come to solicit an exhibition of her powers for the entertainment of his guests.

The party at the whist table were very intent on their game, and for a time were very noisy in their remarks, after Blonde was seated at the piano, with the clergyman standing beside her. But even their attention was soon arrested as a low but distinct thrill of song trembled upon the ear. A heart and a tearful memory were singing. Beside the grave of her dead lover, a young girl was pouring forth to the blue sky her prayer in song. It was the day, appointed by her consent, when her little white hand was to have rested in his, as his wedded wife. And on that day she prayed, from the hand of the good God, other and more beautiful nuptials. She sang of her faith in the Communion of Saints, and earnestly besought Heaven that the soul of the dear slumberer might return to her side, to watch over her lonely life. That in the dim hours of the evening, and in the silent night, a low sweet voice might steal in music over her pillow, and whisper to her the counsels of God. That in the trial hours when temptation hung his luring veil o'er sin, the spirit voice might guide her, and the loving spirit hand smooth her brow tenderly, and soothe her lonely heart to peaceful dreams of God and his angels. And while her trembling lips were breathing out her prayer, her lover's spirit hand appeared to her, and raising from his grave her gift of dewy flowers, made with them on her forehead the blessèd sign of the cross—then left them in her hands in token of her answered prayer. Then louder and sweeter rang her anthem of praise, ascending on the ladder of song to the kind Father, who had warmed her bleeding heart with the gift of that dear and eternal presence, that holy guardian lover.

The voices at the whist table were hushed, and the hands were held motionless by the ruling spirit of the place. The fair girl's attendant clergyman gazed upon her angel beauty so radiant in her emotion, as if he dreamed of the celestial choirs above. But in Judge Peyton's eyes tears glistened fast. As Blonde arose from the wonderful keys and turned away, Mr. Seymour said to her gently,

"My introduction to the town of C—— reminds me of the gate called Beautiful."

CHAPTER XI.

Myrtle Dell was the pride of the county. Isolated from the public highway by a low range of pine covered hills, no wayfarer would have imagined its existence, unless he had chanced to pause at the low brown gate in passing, and peered down the long myrtle covered dell, from which the magnificent property derived its name. Then he would only have discovered an admirable road, covered with carefully pounded slate, and winding along between the low hills, till it seemed, at the distance of a hundred rods from the gate, to lead into a broad reach of green meadows. This was the limited and only glimpse of the Old Dutch Manor that was possible from the highway. The dell itself was scarcely twelve feet wide, and up its gently sloping sides, lay emerald masses of the myrtle, and over it waved on either side the broad arms of the white pines. It was a dark and gloomy drive at night, but in a broad glare of the summer sun, was a cool and delightful avenue of approach to the manor house in the meadows, beyond. Looking upward, one would catch occasionally glimpses of the blue sky through the dense foliage of the pines. The myrtle clung to the sides of this ravine, everywhere in wonderful luxuriance; and a clear spring issuing at one side formed a little stream which flowed along beside the slate road till it escaped into the highway near the entrance gate. This dell and road and glimpse of the distant meadows were the only indications to the passer-by of the noble estate behind the hills. But the more favored individual who might have the *entree* of the place would discover, at the abrupt termination of the cool, shaded dell, that he was entering upon a great meadow or park, bounded on the east by the range of hills through which he had just passed, and stretching away toward the other three points of the compass with the undulating formations of the ground, at least a mile in every direction. Then in the distance the heavy oak and chestnut wood swept its dark boundary line around the park till it met the pine covered barrier which concealed the property from the highway coming out from the town of C——.

The park was gradually rising from the dell toward the western forest, and occasionally at long intervals the gentle swells of the ground were crowned with clustering groups of native chestnut trees which had been left standing by the early settlers who had cleared away the forest.

On the June morning when the reader is presented to the retired manor and its inhabitants, the sun shone in a cloudless sky, and its rays flashed on a tortuous brook slowly wandering away through the green fields. The blooded cattle of the sleek Devonshire stock roamed through the emerald grass or were stretched beneath the clusters of the shady chestnut trees. The twittering birds darted through the branches. The more musical bobolinks wheeled their melodious circles from the meadows up through space.

Quietly grazing alone by himself in his glistening beauty and his graceful wildness, appeared the raven colored steed of the absent Henry Lansing. The new groom who had assumed the guardianship of the stables of the manor was utterly unable to manage Black Hawk, and so the horse was turned loose into the broad fields to follow the bent of his imperial will. He was the only black object in the landscape. He had lost the only two friends he had ever acknowledged, and he looked as sentimental over it as grass-eating would allow. His long black tail and mane had been the pride of his young master and the admiration of the town of C——, and it was a glorious sight to witness them flung to the wild wind in the desperate flights which he took with his bold rider over the surrounding county. Now the scene was changed; and the beautiful clean-limbed beast was without a rider, a friend, or a groom. None who knew the Lansing family and the pride in their aristocratic bosoms arising from the presence on the manor of an heir so gifted in intellect, and so graceful in every manly accomplishment as young Lansing, could look upon this deserted steed in his black, glossy beauty without an emotion of regret. The pride and heir of the manor had fled, and his loss was like the loss of the sun. His father missed him, for he was a fair representative of two noble families intimately associated with the early history of the State, renowned for their talents, civil and military, and for the honorable principles associated with their very names. The father's family pride was centred in his eldest, eagle-eyed boy. Carefully educated and trained for his prospective ownership of the manor, the young heir seemed about to rival the sterling honesty and enterprise of the Lansing ancestral line, and to revive again the memories of the brilliant qualities of General Philip Schuyler, of the Revolution. With this illustrious Schuyler, Henry Lansing's mother claimed near relationship. It was her pride to teach her sons to emulate the virtues and the valor of the beloved friend and comrade of Washington.

But the pride and the hope of the ancient family had disappeared in mystery; and there was a bitter pang in many a heart. Alas! he was not only lost to his kindred. The more poignant regret arose from the reflection that disgrace, burning shame, in the eyes of the world, was associated with his name. The common expression of the public judgment branded him, a *murderer*. No human soul on that broad manor, believed for one instant that he knew any thing of the foul deed. Nevertheless, there was humiliation day after day in the cruel words that were uttered throughout the country, and which sooner or later, traveled up to the entrance gate, and through the myrtle-covered dell, and across the meadows to the ears of the desolate family. The grey-headed sire mourned from pride, and vexation and loneliness. The gentle, noble mother yearned after her offspring because she loved him, his honor, his reputation and his immortal soul. The blue-eyed Gurty missed his companionship, his guiding spirit, and his kindness, at an age when kindness knits itself into an immortal web over a boy's heart. The energetic, nervous, intolerant widow in Israel, his sister, Mrs. Bounce, missed him when a heavy column of domestic figures lay on the table, waiting to be footed up by his prompt hand, or when an unusual case for the display of fearlessness or force arose about the manor. The servants missed his kind words—his ringing laugh—his horse's hoofs pawing before the mansion, in impatience for the wild rider, and his graceful figure bounding over the meadow road, and his rifle's sharp crack behind the great barns of the manor; and away from the bounds of the lordly park itsel., an honest, faithful heart missed him. The being who had grown up from infancy on the place, and knew no ambition disconnected from his young master's prosperity and happiness, leaned his sable face upon his sable hand, and wondered "What *has* become of Mister Henry?"

The old woman at the fatal garden mourned for him as for her own son. An old hag, who lived alone on the mountain, appeared, for the first time in a year, with her stick, in the streets of C——, begging for bread. Her friend was gone. The town's people, who read the pages of the Weekly Chronicle of C——, missed, for the first time, the inspired lines in the "Poets' Corner" of the sheet. "And last, but not least," a fair girl in C—— missed him as she bowed her golden hair over her embroidery, and studied so deeply, with her mysterious eyes of blue, his absence. Ah! she, the graceful witch, could give a reason, if she would, why the pride of the manor had fled.

But the manor house, on this lovely morning of June, demands our attention. The road, after leaving the myrtle dell, turned abruptly to the Northward, and followed the direction of the sombre pines, which formed the Eastern boundary for at least a quarter of a mile. Then its blue slate line, was traced distinctly through the meadows, circling gradually around for another quarter of a mile to the Westward, until it led directly to the broad piazza on the front of the manor house. The mansion itself, was of a very modern style of architecture. A broad square dwelling of brick, painted white standing on a high foundation, with a broad piazza, whose roof was supported by lofty columns of brick, also painted white with Corinthian capitals. Wild vines taken from the forest, climbed nearly to the tops of these lofty columns, and thence were trained, in drooping wreaths, from column to column, presenting to the eye, approaching from the East, a luxuriant front of green leaves. The lawn in front fell easily to the manor brook, a dozen rods away, over which, rustic bridges were visible, and in whose clear waters, darted speckled trout; unmolested, save by the occasional hook and line of Gurty Lansing. The little walk, which led over the principal rustic bridge below the lawn, passed on to a knoll, shaded by immense chestnut trees where rustic seats were placed for the weary or the contemplative Trees had been carefully excluded from the broad green lawn in front, that the view from the colonnade might be extensive, and command the approaching road through the meadows, even as far as the myrtle dell. But the other three sides of the two story, white mansion, were guarded by many rows of the balsam of fir; each tree forming a perfect cone thirty feet in height, and the lower branches lying flat upon the ground. The site of the mansion had evidently been selected from its being a prominent knoll, and from the beautiful balsams found ready grown upon the spot. In the rear of the great mansion, gardens blossomed with flowers and fruit. Many of the fruit trees were of great age; planted, no doubt, by some of the early owners of the manor, who had lived in the old manor house a hundred rods to the southward. Mrs. Lansing would allow no improving hand to touch the old brick manor house · and there it stood in its quaint old beauty, imbosomed in the rank and neglected shrubbery, with the wild vines tangled over its antique gables, and the ivy nodding from its unglazed casements. The manor brook murmured close beside the deserted and venerable tenement of the past; and when the soft moonlight disguised the cracks and the flaws of time's hand, the old ruin wore a wonderfully weird and fascinating look, and had been a favorite termination of the young heir's night ramble. Here, too, at noon, on the shady bank, had he reclined with his book, while his young brother, Gurty, dropped his hook and line in the dark trout holes of the manor brook, close at hand. In the rear of the deserted old manor house, stood the immense Dutch barns, which, in spite of their great age, retained their usefulness; and far behind them loomed up the dark line of the forest, over which a great hawk, was slowly circling his flight, in cautious pursuit of his prey.

That dense and mysterious wood was no stranger to the boys of the manor; and Gurty Lansing could tell of many a gloomy trout hole in the brooks gliding away under its shadows, and knew each knoll and valley in its shady recesses where the wild, red honey-suckle bloomed, and the low yellow balls of the mandrake ripened in the shade. The boy was familiar with every giant chestnut tree, in whose branches the gray squirrel whisked his graceful bush tail; and he knew the low coarse tongue-call which could delude the timid creature from his hole, to become the victim of his unerring fowling piece.

There was not a spot on the great manor where the feet of Henry Lansing and his brother Gurty had not in their respective youths found their way Each had learned of their mother, the wild tales of the Indian skirmishes and the later battles of the civil war, which had left the arrows and bullet marks in the casements and doors of the old deserted manor house; and each boy had in his time dug up the flint heads of the arrows, from the bed of the brook, or cut deeply into the door posts of the old tenement for English bullets. Little bare legs, with pantaloons rolled up above the knees, had waded up the trout brooks with the bagging scoop-net for the lurking fish, and merry little voices had shouted in glee when the darting trout had tickled the little bare legs in their alarmed efforts to escape.

And as their boyhood ripened into graceful youth, there were memories of parties and pic-nics under the trees, of wild races on the blooded horses of the manor, and sounds of merriment from the broad parlors of the new mansion. And later still, were memories of the young heir, Henry Lansing, returning from the graduating class of the distant college, bearing his diploma, for the admiration of the friends at his noble home; and later still, were memories of his graceful figure bounding away on Black Hawk toward the myrtle dell, as he daily sought the town of C— to pursue his course of study for his adopted profession. Every spot on the manor recalled his memory.

No wonder then, that, on this beautiful morning of June, as the Lansing family carriage, and the Lansing livery glittered on their way across the meadows toward the town of C——, there were sad faces, riding in that princely carriage, as the lone raven colored Black Hawk raised his graceful head to see them pass. The mother in her deep mourning dress with her pale face emaciated by sickness and sorrow for her lost son, leaned wearily against the comfortable back seat and watched with her lustrous blue eyes, the beautiful and solitary steed as he assumed his old position by the side of her carriage and trotted along with it as had been his custom when his young master accompanied Mrs. Lansing into town. The tears glistened in the mother's eyes for the lost rider. She held in her hand a large bouquet of flowers, destined for some one in the town. Gurty occupied the front seat with his small oaken box beside him containing his artist's materials. The boy was on his way to the studio of Carl Grayson, which had now become a daily source of pleasure for his young dawning genius. Mrs. Bounce had remonstrated, with the promptness of faith against her young brother being daily brought under the seductive influence of an Episcopalian family. But her mother had pronounced in her equally decided way that the Graysons were a refined family; and Gurty should be allowed to develope his latent powers under the only real artist in the county. The loss of Henry had caused her heart to cling more tenderly and tenaciously around the only boy now remaining to her; and notwithstanding her illness and disinclination to controversy with her stern Calvinistic daughter, she mantained her point in favor of Gurty's intimacy with the Graysons; and the boy was happy.

As the carriage rolled away from the myrtle dell into the public highway, and the further company of the attending Black Hawk was prevented by the closing of the gate, Gurty said,

"What are you going to do with that beautiful bouquet, mother?"

Recalled to the present by his words, she looked down at the flowers in her lap, and said, in her low sweet voice,

"They are for old Hugo—the old man is very ill, and I know he must feel very lonely in that silent house, with no company but a servant."

"But, mother," said Gurty, "why do you pay so much attention to an old infidel who ridicules your religion? Sister says he blasphemes nearly every other word he speaks, and the devil is certain to have him some day."

"My dear Gurty," replied the same gentle voice, "no one is ever injured by kindness; and this lonely old man will not seek the truth or investigate it, because he fancies every one hates him and ridicules him on account of his peculiar views.

It becomes me to meet him, not with doctrinal assertions, which only make him furious, but in the spirit, so far as I am able, of my Lord and Master. If I can win his regard and esteem, he may at last listen to me, and learn to adore the same holy Mediator with myself. Old Hugo is no trifler, but a thoughtful, honest soul, and a close student of nature as well as of books. He uses his reason, which is God's precious gift, and he certainly finds wonderful facts in the rocks, which I know must be reconciled in his mind with revelation before he will stir or arouse himself to save his soul. But it is vain to dispute his facts until I can grasp the subject more perfectly than I do now; and in the meantime my religion teaches me to be long-suffering with him, and kind to him, for he is a lonely and deserted old soul—and for such as he my Lord died on the cross."

Gurty appeared satisfied and said no more, but sat quietly beside his little box on the cushion of the carriage and studied the white clouds, which in one quarter only of the blue sky were heaped up in snowy mountains, rising above one another in successive peaks. At length, just in the edge of the town, the carriage stopped before a low, vine-wreathed cottage standing far back under the fruit trees; and Mrs. Lansing alighted with her bouquet, and the carriage rolled on into the elm-guarded street of C——, with Gurty and his artist's box.

The figure of Mrs. Lansing moved slowly and thoughtfully up the graveled path which led to old Hugo's vine-covered porch. Her step was feeble, and her mourning bonnet added to the paleness of her emaciated face. But her exquisite blue eyes were brilliant and full of sweetness, and would have insured her a welcome even among the most hardened and abandoned. As she neared the door, a great English mastiff moved dignifiedly up to her side and rubbed his nose against her hand for recognition. Dogs and infants instinctively recognize and love gentle natures. Moreover she was no stranger at the cottage, and the fierce-looking brute had, from the first call, made her an exception in his startling vocal challenge to all intruders on the property. She patted the dog on the head with her small black glove, and he walked behind her to the front door. Her gentle tap with the great brass knocker, polished with habitual neatness, summoned to the door a matron of at least fifty years, with smooth gray hair, and a face which bore only one unwavering expression—sorrowful resignation. That countenance seemed to say, "I have suffered—but I am almost home. Never mind me, but go in."

Mrs. Lansing said to her kindly,

"See these beautiful flowers I have gathered for the old man—is he well enough to see me to-day?"

The matronly, resigned expression of the housekeeper never varied as she glanced sorrowfully upon the bouquet; and then raising her cold, gray eyes to Mrs. Lansing, she moved aside for her to pass in, and said,

"He will not refuse *you* admittance—he is better, and sitting up in bed."

The apartment into which the visitor was ushered was small and simply furnished, the principal object which attracted the eye being the great shelves loaded with books. They were extended across the entire room on one side, and opposite to them was an alcove and window, where old Hugo was sitting up in bed, bolstered with pillows. The quiet and resigned housekeeper passed through into another apartment and closed the door behind her softly, and left Mrs. Lansing alone with the old man. As the dark, mourning figure with the bouquet approached his bed, old Hugo turned his shaggy gray head slowly and painfully towards her. His great brown eyes expanded like those of a sleepy old lion, and he evidently was still very weak from the effects of the violent fever which had passed.—He said, in a deep, stern tone,

"Why do you come again? I shall soon be on my feet again, and you are delicate and weak as a kitten. You might have spared yourself this. I need nothing. Why do you come?"

Mrs. Lansing looked a moment upon his calm, white forehead, stamped with intellectual power, and upon his firm pale lips, before she replied. Then she said, holding the luxuriant and fragrant mass of flowers close under his expanding lion eyes,

"I heard you say once you loved flowers; and then I found a great book on flowers on your shelf one day when you were delirious. I know flowers are sometimes refreshing to an invalid, and I thought you would be glad to see *them* if not me. But you will suffocate in this close room. The day is very fine, and the dear birds are singing in every garden. But in here the air is dreadful. I am going to open that window beside you—the balmy air will revive and strengthen you—here—take this bouquet while I open the window."

Old Hugo's sullen expression vanished, as his pale, thin hand closed around the stems of the flowers, and his great orbs were aroused into admiration at sight of their glorious beauty and their great variety, culled as they were from the choice and expensive gardens of the manor. As his appreciative eye wandered over the beautiful present in his lap, the window was quietly raised, and his brow was instantly fanned and cooled by the June breeze which gently drove away the stifling atmosphere of the sick room, and poured into his expanding lungs fresh, balmy life. The soft breeze, too, agitated the flowers in his grasp, and their fragrance was wafted over the room. This poor old deserted child and worshiper of nature was thus gently restored to her arms. He slowly raised his eyes from the flowers, and there she was again—the pale, gentle lady standing beside him in her mourning dress, with her sad, sweet smile, occasioned by his evident enjoyment. The old man, stern as he was by nature in his tone of voice, and hardened to the world as he was by the bitter treatment that world had given him for being a free-thinker, was nevertheless stamped by our common Creator on his left side with that sensitive organ called the heart. His deep, stern voice, was just a trifle husky, as he rolled his great brown eyes upon Mrs. Lansing's countenance, and said slowly and with painful effort, for he was very weak—

"You are a strange woman to persevere so, in coming to this house to see an old outcast from society who has been abandoned by every one, and who might die here as unnoticed as a dog dies. You never torment me with your doctrines—you never bring those wretched little church tracts and throw over my fence for my dog to gnaw to pieces. What are those tracts to me?—they cannot answer my doubts and my facts, which I have pounded out of the rocks with that little hammer which you see yonder on that shelf. If the wise and the learned can answer my facts and reconcile them with the Scriptures, why don't they do it? I will read anything and everything they will write or have written; but these little tracts—what trash to throw to *me*. Tell me, Mrs. Lansing—does your God order you to throw tracts at a poor, lonely old man who has such a library as that across the room?"

He pointed his pale finger at the choice collection of scientific works on the book-shelves, and looked at the same time into the sweet face of his visitor inquiringly.

"No, Hugo, no," she said, sinking wearily into a chair beside his bed, "the God whom I adore loves you, and would have you exercise your strong intellect and your cultivated reason to its highest extent—but you must not reason when you are ill, but only rest your mind and be calm, and enjoy the air of Spring which our God so kindly sends you. When you are well again, I intend that you shall instruct me in all you have learned and gathered from the rocks ; it must be interesting indeed, and your mind is so clear and your judgment so sound, that I do not fear to trust to your scientific knowledge. There is no harm in studying and prying into God's works—and though many will censure me for learning from you, I do not care—I know I am right in learning all your objections to God's holy Word. If my life is spared much longer, will you instruct me in the wonders of the rocks, that I may know on what foundations my faith rests ?"

The old outcast was flattered, and at the same time touched by her words, for he said, with real joy brightening his marvelous lion-like eyes—

"I am proud to find you so independent of sectarian prejudices, and so fearless in your pursuit of truth. You will be charmed with my noble books and the mysteries of my geological cabinet—but tell me, Mrs. Lansing, why have you braved the reproaches of your church, and why have you been so kind to an old man, who was an utter stranger to you, and branded with that terrible name, 'infidel'?"

Mrs. Lansing busied herself a few moments in adjusting the pillows more comfortably about the lonely invalid, and then drew her chair around so that he could see her without effort. Then seating herselt again before him, she said earnestly,

"You have no conception, Hugo, of the God whom I adore. He, the adorable One, is mindful of the most minute existence of creation. And you, yes! you, here alone by yourself, are the especial object of his care. Before my Lord left this earth, he instructed his followers to remember that his dearest favorites were the poor, the persecuted, the lonely, the friendless, the miserable, of every grade and of every country. And one night when I was bowed before Him in prayer, and had entreated that I might know how to win heaven, a voice seemed to whisper to me, 'Old Hugo, one of my dearest children, is lonely, and deserted and sick. All revile him and desert him, and yet I love him better than all your church put together—that lonely old man is my child, and I shall feel bitter indeed if you do not go to him, and aid and comfort him.—He is lonely ; so was I, for all deserted me and fled. Many will reproach you for going to him and listening to his doubts and his facts ; but I love that old man dearly, and you must be kind to him for my sake. I have given him a royal intellect, and he shall have the right to use it—and remember that every weary step you take in kindness toward that old man's door is for me, and shall be remembered—for he is my deserted and my dear child, and the brightest child, too, that I have in this whole town: endure a little fatigue and reproach to aid him, and I will not forget you when I make up my jewels.'"

The invalid looked at the flowers in his hand, and rocked his gray head back and forth as he listened to her low sweet voice with the manner of one who hears after a long interval, the music of a familiar song. As she paused at length, he looked up thoughtfully into her sweet eyes and said,

"I like your God—he is so different from the gods of most people."

"Yes," she said, with her gentle smile, "He is very different indeed, for He is a God of pure love. Now we have talked enough about my dearest friend; let me talk now about one of your friends. Shall I read to you a little while from that favorite book of yours which lies open on the table? The place is marked just where you left off when you were taken with the fever. If you will not talk, I will read from it till you are tired."

The old man was all interest now, and the thought of hearing his favorite author—now when he was so feeble and helpless, was a joy indeed. He listened for a long time to her calm, cultivated tones, looking down all the while at the fragrant flowers in his hand. But at length her musical monotony of voice lulled him to sleep, and his gray head sank back upon the supporting pillow.

Mrs. Lansing lowered the support for his head, and then stood for several moments watching his slumber. Then she softly closed the window again and stole silently forth into the garden. As she walked slowly down the graveled path to the elms on the street, she was whispering to herself softly—"Oh God, my Father, my Saviour, give me old Hugo's soul."

CHAPTER XII.

Mrs. Lansing found her carriage at old Hugo's gate, awaiting her return from the cottage. The coachman had left Gurty at the studio of Carl Grayson, and returned again for his mistress. As Mrs. Lansing seated herself in the carriage, the driver pointed to an immense cloud of inky blackness slowly moving up from the westward, and said,

"We shall be caught, Mrs. Lansing, in that heavy shower before we can get home. I think I had better raise the top of the carriage and draw the curtains."

The pale, emaciated face of his mistress nodded assent to his proposition, and soon the top of the vehicle was raised and the side curtains closely buttoned to secure her from the approaching storm. The coachman gave a low grunt of satisfaction as he surveyed, for a moment, the completeness of the leathern covering in which he had encased his mistress against the rain. Then springing to his seat in front, he gathered up his reins and urged his mettled steeds to their utmost speed. There was no time to lose.

Already the vexed and frightened wind was sounding the alarm as it swept in uncertain gusts through the elm branches, or turned up to view the white under sides of the leaves of the silver poplars. The dust of the street whirled in fitful circles through the air; the dead branches of the trees snapped and fell to the sidewalks, and the early flowers of the garden shivered and bowed their timid heads in fear. The gloom and the darkness gathered fast, and the wail of the wind was followed by keen flashes of electric light from the impending cloud, and then the startling crash of thunder near at hand bewildered all. Then came at last the pattering of great drops upon the carriage-top, and then the deluge of the rain sweeping along in blinding sheets. The spirited horses plunged aside at each successive flash of lightning, and then dashed on again more madly than before. The unprotected driver bowed before the violence of the rain torrent, and the gentle invalid inside the coach shrunk nervously from the little streams which found their way to her delicate form in spite of her leathern roof. On past the dim houses of the town flew the Lansing carriage; on past the open fields beyond the town it rolled at break-neck speed; and still the pitiless rain fell in unceasing torrents till the meadow brooks o'erflowed their banks, and the wavy grass of June was beaten flat and helpless to the earth. Alas! the trembling, delicate invalid inside the carriage yearned for shelter as she in vain changed her position in the cushioned seat to escape the drenching rain. And yet in her discomfort and her apprehension she remembered her God. Amid the howling of the wind and the blinding sheets of rain, her ear was still open for mercy. Hark! the agonized, despairing wail of a child met her ear. Rising distinct and clear over the howling of the wind and the dash of the rain, it came to her mother's heart, and her Christian soul tremulously sad and sorrowful.

"Robert, stop, in the name of my Master. Stop at once. We've passed a deserted child by the roadside."

The coachman, with an effort, brought his flying horses to a standstill, and bending his ear low to the invalid inside, asked,

"Are you sure, Mrs. Lansing? I have seen no child."

"Yes, Robert; I heard the pitiful cry. Turn around, and drive a little way back."

The driver reluctantly changed the direction of his horses' heads, and drove slowly back the road he had come, peering carefully through the gloom of the increasing storm. He soon detected the cry which had attracted her attention, and passing his reins to the hand which she extended between the carriage curtains, he sprang to the ground, and walked to a bush where a little emaciated figure was crouching for shelter, and drenched to the skin. It was a delicate boy of about seven years; and the poor child was a cripple. He held a little crutch in one hand, as he sat upon the drenched grass under the bush, and one of his little legs was shriveled and twisted. Pain, and hunger, and lonelines, were marked too plainly on his pitiful little face, as he in vain strove to ward off the beating storm by crawling under the bush, and drawing his half naked shoulders closely to his pale face. The violence of the storm admitted of no delay, and the sturdy coachman raised the child in his arms, and bore him, with his little crutch to the carriage, soothing his startled cries of terror, by promises of shelter and protection. He placed the little fellow on the seat beside Mrs. Lansing, and then mounting his box again, urged his horses to renewed speed, through the driving rain. The astonished child looked up to the lady's face, and seeing her matchless blue eyes beaming with tenderness and sympathy, murmured some words of relief, which brought the tears quickly to her eyes. There was something so gentle, so helpless, so heart-broken in his trembling accents, that she passed her arm around his wet and ragged figure, and pressed the little sufferer to her bosom. Then she said gently to him, "Little boy, what twisted your leg so? and why were you alone in the fields?"

The child's gentle blue eye looked up pitifully again to her face, and he said, in a faint, sorrowful tone—

"Father hated me, and throwed me down stairs, and that's

what hurt my leg. I go around and beg, 'cause father won't have me in the house, and I'm so hungry."

The little emaciated outcast had not tasted food in three days, and was wandering about like a beast, seeking for food when the storm came on. Mrs. Lansing gleaned from his trembling little lips, the sad story that he had no knowledge of his mother, and that his father, after hurling him down stairs and injuring his leg for life, had driven him forth into the beggar's world, at an age when children have barely learned to walk. An old beggar woman, with four children of her own, had extended to this infant, the charity of an old piece of rag carpet for a bed, and the privilege of sleeping in a corner of her hut, just outside of the limits of the town of C——. The child's gaze was fixed upon the countenance of Mrs. Lansing; at first in wonder, but as she slowly drew from him the sad little history of his sufferings, and as he experienced a comparative sense of comfort under the leathern roof of the carriage, he nestled closer to her side, and grasped her gloved hand more tightly, with his red little fist, and a faint little smile illumined the corners of his mouth, as he studied her features. No doubt that feeble smile was the first smile of his forsaken little existence. Oh! the father's heart yearns towards his little, helpless child, no matter how great the poverty that lingers at the door of his hovel; no matter how desperate the daily struggle for his bread may be. He freely gives his heart and his supporting arm to the little tottler who climbs his knee. But oh! the unfeeling brute who flung this puny child down the stairs with such fiendish violence that the infant's leg was crushed and distorted for life, and the infant's memory of the title "father" meant only, "agony and terror." Alas! for this poor lonely child, there had been no sweet and soothing cradle hymn—no caressing hand of kindness—no hope—no home! A little, trembling, crawling, crouching existence standing alone and helpless before God. And as he sat upon the soft cushion of the carriage, with his little crushed leg, and his crutch resting in the lady's lap, and heard the cruel rain baffled from his shivering form by the leathern roof, and looked up, for the first time in his life, to gentle eyes and tender words, he seemed to realize the presence of that dearest goal called "heaven." Poor little human waif, flung aside by a father's hand, drifting upon the surface of a cruel world, ignorant of God, and happiness and love; he was now to be rescued, and clothed, and cared for, and taught to look up to and beyond the silver stars, where little crushed legs, and little bleeding hearts, would one day be healed, and where a true and loving Father, would gather the lonely and the suffering home. And why had this sun of happiness arisen so unexpectedly upon his little heart, as he crouched in misery and terror under the wayside bush? Ah! it was the sweet echo of those divine counsels, which breathed from the lips of the lowly Nazarene, so many centuries ago. The pale, gentle lady who had rescued the child, was actuated by high and holy principle. She loved God, and yearned to do His holy will. Those wonderful words had burned deeply into her cultivated and noble heart—" Inasmuch as ye have done it unto one of the least of these, my brethren, ye have done it unto me." Jesus sat beside her in his loneliness. The little crushed leg was His; the pale, tortured little face was His; the unpillowed weary little head was His. She took that little head in her arms—she strained it to her bosom—she pressed her soft kiss upon the forehead, and murmured tenderly to the child—" You shall never be left alone in the storm again—you shall live with me, and I will give you plenty to eat, and clothe you, and give you a soft little bed to sleep on, and I will love you: you, poor little wanderer, do you know what *that* means?—do you know what *love* is?"

The bewildered child raised his head from her bosom, and looked up in her face, and said, plaintively—

" No, I don't."

" And do you know who God is?"

Again the wondering little face said,

" No, I never saw him."

A smile of exquisite sweetness swept over her pale face at this innocent reply, and she answered, earnestly,

" He is my friend, and I will tell you all about Him when we get *home;* you have a home now, child, and that means the place where I live."

But the wild, drenching storm went on, and before the carriage arrived at Myrtle Dell, Mrs. Lansing was conscious that her arm and shoulder were very wet from a small trickling stream which found its way between the fastenings of the leather curtains, and made her delicate frame shiver, and filled her with apprehension of evil results to herself. As the flying horses at length dashed up to the piazza of the manor house, and then suddenly halted, she was praying inwardly, " Oh! God, spare me for my children's sake."

The manor house was alive with excitement. The violence

of the June storm was unusual, and the inmates of the great house were watching, in profound interest, for the arrival of the invalid mistress. They had caught a glimpse of the carriage whirling along through the inundated meadows, and when it reached the piazza, there was a grand rush of umbrellas and blanket shawls, to cover Mrs. Lansing's entry into the house. She was escorted at once into the kitchen in the basement of the house, where the grand fire-place was glowing with warmth and comfort for the wearers of wet garments, and where the odors of the approaching dinner, fell gratefully upon the sense. Mrs. Bounce flew distractedly about the house in search of comforts for her mother, throwing the servants into confusion by her nervous calls and directions, and by her still more nervous gestures and manner. When her mother was at length seated in dry garments before the kitchen fire, and warming her feet at the glowing mass of coals on the hearth, Mrs. Bounce found time to inspect the little cripple who had, under Mrs. Lansing's directions, been stripped of his soaked rags, and clothed in a dry suit of Gurty's long disused garments. The stout Irish maid had washed the child's face and hands, and combed his tangled brown hair into a certain semblance of civilization, and the little fellow was now seated in a low chair before the cheerful fire, ravenously devouring the hot soup which had been presented to him in a bowl, and which had been dipped out of the cauldron which hung from the iron crane over the fire. Mr. Lansing, the proprietor of the great house, had a fancy for the immense and old-fashioned fire-places of his boyhood ; and his taste had been gratified in building the great kitchen of the new manor house ; for the fire-place was of enormous size, and capable of receiving several logs of at least a foot in diameter. At one corner of this great fire-place, sat the little cripple with his bowl of soup His crutch had fallen to the floor, in his eagerness to satisfy his poor, craving stomach, and he was too intent on his meal to notice anything that was occurring around him. Mrs Bounce marched, or rather thumped her fat figure along the floor until she stood opposite the child's face, and then surveyed him from head to foot, with an air of indescribable astonishment and disgust. Then she vented her feelings thus :

"Mother, what in the name of goodness, are you going to do with that thing, that child ? He is dressed in Gurty's clothes, and his feet are as red and dirty as a pig. How came he here. and what do you expect to do with him ? He ought to be in the poor house this minute ; poor house pauper is written all over him. He surely can be of no use here with that twisted limb. I only hope he has brought no vermin in the house with him."

Thus delivering her sentiments regarding her mother's charity, she placed her arms a-kimbo, and looked with a dictatorial stare, into Mrs. Lansing's mild, lustrous blue eyes. The little cripple was startled by her loud, harsh accents, and looked up from his soup with the crouching and trembling air which had almost become a second nature to him. But the pangs of hunger were too great for interruption, and he commenced again at his bowl of soup, stealing however, out of the corners of his pale blue eyes, occasional glimpses at Mrs. Bounce's severe countenance, as if he apprehended, at any moment, a sudden blow on his little head. Blows and kicks from his father, had developed caution in his poor, trembling nature, and the little puny cripple was ever on the alert to avoid punishment, or rather cruelty.

Mrs. Lansing detected, however, the child's alarmed manner, and an expression of keen anguish darted to her eyes. She answered her daughter very quietly, however, suppressing some intense impulse of indignation, which, in either of her sons, would have flashed forth in high words on the instant,

"Esther, I found this poor child almost dying, by the roadside, lying out in the storm, and moaning so pitifully. His own father has made him a cripple for life. He is going to stay in this house as long as I live. If I can make him useful, I will do so; if not he may limp about with his poor little limb and enjoy himself. We have every thing that heart could desire here, and we need some poor tortured little specimen of humanity in our midst, to teach us, by contrast, how to be grateful to Almighty God. I desire that my dear Gurty shall always be sound of limb, and strong in health; and perhaps God will accept my services for this poor little outcast as a pledge and offering for the happiness of my own child."

There was a quiet and yet imperial dignity and force in her manner, as she uttered these words in her low, silvery voice, which conveyed at once to the daughter, the conviction that this was one of the questions which were not open for discussion and opposition, and that her mother's mind was indeed made up and determined. Mrs. Bounce looked confused and annoyed before all the servants, who happened, at that moment, to be collected in the kitchen, and who were always inclined to rejoice over her discomfitures, which, latterly, had become very few. She contrived, however to appear calm and unconcerned as she said—

"Well, I suppose, then, we must provide some place for the child to sleep. He had better have a cot in the room with the coachman, in the stable loft."

"No!" replied Mrs. Lansing, quietly. "I will never permit that little crushed leg to travel up and down stairs. My little dressing room at the end of the lower hall, is not necessary for me. I can use your father's dressing room, for he says he cares nothing for it. Put the child in that little room, and make it very comfortable for him. What is your name, little boy?"

The little cripple had finished his soup, and was watching his new friend's countenance with intense interest, as he discovered comfort for himself in her soft, gentle words. He replied, at once, in a quiet but distinct accent, while his little red hands clasped both sides of the empty bowl—

"The boys called me Twisty, and the old woman does, too!"

"Well, then," said Mrs. Lansing, "we will call you Twisty, too, until we can find a better name for you. What are you looking at, child, so earnestly?"

The little cripple raised his hand, and pointed with his delicate little finger across the kitchen to a large bass-viol, which hung from a wooden peg in the wall. It was the property of one of the servants, and figured often in the kitchen frolics, which Mrs. Lansing tolerated rather than approved, on public holidays. The child's blue eyes brightened, as they followed the direction of his pointing finger, and he said, with animation—

"Don't you see that music on the wall? I can play. I know how."

All eyes were directed at once to the child, for he spoke so confidently of his power, that all were impressed. But Mrs. Bounce ejaculated, impatiently.

"Well! what assurance that child has. Mother, I am very much afraid you have secured anything but comfort, in bringing this beggar here to live."

Her mother answered only by directing the bass-viol to be brought to the little cripple, to test the truthfulness of his assertion. The instrument was placed with the bow in his eager little hands, and he instantly proceeded, with the air of a master, to put the bass-viol in tune. He evidently knew what he was about, and all his subdued and shrinking manner vanished the instant his hands grasped the coveted instrument. Expressions of amazement appeared on every countenance, at the puny creature's change of manner, and his absorbing interest as he carefully turned the screws in adjusting the strings to the proper tone. In a few seconds, he reached his hand down to raise his crutch from the floor, where it had fallen. Standing then erect, by the aid of his crutch, he rested the bass-viol against himself, and drew the bow across the strings. His little shrill voice broke forth in a strange wild song, descriptive of a battle where mountaineers hurled rocks in a narrow defile upon the heads of the invading army. He accompanied himself with his bass-viol in perfect harmony, thrilling the hearts of his audience, as they all gathered in a circle about him, by the intense pathos and sublimity of the words, and the wonderful power and appreciation with which he sang them. The audience were astounded, thrilled, delighted in rapid succession. Even Mrs. Bounce exhibited a smile of pleasure, as his infant voice mounted to the high key notes of triumph, at the repulse of the foe, and then suddenly paused. The surprise was indeed complete. This poor, distorted, helpless little specimen of humanity, trampled upon, hurled forth upon the lonely world, an outcast, a beggar child, was, nevertheless, the casket which enclosed the priceless gem, *music;* dear, sighing, whispering, moving, triumphant *music.* Power was in the little red, trembling fingers ; the pale, hunger-worn, infant lips ; the power to move the inmost soul to grief, or joy, or worship. God, the All Wise, had suffered this trembling and persecuted child to wander without an alleviating smile, along the thorny paths of life, starving and moaning away its little existence ; and yet He had given to the deserted cripple, a pearl which all the wealth and the influence of the proud Lansing family could never buy.

From that hour, not a soul on the great manor, regretted the charity of heart which had induced the gentle mother to rescue the abandoned child. Little "Twisty" became the pet of the household. Every bright day, the little fellow could be seen hobbling about the lawns and the gardens of the manor, peering into the faces of the beautiful flowers, which seemed to occupy a great part of his affections, gathering the various fruits in their seasons, and bringing his heaping baskets to his beloved mistress, mocking the birds with his sweet, shrill voice, watering the plants of the conservatory with his little blue watering pot, and watching every look of Mrs. Lansing, that he might anticipate her slightest wish, and save her the least inconvenience. His little dwarfed nature expanded under the genial sun of kindness, and he soon forgot to shrink and tremble when a voice addressed him, and became the merriest, sweetest little humanity on the manor. His musical talent was carefully encouraged and cultivated, and Mrs. Lansing procured him a place in the choir of her own church in C——, where his bass-viol became a prominent and indispensable favorite with the congregation on Sundays.

But often in dreamy moonlight evenings of the summer, his warbling little voice could be heard, under the silvered mass of shrubbery in the garden, uttering his low, sweet songs, in company with his beloved bass-viol, which moaned and murmured and triumphed forth strange melody upon the quivering night air ; and Mrs. Lansing would sit on her piazza, holding Gurty's hand in the soft moonlight, and listen to the child's music under the shrubbery, and wonder and sigh and weep. Alas ! music recalled the memory of her wandering, lost, idolized, eagle-eyed son, Henry Lansing, the mysterious, lonely fugitive over the broad world.

Little Twisty's life seemed made up entirely of love for the pale, fading mistress of the manor, who had saved him from the material and spiritual storms of life. Every night before he limped away to his little bed in his mistress' dressing room, he would kneel in the great hall of the house, before her bedroom door which had closed upon her weary footsteps, and lay his crutch beside him on the floor, and clasping his little hands in prayer, would say—

"Oh ! my good God, please make her well once more, for you know she is the only one poor little Twisty has to love him."

CHAPTER XIII.

Glorious, golden August still hovered over the town of C——. The last month of summer lingered in warmth and beauty, bringing a flush to the cheek of the rapidly softening peach, and adding a darker hue to the purple clusters of the grape. Luscious pears, pendant from the trees, tempted the passer-by with their yellow plumpness, and occasionally a golden pear of a rarer species swung in the sunlight with a bright red flush upon its polished skin. Dahlias of crimson, or scarlet, or yellow hues nodded gracefully in the gardens to every wandering breeze ; and the juicy melons on the earth lay voluptuously still in the warm embrace of the ripening sun

The last day of summer was close at hand as an elegant carriage, drawn by two fiery steeds, dashed up to the gate of old Rosy's garden and deposited two gracefully dressed ladies, and then whirling around again, rolled back to the town of C——. The ladies left at the gate were Blonde Grayson and her friend Clara Peyton. They were attired in plain white muslin dresses, and wore white crape bonnets trimmed neatly and simply with purple leaves and small bunches of grapes. Each lady was belted with a blue ribbon secured by a gold buckle. Simplicity and comfort had evidently been studied in this day's attire, for the friends had been invited by old Rosy to come and enjoy a few hours' easy and uninterrupted intercourse with her in the cottage and under the trees and arbors of the garden. The dial near her gate indicated the hour of noon as the two walked slowly under the dense shade of the young maples up toward the cottage. The startling crime which had invested the neighboring wood with horror for the past three months, and the mutual disposition to defend the young heir of the manor from the dreadful charge of murder, had drawn old Rosy's heart warmly and ardently towards Blonde and her friend. On several occasions during the summer had the two friends visited the owner of the garden, and indulged in conversation regarding young Lansing, his character, his history, and his innocence. He had communicated to the old woman at different times before his abrupt disappearance, and during his frequent visits to her garden, many of his secret thoughts and acts. He had formed an earnest friendship for old Rosy and her flowers, and his unrestrained discourse in her presence had revealed to her much of his real character and principles. She understood his fearless and impulsive nature, his generosity, his pride, and his love for the sublime and the beautiful. She extenuated the faults and the misfortunes arising from his impetuosity, and defended him with warmth. Thus had these two young ladies gained a favorable insight into the character of the young heir in whose defense they had volunteered before the excited town of C——. Their first impulse had been to vindicate young Lansing, because he was a high-toned gentleman, a member of their own circle of society, and one whose open and candid traits of character precluded the possibility of his committing a secret and cruel murder. But now their intercourse with the old woman had elevated still higher their regard for the wanderer, opened to their gaze, his earnest and true heart, and exhibited to them the strange wild fires of genius which played so constantly in his brain, and ambitiously were cultivated in the late studies of his private room, and beside the flickering lamp whose light had often paled before the eastern dawn. They learned from her that his keen intellect would never succumb to the excesses of dissipation; that his nature was rapidly flinging aside his faults, when the fatal day broke on the town of C——; and that his professional career would some day astonish those who knew not of his intense study and his patient research in the realms of science. Making due allowances for old Rosy's partiality, the two friends were nevertheless impressed by the facts of his history, and their satisfaction was still greater that they had not faltered in lending their support to his friends in the days of trial and reproach.

But the graceful Blonde knew, almost to a certainty, who the real perpetrator of the murder was. Judge Peyton shared her secret. The negro boy, Norman Prince, unquestionably must hold a valuable clue. Why were these three silent? Weeks and months were gliding by, and the mystery of silence still rested on their lips. The stain was becoming irrevocably fixed upon the noble and esteemed and powerful Lansings. The dashing heir of the manor returned no more. A pall hung over the great estate more solemn, sadder than death; it was the pall of *shame.*

How much longer were the three to wait before the dreadful name should thrill the community? Had the truthful and the prayerful Blonde no pity for the pale and fading mother on the manor? Had the irreproachable and the unpurchasable judge, whose virtues and whose praises were on every lip, no sympathy for that orderly public, whose rights every crime outrages? Had the negro boy, Norman Prince, no memory of his kind young master and friend, whose name was unnecessarily stained with blood? Why did he remain so passive, so mysterious, so still? Alas! there must be some fearful conflict of duties in the consciences of this singular and irreproachable trio to permit a noble and an honored family name to lie crushed and dishonored in the dust of shame.

Whatever may have been the mysterious motive which sealed the lips of Blonde Grayson, certain it is that she experienced no remorse of conscience, or, at least, manifested none at the constant reflection in her mind that she was concealing a murderer from justice. From the very moment she had shared her secret with Judge Peyton, ease of conscience returned to her, and now, as she slowly walked with her friend under the maples towards the old woman's cottage, her eye was clear and bright, her complexion brilliantly white and beautiful, and no trace of sorrow on her fair face. But occasionally her blue, mysterious eyes grew thoughtful as she listened to Clara's ever-ready tongue, and before she reached the door of the cottage Clara once detected her in an abstracted mood, with her eyes fixed apparently upon the distant blue hills. She made no reply to Clara's question, but the young girl was not disposed to notice her abstraction, and continued to chatter in her spirited way until they reached the door of old Rosy's cottage. Clara imagined that within the past two months her friend was often thinking of the absent Henry Lansing, but desired not to have it known. It would be difficult to indicate upon what state of facts this imagination was founded. There never was a tremor in Blonde's voice when speaking casually of him. There was no effort to avoid mentioning his name, and no effort to intrude his name into their daily conversations. And yet Clara believed these occasional abstracted mood of her friends arose from secret thoughts of Henry Lansing. Whether the fair girl surmised correctly or not, the sequel must determine.

Old Rosy discovered the approach of her visitors, and came out to meet them. She wore a dark blue gown and a small white apron with pockets. Her gray hair was surmounted by a white lace cap with a blue ribbon run through it; and under this cap her hair was parted smoothly back covering her ears from sight. She evidently had passed the age of fifty, but her dark eye was full of fire and spirit, and her whole appearance, ladylike and prepossessing. She made a graceful courtesy to each of the young ladies, and then extended to them her strong, labor-hardened hand in welcome.

"Come in—come in, young ladies. I declare, you are as prompt as the sun itself. I had no idea you would be here in an hour, yet; but come like all fine ladies, after the time, and when my poor little dinner would all be cold, waiting. It's a good sign, young ladies, this being prompt, and you'll surely escape a deal of trouble in life, if you follow it up. Come in—come in—you surely know the way by this time."

Thus speaking in her cheerful tones, she ushered the two friends into her principal room, where the sad inquest had been held over the body of Hartwell. The scene now was indeed changed. The floor was covered with fresh looking red and white matting. Three or four cane bottomed chairs stood against the walls; also a lounge covered with blue and white calico. In the centre of the apartment, stood the square dining table, covered nearly to the floor with a snow white table cloth, and covered with the white china plates, and the white handled knives and forks, which the old woman only used on great occasions like the present. She had taken a great fancy to the two friends, and was determined to prove to them, as she remarked "that poor folks have an idea of comfort, as well as the best people in the land."

Blonde noticed in passing, that beside two of the plates, little bouquets of the choicest flowers from the old woman's conservatory, rested in glass tumblers. The mistress of the cottage conducted them across her dining room to her little bed room, where they could remove their bonnets, and adjust their disordered hair before her little looking-glass, the frame of which she had covered with a wreath of her evergreens. The little bed was remarkably white and inviting, and the only window was honored with white muslin curtains, sliding back and forth on a piece of white tape, nailed across the top of the window frame.

As Blonde Grayson removed her white crape bonnet and commenced to adjust her golden hair before the little mirror, old Rosy exclaimed—

"The most beautiful hair I ever saw! Why! Miss Grayson, you ought to marry nobody but some prince who could afford to exhibit that head of hair over his whole kingdom."

Blonde laughed heartily, as she answered this compliment—

"Well, Rosy, if you'll find me a prince I'll promise to marry him. A regular prince is just the thing I want. I must marry something grand, or never marry at all."

"That's as true as the gospel," said Clara Peyton. "Blonde has refused nearly every one in this town, that is certain. I don't know what the child means. But it seems, really, as if her mind was made up to live and die an old maid. Rosy, what a sweet little bed room this is. I would like to sleep in that clean, white bed, this very night."

"Ah!" sighed the old woman; "those very same words were said by Mr. Henry Lansing, once, and I let him sleep there that same night. He was very tired, returning from a long hunt, and said he wouldn't go home that night, because he was miserably blue and cross. He flung himself down on my lounge, with all his hunting clothes on, to sleep; but I made him come in here, and go regularly to bed. He said it was the sweetest sleep he ever knew. I peeped in here after he was asleep, with my candle in my hand, for I was frightened at his way of talking, and I feared he must be sick; but no—here he lay as quiet as a lamb, with his graceful arm flung on the pillow above his head, and with the sweetest smile on his lips I ever saw on a human. I surely believe if I had been a girl and found him sleeping with such a beautiful smile on his mouth, I couldn't have helped giving him my heart that very minute. He looked that minute, just the picture of his beautiful mother when she smiles. Now—you spoke about a prince, Miss Grayson; if there ever was a prince, he's the very one Why, he's formed and shaped the most beautiful you can think of. He came in here one day, with his gun, in winter, and the water from some swamp had run in between his leg and his boot, and then froze up; and his hunting knife had slipped down his leg, and cut into his knee. He jerked off his frozen boot, and then rolled up his pantaloons' leg to stop the blood; and I declare to you, his leg was as beautiful and as perfect as a king's—indeed I doubt very much if there ever was a king who had such a leg. That makes you laugh, does it. Well, it's true, I assure you."

Clara Peyton roared with laughter; but Blonde was remarkably busy, at that moment, before the glass.

At length the two friends completed their toilet, and were then conducted by the old woman, through her dining room again, out upon the lawn under the young maple trees. The stillness of noontide was upon the garden, as the three seated themselves in the cane bottom chairs, placed in the dense shade of the maples. Old Rosy had given a moment's attention to her dinner, which was cooking in the little closet, which she denominated, "My kitchen." Then she had conducted her guests to the shade trees and said,

"We will have a nice talk, now, for it will be a full half hour before dinner is ready. Do you know I have sold more flowers this summer, than I ever did before? All the young gentlemen in town, seem to be crazy on the subject of giving their sweethearts the most expensive bouquets; and then there has been so many parties. I shall live quite comfortably this winter, I'm sure. This new rector of St. Paul's has a remarkable fondness for flowers; he comes here often after them—I never knew any body so devoted to flowers, except poor Henry Lansing."

This latter name seemed to occasion serious thoughts, for all remained silent and thoughtful for a moment. Then Clara, catching a glimpse of a young tree near at hand, said in her quick way, pointing her white finger toward the garden,

"Rosy, tell me, is not that a locust tree? I heard something a few days ago about that tree. The language of the locust is something very singular, or very beautiful—I don't know which—do you, Blonde?"

Her friend confessed her ignorance of the symbolical meaning of the tree, but the owner of the garden exclaimed,

"Yes, that is the locust; I do not know its meaning, but I can find out in a minute. Wait two seconds."

She disappeared for a few moments inside the cottage, and then returned with a flat, red-covered book, resembling one of her account books. As she seated herself again under the maples, the friends discovered on the cover of the book words printed with a pen, and reading thus—

"A SINNER'S JOURNAL."

"This," said she, opening the book, "is a journal kept by Henry Lansing. He asked me to keep possession of it for him. He said he would not keep it at the manor for fear Mrs. Bounce would get hold of it. He told me to read in it, if I pleased, but to be careful that no illiberal minded person got hold of it. He told me once, when he was writing in it here under these same trees, that he was putting my locust tree into his book, and he said something about the language of it. I had forgotten all about it until Miss Clara spoke. And now we will find the language here, I have no doubt. He was the most singular young man you ever knew—not a flower of the field or the leaf of a tree, that he didn't know all about; and he was forever boiling leaves and wild plants in my little kitchen, and carrying off the juices in little phials. He made a mixture once from some wild plants which he came across in his hunting days, which cured the most violent nervous headache I ever had. He has a gift that way, I am certain. Here—here it is. I told you so. I knew it—see? 'Locust and its language.' You read it, Miss Clara—my eyes are getting rather dim these days."

Clara Peyton took the book, and leaned back in her seat to read. Before commencing, however, she glanced at Blonde's countenance, and detected signs of intense interest in those blue, mysterious eyes. Blonde saw the quick meaning in her friend's eyes, and slightly averted her face. She knew for the first time that she was watched with reference to Henry Lansing, and her uneasy look told Clara plainly enough that Blonde knew it at last.

Clara's low, sweet voice in reading, floated tremulously and dreamlike in the utter silence of the noontime under the shade of the sleeping trees.

"LOCUST.

LOBINA, CARAGANA.

(Green leaved) Class 17. Order 10.

This genus is mostly indigenous to tropical America. Caragana is a North American Species—and there is one in India and one in China.

The language of the boughs is this:

Affection beyond the Grave.

"The fresh boughs of the Locust tree
Do image forth his memory in my heart."

I never shall be loved this side of death. The fluttering leaves of the trees whisper this sad destiny to me. My nature craves the pure and deathless love of woman. I know a treasure lies within my daily grasp, priceless and beautiful as the light of stars. I press that treasure daily to my heart. I look up to the blue sky, and thank Him who gave it. That peerless, that unmatched loveliness, is my devoted, my holy mother. I tremble to own this treasure. I feel a keen and darting agony when she draws nigh, for I can see, with scientific eye, those blue veins in her neck and arms are fast preparing for their last sleep beneath the sod. Oh! I shall be alone, and the night breeze will murmur to me that soul's desolation—'Gone!—gone!'

But other mortals replace this dead love with another. Most men may find peace, hope, and quiet joy in the gentle love of some fair stranger to their blood, and linking their destiny, their hopes to her, live on in mutual joy till Death, that spectre-horror, steps in to mar the light. But I, alas! the favored child of fortune, with rank and wealth, born to no toil, or care, or want, look forth like a deserted child upon a boundless sea, without one coming sail of love. My wealth may win fair hands and fairer cheeks. But I, a human soul, with eager hopes and silent yearnings, capable of loving woman with a madly reckless passion, fear and shrink, and oftentimes despair of winning unselfish love. Oh, could I be loved purely and devotedly for myself alone! Could another existence be bound up irrevocably with mine, so that when I shall die, that other existence must necessarily accompany me through the dark vale, through pure inability to breathe here without me—Oh! then my dream of life would be complete in its fruition.

But these sad locust leaves are ever whispering to me, 'The love of woman will never come to thee—never, oh never!' and this reflection maddens me amid my ambitious dreams; for if I have none to share my pride and ultimate success, why struggle on? I would be useful, honored in my day, and crowned with wreaths of praise for scientific power and service to my race. But my lone heart is ever murmuring for a bright sweet face to be the reflex of my joy; for a gentle form to steal softly, noiselessly to my side in quiet hours, and fill a void which comes with my very nature to be filled. And will *I* ever love? Will this craving find its idol clothed in human form, and rising to my vision like a new flower born to a wondering world? I feel that this will be. She will come to me radiant and hopeful as the morning. I will love her, and see in her the promise of a new life. Alas! alas! sad locust tree, will you never cease your warning notes of woe? She will not give to me the answering gift for my poor heart. I shall not receive the balm of love this side of death. Sad locust leaves, your language is 'Affection beyond the grave.' My race will be run in loneliness and despair; the low, craving cries of my nature will be drowned by the green sod which shall cover me—and then, ah then, by the power and the magic of thy leaves, oh! murmuring locust tree, she shall be led to my lonely grave. The light of heaven shall open to her the depth and the fondness, and the eternity of that offering which I so vainly offered to her angel beauty and her pure heart in life. And kneeling, she shall stretch across my grave her fair hands, clasping a branch of thy mysterious leaves, oh locust! to tell my disembodied spirit of her coming love and tenderness beyond the grave."

Clara's low sweet voice trembled as she neared the end.—She looked up and found old Rosy in tears. But Blonde, the fair and graceful lily, with her clasped hands resting in her lap, and her averted face turned to the blue outline of the distant hills, listened as one who hears celestial music calling her away from earth and its sorrows to a far-off home.

Old Rosy dried up her tears on her snow-white apron, and then walked rapidly away to attend to her dinner arrangements. Clara turned over the leaves of this strange journal, seeking with eager curiosity to peer more deeply into the records of this strange wild heart which had so fearfully agitated the town of C——, and which yet appeared so full of pathos, gentleness and love.

But Blonde, without a word, moved slowly from her seat,

and passed across the soft and velvety grass to the locust tree. A small branch of the leaves hung low, and drooping towards the ground. She reached up and broke off the branch, and brought it slowly back to Clara's side, and said softly, as she studied the formation of the leaves, "Clara, we will never forget the language of the locust after this. How sad it is to be hopeless and alone."

Clara looked up from the journal, but met only the gaze of sweet, blue, unfathomable eyes, beaming with gentleness and mystery.

CHAPTER XIV.

The Rev. Marcus Seymour was a favorite among the elegant congregation who worshiped at the chapel of St. Paul. From the first Sunday after his appearance in C——, he was respected and admired for his eloquence, and loved for his gentleness, his faithfulness, and his zeal for the prosperity of his church. His social qualifications were of a high order; and both the literary and festive portions of his congregation were delighted with his acquirements and his toleration of all reasonable festivities which did not intrench upon religious duties. The elderly ladies of St. Paul's chapel found constant interest in his civilities and his dignified conversation; and the young ladies eagerly sought his society for his sparkling wit and merriment, for his enthusiasm for all that was refined and beautiful, and for the sake of glimpses into his marvelously brilliant, dark brown eyes. Those clear, truthful eyes in society, fascinated by the generous emotions which lighted them, and flattered by their genteel and respectful approval of excellence in music, and skill in art, and dexterity in embroidery. This keen perception of excellence in every department of life enabled him to make rapid progress in paying off the indebtedness of his church. For what lady would not weary her fingers to work for his fairs for the church when he bowed so gracefully over every piece of difficult work she did, distinguished and remarked upon its excellencies, and encouraged her by his kind words and compliments? He was a candid and an outspoken priest. He encouraged, he denounced, he implored Few cared to absent themselves from the services of the church while his musical voice read the solemn service and his eloquent finger in the pulpit pointed heavenward. His burning utterances made sin appear absolutely hateful, his alluring visions of Heaven stimulated to faith and good works among the suffering poor. What wonder, then, that the fair girl who wept at his inspired words on Sundays, and laughed at his keen satire and his genial humor during the week, should sometimes experience an emotion of tenderness in his regard, should deem it possible to be happy as the wife of a poor clergyman. In fact, a dozen girls who swept their trains so gracefully up the aisles of St. Paul, were really or partially in love with the Rev. Marcus Seymour before he had been settled a month in C——. But all the young ladies, or rather all the marriageable ladies of St. Paul's, soon discovered that their reverend pastor was no fool. It would not do to palaver him. It did not suit his style or calibre of mind. Persistency or grossness in flattery towards him evidently offended him. His favorites were the refined, the gentle, the modest. This discrimination and good sense secured him, for a wonder, the good wishes of the male portion of his charge. He was a deserving and universal favorite in his church. Many were the speculations indulged in as to his probable intentions in regard to marriage.

An old maid of his congregation who had grown gray in the service of church fairs and Sunday-schools, and who, from the length of her tongue and her quick perceptions, had been universally recognized as a species of oracle, had pronounced her opinion on the subject of his wedding propensities thus:

"I will tell you, girls, just exactly what Mr. Seymour will do. The first move he makes will be towards Blonde Grayson. That you may depend on. Every single gentleman of real decency and eligibility in this town takes his first look at that girl She is beautiful and she is good; don't one of you jealous things dare deny it to *me*. But she rejects most everybody, though she is most twenty-five. I can't tell you all why, but I surmise she's engaged out of town, or has got a dead lover. Well! I tell you Mr. Seymour will propose to her some fine day. She'll refuse him, just as sure as my name's Sarah Legget. When he gets his cooler from her, then we will stand our chance; that is, some of you young things, for I'm too old. Just look under my front hair, and you'll see the gray hairs preparing to show themselves before many months. Now mind what I tell you. Blonde Grayson will have a chance to refuse him—and she'll do it. She'll never marry a poor clergyman; it ain't in her, and I don't blame her."

One of Sarah Legget's auditors ventured this reply:

"I don't see why people think Blonde Grayson possesses all the beauty in C——. For my part, I think she's too tall."

"Oh, Mary McClure," replied the quick old maid, "I know how sweet and pretty you are, and I know that man will be happy who secures your love, right well; but you know that Blonde Grayson is graceful just in proportion to her height, and that she's a regular queen of grace and elegance. I dislike a tall person who isn't graceful just as much as you do; but her height becomes her style, and she is just as sweet as she can be. She's only a little too mysterious at times—but that's her nature. She's a lady, every inch of her, and a good pious girl, too."

As the new rector made no visible motions towards marriage, other than a slightly evident disposition to linger in Miss Grayson's society whenever he chanced to meet her, the marrying public waited patiently through the summer months for the fulfillment of Miss Sarah Legget's prophecy. But the reverend young clergyman, no doubt conscious of the many curious eyes that watched his movements, visited no oftener at the residence of Mr. Grayson than at any other residence of his parishioners.

But it chanced that on the identical day old Rosy was entertaining at dinner Blonde Grayson and her friend, the rector of St. Paul's was wandering along his usual walk through the meadows towards the old woman's conservatory for a bouquet of his beloved flowers. He had a passion for adorning his open study window with flowers, and enjoying their odor wafted over the room as he studied or wrote. It was his custom to enter the garden quietly by the meadow path which led over the old woman's stile, and wander about the garden selecting such flowers as pleased him, and then returning to the cottage to pay for those he had chosen and tied together. He carried a small pair of scissors with him, and inasmuch as old Rosy knew him to have a careful and delicate hand for such selections, he culled at his leisure the flowers that suited his fancy, whether in the conservatory or in the open garden.

While the two friends were enjoying the excellent and abundant viands on the cottage table, the Rev. Marcus Seymour crossed the stile unnoticed, and wandered about the grounds with the deliberation and coolness proper for an August day, culling his favorite flowers. When his bouquet was at length complete, he strayed away to the cool spring in the corner of the garden, and, seating himself on the shaded grass beside it, placed the fragrant flowers, which he had tied together, in the bubbling waters, to retain the necessary moisture. The heat of the dying summer was so excessive, and the shady recess about the spring so alluring, that the clergyman lingered long upon his grassy seat, and at length fell into a reverie. How long he remained in this state of reflection or dreaming, he never knew. He was awakened from it by hearing voices close at hand, under the shrubbery, and apparently approaching his cool retreat. He listened a moment, undecided whether to remain as he was or to rise and follow out the shady path in a more dignified manner to meet the intruders. His ear detected the sound of Clara Peyton's well known voice pronouncing his own name. Curiosity, or an instinctive disposition to remain quiet when concealed, prompted him to remain seated on the grass by the spring. This much of the conversation met his ear:

"Mr. Seymour would make you very happy for life, Blonde; I know it."

The clergyman listened eagerly for the reply, for he knew there could be but one Blonde in company with Judge Peyton's daughter. But the fair girl's answer was given in a much lower key than her friend's voice, and could not be overheard. The voices were receding now, so that he could distinguish no more words, but only discover that Clara was speaking earnestly and impressively to her friend. How eagerly he waited for Blonde's reply, and how faint of heart when he could hear no word that might light the torch of hope in his bosom. He listened to their receding footsteps for a while, and then sprang to his feet, determined to learn from Blonde before she left the garden, whether or not he might hope to secure her love and her hand. If personal, and intellectual and religious attractions could win her, Mr. Seymour held a splendid hand of matrimonial cards. The young clergyman was perfectly aware that the beautiful girl, who had attracted his admiration on the first evening of their acquaintance at the residence of Judge Peyton, had manifested towards him no other evidences of partiality than were natural and necessary to indicate her great respect for his intellectual powers, and her esteem as a strong churchwoman for a pastor whose shades of opinion and whose ideas of life and character coincided so accurately with her own. She sang in her exquisite style for him as often and as willingly as she did for other gentlemen, who enjoyed her respect and intimacy; but no more willingly, and no oftener. He could read in her blue eye, at times, that involuntary admiration of his face and figure, which every attentive and appreciative woman at some time manifests towards a gentleman of her circle who bears a reputation for grace and prepossessing looks. Her beautiful eyes had brightened at his approach, and her graceful hand was often extended to him in meeting. But those eyes had never softened in expression to indicate an unusual predilection for him which might lead to an acceptance of his hand for life. On the contrary, she appeared always so calm and self-possessed and lady-like in his society, that he had never been able to muster courage to lead conversation into those delicate channels regarding love and matrimony, where so many secrets may leak out, and so many soft words may be uttered, which form the basis of future love raillery and marriage negotiation. She was just so dignified, and so queenly and so sweet in every act of her life and every motion of her exquisite figure, that the familiarity of a love proposition appeared to him like downright presumption. He experienced the slightest degree of awe in her captivating presence; and he felt often that although his heart must follow her during the remainder of his existence, it must be at a respectful distance. The more refined and delicate the emotions of a true gentleman's heart are, the more elevated does a lady's character and position appear in his estimation. He shrinks sensitively from any act which may pain or startle her, or render her uncomfortable or uneasy. He may crave her love in his secret thoughts, but he waits long and patiently for that moment to arrive when his heart offer will be consonant with refined and natural manners, and when he may rather be led and allured into his proposal, than to force his own way rudely and indelicately. The young clergyman had, on two or three occasions, been on the point of offering himself; but those calm, unmoved, mysterious eyes ever restrained him, as they looked so kindly, so sweetly, so queenly into his countenance.

But as he sat beside old Rosy's dancing sparkling spring, and heard the fragment of a conversation regarding himself, and a life union with the gentle lady who haunted him in his dreams; when he knew that a heart union with himself would not be novel or startling to her, he started up, and impulsively determined to follow up the two friends, and contrive, in some way, to disengage Blonde from her friend, and compel her to resume the consideration of the same subject of conversation wherever Clara might leave off. He had overheard enough to convince him that Clara was his advocate. That radiant, sparkling beauty of seventeen, who often slept in his idol's bosom, knew many, if not all, of her maiden secrets, received and owned the full tide of Blonde's affection; that same beautiful, intimate friend had the moment before, been urging upon Blonde, a favorable consideration of himself, as a life partner Why, or wherefore, or in what way, such a remarkable conversation regarding himself should have arisen, he could not conjecture. Perhaps Blonde had divulged to her friend, a dream of him; perhaps he had made an impression on the heart of the graceful lily, which had caught Clara's keen eyes.

The young clergyman slowly paced along under the shrubbery, following the general direction that the two friends had gone. He feared to follow them too closely. They might imagine he had been listening to them, otherwise than involuntarily. He waited until several minutes had elapsed, before he quickened his pace; and then he took a circuitous path, which led around to the stile, hoping to intercept their walk, if they should be taking the direction of the meadow path towards the town. When he reached the stile, the two friends were not to be found. He glanced anxiously across the meadows towards the town, to discover the figures somewhere along the meadow path. They were not to be seen in that direction. Then he listened for their voices or their footsteps in the garden behind him; but no sound met his ear, save the low hum of the garden insects, or the whisper of the summer breeze to the low shrubbery. Where could they have gone? He turned towards the cottage; ah! a flutter passed over his heart. There under the maple trees, without bonnet, or scarf, or gloves, robed in spotless white and blue girdled, with her golden mass of soft, wavy hair, sweeping back from her brow in misty puffs sat Blonde, like an angel. She was alone. The cottage in the background was apparently deserted; no other face was in sight. There she sat, with a small locust branch in her hand, in the contemplation of which, she seemed utterly engrossed She was unconscious of any presence, and Mr. Seymour's salutation on reaching her side, was her first intimation that a gentleman was on the premises. She started in surprise, and a faint blush tinged the snow of her cheek. Then recovering instantly, her habitual self possession, she extended her lily hand to the clergyman, and said, laughingly, while the cunning dimples played about her graceful mouth—

"I never was taken so unawares before—you must possess the invisible slippers of the fairy tales, to be here at my side without a sound or motion. I dreamed I was alone. Clar Peyton and old Rosy have just left me for the conservatory

Ah! how tasteful your bouquet—did you come, now, from the conservatory?"

The young clergyman extended his bouquet to Blonde, impulsively, and said,

"I am glad you admire *my* taste. Will you not be charitable enough to honor me by accepting it?"

She took the proffered gift in her hand, and said, with a gratified manner, which encouraged him—

"Any lady would feel honored to receive such flowers, from such a hand."

Mr. Seymour's brilliant eyes were full of meaning, as he answered this brief adulation, looking directly into her calm, upturned, pleased eyes:

"Miss Grayson, if you feel honored to receive flowers from my hand, will it be presumption in me to offer you something which will never fade, like these flowers? Something which requires no air, no sun, to nourish it; but which flutters and expands in darkness and in silence, and will ever live?"

A revulsion of feeling passed over that fair, upturned face. The smile vanished. The long eye-lashes drooped guardedly over the blue astonished eyes, and she looked down at the bouquet, which rested on the locust branch in her lap, confused and bewildered as a startled bird. When she at length broke the stillness, the words trembled on her sweet lips, and she was obliged to pause again, to recover her self-control. Then she said, seriously and earnestly, with her eyes fixed upon the soft, waving grass at her feet:

"Mr. Seymour, your words and your looks combined, leave me nothing for conjecture in regard to that which you are about to offer to me. Will you listen to my words, and at their conclusion, leave me, with a prayer in your heart, that God will bless me?"

The unfortunate clergyman knew that his doom was already pronounced, and that he was rejected. His lips quivered as he looked away towards the setting sun, which already was casting long, trailing shadows of the trees across the garden paths. He said in a low whisper,

"God will always bless *you*, Miss Grayson. I will always pray for you; tell me the sad words, and I will never cross your path again in entreaty, or request, or offer, but only in silent agony."

The low, despairing whisper, touched her heart. The reflection fluttered nervously to her mind: "Oh! will my poor heart be thus rejected, when its day shall come?"

Her calm, clear sense of right and duty soon returned to her and she said, calmly looking down at the clergyman's gift,

"I never can, I never will accept the love of any man, for which I cannot, in return, give my whole soul. I firmly believe most girls are differently constituted from me; I know many are. With me, love is life, and light, and air. Independent of it, I can see little of pleasure in life, except to do God's holy will. Mr. Seymour, I cannot love you, because God does not intend me to love you. I never had an emotion in your regard, except the most profound respect for you as a Christian priest. My day to love has yet to come. You shall live to know that I am your sincere friend. May God bless you; go now, for your own sake, and to save comment, for in intrusting me with your secret, you have trusted to the silence of the grave, and I already hear voices approaching who may not be as discreet. If you will allow me, I will retain your bouquet, as the gift of my pastor and my friend."

The clergyman's ear detected the sound of voices approaching through the shrubbery, and he said, hoarsely, "For me there is nothing now to live for but heaven. Farewell! I am wounded, but not offended; I am proud of your friendship, though its track leads over the ruins of a desolate heart."

He bowed sorrowfully to Blonde and then turned down one of the narrow garden paths, and walked rapidly away, to avoid the approaching footsteps. His figure had scarcely disappeared from sight when Clara and old Rosy made their appearance with large bouquets from the conservatory. Blonde had concealed Mr. Seymour's gift in her bosom, to save unnecessary comment.

CHAPTER XV.

THE morning of the sixth of October opened in unwonted splendor upon the Lansing manor. The white, thin frost which night had spread over the broad meadows and the green slopes of the great estate, glistened diamond-like in the rays of the rising sun, and then speedily vanished in the increasing warmth. The day promised to be unusually balmy and delightful. The burs of the great chestnut trees which crowned the gentle hill tops of the park had been opened by the power of the night frost, and the brown chestnuts were occasionally rattling down upon the dry and crisped leaves on the earth. As the genial sun ascended over the tops of the dark pines which concealed the manor meadows from the public highway, the oak and chestnut and maple forest appeared in a dress of wonderful richness and beauty to greet his coming. The encircling woods in the rear of the great barns and the manor house were glittering with the gay colors of the autumn. To the carnival of nature the maples wore scarlet and yellow, the oaks dark red or purple, while the pines declined to change their dress, and wore dark, solemn green. The cone-shaped evergreens about the manor house stood solemn and unchanged in their dark green mantles. But the young maples, and the younger elms which had been planted in a circle about the evergreens, now wore leaves of brilliant yellow; and the long, climbing vines which were wreathed about the columns of the manor house and festooned from column to column, were now draped in one dazzling mass of scarlet leaves. But the most wonderful handiwork of the autumn was visible upon the old manor house which, far away through the meadows, thrust up to view its quaint old chimneys through the matted vines and neglected shrubbery. Its leafy robe was one great mass of red and golden fire. Ah! the old abandoned manor house was tenanted on this glorious morning. Shortly after the sun had made its appearance over the pines, bordering the myrtle dell, the fiery drapery which hung over the front entrance of the deserted house was violently agitated, and the unknown inmate made his way slowly out to view. It was the graceful, clean-limbed, raven-colored steed of the absent heir. No one on the manor could tame his wild nature since Henry Lansing had disappeared. He had been abandoned wholly to his own keeping, and following his lost young master's tastes, he was accustomed to haunt the deserted old tenement of the Lansings, unmolested and solitary. He always appeared in the daylight wandering about over the green fields, and to the amazement of many on the estate, with his dark coat always nicely rubbed down and glistening in the sun. How this happened Mrs. Lansing knew, and the keen-eyed Mrs. Bounce surmised. The faithful negro boy, Norman Prince, secretly solicited from the mother of his lost young master, the privilege of coming quietly by night and caring for the wild and lonely steed he so dearly loved. He had made a comfortable stable for his favorite in the deserted manor house, and in each still and lonely night he could be found under the dense and lonely shrubbery, endeavoring to keep Black Hawk in the condition the young heir had always insisted upon. Sometimes, in dark and lonely nights when there was little danger of meeting unwished-for faces on the highway, Norman Prince would lead the noble beast cautiously out from the manor, and leaping to his back, go flying along the country roads at the break-neck speed once so habitual to the young heir. His honest heart was ever consoling itself with the reflection, "How proud I shall be when Mr. Henry comes back and thanks me for loving his favorite horse. Mr. Henry's a regular prince—so is Black Hawk. Mr. Henry has the best of blood—so has Black Hawk."

Sometimes, in the old manor house, late at night, the negro boy would place his lantern on the oaken floor, and seating himself beside it while Black Hawk was feeding, lean his sable face upon his sable hand, and wonder what had befallen his young master that he never returned to his home. Occasionally Gurty Lansing would steal quietly away to the old manor house at night, and leave a broad piece of gold in the negro boy's palm, and say,

"Norman, never desert Black Hawk—mother says so. You're the best nigger in the county, and she says I must never let harm come near you; and Norman, I won't—trust me."

One night Gurty marched into the old tenement, and found the negro boy sitting beside the dark steed, and buried in one of his reveries. He came up quietly and slapped Norman on the shoulder. The negro started to his feet in terror, but Gurty only laughed and said,

"Here, Norman, I like you for my brother's sake. Take this—it now belongs to you."

He placed in the hands of the bewildered servant his own elegant fowling-piece. The negro looked at the gun and then at Gurty. There was no mistaking his good luck—the donor was in earnest. The faithful boy had coveted the possession of a gun above everything else. He was one of the best shots in the county. He took off his hat, bowed with his wonderful grace, and attempted to speak—but the words choked him. He burst into tears. At length he said,

"Master Gurty, I'm a poor boy, and I can't never return much for your kindness; but you're growing every day like Mr. Henry, and I'm going to try and think you're him till he comes back. You just tell Norman Prince to go through the fire for you, and see if I don't do it. You're both princes—both of you"

The October day which dawned so auspiciously upon the

manor was an exciting day for the Lansing family. From time immemorial, the anniversary of the birthday of the boys of the manor had been celebrated by a grand dinner to the friends of the family, and by rural festivities. There appeared to be sufficient reason this year to let the birthday festival go by unnoticed. Sorrow and pain had laid cruel hands on the ancient and aristocratic family. Mrs. Bounce, who had a most remarkable penchant for economy for one of her position in life, and who desired on all possible occasions to do away with those observances of her ancient family which were not consonant with the customs and ideas of that new people from the Eastern States who were gradually driving to the wall the citizens of New York State who prided themselves upon their Dutch and Huguenot descent, desired Gurty Lansing's birthday to be passed by this year in silence. She urged the sad condition of affairs as regarded the absent heir, and pointed out plainly enough that many could not be invited who were customary guests, on account of the faction they had joined against the heir, and against his innocence in the matter of the murder.

Mrs. Lansing listened patiently to her daughter's objections, and then said with an unwonted fire in her wonderful soul-eyes,

"My boys are born gentlemen, with the high and honorable privilege of maintaining a dignified position by their talents, by their courtesy, and by their upright conduct in life. There will be an additional inducement to be prominent and useful in life, in looking back to an ancestry honorable and honored.—They are born gentlemen. I pray earnestly that they may be Christian gentlemen. But they are honorable from their family, and I desire them to think so and to remember it. I love ancient observances which are calculated to maintain family pride; and now, with my noble Henry absent, and suffering unmerited reproach, now is the very time to hold one's head high, and live down this foul calumny against the heir and the heir's family. The Lansings have never stooped to dishonor—my son is no murderer, and his home is not afraid to keep the family observances. Let those who discover stains of shame on this house remain away, and may God forgive them. Let those who have hitherto been omitted come now, for the noble charity they have extended to my boy in his trouble. Let Gurty's fourteenth birthday be celebrated with unusual style and expense—and when I am laid beneath the sod, my boy will remember that his mother's heart and his mother's family pride never faltered under reproach and persecution towards him. I will brace my feeble health for the sixth of October, and then retire to the quiet and the rest which becomes a soul so near its final account."

And so the sixth of October dawned in excitement and preparation on the Lansing manor.

Before the hour of noon three great tables had been arranged for the expected guests, and covered with white cloths and plates and bouquets, preparatory to the reception of the enormous and delicious dinners in course of preparation in the great kitchen of the manor house. Early in the morning additional cooks and servants had been arriving from the town, and for hours the savory cooking had been going on for the expected crowd of guests. A score of ladies and gentlemen came early in the forenoon, who were relatives of the Lansings from distant cities, and from estates a few miles away. One table had been spread the entire length of the great hall for the grown guests; another was extended under a group of chestnut trees in the park for forty young boys and girls of Gurty's age; and in another direction, under the broad chestnuts, a long table was placed to entertain the tenants who paid the Lansings rent for the rich farms in the neighborhood. The manor gardens were stripped of their flowers to adorn these tables, or to swing in wreaths from the chestnut branches overhead.

Mrs. Lansing, pale and weary, but resolute, sat in a comfortable seat on the great piazza, from which she commanded a view of the table in the great hall, and the two less pretending tables spread under the chestnut trees. Ah! how she missed in this festival time, the quick eye, and the correct taste, and the calm, instructing orders of the absent heir. His ever ready tact, and clear, condensed orders had ever been in requisition to guide aright the feet and hands of confused and hurrying servants. But now Mrs. Bounce, nervous and fluctuating, was flying around like a possessed person, worrying and tormenting the servants into stupidity and confusion every minute, which her mother was forced to undo again, at the sacrifice of her feeble voice and her weary frame. The young Gurty in whose honor the fete was given, was superintending the placing of targets for the riflemen, and arranging the details of the races around the park, for which the manor was to furnish the fleet and blooded steeds. The races were ever of the most interesting character, from the number of ladies who rode for the prize.

Punctually at half-past one o'clock, which was just one half hour before the time appointed for the great dinner, a stylish carriage, containing Judge Peyton and his beautiful daughter, dashed up to the piazza of the manor house. In a few seconds another equipage made its appearance, driven by the negro boy, Norman Prince; and in it sat Mr. Grayson and his son the artist, and the elegant Blonde. The graceful lily was radiant in a scarlet silk, which, as she ascended the steps of the front piazza, exhibited precisely the hue of the vine leaves festooned above her head on the great Corinthian columns. These two carriages were speedily followed by a line of elegant vehicles of every size and pattern, rolling rapidly from the myrtle dell across the meadows, and flashing in the dazzling sunlight. The green fields were already alive with groups of the tenantry, with their wives and daughters, some seated under the broad chestnut trees, or engaged in games of base ball, or throwing quoits, or wandering about examining the sleek Devonshire stock which roamed the meadows. Small parties of neatly-dressed girls from the neighboring farms were strolling away with their beaux in the direction of the highly-cultivated gardens and the hot-houses of the manor, or gathering the large red apples which were scattered about in the abundant orchards. The shouts and laughter of children rang out from the high branches of the chestnut trees, where they clung with their little hands, and stamped upon the swaying branches till the reluctant brown nuts rattled down through the leaves for the little anxious faces below. On every side laughter and merriment sounded; and the only creature that appeared lost, and lonely and bewildered, amid all this revelry and excitement, was a dark, graceful figure, standing apart on a knoll by the old deserted manor house, and contemplating the unusual scene motionless and silent. It was the lone steed Black Hawk.

At length the appointed dinner hour arrived, and within and without the great mansion the guests gathered about the luxurious tables to enjoy the good cheer. Gurty presided at the juvenile table without, and his father, the gray-haired proprietor of the manor, sat at the head of the long and sumptuous table in the great hall, and the fair, blue-eyed, suffering mother sat at the foot of the table with her venerable and aristocratic-looking kinsmen about her. On the right of Mr. Lansing sat the Rev. Marcus Seymour, in attendance upon the beautiful daughter of Judge Peyton. On the left of Mr. Lansing sat the Rev. Thomas Delaplaine, attentive to his neighbor, the raven-haired beauty Mary Livingston, a dark-eyed belle of twenty, and heiress to a great estate upon the Hudson. She was the gifted and graceful girl upon whom Mr. Lansing and many of his relatives had looked with favor for the past two years as a suitable and desirable match for his eagle-eyed son and principal heir. The dark-eyed girl was aware of this partiality in her regard, and dreamed of fascinating the handsome Henry Lansing when his wandering freak should have terminated by his expected appearance again on the manor

The Rev. Thomas Delaplaine, pastor of the Presbyterian Church of C——, was a gentleman of medium height and slight figure, with clear hazel eyes and dark red hair. He was smoothly shaven, and his expression was gentle, and winning, and intelligent. His manner, at first, was timid with strangers; but when conversation and coincidence of views were firmly established, he became natural and genial. He was kind of heart; and liberal for one of his peculiar sect, but he had many in his church who overawed him by their intolerance and checked his natural flow of spirit by their severe comments. But though he was influenced much by the majority of his pastoral charge, they never had succeeded in forcing him to take part against young Henry Lansing. He always admired and loved the heir from his childhood, and confidently looked for riper years to dispel the wildness of his character. He had never vehemently taken the side of the heir in the matter of the murder, but all efforts to make him believe young Lansing was guilty had proved utterly futile. and he had been recognized as one of the Lansing clique.

But on this festive occasion, surrounded by sympathizers with the family, and untrammeled by the presence of the intolerant, his natural impulsive Huguenot blood revealed itself in words. As he was called upon to say grace preparatory to the great dinner ceremony, he arose, and after invoking the blessings of heaven upon all present and upon the viands so bountifully spread before him, he concluded, with a strong accent upon the adjectives, thus:

"And we beseech Thee to return in health and happiness right speedily, the *manly, honest* and *innocent* heir of the Lansing manor. Amen!"

It was a happy hit for the Rev. Thomas Delaplaine in that assembly. When he had concluded and seated himself again, beaming eyes were directed towards him from every part of the long table, and murmurs of approbation were whispered on every side. But as he chanced to look away towards the extreme foot of the table, he detected a pair of large, lustrous blue eyes fixed upon his countenance with the absorbed, tearful interest of profound gratitude.

Blonde Grayson was seated near the foot of the table between her brother and a handsome young widower, who rejoiced in the name of Henry Livingston, and who was a cousin of the dark-eyed Mary Livingston near the other extremity of the table. This elegant young gentleman with brown hair and moustache and keen gray eyes had been fascinated by Blonde's appearance and conversation previous to the summons to the dinner-table. He had contrived to escort her to the table, and now devoted his looks and conversation almost entirely to his agreeable companion. He was familiar with her favorite cities and galleries of art in Europe, and their conversation during the entire dinner was almost exclusively devoted to their respective tastes and experiences in life. When the grand gastronomic ceremonial was finally concluded, and the guests commenced to leave the table for the exciting scenes soon to be witnessed outside in the great park, Henry Livingston said to his companion,

"Miss Grayson, do you expect to be a participant in the races this afternoon? I understand several ladies are to ride, and have brought their riding habits with them.'

"Yes, indeed!" she replied, with animation; "riding is one of my passions. My friend, Miss Peyton, is to ride, and Miss Van Vorst, and Miss Graves, and I know not what others."

He remarked again, as they arose from the table and sauntered out upon the front piazza,

"You all will have a formidable rival this afternoon. My cousin, Miss Livingston, is one of the most superb horsewomen I have ever met. I do not say this in banter, or to arouse your jealousy, but because I know her to be absolutely superb in the management of a horse. Indeed," he added, in a low tone, "that accomplishment is expected to go a long way in fascinating the heart of the heir of this manor when he returns from his strange wanderings. For it is whispered that she is a favorite with this family, and they hope to see her united some day with Henry Lansing. He is a daring rider, and I heard him, myself, say that he would never marry a woman who couldn't accompany him on horseback. He is a fine fellow. I suppose you know him, Miss Grayson?"

"Yes," she said, calmly, "slightly." Then her eyes wandered slowly over the figure of Miss Livingston, who was standing near her on the piazza among the guests who had crowded out to gaze upon the picturesque scene in the park. This inspection satisfied Blonde that the young heiress was beautiful, and as beautifully formed as her aristocratic birth and her high aspirations demanded. Miss Livingston was not quite the height of herself, but grace and elegance appeared in her every movement. Her eyes were large and almond-shaped, radiant with passing emotions, filled with thoughtful shadows, or brilliant with excitement. Her face was a perfect oval, and her complexion dark; her lips full, red, and voluptuous, her nose Grecian, her neck and throat faultless. Her hand, which rested on one of the columns of the piazza, was small, plump, and dimpled. Her dark dress fitted her plump figure exquisitely, and was bordered and trimmed with straw on the lower edge of the skirt, and up the front of her dress to the neck, and the same woven straw trimmings were on her arms and her breast. At the high neck of her dress a bunch of golden wheat was secured by a simple pin of gold, and a bunch of golden wheat was fastened near the part of her glossy black hair. She was an attractive picture, and the fair, golden-haired girl who was studying her, admitted it, in a low whisper, to Henry Livingston.

The group of guests remained for several minutes on the front piazza of the mansion watching the foot races and various games with which the tenantry were amusing themselves, or listening to the sharp crack of the rifles across the park, where forty or fifty gentlemen and farmers were firing at a target for the prize, a silver mounted rifle. At length several of the young ladies withdrew to Mrs. Lansing's bed-room to don their riding habits for the race. The intelligence was rapidly passed from mouth to mouth around the park, and the guests of every rank and age were hurrying across the fields to secure advantageous positions to witness the novel scene. The manor park was almost a perfect circle enclosed by the oak and chestnut forest, and by the pines which bordered the public highway. A carriage road had been carefully laid out around this circular park, and its course followed the outline of the encircling forest trees. It was nearly three miles' ride around this magnificent park by this carriage road which had been cleared and smoothed for the race. The starting point was at the myrtle dell, in full view of the manor house colonnade, and at that point a richly chased golden cup was suspended from one of the pine boughs by a slight thread, so that the foremost rider, in passing, could easily detach it and secure the prize as she came in ahead.

The sun was still high in the west as the beautiful steeds of the manor were brought around to the front of the mansion to await the pleasure of the fair girls who were to compete for the golden cup. Ten blooded horses with glistening coats of black, or white, or chestnut color, were led up to the front piazza, and stood pawing the graveled road in conscious grace and beauty, impatient for the coming of their gentle riders. Norman Prince, the graceful negro boy, had secured a favorite chestnut-colored gelding from the manor stables, whose speed and gentleness he was well acquainted with, for his new mistress, Blonde Grayson, to ride. He was determined to give the fair girl the chance which he deemed best to secure the prize. The groom who had succeeded him in the care of the manor stables held for Miss Livingston a powerful black steed which had been fortunate enough, on a former fete day, to win the prize for his rider. The groom also felt confident that his fleet steed would win the race for the dark-haired girl who was understood to cherish reasonable expectations of some day securing the hand of the heir. Clara Peyton was to ride Gurty Lansing's snow white racer, and Miss Van Vorst had selected Mr. Lansing's iron gray; Miss Graves had chosen a bay mare which Henry Livingston pronounced to be the fleetest on the manor. The remaining five young ladies had selected steeds which also bore high reputations in the sporting history of the Lansing estate.

The excitement was great, indeed, as the ten young ladies, in their riding habits, finally made their appearance at the front of the mansion and successively mounted to their saddles and cantered away towards the starting point under the golden cup at the myrtle dell. No more imposing cavalcade of graceful ladies had ever entered the manor races before. By the established rules and regulations of the race, the ten were not confined to the beaten road for the first twenty rods after starting; after that distance was attained they must rein their horses into the road, and keep in it till they came around to the golden cup. The first two miles of the circle the riders must rein their steeds to a gallop. The last mile must witness an exciting, wild, tearing *run* in for the prize.

CHAPTER XVI

At the appointed signal from Gurty Lansing's white hand kerchief, the ten graceful competitors swept off abreast to wards the great chestnut tree which marked the first twenty rods of the course. So beautiful and exciting was the pageant, dashing away with their long dark and white feathers in the full blaze of the Western sun, that a great shout went up from the spectators on the park. Each eager rider endeavored to reach the great chestnut tree first, for after that point was attained only four could ride abreast from the narrowness of the road. Miss Livingston's powerful black steed first reached the chestnut at least a rod ahead. As she passed Blonde Grayson's chestnut-colored gelding, she bowed and waved her riding-whip. Blonde detected a certain hauteur in her bow and manner as she dashed by, and she thought to herself, "That proud girl feels confident of her power to outstrip me in this race ; but we shall see."

Blonde applied her whip vigorously to her steed, and the fiery gelding dashed ahead with augmented speed. Before her horse had traversed sixty rods she was beside Miss Livingston again with her beautiful face flushed with excitement. Clara Peyton and Miss Van Vorst were close behind her. When the rider of the black steed realized that Blonde had overtaken her, she looked surprised, and whipped her horse right smartly. Blonde did the same—and away they flew in a tearing gallop till the October wind whistled shrilly past them and renewed cheers and cries from the distant spectators sounded over the park. On, on, past the conservatory and the gardens, on past the teeming orchards and trout ponds of the manor, they sped. Their horses' hoofs sounded hollow and quick over the little bridge which spanned the manor brook, then were muffled again in the soft earth of the track. On in eager and passionate rivalry they dashed towards the shade of the encircling forest, whose leaves flashed golden and scarlet in the sunlight. The long branches nodded and bowed to the beaming-eyed riders. The leaves rattled and fluttered above their mad course, and the wind of their flight tossed up and trailed out their cap feathers. But still the two leaders and rivals flew on unflagging, unyielding and equal. For the last mile the black steed and the chestnut gelding had galloped side by side with no perceptible advantage gained by either. Miss Livingston had encountered, for the first time in her life, her equal. Blonde, stung by the supreme and graceful contempt of her rival's passing bow, bent all her energies and skill to the guidance of her chestnut gelding. The dark-haired beauty bounded on, still confident of her superiority in her equestrian powers and her ability to keep up this violent pace till her fair rival should fall behind before the point was gained, where the running of the horses was to commence. Vain, unfounded hope!

The signal flag of white, which was to terminate the exciting gallop, fluttered ahead at last, and neither of the two had secured the least advantage. Nearer and still nearer fluttered the boundary flag; faster and faster bounded the eager steeds, and brighter and wilder flashed the eyes of their flushed riders. Ah! here it comes at last; quick blows, sharp words, one skillful, convulsive effort, and away they flash into a wild, reckless, mad, tearing *run*.

The spectators left their knolls and their tree tops, and hurried in towards the closing race, to see the golden cup snatched from its pendent thread. Fearlessly, eagerly, triumphantly, streamed, through the whistling wind, the plumes of the riders. Nearer, clearer, and glistening in the sunset, swung the golden prize cup. See! an advantage! The fair rider, with disordered golden hair, uttered one talismanic word, and the chestnut gelding passed the black steed in an instant, and dashed in ahead. Blonde raised her trembling hand, and struck the golden cup. It glittered forward, fell upon the chestnut gelding's neck; then rattled to the ground.

On past the fallen prize cup, and the myrtle dell, she flew, in efforts to rein in her steed. At last she stopped him in the road. Hark! A scream of terror! piercing and thrilling arose behind her. Then a shout from the men: "Look out, Miss Grayson, look out!" The cry chilled her blood. She reined her horse around towards the prize cup, and her danger was revealed. Her dark haired rival was flung bleeding to the earth, and the steed she had ridden was bearing down upon Blonde in frantic company with the incarnate black demon who had occasioned all the mischief.

Black Hawk, solitary and untrammeled on his hill top, had

witnessed the whole affair. Jealous and neglected, excited and uninvited, his wild blood had induced him to participate without an invitation. He stood on the hill top, tossing his black mane in the air, and with his wild eyes starting from their sockets, as the two foremost riders neared the white flag. But when they broke into a run, it was too much for his equanimity. He felt confident of his ability to beat both of them. Down the hill side he bounded, with an occasional spasmodic kick into the air, at any stray spirits who might be following him in remonstrance, until he reached the race course. Then he flung himself frantically forward in pursuit, and overtook Miss Livingston at the moment Blonde was reaching out her hand for the golden cup. One well aimed kick at the young heiress in passing, hurled her to the earth, and released her horse, which immediately, in startled terror, joined the black devil in still another raid upon Blonde Grayson ahead.

There was not an instant to lose. With consummate skill and quickness, the golden haired girl reined her horse's head from the road, and applied the whip. The gelding dashed out of the road, and the two wild brutes flew by on the instant, at a distance of only a few feet. As they passed, however, Black Hawk delivered himself of one of his wild screams, and that with his frantic bounds, and his heels flying up in the air, were sufficient to persuade the gelding to join the runaways. In spite of Blonde's strenuous efforts and struggles, her horse broke away from her control, and followed Black Hawk. Cries, shouts and lamentations broke from the crowd, but Blonde was soon out of hearing, clinging to her mad horse, as he went bounding and plunging over the meadows in pursuit of his black tempter. Down through the meadows, down through the gullies he leaped, and struggled, and floundered, and rose and dashed on again more madly, striking fire from the stones with his heels, and threatening every instant to unseat his rider. Black Hawk madly leaped the meadow brook, and dashed up towards the manor house, where a group of guests and children were gaping in horror. The gelding followed. Still more excited by the frightened cries of the guests, Black Hawk crashed through the low boughs of the cone-shaped evergreens about the house, and Blonde was compelled to follow. The stiff branches nearly swept her from her horse. But she clung desperately and successfully to her saddle. They cleared the evergreens, and launched forth again into the broad fields.

But no! the mad demon who led, remembered an old feat of

the absent heir of the manor. He made for a four barred garden fence, and leaped it in an instant. The chestnut gelding leaped it too, with the terrified Blonde clinging to his back. Unharmed she flew on, whispering with white lips, prayers to her God, using at the same time, those tenacious qualities and that firm grasp on the reins, which had become her second nature on horseback.

Away they flew in a mad circle around the garden shrubbery, which bent and crashed under their feet, and then out through an open gate into the park again. One terrific sweep around the old vine clad manor house ; and then Black Hawk mounted to the top of the hill from which he had started and suddenly stopped, panting and trembling. The gelding with the unyielding, clinging girl, paused also. Blonde quickly released her foot, and leaped to the ground, firmly holding on to her reins. She was afraid another heat was in contemplation. But no! the infuriated Black Hawk was satisfied. He stood panting and weary, contemplating Blonde's triumphant countenance with an expression which seemed to say—

"Girl, you are ahead of my time. I believe you will do to ride with my master when he comes back."

Blonde stood for a few moments, holding her exhausted and trembling horse by the bridle, and watching Black Hawk narrowly, in anticipation of some new deviltry. But the black, glittering brute, appeared content with the mischief he had done, and after a while, trotted slowly away. Then she turned her eyes towards the manor house, and discovered the gentlemen and servants streaming over the fields towards her. Henry Livingston and Norman Prince, were far in advance, having followed her from the terrific moment she had crashed through the evergreens about the mansion, and expecting every moment to see her flung, crushed and lifeless, on the earth. What was their surprise and joy to see her leap to the ground, and in a few seconds wave her white handkerchief to the people collected about the myrtle dell, and to the eight ladies who had fortunately been left behind, in the race, and had reined in their horses, when Black Hawk descended to the road ahead of them. Before Henry Livingston and the negro boy could come up, Clara Peyton and her companions, rode up to the pale but undaunted girl, and relieved her hand of the gelding's bridle.

Clara's eyes were beaming with joy as she spoke : "Oh! I am *so* happy, Blonde ; you are magnificent. I gave you up twice ; once, when your horse stumbled on the pile of stones ;

and then when you went over the evergreens. But poor Miss Livingston, her shoulder is dislocated, and her right arm shattered at the elbow. Doctor Cramer, fortunately, had arrived a few minutes before it happened, and he says she will recover. There! they are carrying her towards the house now. But can I do anything for you?—you are very pale, though your eye flashes like a star. Here is your gold cup. This day will not soon be forgotten on the manor."

Blonde declined all offers of assistance, and said,

"There comes Mr. Livingston. When he arrives, I shall lean on his arm, and walk with him to the house. Norman Prince, my servant, is coming with him—I am too nervous just now, to ride back to the piazza."

She took the prize cup from her friend's hand, and examined it closely. It was very heavy; four inches in diameter, and a trifle over seven inches deep. It was solid gold, exquisitely chased, with a bent riding whip for a handle, and a horse's head for a spout. It bore the Lansing arms in relief. The sun was just disappearing in the west, and its slanting beams flashed upon the cup in the fair girl's hands.

Miss Van Vorst reined her iron gray steed around to Blonde's side, and said, pleasantly,

"We all envy you, Miss Grayson, but it was fairly won. Perchance you may not know that the design of that cup was drawn by Mr. Henry Lansing's hand. It was, however, for I was visiting here, and saw him sketch the plan. He laughed when he was drawing the design, quietly to himself, and I asked him what he was amused about. Finally, he answered my importunity by saying:

"'I was thinking of a beautiful girl, and wondering if she was horsewoman enough to win such a prize. I do not even know if she rides at all. But I would take great pride in seeing her win this cup.'

"He was so mysterious about it, that I could get nothing further from him, only that she was very lovely, or very beautiful, or something of that kind."

Blonde was intensely absorbed, at that moment, in studying the details of the golden cup; but she asked, slowly, with her mysterious eyes fixed upon the glittering prize,

"When was the design of this cup made? At the last birth day races in October?"

"No, this last spring, when I visited here," replied the rider of the iron gray. "He was forever sketching something, and he draws right well; but Gurty, oh! that boy is a real genius. He has just completed a small oil painting which I saw for a minute to-day. It is very spirited, indeed. A handsome brigand with a black slouched hat, and mounted on a black horse, is escaping up a mountain, just ahead of two pursuers; a terrific storm is coming on, and a slight figure is crouching under a ledge of rocks, peering out after them. It is very fine, indeed; he will be a master, I'm sure, some day."

No response was made to these remarks. The allusion was unfortunate. Inasmuch as some of the young ladies present were relatives of the Lansing family, those who surmised the real import of Gurty's picture prudently remained silent. But Blonde was absorbed in the study of the cup. She turned it over and over again, and remarked upon the taste and elegance displayed in its construction. Mingled with her gratification at the result of the race was a secret desire that the heir of the manor should also know of her success. It was evident enough that whatever might be the general opinion of the townspeople regarding Henry Lansing's character, this group of female equestrians held him in high estimation. His tastes and his prominence in festive scenes like the present, were constantly remarked upon by the group of riders surrounding the successful holder of the cup. It would have puzzled any keen observer of the human face, to conjecture the emotions in the breast of that fair and successful rider, who stood in the centre of that graceful group in silent study of the golden cup. Her golden hair in captivating disorder fell away from her velvet riding cap with its dark plume. Her slight figure was enclosed tightly in her dark riding habit, whose skirt fell carelessly away upon the green earth. Her left hand grasped her ivory-headed whip, while her right held up the prize cup. The discriminating hand which had planned that cup had been offered to her for life. Her refusal had made a lonely family and an incomplete festival. Might she not have accepted that ardent offer, even though it had been a surprise offer, and become the mistress of this beautiful estate, which in the sunset of October gleamed away before her with the misty, softened beauty of a dream? Was not that high and spontaneous affection which she expected some day to rise up in her heart towards a congenial being, only pure sentiment, and utterly devoid of that practical character which is suited to meet the vicissitudes of life? Might she not have accepted this young man, gifted, wealthy, and attractive as he was, and learned to love and cherish him by the familiarity of daily intercourse, and thus have saved him all the troubles and the desolation which had fallen upon his reputation and his heart? These reflections traversed her brain as she stood in the midst of that gay circle, with the long-coveted prize cup now her own. But then a still, small voice of caution whispered to her, "You were right—fling not away your life happiness for a brilliant offer or a great estate—test and prove the sincerity and the stability of an offered heart before you take the step from which there is no further escape but the grave, if you are once deceived." And this still, small voice of caution now, as it had ever before done, swayed the sceptre over her impulses, and she involuntarily sighed in uncertainty of heart and of purpose.

At length Mr. Livingston, in company with the negro servant, made his appearance on the scene with his hearty congratula ions at her escape Blonde requested the support of his arm in her walk towards the mansion—and as the two walked slowly and leisurely away, Norman Prince mounted to the gelding's back, and in company with the female equestrians dashed off towards the same destination.

The young widower on whose arm Blonde was leaning, said as they walked—

"I never dreamed of your ability to ride with my cousin, when I mentioned her accomplishment to you on the piazza. She is reputed the best rider on the banks of the Hudson, and when I saw you keep up with her, and then come in ahead, I was astonished indeed. I saw her fall, but my interest was too absorbed in your mad flight to allow me to run to her assistance. I hoped to be able to seize your bridle at one time, but a higher power than mine was interested in your life. Do you see them yonder carrying her into the house? Poor girl, if she survives her injuries it will be only to die of mortification at losing the cup. But you have accomplished a greater triumph than winning the race. Your self-possession and the magnificent manner in which you retained your seat in your dreadful runaway, will make you a higher reputation on this manor and in this neighborhood than fifty races. Even in the midst of all the apprehension every one felt on your account, I could hear such exclamations as 'Superb!'—'wonderful!'—'God save that wonderful horsewoman from death!' Ah! do you hear that?"

The two were approaching the crowd which was hurrying over the fields to meet Blonde, when a wild, thrilling shout went up from a hundred voices in an applauding cheer at her wonderful riding and her escape. The eye of Henry Livingston lighted at the inspiring sound, and he turned to speak to his graceful companion—but she withdrew her arm from his, and hastening forward, threw herself into the arms of one of the foremost of the advancing crowd. It was her father. The old man was too overcome to speak. He clasped her in his arms and cried for joy. Then he led her away towards the manor house, the crowd of gentlemen and tenants following in a confused procession, cheering and uttering warm words of congratulation until they arrived at the great colonnade.

Blonde received the congratulations of the ladies, on the piazza, who came forward to greet her, and immediately inquired for the room where Miss Livingston had been taken. She was directed to a door opening into the great hall; and gathering her riding habit up from the floor, she passed rapidly across the hall and pushed open the door. She found the unfortunate Miss Livingston stretched on a bed, attended by Dr. Cramer and Mrs. Lansing, and a score of ladies anxious to render assistance to the poor sufferer. The physician had succeeded in replacing the injured shoulder and the broken bones of her arm, and was now giving directions to the pale mistress of the manor, who sat upon the bed applying soothing restoratives to the forehead and neck of the beautiful, raven-haired heiress. As the successful winner of the cup approached the bedside, Miss Livingston saw her, and whispered softly for her to come to the bed where she might speak more conveniently to her. Blonde kneeled down beside her, and the poor helpless girl said, while the tears gathered to her eyes,

"I was proud, and God has humbled me for my own good. But the sympathy in your eyes, Miss Grayson, is more than sufficient to compensate me for the pain of my defeat—if you had commenced to go through the customary words of pity and distress at my condition, I should have hated you. But you stand so gently aside, and your eyes are so gentle and sorrowful without one word, that I love you—indeed I do. Kiss me."

Blonde leaned forward and pressed her soft warm lips to the pale lips of her rival, and then bowed her golden hair upon her pillow and sobbed bitterly. Then she raised her gentle face again, and said,

"There is no power on earth that can or shall prevent me from presenting this cup which I hold in my hand to you. We came out so nearly even, that nothing has been really decided. Promise me that you will accept the prize from my hand, not as a prize, but to confirm those words you have just uttered—'I love you—indeed I do.'"

The poor, pale lips of the sufferer murmured in reply, as her dark eyes looked into Blonde's face in gratitude,

"I will accept your gift, and inscribe upon it these words—*Won by excellence, given away by generosity.*"

From that hour Blonde Grayson never left that sick room until the dark-eyed heiress was entirely restored to health.—She hung over her pillow during the long weary nights after fever set in, and when the patient's life seemed balanced on a thread. She soothed and caressed and watched her for weary days and weeks, gentle and noiseless in the sick room as an angel nurse, And when at length the fever wore away, and health and bloom returned to the cheek of the high-born and aristocratic beauty, the golden-haired girl traveled away with her to the distant Hudson, and for many weeks tarried with her in her noble home, cultivating into higher beauty that germ of love and sympathy and nobleness which had come to life amid the rivalry and excitement and disasters of the memorable race upon the Lansing manor.

CHAPTER XVII.

THE sad, moaning wind seemed never weary. Its wailing notes were ever sounding in the tops of the leafless chestnut trees, or dying away in sighs across the chilled and dying grass of the manor. Leafless and cold stood the tall shrubbery of the gardens, and the slender stems of the dead and fallen flowers shivered and trembled in the cold breath of the passing and fitful wind. The yellow leaves of the chestnuts and maples had been stripped from the branches, and now were driven before the November blast, hurrying and rattling over the hard frozen ground. The sky was overcast with pale, gloomy clouds, betokening the speedy coming of the first snow storm of the rapidly declining year. And yet the expected snow lingered, and the wind wailed on unceasingly its chill notes of woe.

Far away over the lonely meadows wandered a solitary and deserted steed. It was the graceful Black Hawk of the lost heir of the manor. The cold, sweeping wind flung aside his magnificent black mane and long, glistening tail, as he moved slowly along with the dignity of a deserted emperor.

There was an indescribable aspect of loneliness over this superb and wide-reaching manor, under the frown of the pale snow clouds, and breathed over by the chill moaning wind. No human figure moved upon the scene. The great piazza of the mansion, with its tall, solemn pillars of white, wreathed with bare and leafless vines, was utterly deserted. No face looked from the windows, and the only sound from the great house was the occasional low, grating noise of the window shutters on their iron hinges, as they moved slowly back and forth in the rising or receding force of the cold, shifting wind. The evergreens about the house were dark and gloomy in the frown of the approaching storm, and their wide-extended branches swayed mournfully in the chill breeze, and whispered and sighed. Away in the distance was faintly traced against the gloomy sky the outline of the naked, leafless forest. The old manor house had flung aside its golden and scarlet mantle, and now stood revealed through its net-work of vines, each odd and old-fashioned door and window meeting the eye, and revealing more plainly its utter desolation and abandonment.—The manor brook which rippled beside it, bore upon its chill bosom the red and yellow leaves swept from the trees by the frost and the wind long weeks before, and which were scattered and tossed by the gale, till now they floated calmly along down their river of death, far, far away from the bounds of the lonely manor.

And still the lonely wind moaned over the meadows, and the gray branches of the chestnuts shook, and the dying grass sighed. Alas! Nature mourned for the pure and the lovely one who was passing away, for ever.

In a dim and silent chamber of that silent manor house, the pale, suffering, holy mother was dying. The dark angel stood beside her with his last awful summons. Struggle, oh! chestnut branches in your convulsive grief—sigh, oh! grass of the fields, bowed down and desolate, and whisper in grief, oh! encircling evergreens—for the eye which reveled in your beauty, and in your wonderful formation found the hand and the power of her God, is fast closing upon you forever.

The gray-haired sire stood by, and the widowed daughter bowed her head in grief, and the boy Gurty clasped his dying mother's hand. That true-hearted clergyman of her church who had never deserted her or her son Henry, and who had never bowed to the storm of reproach which swept so fiercely over the Lansing family, stood by her now to see her die. And many of the high-born and aristocratic people of her honored race, who knew her virtues and the elevated tone she always gave to family and rank, gathered about her in that passing hour. Ah! that pale, emaciated, wasted wreck of beauty, had never forgotten God's dearest friends, the suffering and the poor. He could not forget her now. Lowly, sweetly she spoke of her hope confirmed, and her love of God intensified in her last dying hours.

"God is holy. I am weak and sinful; but I love Him, and for that love I trust and believe He will receive me, through the merits of the all-sufficient Mediator. Oh! my boy, my precious Gurty, all the beauties and the splendor of this world are nothing, unless you strive in life to please God. Oh! tell my wandering noble Henry when he comes back, that his mother loved him and defended him, and when she died left him in the hands of her God, and her Father, and her Friend."

Her spirit seemed to linger for a service yet unfinished. As the sad moments glided past, she whispered, "The lonely and the deserted are all God's children. He loves them all. Let no one dare revile or persecute or shun the lonely of any grade or any rank. Hark! I hear a footstep."

A heavy tramp was in the hall of the manor house; slowly, firmly, evenly it sounded till it reached her door—then paused. Mr. Lansing turned to answer the low, cautious knock upon the panel. He returned with a venerable figure of an old man leaning on his arm. The stately, solemn figure held in one hand a low-crowned hat, which he had removed from his abundant and shaggy locks. The other hand held a small steel hammer. It was old Hugo. He had come to see her die. Gently she whispered him to her bedside, and pointed upward with her dying finger: "I go to Him, my friend; and in the sunlight of His presence I will pray for you."

The lion eyes of the old outcast followed the direction of her finger, for the impress and the majesty of truth were on her dying lips. He thought to see the divine presence which seemed revealed to her. But as he looked, the spirit of the pale, gentle lady passed away forever. He looked at her again; but she was gone. His venerable head dropped upon his breast, and he murmured, "I believe in her God, now and for evermore."

But listen to that low, sweet strain of solemn music! Can the harmony of the better land be heard this side of death?

Can mortal ears drink in the sound of heavenly harps, and mortal aspirations breathe forth in the divine notes of the immortal land?

A low, sweet voice was singing, and with it moved in strange, wild harmony, an accompanying sound, which rose and fell upon the rushing blast with tremulous solemnity, and then suddenly ceased. Then trembled upon the ears of all the despairing wail of a child. Gurty Lansing removed his hand from the hand of his dead mother, and walked away to the window; and there he saw a little, crouching figure seated on the ground, with only a bass-viol and a little twisted, helpless leg.

The child had been playing the holy woman's dirge. She was his all, save God.

* * * * * * *

The solemn clang of the distant bell in the church tower sounded dismally over the snow-covered meadows of the Lansing manor, and then all was still again. After a long interval the heavy, solemn stroke was heard again, and then the sound vibrated itself away upon the air into silence once more. At the first stroke of the funeral bell the procession commenced to move away from the manor house in attendance upon the dead. Slowly and mournfully sounded the distant bell; slowly and mournfully moved the long line of carriages, through the thin coating of snow, away over the meadows towards the myrtle dell. Alas! the lovely and loving mother was leaving the beautiful and noble estate behind her, and she would never return again. Never more would her blue eyes beam in kindness; never more would the warm kiss come from her lips. Poor, lonely boy, the world looked dark to thee when she was gone. She was thine all when Henry fled. Dost thou not remember thy reverie upon the mountain side, and the words whispered in thine ear: "But these may pass away in death, and thou be left alone. Start, then, with God."

With the painful pressure on thy heart, and with that choking faintness in thy throat, look out upon the slowly passing scene, and learn how best to die. Thou wilt be rich and powerful some day; learn now, following in thy loved mother's funeral train, how the rich may live in fortune's smiles, and yet at last lie down to die: in the protecting arms of God and his angels, for all eternity.

The funeral train of slowly moving carriages, reached, at length, the gate leading from the myrtle dell, into the public highway. Ah! what means this new gathering outside the manor gate, to offer honor to the holy dead. These are uninvited guests. No lofty and luxurious parlors ever echoed to their tread; no gilded carriages ever bore their shivering forms. They rarely congregate in the presence of refinement, or pass in review before the marshal of great funeral trains. They are only God's suffering poor. But lonely and forsaken as they are, no human power can keep them from Mrs. Lansing's funeral train, as it moves out upon the highway, to the solemn music of the funeral bell. Little wan faces of shivering boys, little hollow blue eyes of half naked girls, have gathered beside the manor gate to see the great lady pass to her grave. Ah! they remember the bread she put in their trembling and half frozen hands. They remember the little warm shawl she placed about their shivering shoulders. They remember those dreadful nights when she came to their suffering mothers who were crying in pain. They remember when she left the door again, their mothers were hushed and smiling And they have gathered now to honor the pale, gentle lady, who, in life, was not ashamed to honor them. They follow at a distance, the slowly moving procession, and they are whispering to each other, as they trudge with their little feet through the snow, "She has gone way up there, where she told us the good will all go.'

Yes! little, thoughtful, suffering faces, she has gone farther beyond the clouds than your little eyes can see. And she has won her crown there because she loved poor little tottering, helpless things like you. You were her Master's little ones, and for His sake, she loved you, and won eternal life.

She might have stored her mind with abstruse knowledge, and become a celebrated dogmatist to startle and denounce. She might have made predestination still more awful, and human depravity still more discouraging to her listeners; and then at last have died wrapped in the shroud of dogma, and enfolded in the pride of stern sectarian hate. But no! her God was love, and in her love for Him, the crucified, she learned to love, and to love all.

Hurry on behind her funeral train, little ones; hurry on, aged and tottering poor, for above you in the unseen Heaven, a great angel, with a golden pen is writing, and looking upon you as you pass. The angel is counting you one by one, and your names are being entered in a great book to the credit of her sweet holy name. And beside him as he writes, another spirit, her guardian angel, is standing and watching the entry in the great Book of Life. And as he watches, a radiant smile of joy is on his dazzling face.

CHAPTER XVIII.

The glimpse which Clara Peyton had been granted, into the private journal of Henry Lansing, under the maples of old Rosy's garden, had excited her curiosity to know more of its contents. After she had finished the reading of the article on the language of the locust tree, she had hastily turned over the pages of this private daily record, and many strange headings had met her eye; some suggestive of serious thought, and others evidently pointing to comical and ridiculous phases of the writer's experience in the town of C——. She had importuned old Rosy to allow her to take the journal home with her, and read it at her leisure; but the old woman had obstinately refused, stating at the same time, her apprehension that she had already allowed her young friend's secrets to be exposed too freely, without a consultation being first held with the writer.

But as the months rolled away, and no sign of the heir's return appeared, and as the bonds of friendship steadily grew firmer between herself and the two young ladies, old Rosy relented and yielded the journal, at last, to Clara Peyton's importunities. She, however, bound the young lady to utter secrecy regarding the contents of the private record, saying—

"You must promise, Miss Pey on, not only for yourself, but also for your friend, Miss Grayson, that my young gentleman's secrets shall never go farther than you two. He instructed me to let the book fall into no illiberal hands, and I don't intend to do it. But I'm sure you two sweet things are not illiberal—and he couldn't object to you by any manner of means."

"All right; all right;" replied Clara. "I promise for myself and Blonde, both—there—give me the book. I'll never breathe a word—depend on *us*."

Joyfully she seized the book, and hiding it under her cloak hurried away over the snow fields towards the town. Darkness was rapidly falling upon the earth, but she hastened along the streets of the town, till she reached the Grayson mansion. With her fair cheeks flushed into rosy hues by the winter air, and her violent exercise, and her violet eyes flashing under her fur bordered bonnet, she bounded along the main hall, and pushed open her friend's door. Blonde was sewing industriously by the lamp light at her black marble table, and Clara gave her one kiss with her cold, cherry red lips, and said, flinging the book upon the table—

"There is a prize I have drawn for you and me—we will go halves. I've overcome old Rosy's scruples at last, and there is Henry Lansing's journal. See the name on the cover? 'A Sinner's Journal,' and a big sinner I reckon he was, too, for such a gentleman and scholar as he is. Poor fellow! I wonder what has become of his handsome face. Do you know," she continued, drawing a chair up to Blonde's cheerful coal fire in the grate, and holding up her little feet, alternately, to warm them at the glowing mass of coals, "that I heard to-day of one of Henry Lansing's capers, that I couldn't keep from laughing at, although it was so wicked and thoughtless. 'You know what great Democrats the Lansings are? Well! I heard that at the last election when he cast his first vote for governor — Oh! I forgot, Blonde, that your father's a Whig—but you won't mind if I do laugh, will you?—we girls care little about their politics, any way. Well, the Whigs were going to have a grand procession to outdo the great procession the Democrats hadthe day before. They sent for a fine band of music forty miles off, and they had a new band wagon all decorated with flowers, and gilt eagles, and a velvet cloth hanging over the sides to hide the wagon wheels. They had a goddess of liberty all dressed up, in front, with a crown of roses, and the reins appeared to be held in her hand. This wagon was drawn by sixteen gray horses, and was expected to be the greatest sensation in the way of a political demonstration, that was ever seen in this town. Well, now, what do you think my fine young gentleman did, but make up his mind to spoil this band wagon, and the great Whig sensation in the procession. He told a crowd of boys and Irishmen, who worked for his father, to go ahead of the procession and wait for his signal, and then to yell hideously and distractedly. The procession started off in grand style. The trumpets and the trombones tooted forth in triumph, and the drums beat, and the goddess of liberty held the reins. The people shouted and rejoiced, and the Democrats looked crest-fallen and fairly beaten, when suddenly down the road came Henry Lansing mounted on Black Hawk and flying like the wind. He dashed alongside the band wagon and the sixteen gray horses, and when he was most at the heads of the leaders, he shouted something to Black Hawk. Then his horse, at the sound, gave a scream or a yell, and commenced kicking the gray horses right and left, and then bounded on madly ahead. It so frightened the leaders that they ran away, and the whole fourteen other horses ran with them. The reins were so entangled in the figure of the goddess of liberty, that the real driver couldn't stop the runaways. Down the road they tore till the band wagon with all the musicians, was tumbled over into a ditch. Away went the goddess of liberty head first into a fence. And the big drum had a hole knocked in it as big as your head. The boys kept shouting at the horses, till they all broke loose from the band wagon, and scattered in terror all over the country. No one was badly hurt, but the Whigs were furious about it, and father thinks some of this spite against Henry Lansing concerning the murder, may be traced to this wild caper. But you know father is a great party man; and no doubt that feeling gives him that idea about the murder."

Blonde laughed at all this, and said, "I know it is wicked to laugh at such things, but I believe I should have laughed even if I had seen my own father in the wagon—but take off your things, and come and read to me out of this journal. I didn't dream Rosy would let us have it again. I shall be entirely alone this evening, so I will have tea brought into this room, and we will have a cozy time all by ourselves."

Blonde rang the bell, and after giving directions to the servant who answered it, regarding bringing up tea to her boudoir, returned to her sewing at the black marble table. Clara soon removed her winter outside garments, and appeared at the table with her exquisitely plump figure tightly cased in a dark brown merino with white linen collar and cuffs. Blonde glanced up from her sewing and said, "That is the most becoming dress I ever saw you wear. Have you light enough to read there?"

"Oh, yes; plenty," said Clara, seating herself and taking up the journal. "Blonde, who fitted your merino? Miss Pitney? I tried to find that shade of blue at Merriam's, but they never have anything there."

"Yes, Clara; but go on. I confess I am curious to hear the contents of that journal. I'm afraid, however, it's a species of robbery to take those secret thoughts without his consent. Well! old Rosy is responsible, for he made her his executor. Go on."

"A SINNER'S JOURNAL.

"*December* 10*th.—The Sewing Society.*—Last night I met Lizzie Doten at Mrs. Cramer's. She invited me to accompany her to the sewing society in aid of the Presbyterian organ Lizzie has an imperial way with her, and I dared not refuse. She has the most fascinating pair of eyes in this town, save one, and that one is Clara Peyton."

"Don't laugh, Clara," said Blonde. "If you begin to laugh this early in the book, we shall never get through."

"So up the steps of Mrs. Farnum's two-story whited sepulchre, which stands with its gable-end to the street, marched captive I, chained to Lizzie Doten's fair arm (the fair is a poetic word—but its appropriateness in this connection I cannot vouch for, as the arm had a long sleeve over it—still, I believe Lizzie's arm to be fair). I *know* that Lucy Filmer's arm cannot be fair, for the girls say she never—she never—— Well, let it pass. Girls do slander one another so.

"As we entered the hall I whispered to Lizzie, 'Tell me what kind of an expression I must put on in this place, for I never attended one of these affairs before. Shall I look eminently pious and meek, or only semi-religious, or may I assume the expression of the wicked world, that is to say, a frivolous, human sort of expression?'

"Lizzie laughed with her pretty eyes, and whispered back, 'Hush, you sinner; don't you see Mrs. Farnum sewing in that door behind you? She has ears that hear a mile. You wait till I come down from the ladies' chamber, and then go in and sit with me. There are no religious services here, and you may laugh to your heart's content. They are very boisterous here sometimes, and laugh and carry on like the mischief. You must know there are two rival parties in these sewing societies. Your sister, Mrs. Bounce, leads one clique, and Mrs. Fierygrim the other—and it's all about the organ, who shall play it, and what color it shall be painted and all that sort of thing. You will be, like the other gentlemen who come, solicited for some small contribution to pay for this organ, for which the ladies are sewing and getting up a fair. Give much, little or none, just as you please—some gentlemen give nothing. Now I have given you an inkling of the affair—wait here till I come down stairs.'

"Lizzie hurried up to the ladies' room, and I hung my hat in the hall, and looked around me. I could see that the door at the end of the hall was open, and there was a room full of feminines of all ages, sizes and conditions, sewing, chatting and laughing. Some of the old women I recognized as the solemn and religious faces I have seen in church and on the streets, always looking as if they were near their latter end. But now, strange to say, these same faces wore an interested expression, and in some of them the corners of the mouth had actually curved upward, and reminded me of a cheerful crescent moon arising upon the lowering and gloomy face of nature. I recognized in the short figure, standing by a tall basket of work, Mrs. Fierygrim. Oh! yes! I know *her* and she knows *me* of old. She wears spiteful looking short curls, and practices the most rigid economy in marketing, to keep her figure down and her dry goods bill down, too. Lizzie Doten visited a young lady at her house one evening, and accidentally upset and demolished a lamp; and she made Lizzie pay for it. Lizzie was furious, not at paying for the lamp, but at the way she commented on the accident. Mrs. Fierygrim is all eyes, ears and tongue. What she doesn't know of affairs in C——, there is no use in knowing. The Lord has endowed her with a tongue like a two edged sword, with which she slashes the neighborhood right and left, for the honor of His name.

"Just beyond this lady, I recognized an elderly gentleman sitting on a low ottoman, and holding a skein of yarn at arms-length, for a pretty young girl who was laughing and winding it into her ball. His face would have delighted Talleyrand, it was so emotionless. No human could ever fathom his thoughts from his countenance. I never knew him to be excited except in one contingency. I often sat beside him in the choir of the church, and heard the preacher overwhelm the audience with grief, and move even to tears. It never occasioned one change of a muscle in his countenance. But when the hymn or psalm was given out to the choir, 'a change came over the spirit of his dream.' He would cram a ball of tobacco into his cheek, and grasp his immense bass-viol with a nervous, excited manner, and his grey eyes would begin to roll. He was steaming up for devotion. He would give a little hitch to one elbow of his coat to clear his coat sleeve from his hand, then a little hitch at the other elbow. Then he would arise quickly from his chair, and stand impatient for the chorister to lead off. When his solemn instrument was fairly under way, he looked the animated picture of elbow devotion; his eyes rolling back and forth with the motion of his fiddle stick. He was utterly absorbed in his instrument worship. It is the only expression

I ever beheld on his calm face. I' have always styled him 'Praise the Lord Catgut.'

"Presently Lizzie came down stairs and took my arm, and conducted me into the midst of this chattering and industrious crowd. Several pairs of bright eyes looked up from their work and recognized me, and appeared to be pleased to see us. But some of the old saints cast guarded looks towards me, as if they discovered the odor of approaching sulphur. I had a history among some of them, and I knew it. But I put on an expression of amiable and affable devil, and sat down among them. I chatted with them about the beauty and the grace of the baby stockings they were knitting for the fair,—and when the old maid came around with the subscription list for the new organ, I gave her five dollars. She was all thanks and smiles, and didn't appear to notice any sulphur perfume in the bank bill I gave her, different from the odor of the other bills which she collected. After all, the filthy lucre, the root of all evil, carries its own recommendation on its face, and is as welcome among saints as among sinners.

"In a few minutes a sensation arose in a small room adjoining the large parlor where I was seated. At first I heard a loud shrill female voice saying in entreaty,

"'Now, Mr. Bombo, please put your name down for *red.*'

"Another female voice equally loud and distinct, remonstrated—

"'No, no, Mr. Bombo, blue is the color—say *blue.*'

"Then a loud hearty laugh of a man ensued, and he said,

"'Give me time—give me time—let me hear both sides.—What do others say about the color?'

"Then I recognized the voice of Mrs. Fierygrim. It was a perfect cat whine.

"'Now, Mr. Bombo, do say *blue*—that will be tasty, and so appropriate, you know.'

"I asked a young lady seated near me, who was listening to the loud, excited voices, what the colors meant. She informed me that the new organ was yet unpainted, and the color was to be determined by the votes of the subscribers.

"The noises and the confusion were approaching nearer.—They were evidently coming into the large parlor. Others were participating in the altercation, and some laughing heartily.

"'Don't let Mr. Bombo go—stop him—*make* him say—say blue, Mr. Bombo—no, red, Mr. Bombo. There's a good Mr

Bombo, say blue—red—blue—Bombo. Ha! ha! grab him—make him say red.'

"The crowd in the parlor arose to their feet in excitement, and rushed towards Bombo. Shouts, laughter, and remonstrances sounded on every side. Presently I caught a glimpse of Bombo, forcing his way through the crowd of importunate and screaming ladies. He was an enormously fat gentleman, with a red, jolly face, round as the moon, and covered with perspiration from his excitement and struggles with his tormentors. Some had hold of his arms, some his coat tails, some his hair, and some his watch chain; and all screaming and laughing, 'red—say blue, Mr. Bombo—say red—don't let him go—ha! ha!—look at him, he is going to say red.'

"The good-natured countenance of Bombo was alternately smiling and frowning, and all the while he struggled to be free of the hands straining at his arms and coat tails. He plunged frantically across the parlor, but a score of ladies clung to him. He reeled away like a drunken man behind the centre table. All in vain! They clung to him, and begged and shouted and laughed. One more turn around the table, and then came the cry

"'Look out! Mr. Bombo—the stool! the stool!'

"Too late for the unfortunate and undecided Bombo. His retreating legs struck the low stool, and over he went, crash! his full fat length upon the floor, dragging two clinging ladies on top of him, and falling heavily upon a third old spinster seated on another stool behind him, with her knitting needles in her hands. One convulsive shout of laughter ensued. Mrs. Fierygrim picked herself up, and bending over the astounded and shaken Bombo, shouted,

"'Will it be red now?'

"Bombo looked up quizzically, and said, 'I should think it would—very red.'

"I laughed myself sore. Then I asked an old lady near me,

"'Mrs. Wilder, why do you all discountenance dancing?'

"'O mercy!' she exclaimed, 'it's so very distracting to the mind; it's inconsistent with a spirit of prayer.'

"Then I said, 'Please get some one to pray now, Mrs. Wilder, before Bombo gets up. It will be so appropriate.' I couldn't hear what her reply was, there was so much giggling and shouting over Bombo."

Clara Peyton laid the journal on the table, and exclaimed, "I'll vouch for the accuracy of that description. Mary

Sedgwick was present at that very sewing society, and described the whole performance to me. She declared there was more noise and shouting over Mr. Bombo than full band of dancing music could possibly make. But, Blonde, that Mrs. Fierygrim is one of those persons who have made themselves so conspicuous in charging that murder upon Henry Lansing. She ascribes every conceivable mean motive to me and to you, for the part we have taken in defending him. She moderated in her expressions very much after poor Mrs. Lansing went to see her about the violent language she had been using; but since Mrs. Lansing's death she has broken forth worse than ever. Do you know, Blonde, that I never can divest my mind of that dreadful death scene. It seems to me that Mr. Hartwell's ghastly face is ever coming up in my dreams, and I can hear him begging for mercy, as he did in the wood. It is dreadful to dream of it so often. I sometimes lie awake nights, and puzzle my brains, wondering and surmising who could have killed him. Do you know that your servant, Norman Prince, acts very strangely about this murder? I have tried several times to engage him in conversation about it, but he seems very reluctant to say one word on the subject. You would think he would feel anxious and willing to talk about it, for he was so attached to Henry Lansing, and if the real murderer could be found out, it would bring such joy to that lonely family. But all I can get from his lips is something about its being a dreadful business, and that God will make it all right some day, and clear Mr. Henry's name. What makes you so quiet and thoughtful, Blonde?"

The fair girl who was possessed of the dreadful secret, was bending low over her sewing, and striving to appear calm and self-possessed, but her heart beat quickly and painfully, as it ever did when the mysterious tragedy was mentioned in her presence. She determined, however, when she heard that Norman Prince's manner of maintaining silence on the subject was subjecting him to the suspicion of mystery, to avoid that reserved manner herself. When Clara inquired the cause of her own silence, she looked up from her work and said earnestly, and without the least flutter in her tone, although it cost her a fearful effort,

"I cannot but study this tragedy deeply. The victim was so well known to me—his own dying words regarding myself were so mysterious—I cannot even dream what he meant by speaking of his unsuccessful attempt to injure me. Oh, Clara, if this whole mystery could be cleared up, how many happy hearts there would be. Gurty Lansing, poor boy, comes here so often since his mother's death, and puts his face in my lap, and cries as if his heart would break. He thinks if his brother could only be restored to him, he would not grieve so about his mother. His sense of family pride is so remarkable for a boy. He says it is the first stain on his family record that has ever been known. He confided to me that he is not treated with anything like the consideration on the manor that he was before his mother died. Mrs. Bounce rules there with a high hand, and is anything but zealous in vindicating the character of her absent brother from this charge. Her mother's friends have been dropped, and her implacable enemies taken into confidence by the daughter. Gurty is scolded and tormented about his visits to me, but he declares he will never desert Carl's studio nor me. He asked me if I would become his sister and love him, poor lonely boy, and I told him to come here just as often as if it was his own home. You must notice him, Clara, for he is the most desolate little soul I know. But he is as firm and decided in his likes and dislikes as his brother. Nothing can frighten or discourage him about his friends. I would rejoice if I could bring his brother back to him. But, Clara, don't you think if Henry Lansing was to return now, that it would go very hard with him on a trial for his life, with all the feeling there is against him, and with the singular evidence they have accumulated against him?"

"Yes indeed!" replied her friend, "I wouldn't have him return just at this time for the world. I feel confident they would find him guilty. Poor Gurty! I can sympathize with him about his family pride. I believe it any of my relatives were accused of a crime persistently, or of a dishonorable or shameful deed, I would go distracted. I am like my father in that respect. He would rather lose all his wealth than have one of his family or kin spoken of disreputably. Blonde, I would rather see my father lying dead on that floor, than to hear the public charge him, with any plausibility, of being dishonorable, or of being anything else than the upright Judge he is. My father's ancestors and my mother's are without a stain, and I *glory* in it. If we become poor, I can work, I can do anything; but dishonor—oh! that would kill me."

Blonde interrupted her friend, vehemently exclaiming,

"Oh, you agree with me so completely. Give me a fair name among fair and reasonable people, and I could beg even for my living. But think of poor Henry Lansing—he even doesn't know that he is charged with disgracing his proud family name. How he would come flying back here if he heard of this charge. But here comes our tea. Why doesn't your father come here and take tea with us oftener ?"

"He very rarely indulges in an evening meal. He tells me to come here and make myself social with you, for he is too busy to see me in the evening."

The two friends cleared off the marble top table, and the servant placed their elegant supper upon it and then left them alone to themselves.

As Blonde Grayson ate and chatted volubly with her friend for the next half hour, no one could have discovered in her manner the slightest trace of the storm of emotion which had been sweeping over her heart during that brief conversation regarding the murder. Her soul was a soul for great secrets. Trivial emotions flashed to her eyes. Great emotions and profound secrets served only to render those blue eyes still more mysterious and unfathomable. Her heart was a courageous heart, capable of enduring any pain for one she loved, and enduring calmly. As she sits so cheerfully beside her violet-eyed and beloved Clara, gentle reader, glance once more into her sweet, mysterious eyes of blue, note the wonderful and misty luxuriance of her rippling, golden hair, and admire the gentle dimples which come and go with her smiles, and the lily grace of her tall form, for we design to bid her farewell for a time. The thread of our narrative is broken, and we shall not take it up again until long years have passed away. For years the fair Blonde and the upright Judge and the faithful negro boy concealed the name of the real murderer from every human being. The opening of the next chapter is at a period nearly four years after the gentle, holy Mrs. Lansing went to the arms of her God.

CHAPTER XIX.

Mrs. Bounce was alone. In a great window of the library of the manor house her plump figure stood partially revealed under the heavy drapery of the window curtains. The window was open, and she stood gazing out upon the beautiful landscape of the park, in the soft light of the summer sun, which just lingered above the tops of the forest trees in its descent to the Western horizon. One arm was raised in the attitude of holding aside the window curtain that it might not impede her view. She was dressed in deep mourning. The dark robe fitted tightly to her bust, and her round plump arms, revealing the outlines of a figure more suggestive of robust health than grace. Her waist was far from slender, and the small hand which held aside the curtain, was very white and fat. Her height was of the medium order, and the foot which stole out under the dark skirt of her mourning dress, was cased in a dark gaiter, wonderfully small for the heavy plumpness of her figure. Indeed, her feet and hands were both very small, and were the only indication of gentle birth about her person, except the whiteness of her skin. All else was heavy, gross and sensual. Her face was round and her cheeks fat. Her lips full, red and voluptuous. Her chin was double. Her nose short and straight. Her large eyes were dark, under heavy dark eyebrows, and in moments of repose or pleasure, gleamed with a snaky, or a sensual light. Her dark hair was pressed smoothly back from her low, white forehead, till it fell away in heavy curls upon her neck. Her age was not a day beyond thirty-two. It was her birth-day evening. Her expression was ordinarily stern and cold. But in moments of relaxation, her eyes could soften with fondness or with passion. A casual observer could not fail to pronounce the widow a cruel and a sensual woman. As she looked out upon the beautiful manor, and the occasional chestnut trees, and the half concealed and deserted old manor house, a flush of pride and pleasure came to her face. That beautiful landscape over which the departing sun was pouring slanting and misty showers of light, with its groups of magnificent old trees, and its sleek roving herds of blooded English stock, was all under her especial supervision and control. Her father was too engrossed in the management of his other property, to devote his time to the manor, and the full care and superintendence of this lovely estate was entrusted to her hands. There was every indication that she would control it for years to come. The heir had been gone so long that reasonable apprehensions were entertained that he was dead. No word or letter had ever come from him, save the brief note found in the mane of Black Hawk. Gurty Lansing, now a graceful, handsome youth of seventeen, was a college student, and several years must elapse before he could be in a situation to undertake the care and management of the estate. The young widow, in her mourning weeds, as she studied the fair scene from the library window, pondered all this, as she murmured at length to herself:

"Now is my time to win a heart and a hand. Henry is no doubt dead. If he returns, he will unquestionably swing. He must have murdered Hartwell on Blonde Grayson's account. I shall rule the manor until Gurty attains his majority. The prestige of my guardianship of this princely estate, coupled with my expectations of the competency which will come to me in stocks and bonds by my father's will, must enable me to win any desirable man who may cross my path. This doctor is that man. I pronounce him forty-five. There is just gray tinge enough in his splendid beard and in his hair to give him an aristocratic look. He is a skillful physician, and I see his practice increases fast. Doctor Cramer resigned his practice into superior hands. He is not so successful in the treatment of infants, but in everything else, he is Doctor Cramer's superior. His family reputation is excellent. His cousin Emily was my schoolmate. He will be rich without my property counted in, from his profession alone. He has a manly figure. I won't marry anything else than a fine figure. His only fault is that he is too good—too gentle. Oh! if he knew my plans in regard to him, he surely would never let Gurty rise from that bed again. But he won't arrange that matter. I feel sure; I know it. He is too gentle. I wouldn't hint it to him for the world. And yet if Gurty was out of the way, I should inherit this whole estate, and all the other estates. Everything would then be mine. Wouldn't I lord it over Mrs. Fierygrim. I would make that church run to me instead of to her, *indeed* I would. Ah! I hear his footstep coming down. Now we will see what his prescription is for Gurty."

The widow relinquished the window curtain from her fat hand, and turned away towards the hall door.

The doctor, who had superseded the family physician of the Lansings, was, as Mrs. Bounce had surmised, a superior man in his profession. Dr. Cramer had introduced him to his friends upon retiring from practice, as one eminently qualified to take his place. His dignity and gentleness of manner, his calm and cautious judgment, and his unflinching faithfulness to his patients had, in a very few months, insured him a wide popularity. He was, moreover, a cultivated scholar and critic, and was well received in the extensive literary circles of C—. He was nearly six feet in height, and firmly and powerfully moulded. His dark brown hair was slightly mixed with gray

His long, heavy beard and moustache bore traces, also, of Time's gray touch. His dark eye kindled in animated and exciting conversation, but its ordinary gaze was calm and serene. His entrance into a sick room was like a glance of subdued sunshine to the invalid. He walked noiselessly, spoke gently, and cheered by his very presence. He was very guarded in avowing his political and religious predilections. Though understood to be a Methodist, his practice rarely permitted him to attend that church. This reserve and consideration in regard to expressing his opinions established him firmly in the families of his patients, who were connected with some one of the dozen rival churches of C——. Dr. Mosely was a favorite.

As he came to the library door, which stood open, in quest of his patient's sister, she came forward from the window to meet him, with her face wearing its sweetest smile, and her eyes raised to the doctor's calm countenance in an expression of the passionate fondness she really entertained for him. No man could hesitate a moment how to construe that devoted expression. The doctor had already on several occasions observed her predilection for him; but now her manner and her gaze were so marked that he was slightly embarrassed. He averted his eyes as he said,

"Your brother will have a high fever to-night. I am concerned about him, and will drive out here about eleven o'clock. I have a patient on the road, nearly as far out as the manor gate, whom I must see about that hour. The proper medicine for your brother I will prepare myself, and bring it out with me. You have an excellent girl with him—I know her capacity for nursing very well. But I think your brother feels lonely, and requires your own presence occasionally to cheer him up. Your weighty cares concerning the manor must engross your entire time; but I would drop in to see him once in a while, if you can. He will be very sick to-night. Poor boy, he has been talking to me about his mother and his brother, and he appeared to be very much affected. Those paintings in his room are certainly wonderful, especially the one he says he painted some years ago—the brigand escaping up the mountain. Oh! I had nearly forgotten his request. He desired me to notify Miss Grayson of his illness and request her to come and see him. Is it a proper request?"

The physician's inquiry interrupted for a moment the display of Mrs. Bounce's affection for him. At the mention of that detested name, the widow's eye grew cold and stern, and she said emphatically:

"The boy must be crazy to make such a request. That young lady never visits this house. She may be a very nice girl for all I know, but she was never deemed by my mother of sufficient standing and position in life to be intimate with this family. I beg of you, doctor, that you will dismiss the subject from your mind and pay no further attention to Gurty's whims. Miss Grayson was never invited to the manor except on one extraordinary occasion. My mother invited several girls from town to participate in the race for a golden cup on the occasion of Gurty's birthday several years ago. This young lady succeeded in winning the prize. The cup had been made under Henry Lansing's directions, and was therefore the occasion of great rivalry. She won the cup as the fastest rider. That is the last and the only time she was ever invited to the manor; and on that occasion, every class and condition of people came."

Dr. Mosely bowed approvingly as he answered,

"Of course it is no concern of mine. Your brother feels so lonely, that it struck me as being an innocent request. The young lady has been one of my patients for a time, and I found her very agreeable and well educated. I hope you will pardon my repeating his request to you. I supposed they were intimate friends of your family. I am still such a stranger in C——, that I have not fairly learned yet the boundaries and regulations of society."

The widow's loving expression returned again, and she smiled sweetly as she said,

"You are perfectly excusable, doctor. But speaking of society, there is no circle to which your countenance and your accomplishments will not be a ready passport. I am certain you can aspire to any position in C——. Of course you will marry here; for I believe all doctors marry at some period of their lives."

She said this half seriously, half quizzically, looking at him all the while to detect any clue in his expression to his secret purposes in regard to matrimony.

The physician appeared not to observe the interest in her tones and manner, for he said, smiling, in his own gentle way,

"I have really considered that interesting subject since my arrival in your beautiful town. If I could fancy a *young* lady for a partner, I should have been long since captured for life, I'm sure. The girls here are beautiful and fascinating. But

I want a companion nearer my own age. Do you not think, Mrs. Bounce, I am reasonable in this?"

The widow blushed deeply and looked down. There was not so great a distance to traverse to win his heart, after all. He would not marry a girl. Might he not already be thinking of securing herself? She did not raise her eyes, for she knew he was regarding her. Her bosom rose and fell under his glance with her secret emotion. At length she looked up coquettishly and said,

"I surmise from your question, doctor, that you have already made your selection, and only ask me to confirm your judgment in the matter. If you think best to make me your confidante, I may be able to assist you in your suit; you know we widows are considered great and efficient managers, sometimes, on behalf of gentlemen. Come now, doctor, own up—who is the fortunate fair one, near your own age, who has secured your heart already in this town? I will be a true friend and assistant to you in the matter, if you are not already quite sure of her."

He averted his eyes slightly again from the eagerness and the ardor of her passionate gaze. But he laughed and said,

"Don't make me commit myself; I might startle you. But really, Mrs. Bounce, you have no right to draw out my secret now, even if I had a secret; no, no!" he said, turning away towards the hall door and laughing. "I am not going to divulge anything now—I must go. But we will renew this subject, perchance, at another time. Good evening. I will come again at eleven to-night."

Thus speaking and laughing he bowed himself out of her presence, and in a few seconds she heard the wheels of his vehicle rolling rapidly away from the manor house. The widow returned to her open window again and looked out towards the myrtle dell. As a turn in the meadow road brought his person again in sight, he looked back and saw her at the open window. He bowed, waved his hand to her, and drove on.

Mrs. Bounce remained a long time at the open window in a thoughtful mood. She had elicited nothing from the physician except his intention to marry, and not to marry a young lady. He might be enamored of herself. Who could tell? She thought if she was the fortunate holder of his heart, he would have lingered longer. But then he was so prompt and punctual in his professional calls, that this conclusion might be utterly erroneous. There was this much consolation—he had promised to renew the conversation again. But a painful reflection intruded itself, and ran its keen point through her jealous heart. The doctor had expressed admiration of Blonde Grayson's manners and accomplishments. Would he consider and class her among the "young"? The widow considered a moment, and recollected that the fair Blonde's age was about four years less than her own. She knew that Miss Grayson's charms were as brilliant and ensnaring as ever. No one disputed the fact. She knew that Blonde usually had the first choice of new suitors who arrived in C——. Had the popular physician fallen into the customary snare? Hope, fear, jealousy, rage, agitated the mourning figure seated in the twilight in the library window.

As she appears so absorbed in her meditations at the window, and as the hastening shadows of the night rapidly render her figure dim and lost in the darkness of the great manor library, we shall steal away through the broad hall and up the wide oaken staircase to the neglected brother's room in the second story, which looks out upon the vine-clad colonnade at the front of the mansion.

Gurty Lansing was alone in his spacious room, stretched on his bed, feverish and sad. His windows opening upon the colonnade had been raised to give him air on the sultry summer evening, but the shutters were closed. A shaded lamp lighted the apartment, and through the open slats of the window shutters the dizzy chirp of the crickets and the answering calls of the tree-toads came to his ears through the stillness of the summer night. He had returned home sick from the distant college, and his malady had finally sent him to his bed. It was the second evening of his confinement to his room. As he turned uneasily from side to side, intense pain and throbbing in his head were coming on, and his forehead and hands were growing hot and dry under the influence of the hastening fever. At length he moaned in pain and loneliness. The faithful and attentive nurse, whose services had been secured by Mrs. Bounce to relieve herself of trouble, had just left the room, at Gurty's request, to get her tea. During her absence the dreadful fever stalked in with the evening and embraced the lonely boy. He whispered low and sorrowfully,

"Oh! my mother, in heaven, take pity on me, for I am growing crazy with pain."

Then he turned his hot cheek to the pillow, and moaned again. The walls of his room seemed to whirl in circles. A hard grasp like an iron vice seized his temples, and the shaded lamp on his table appeared to reel and stagger before his eyes.

A more agonized and louder moan escaped him. It was heard. A heavy but cautious step was approaching his half-opened door. She had come, slowly and carefully up the back stairway of the house, and as she neared his door, the moan had reached her ears. It was the corpulent figure of an old negro woman, the faithful and trusted servant to whom the departed Mrs. Lansing had confided the care of her larder and her cooking department. The fat arm of the old cook pushed open the door, and she waddled into the sick-room puffing and blowing She came close to Gurty's bedside, and asked in the fondling tone of a nurse—

"What is the matter with aunt Roby's baby? Just heard all about it—never sent for aunt Roby—cruel Gurty—what's the matter, baby?"

Gurty turned gratefully towards the old woman and whispered,

"Oh! aunt Roby, I'm so glad to see you, I'm going to die and go to mother; do you believe I'm good enough to go where she is?"

"Hush your nonsense, child, don't you be talking that style to me. Why, baby, you is just as hot as coal of fire. Lord save us, but you's going to have sure enough, fever. There's some in this house as ought to feel ashamed the way my baby is left all alone; Nurse says so, and I says so too. Aunt Roby wants to fix up some nice thing for you to eat, baby, but it's no good with such high fever as this."

"No, no," moaned Gurty, "don't mention anything to eat, I can't put a thing in my mouth. Oh! aunt Roby can't you put some cold water on my head, I believe I shall go crazy."

The old woman waddled away to the table and brought a pitcher of water, and bathed the temples and neck of the sufferer. The water seemed to give him temporary relief, and under her fat, soothing hands, and the consciousness of being attended by an old friend, Gurty, after a time, fell asleep. She watched his heavy breathing, and put her hand several times on his feverish head, and then muttered to herself, and shook her head deprecatingly at some absent individual, who had provoked her ire. Finally, as the boy seemed likely to sleep for some hours, the old cook seated herself upon the floor, and resting her aged head against his bed-side, gradually gave way to the influence of sleep. She had promised the nurse to relieve her, for an hour or two, of her watching, and this was the way the weary, affectionate old soul fulfilled her promise.

After the two had slumbered on for more than an hour, and

the lamp on the table was rapidly growing dim from want of attention and replenishing, another footstep approached the door of Gurty's room. The tread was heavy and careless, and sounded, thump, thump, thump, along the hall to the door. There was no consideration for sickness in that plunging tread. It was Mrs. Bounce's heavy mourning figure. She paused at the door, and said in a loud, harsh tone, devoid of kindness—

"Well, Gurty, how do you feel now?" No answer came from the sleepers in the dimly-lighted chamber. She spoke again, and in a louder tone—

"Gurty, do you want anything? Gurty! Gurty!" Still no reply. She muttered to herself, "He is asleep, I won't disturb him. Where is the nurse?—gone, I declare; I'll teach her to loiter in this style."

And away the widow went back to the staircase, thump, thump, thump. She considered that her visit to the sick-room had been well performed, and she turned away to more congenial business than watching and nursing invalids.

The stillness of the summer night continued. The hum of the distant insects outside the mansion was gradually subsiding, and the dim rays of the fading lamp burned lower and fainter in the sick chamber. Gurty, flushed and breathing heavily, still slumbered on his couch, and the half-hidden figure of the old cook still slept against the side of the bed. The nurse had looked into the apartment once, and finding everything disposed so comfortably, had returned again to the kitchen to continue her gossip with the housemaids and the coachman. At length the invalid opened his eyes and stared about him. His eyes were bloodshot and his tongue parched, and he seemed bewildered. But finally he discovered aunt Roby sleeping against his bed, and he composed himself once more and lay on his back with his white bare arm beneath his head and gazing upward at the flickering shadows on the ceiling. Suddenly he heard the distant howl of a dog, mournfully repeated in the silent night. He shuddered, for he knew the popular superstition which attaches to the howling of a dog at that ill-omened hour. The pain and the throbbing in his head returned with increased violence, but he was too considerate to arouse the sleeping old woman. He reflected a long while on his condition, and then he wondered if Blonde Grayson his friend would come in answer to his request. After awhile he heard the solemn clock in the town of C—— striking the hour. He counted the heavy, distant strokes, as they slowly fell upon the night air, till they marked the hour of eleven. Then a smile came to his flushed face, and he thought to himself:

"That good doctor will come soon and relieve me of my pain. I have such faith in him—he is so calm and wise, and knows what is the matter with me."

The pleasant thought tarried, and before it was forgotten in his sufferings, he heard the sound of the physician's wheels rolling over the meadow road towards the house. He heard the sound till it ceased before the door, and then he detected voices below in the great hall. Presently the delinquent nurse hurried into the room and aroused the sleeping cook and sent her away, and then hastily trimmed the fading lamp till it illumined the sick room again. She was just in time, for as she turned away from the replenished lamp, Mrs. Bounce and the physician entered the room. The widow was all smiles and gentleness now, for she was acting a part before the doctor. She approached her brother and stroked his forehead, and inquired caressingly concerning his condition. But Gurty turned sullenly and bitterly away from her touch. He understood her too well. That trait in his character which nurtured by kindness on her part in the past would have been now devotion and love, was, from bitter experience of her treachery and intolerance, turned into loathing and contempt.

Doctor Mosely raised the shade from the lamp, and then came to the bed and sat upon its side. Gurty extended his small graceful hand to the physician, and murmured:

"I am so glad you are punctual; my brain is on fire—please cure me, doctor, right soon, or I shall lose the prize at college. You are the only friend I have in this world except the Graysons and my lost brother."

Mrs. Bounce compressed her lips with vexation at these words, but she prudently refrained from insisting upon having herself included in the category of friends. Gurty would have stormed forth stern facts if she had dared to attempt it. She knew him to be a long-suffering youth, but capable on occasions like the present of hurling furious shafts of sarcastic ire.

The doctor made no reply, but studied carefully the features of the invalid, pressing softly and kindly the boy's hand. That touch meant every thing to Gurty. He tried to smile, but pain rendered it a feeble smile. The physician, after a few minutes of silence, said with sudden and unexpected force:

"Mrs. Bounce, I shall bleed him at once—please prepare a bowl and bandages. Gurty, I will cure you if you will not worry your mind about any thing which is disagreeable to you. Think of what pleases you alone, and follow my directions. You are a great artist, and I mean to save you. You must live for art and that alone. You have a genius for painting, and God designs that to be your profession. Your mathematical prize at college won't be worth to you the snap of my finger. Trust me—I am older than you. Don't worry about that prize one minute longer, and don't strive for it even if you are well in time to compete for it. You must give your time wholly to the study of art. As soon as you are well, I will persuade your father to send you at once to Europe. You have had enough of college and mathematics."

The face of the sufferer lighted through his pain. He looked triumphantly at Mrs. Bounce. She had always opposed his artistic studies. He at once forgot the college prize, and smiled as he bared and extended his white, graceful arm to the physician's lancet

When the operation was concluded, and the invalid youth appeared to experience some relief from the excessive pain in his head, Doctor Mosely took Mrs. Bounce to the window, and said, in a low tone, "Leave these shutters just as they are, if the night continues warm. Your brother is in great danger of dying. This little vial of medicine, which I hold in my hand, you must give him at two o'clock precisely, clear and unmixed with any thing, just as it is. A failure to give him this would probably cost him his life. I have known such neglect to prove fatal. Remember and give it to your brother at two o'clock."

Mrs. Bounce took the vial of red fluid and promised to sit up with Gurty and administer it to him at the proper time. The doctor remarked to her at leaving that delirium would soon manifest itself in her brother's case. His last words were:

"You realize the vital importance of giving him the red vial."

CHAPTER XX.

HARK! Was not that the expected stroke, trembling solemnly upon the hushed night air. She started from her seat to listen, and her heart beat fast. She smiled grimly at her nervousness, and her foolish fear, and sank back again, into her chair. The silence was fearful, and profound. Her heart pulsations were so loud she could hear them, and the muffled sounds were only hushed to her ear when the heavy breathing from the bed echoed louder from the exhausted slumberer. She started at the rustling of her own mourning dress. Why should she fear ? The door was locked on the inside, and the nurse long since gone. She was entirely, safely, *triumphantly* alone. For the manor was just within her grasp. The pride of the county, the far-famed, magnificent myrtle dell, with its meadows, and woodlands, and its princely income was offered to her at a trifling expense. Its actual cost, at that solemn hour of night, was enclosed in the palm and fingers of her small, white hand. She glided quietly across the floor to the silent, faithful light of the watcher's lamp. She held up to that lamp the price of the great manor. It was the ominous color of *blood !* She shook it in the lamplight, holding it up before her. It still revealed the startling hue of human blood Ah ! why that start ? Did she see anything ?—or was it only that imagination, that foolish, fevered imagination, which is nursed and grows strong from the study of religion and of the invisible life. It must be that. But oh ! it seemed to her as she fixed her sinister gaze upon that transparent hue of blood, that a wing swept through the air, and brushed against the little vial in warning. Hush ! Was not that the dead mother's whisper that passed with the wing ? No ! weak, foolish, conscience, it was only the slumber-sigh of the helpless, doomed brother. She laughed again at her fevered imagination and her foolish fears. This night watching must be trying to the unaccustomed nerves. It was so new to her. She glanced at the ticking watch upon the table. The hands moved very slowly, and the test hour was still distant. Why feel so excited yet ? Plenty of time to think it over, and weigh its dangers and its advantages together. Hush ! beating heart ; there is no cause for fear

She grasped the fatal vial tightly in her palm and fingers once more, and, removing the shade from the lamp, walked slowly to the bedside to study the features of the sleeping boy. The face was flushed with the fever, and the closed eyelids looked so sunken and pitiful, and there was the distorted expression of suffering about the small, refined mouth. How white and beautiful the smooth round neck, and the slender arm, bare below the doctor's bandage. How striking the resemblance of the sleeper to his dead mother ! Was the belief in guardian angels utterly unfounded, or did that mother indeed hover over that sleeping boy in unutterable tenderness and constant prayer? How tenderly, how touchingly, had that mother's heart clung to her boy. How ardently had she prayed that he might have protecting and soothing love when she was gone to her grave. Could the barriers of a distant heaven hold her from him now, as he lay in painful, unrefreshing slumber, and the death angel was already looking enquiringly into the face of God?

How fearful the silence of the sick chamber to the holder of the red vial. She could hear the ticking of the watch now. She left the bedside at the sound, and went to examine it again. *Fifteen minutes of two o'clock!* She started at the figures. She clutched the red vial. She held it again to the light. Why did she look behind her? There was no one in the room but the sleeping Gurty. No prying eye was watching her, and she only held up to view the healing medicine for her poor, exhausted brother. It was nearly time to arouse him and administer the life-giving potion. Her hand dropped away from the light, clasping the vial. She turned away thoughtfully from the lamp, and sought her arm chair once more. She leaned back in it, and her dark eyes glittered, as they studied more deeply her dreadful purpose. Her eyes grew calmer, as her mind wandered away in reverie to some less sinful purpose.

A mournful *clang* sounded in the distance over the meadows from C——, and then trembled away into silence. *Clang* again sounded the bell. She sprang to her feet, shivering with terror. The dreadful hour of *two* had come. The solemn, lonely sound vibrated itself away, and then silence reigned as before. She hung her guilty head and reflected. Give Gurty the contents of the vial, and he would live. Pour it away, and the poor boy would die. And then? What then? The recording angel would write in the Great Book opposite the name of Esther Lansing—"*Murder.*" For a moment she wavered in her purpose. But the manor, as she had seen it from the library window, bathed in the glory of the western sun, loomed up in matchless beauty. An attentive fiend grasped her by the elbow, and pushed her impulsively towards one of the windows. She pushed open the shutters, poured the contents of the red vial out upon the grass, and then, closing them again, returned to the table, and placed upon it the empty vial. The fiend chuckled in triumph. But her calm, patient guardian angel shrieked and fled.

The deed was committed. Her mental struggles and her anxiety were over She now could make her dispositions for the remainder of the night, calmly and without any further caution. No one would surmise that she had not administered the potion to the invalid at the proper time. Before the nurse had retired to another room at her suggestion, to sleep, she had witnessed the manifestation of Gurty's delirium. If the invalid should be able in the morning to converse, he would be told that he had taken the contents of the red vial during his temporary alienation of mind, from the hand of his sister. Mrs. Bounce smiled complacently to herself, at the ease with which she had disposed of her obstacle to the ownership of the manor. She had given Gurty nothing to take away his life—her offence was merely one of omission. She waited for a few moments in silence, then she arose, replenished the night lamp, and retired to her own apartment, leaving her brother's door a-jar, that she might hear any call from him before morning. Just before leaving, she cast a hurried glance around the room, her dark snaky eye searching every shadow, to see that all was right and secure. Strange it was, she did not see that glaring eye fixed upon her countenance with the wild ferocity which lights the terrible eye-ball of the concealed panther when it gathers itself for the fatal spring upon the man who dares to molest its young. There, between the open slats of the window shutters which opened upon the vine-clad porch, not the side window through which she poured the contents of the red vial, but the front window, where Doctor Mosely gave her the special directions and the vial of medicine, there! there! it burned and glared upon her guilty face, and she did not see it—that terrible eye. It had been there when the physician conversed with her in the window. He did not see it. It had returned again, raising itself slowly to the level of the first slats just before the solemn clock struck two. It had witnessed all her struggles, glaring into her agitated, guilty face, as she raised the red vial to the light. It had witnessed the destruction of the life-giving potion. It now followed her every motion, to see her final arrangement for the night. When she disappeared from the room, leaving Gurty alone for the night, the eye disappeared also, dropping away from the shutter. A dark figure clinging and passing from vine to vine, with the agility and caution of a cat, slowly decended between two pillars of the colonnade. The dark figure moved noiselessly and cautiously downward, till it reached the steps of the piazza. There it paused and listened. No breathing thing was near. It stealthily crept down the steps of the piazza, reached the graveled walk stole away down the soft grass of the lawn.

leaped the manor brook. and then darted away over the dark meadows. Every vale and rise of ground seemed familiar. No pause, no abatement of speed—on, on, to the myrtle dell. The shadowy figure hastened along between the banks of myrtle till it reached the brown gate. No pause to open the gate. The figure bounded over the manor fence and landed in the highway. Down the lonely highway the strange nimble shadow glided on some pressing errand. There was no one to molest or wonder, abroad, at that late hour. The figure hurried on till it reached the elm-guarded street of C—, bounded along its deserted pavement in mysterious haste, and penetrated to the interior of the town. At last, in the profound darkness, it paused before a low brick house, and stood panting from exhaustion. A light in the second story of the dwelling, gleamed faintly through the closed shutters. The mysterious figure looked up to it for a while, and seemed perplexed. A few minutes' longer pause, and then the figure groped around upon the pavement. It rose upright again, and a fragment of brick rattled against the shutters where the faint light was. A fortunate throw, and well aimed. The inmate of the room heard the sound, for the light moved nearer to the window. The shutters were pushed open, and a man appeared with a lamp.

"Who is there? and, what do you want?"

The dark figure came forward into the light, and answered,

"I'm Mr. Grayson's coachman. For God's sake, come down to the door."

The lamp was extended further out from the window, to identify the person of the last speaker. The examination appeared to be satisfactory, for the light was withdrawn, and soon disappeared altogether. Presently it appeared again in the lower hall, and the key turned in the front door. When the door opened, there stood Doctor Mosely in full dress, confronting the negro.

"Norman, who is sick? and why didn't you ring the bell?"

The negro removed his straw hat and bowed with his wonderful grace. Then he said quietly—

"Mrs. Bounce threw away the red medicine for Mr. Gurty Lansing, and I saw her."

Doctor Mosely started and exclaimed

"Impossible! But, Norman, your word is as reliable as a nobleman's. Tell me about it."

The negro related the whole occurrence minutely, from the moment he overheard the physician's directions at the window, to the time Mrs. Bounce retired for the night. The doctor listened eagerly, and then said:

"Why were you up there on the vines, at that hour of night?"

The negro answered pathetically,

"Norman Prince loves Mr. Gurty. Mr. Gurty is kind and good. He hasn't no friend on the manor since Mrs. Lansing died, and Norman Prince loves to watch him. Doctor, I keep a bright eye on that young gentleman, and I never had much faith in Mrs. Bounce."

The physician looked at his watch, and said calmly,

"There is time enough yet. Here, Norman, is the key of my stable—you know where it is around the corner—wait here till I bring you down my lantern. I want you to put in my horse as quickly as possible, and bring him around to the door. Then you must go with me."

The negro took the key and bowed. Then he chuckled to himself and said,

"Norman Prince's heart is just as light as a feather. I'll bring him round quicker nor lightnin'."

The negro stood on the door step, twirling the stable key around his forefinger, and chuckling repeatedly while the doctor ascended the stairs again for his lantern.

The physician was very expeditious, and soon returned with the lighted lantern. The negro seized it and hastened around to the stable. Before the doctor had prepared another vial of the medicine his buggy wheels rattled up to the door. The negro was evidently anxious about Gurty Lansing. Presently a dark figure closed the front door of the dwelling and walked out to the buggy. He stepped in beside the negro and took the lantern on his lap.

"Now drive away, Norman, as fast as you like."

The horse started out at a fast trot. The physician, with the lantern in his lap, remained silent. He was studying his plan of operations. The light of the lantern flared strangely upon the passing buildings that lined the street, and fluttered through the dense foliage of the great elms as they seemed to glide past. On, on, without a word to break the monotony of the drive, they rattled through the darkness till the broad fields were reached at last. Then the lantern light danced along the hedges and streamed away over the fields, and Norman Prince urged the horse to renewed speed. Still no word was uttered, for both riders were studying deeply their errand and its difficulties. At last they reached the brown gate of the manor in the profound darkness, and the physician swung out ahead the lantern to guide their further route.

"Here, Norman, drive up to that gate post and hitch my horse. We are going to walk from here."

The quick-witted servant had been thinking of the same preparatory step of caution, and said,

"All right, doctor. Two men, but both thinking of same thing. The lantern won't show till we get most through the myrtle dell. Whoa, sir! Whoa!"

The doctor's horse walked up to the gate post, and the two occupants of the buggy jumped to the ground. The horse was secured to the post, and the two opened the gate and passed into the myrtle dell. The lantern proved serviceable indeed for the pedestrians. The myrtle-covered ravine with its overhanging branches of pine trees was as dark and gloomy as a cavern. The rays of the lantern glistened upon the smooth masses of the myrtle and flashed upon the bosom of the little stream which flowed beside the hard slate road. As they approached the termination of the myrtle dell, the physician, who was walking ahead with his lantern, paused and looked around him. Finding no cavity in the sides of the ravine to hide his lantern, he placed it in the middle of the slate road and left it burning there, in the anticipation of its being serviceable upon his return. The two walked on and were soon in utter darkness again. They groped their way however through the ravine, and soon emerged into the meadows. They could see now the light dimly shining in the distance, through the window shutters of the invalid's chamber. As they walked rapidly through the meadows the physician detailed to his attendant the part he was expected to perform. The negro was to climb as noiselessly as possible up the tall vines on the colonnade to the invalid's window, and see if Gurty was still alone. If the coast was clear, the agile servant was to swing himself by the tangled vines against the shutters and effect his entrance into the apartment as best he could. He was then to close softly the door of the apartment and awake Gurty and administer to him the contents of the vial, and inform him that Doctor Mosely had sent it to him. If the invalid was delirious the negro was to force the fluid down his throat, and then make his exit by the window, as he had entered. The utmost caution was requisite in entering the window, for Mrs. Bounce might still be awake, and was supposed to have left her own chamber door ajar also, to detect sounds from Gurty's room. Both physician and servant were convinced that the widow intended to destroy her brother's life. If she overheard any sound she might thwart their plan to administer the potion which was to save him. The negro was informed that the delay in administering the contents of the red vial must not be permitted to extend beyond an hour longer. The remedies which had been already given to the invalid were very powerful, and the red potion must be taken immediately to counteract their baneful influences. If they were allowed to operate upon the exhausted system of the boy much longer, unchecked, they would settle the unfortunate invalid's fate before morning. He would be lost.

At length the lawn in front of the manor house was reached, and the servant stole quietly up to the piazza to reconnoitre. All was silent as the grave. No motion, no sound of life. Only the faint light glimmered through the shutters of the upper window. With that exception the whole mansion was buried in gloom. The negro uttered a low whistle and the physician answered it by approaching cautiously up to the piazza. The vial of the precious fluid was handed to the negro, and thrusting it into the bosom of his shirt, he grasped one of the large vines and commenced slowly and cautiously to ascend, passing one hand above the other and clinging with his bare toes to the vine which circled about the column. He passed several times around the column in his difficult ascent, following the curving direction of the vine, which in some places clung so tightly to the pillar that he found great difficulty in grasping it with his sinewy fingers. The ascent was fatiguing in the extreme until he reached the second story windows, where the vine had partially followed its own will, straying off in branches which had been carelessly secured to the window frames. At last the more difficult climbing was over, and he seized one of the imperfectly trained vines which swayed away towards the shutters. He now had a firm grip with his hands, and struggled cautiously among the tangled web of vines and leaves slowly towards the window. He raised his head slowly to the level of the window sill and looked eagerly through the shutters. The room was silent and deserted as when he last saw it. The invalid was quiet, and the night lamp burned under its shade. The honest heart of the negro rejoiced. All was now clear sailing, and his dear young friend would be saved. He raised his dark figure higher through the leaves, to secure a foothold near the window. The tangled vines impeded him, catching him around the shoulders as he shov.d his figure through, and brushing against his shirt and his bare ebony neck. He felt his clothes lifted and twisted around by the reluctant separating vines. A *crash* on the piazza beneath him met his ear. He paused, thrust his hand into the bosom of his shirt, and felt for the red vial. It had brushed out of his bosom, fallen to the piazza, twenty feet below him, and broken into a thousand fragments. A low cry of despair escaped his lips, and the cold, clammy perspiration started to his forehead. *Poor, unfortunate, doomed Gurty!*

The physician had been standing motionless below the window, endeavoring to follow with his eye the dark climbing figure of the negro. His own reputation was involved in the negro's success. The death of the invalid would be ascribed to him. He had employed remedies which most of his profession would not dare to administer. Their successful use depended upon the counteracting vial of red fluid being administered at the proper time and promptly too. When the priceless vial fell, shattered at his feet, a cold shiver passed over him. Alas! it was too late now to go back to the town for more. Indeed there was serious question if the present moment itself was not too late for any antidote to operate successfully. Many of his profession would have abandoned the helpless boy as beyond all hope. Active intellects, nervous temperaments, and genius win their ends by the use of the same brief word, *Action.*

Doctor Mosely whispered up towards the clinging negro,

"Norman!"

"Sir!" came faintly whispered back from the unhappy, unnerved servant.

"Come down this instant, and wait for me on this piazza. Down with you, sir, at once, and don't you stir from these steps till I return."

Without waiting to see if his command was obeyed, the energetic physician leaped down the steps of the piazza and disappeared in the darkness. His flying tread was heard by the negro descending the path to the manor brook. Then it was lost in the soft meadow grass beyond. Wonderful speed for a man of forty-five! When he was a boy, he must surely have excelled in the leap and the race. But his soul was on fire. A beautiful life was suspended by a thread; its only salvation depended on his speed, his luck, and his God. Science, pride, humanity, goaded that earnest heart as he bounded away in the darkness over the unfamiliar meadows. How earnest, how eager, how violent his struggles. Away, away. Dear life lingers, and may be saved. Oh, mothers, as you recall the memory of those fearful nights when your ears listened in agony for the footfall of the man of science to relieve and save the little fluttering life in your arms, pray for the good doctor who plunges so bravely and nobly over the dark meadows to save the motherless dying boy who is passing away for ever by a guilty sister's sin. Ah! he prays in his flight. There is something higher then than science in that noble heart. He believes in God. The grass bends, the flowers of the field are crushed, and the rattling pebbles fly before his rush of agony. On, on, beneath the broad arms of the great chestnuts, up the painful rise of the shadowy park, and down its unseen slopes he strains forward to save dear life. A cry escapes him. He is conscious of his failing breath and strength. "Oh, God, help me." See the dazzling answer. A form is poised above him, misty and beautiful, in the darkness. It flies with him. Its angel finger points his way. It whispers of the unseen obstacles, and he avoids them. A white wing fans his heated forehead. Oh, God, it is the wing that brushed the red vial in warning. The Eternal has sent the boy's blue-eyed angel mother.

He reached the myrtle dell. The solemn clock of C—— tolled *three*. The dreadful sound increased his speed. He hurried through the dark ravine; the lantern light met his glad eye. He stooped for the light, grasped it in his hand, and bounded on. The myrtle glistened, and the brook sparkled, and the misty angel mother pointed on. At last, at last the eager doctor stood beside his horse. He swung his lantern under the carriage seat to find his leathern case of vials. God grant a tiny vial of the red life fluid may be there.

Norman Prince slowly descended the curving vine of the colonnade, trembling and sad. Then cautious, still and catlike, he sprang with his bare feet to the piazza. Seating his dark figure upon the steps, he muttered mournfully to himself, "Mr. Henry's gone, and now little Gurty is going, too." He heard a distant sullen sound from the old deserted manor house. "Yes; that's Black Hawk's hoofs. Norman Prince must take good care of him. He's all that's left now."

Look up, faithful, honest, sable face. Your true heart has clung to the old Dutch manor, where you were born, through its troubles and its joys. You have never faltered in its defence—you have been true to its pride, and its honor, and its children. Look up now, for there is light ahead. Over the meadows it comes, guiding faithful footsteps. They are hurrying, and will soon be at your side. Oh! he would not come so fast if there was no hope. Hope, precious hope, for the gasping, motherless boy. The light is at hand. Over the brook it leaps, and rushes up the dark lawn and stands beside you. It flashes upon a red glistening object in his hand. The vial is only half full; but Mrs. Bounce, the murderess, *shall never own the manor.* Stand aside, Norman Prince, and quench the light. A tinge of gray hair and a tinge of gray in the long beard can climb nearly as well as you under the impulse of professional pride, and science and humanity.

The intrepid, wary doctor threw aside his coat, and laid aside his hat, and cast off his heavy boots. He put the vial in his mouth, and held it firmly there. Then he grasped the clinging vine and began to climb, leaving the astonished negro standing alone on the piazza. Slowly, but firmly he overreached his hands and clung with his feet, drawing himself farther and farther up. He had not forgotten yet to be a boy. At intervals he would pause and pant and listen. All was still, save his rustling of the vine leaves. Then he mounted higher on the colonnade, and higher still. The window was attained at last, and he peered in. The gasping Gurty was alone, and the lamp burned. The sight of his helpless patient restored his professional calm and his scientific hope. He raised his figure higher, and tried the shutters. They flew open to his touch. He placed his arm upon the window-sill, and cautiously drew himself into the chamber. He listened again. No sound but the gasping boy. He glided across the room, and closed and bolted the door. Then he removed the lamp shade and approached the bed. The countenance of the innocent youth occasioned a look of sadness on his bearded, searching face. He raised gently the head of the deserted boy and whispered, "Gurty." The blood-shot eyes opened, but did not know him. He was delirious. There was no time to lose. The physician raised his eyes to God for an instant, and then sustained the unconscious sufferer with his arm until he had poured the red contents of the vial down his throat. He laid his head back again upon the pillow, and leaned over him in earnest study. The gasping painfully continued. He watched him still. Seconds, minutes, quarters fled, and still he watched him earnestly, looking for a change. The distant solemn bell struck *four.* The sufferer ceased to gasp. Then he turned over on his side and sighed. Then he slept peacefully and calm. The physician leaned over him again and smiled, and then he pressed a warm kiss on his hot brow.

Cautiously he opened the door and left it as the murderess left it. He walked to the window with his empty vial, and slowly disappeared from sight, closing the shutters behind him as he descended the vine.

When he reached the piazza he told the negro that his young friend was safe. The negro chuckled, and cried, and kissed the doctor's outstretched hand. Then they parted, the physician taking the lantern and the road leading to the myrtle dell, while Norman Prince stole away in the direction of the deserted old manor house. The faithful negro desired one glimpse of admiration at the concealed gift of Gurty Lansing presented years before. He chuckled to himself with the grateful tears in his eyes, "Norman Prince has paid now for Mr. Gurty's fowling piece."

CHAPTER XXI.

Blonde Grayson had improved in appearance. Four eventful years had glided by, and still she was generally acknowledged in C—— to be the most beautiful woman in its attractive society. If she had really grown thinner, as some asserted, it only served to give her beauty a more spiritual type. Her rippling, golden hair still marvelously waved, her pearl teeth still glistened at her dimpled smile, and her blue eyes still charmed by their sweetness and their mystery. She had made many friends. In her own church people were unavoidably brought often in contact with her, and no one could know her without recognizing her goodness of heart and her elegant manners. It was well known that her regard for her church was uppermost in her heart. Not only was she high church in her principles, but in her daily life she evinced her desire to have her church ever before her, and to have church going and church exclusiveness cultivated to the highest point. The rector of St. Paul's could suggest no extra or devotional service for his flock that Blonde Grayson did not endorse and aid. Her class of children in the Sunday school were the best behaved and the best instructed little brood of churchmen in the parish. By constant words and gifts she made these children love and venerate the festive day of Christmas above every other day in the year. Every Christmas morning, when she arose from her bed, she bowed her golden hair and cried like a child with joy and gentleness of heart. All this church feeling was, of course, no great recommendation for her to the wealthy and influential congregation who worshiped at the Presbyterian church of C——. She nevertheless had ardent admirers and a few warm friends even in that society. Her charities extended to the poor of all churches. Thus was she universally recognized in C——, as a beautiful, high church, charitable, accomplished lady. Many added to these adjectives the word " ambitious." For her repeated refusals of marriage offers occasioned the opinion that she aspired to marry some one of great wealth or position if she should every marry.

Her friend Clara, who was now married and a mother, frequently said, " Blonde, I sincerely wish you would accept some one of these men. I know you would be so happy and superb as a wife." But the blue mysterious eyes would look so provokingly calm as the lily replied,

" My sweetest friend, I must *love* before I can marry. It would be exceedingly unpleasant for me to marry a *poor* man. I trust I never shall. But I will never, I can never give myself to any man unless I love him, and love him as you love your own gifted husband."

Then Clara would exclaim :

" You beautiful witch—you are now an old maid, and an old maid you will remain. But if you were sixty, and I a young man, I would just furiously worship you. Indeed, indeed I would. I'd marry you when all that gold is turned to gray, and be right happy of the chance."

Mrs. St. Clair, for that was now the name of Blonde's violet-eyed friend, continued, after her marriage, to be Blonde Grayson's shadow. Loving and faithful wife as she was, she found many opportunities to follow Blonde. Her lily friend was the god-mother of her little daughter, ever welcomed by her husband, and enquired for by her father, Judge Peyton. The wife was impetuous and proud, and forever having some difficulty with her neighbors on that account. When contentions had gone far enough, she always came to Blonde for advice to get her out of the trouble. Blonde would laugh at her, and then point out to her some sensible plan of reconciliation. Her friendship proved more beneficial to Clara as a married woman, than it had as a maid. Blonde was happy when she could have Mrs. St. Clair all to herself. Then she was perfectly without restraint, and gay. But when Clara's husband was present, agreeable and intelligent and kind as he was, Blonde's eyes often turned, unnoticed by him, to study his features. Then the mystery in her sweet eyes deepened, and some far off reminiscence, seemed to trail a shadow over their blue depth. She would glance at the remarkable breadth of his shoulders, and the extraordinary muscular development of his arms. He was a finely formed man of forty; a lawyer of reputation and wealth, and high in public esteem. His strength of arm was wonderful. No man in C—— could compete with him in lifting. His hands and his arms were compared to iron by public remark. Blonde could never approach him without her eyes wandering by a species of fascination to his remarkable arms. Some mystery was connected with this strange look, and she never was perfectly natural in his presence. Clara had detected that unaccountable look at times, but never had succeeded in obtaining a satisfactory explanation. When Blonde studied St. Clair, she studied the unfathomable past.

While Gurty Lansing slowly recovered from his dangerous sickness, under the supervision and skill of Dr. Mosely, Blonde Grayson was slowly and discreetly preparing to astonish the citizens of C——. The hospitality of the Grayson family was proverbial through the town. During the winter season, no more elegant and frequent entertainments were given than by that new family. The gayety of the past winter, however, had been interrupted, so far as the Graysons were concerned, by the death of Blonde's father. The kind, genial old man, had gone to his rest while the snow lingered on the ground. The young men and widowers of the town who had not succumbed to the fair lily's charms were now forced to admit that Blonde Grayson in mourning was irresistible. If the fair girl had captivated and ensnared hearts in the sleeves and the waists of her exquisitely tasteful dressing in colors, what was to be expected now, of her fair, dimpled face, and her white throat, and her golden hair, and her slender waist, and her tapering hands, contrasted and set off with the sombre hue of her mourning robes? The festive halls knew her no more. The beautiful orphan was rarely seen on the promenades of C——. Her brother and herself were busily engaged in closing up and settling her father's intricate financial affairs. But on Sundays she was visible at St. Paul's chapel; and when her little class of scholars marched before her around the Gothic church, to the Sunday school, the orphan teacher was so beautiful it was a terrible temptation to be rude, and gaze after her graceful, mourning figure.

One bright summer morning Blonde sat in the parlor of the

Grayson mansion in her graceful mourning robe, and her white linen collar and cuffs. Mrs. St. Clair was present, and her little daughter Clara was wandering about the parlor. Presently the sable face of the negro coachman appeared at the door of the drawing room. He had been in the employ of the Grayson family several years, and Blonde considered him invaluable as a servant. He was dressed neatly and simply in black. He bowed with his sable, inimitable grace, and said,

"I understand Miss Grayson wishes to see me in the parlor."

"Yes," said the mourning orphan mistress. "I wish to discharge you from my service, Norman. I intend no longer to keep a carriage and horses. Will you take the trouble to sell my horses and carriage for me on as favorable terms as you can make? I will pay you for that service, as you know their value much better than I, and I am sure that you can make a better bargain than I. I am very sorry to part with you, Norman; I sincerely wish I could keep you all my life."

The servant replied: "You have been very kind to me, Miss Grayson. This place is my second home. I expected the horses to be sold, but not so soon. I would like to sell them for you; because they ought to bring a high price, and you might be taken advantage of, as you say. Do you want me to leave to-day?"

"No, Norman," she replied, "I will pay your wages up to this day, and you can remain here, free of charge, until this house is sold, which will be very soon. I am going to take a smaller house. I will endeavor to find you a new place as coachman, if you would like me to do so."

The faithful fellow now discovered that the Graysons were in more trouble than he had anticipated, and he brushed a tear from his eye, before he replied: "I promised Dr. Mosely, if I ever was out of a place, to work for him. I know he wants me. But I don't like to see this fine house broken up—indeed I don't, Miss Grayson. I take just as much pride in this place as anybody; and nobody will ever take care of me as you did when I was sick with the fever. I'll pay you for that, Miss Grayson, before I die; you see if I don't. Norman Prince always pays for kindness, some day," and the honest, sable face was covered by his hands, as he cried bitterly. The beautiful mourner was touched at the poor fellow's sympathy and attachment to herself, and her blue eyes softened with the faintest mist of a tear, as she said,

"Changes must come in this life. It is best to be always prepared for them, Norman. You know that better than I can tell you. You lost the most beautiful home in this county, which your whole life was identified with. This home of mine is only one of the many homes I have had. I can soon reconcile myself to another. But, Norman, don't you fail to go to Doctor Mosely. He is a gentleman who will be more than an employer to you—he will be your friend. I know his gentleness and his goodness, from the experience of my friends. You are fortunate to be able to secure a place there. You may go now. I leave my horses entirely to you. Whatever you sell them for, I will ratify the contract."

The servant wiped his eyes, bowed inimitably, and retired backward, out of sight.

To Mrs. St. Clair, who had listened in astonishment to this conversation, the news of her friend's financial embarrassment came with the sudden force of the thunder-bolt. Her look was startled indeed, as she exclaimed, after Norman Prince had bowed himself out:

"Blonde, you frighten me by your words and your calmness. Have you met with irreparable loss, that you surrender this fine house, which your father has so much added to and improved, and all the improvements of the grounds? and the horses too? what does it all mean? what have you been keeping back from your friends?"

Blonde took Clara's hand in her own, as she answered, quietly:

"I did not wish you to worry about my father's embarrassments, until Carl and myself were absolutely certain that we must give up this place. But now we have ascertained beyond a doubt, that my father's partner has made way with all our interest in the firm. He has contrived to appropriate and conceal his own share of funds in the firm, and also my father's entire interest. This reduces my means of support and my brother's, to a very small figure. With the little we have remaining after canceling my father's private debts, and my brother's income from such portraits as he may be called on to paint, we can live barely comfortable. I have engaged a dear little cottage, at the end of Main street, and you will admire it, I know. I believe little luxuries and conveniences have become almost a necessity to me. I have had everything I desired since I was a child, and it will require a great effort to abandon some of them, I know. But it is so plainly my duty to discharge all of my father's obligations in this town, that I must do it at the expense of myself and my brother. I love to enjoy life. I have the keenest zest for society and entertaining my friends, but I have another world to look to, and everything must be made to bend to that. Don't look so distressed, darling Clara; while I have you and my religion, I still have the enjoyment of my two greatest comforts in life."

"You shall have more," burst from the lips of the impetuous Mrs. St. Clair, "my father seldom rides, my husband never. I will bring our carriage around to you every day—we will ride and go where you like—what is a carriage to *me* without you sitting beside me, sweetheart. I will never put a foot in a carriage, if you don't ride with me; indeed I *never* will. Father will feel distressed enough when he hears of this, I can tell you."

Clara laid her head on Blonde's shoulder and cried till her little daughter commenced to scream with sympathy for her mother's distress. Blonde raised her little god-child to her lap and soothed her into silence: then she said,

"Clara, I know how dearly you love me, and desire my happiness; but do not unnerve me, now. Dry up your tears and come with me, till I show you what pictures and books I am going to take with me to the cottage. I have a little picture too, which you have never seen. I prize it so much, for it is the face of a friend in heaven—come, don't be foolish, sweetest, or you will make me helpless too, and I have so much to do—come."

Mrs. St. Clair followed the graceful mourner through the various apartments of the mansion, and Blonde pointed out to her, the many beautiful paintings which she had brought from her tour in Europe, and the little marbles and bronzes, all of which were to grace the rooms of the little cottage in the edge of the town. She pointed out also the extensive library of her brother, for which a little room in the cottage had been selected. Several small tables of Italian manufacture, inlaid with variegated marbles, were designated by her as proper to be removed. But the great bulk of the splendid rosewood and mahogany furniture of the mansion, was to be sold for the benefit of Mr. Grayson's creditors. The elegantly-carved buffet of black walnut, with its mirrors, and silver plate and cut glass and gold-bordered china sets, was to follow the fate of the furniture, and be sacrificed to the auctioneer's hammer. Then Blonde opened a little drawer of her dressing-table, and took out a small oval miniature painted on ivory, and said,

"I will show you my friend's picture after we are in the garden—come to the little grape arbor by the fountain, where we have passed so many happy hours together. It may be the last time we shall sit together in that familiar little nook. I am going to carry little Clara, she is so tired following us up and down stairs."

Blonde raised the little girl in her arms, and the child put her fat white arm around her god-mother's neck. And thus they descended to the hall and out into the garden, Mrs. St. Clair following sadly behind. They entered the octagon grape arbor and sat down. The little daughter played with Blonde's great Newfoundland dog, which had solemnly followed them from the door-steps.

"Do you know the face, Clara?" said Blonde, extending her hand with the miniature. Mrs. St. Clair examined it. It was a fair lady, apparently twenty-five or thirty years of age, with regular, delicately-chiseled features, and dark-looking hair, simply dressed and smoothed back from the snowy forehead. The figure was full length, slight, dressed in dark velvet, and standing alone in a green meadow. The eyes were large, radiant with love and character, and gleaming with the soft azure of heaven. Clara pronounced it to be Mrs. Lansing, before her ill health came on.

"How did you obtain possession of it, Blonde? I should think the family would consider it too precious to leave their hands."

The fair mourning figure placed her arm around Clara's waist, and looking over at the miniature in her friend's hand, replied:

"Gurty Lansing copied it for me from the original, which his mother gave him during her life, and which she charged him to give to Henry Lansing, if he ever returned."

"Is it possible, he can execute so delicate a work as that? The touches on these eyebrows and corners of the mouth are very delicate, and the blue of the eye is something so lustrous, that I never saw it equaled before. He is only seventeen, I think."

Blonde answered, enthusiastically, "Oh! that is nothing for *him* to do: he cares nothing for copying—that is mere play. He can originate with great power and beauty. He seldom exhibits his pieces, for he has peculiar ideas of when the proper time shall come, to display his gift to the world. But I am trespassing upon his secrets. You have seen, however, his painting of the flying brigand—you know what I mean—that was painted long ago. He is wonderfully improved since then. He is a noble-hearted youth, and he is very fond of me—but Mrs. Bounce provokes and torments him so about coming here, that he is really unhappy. He is independent enough; but his nature is delicate, and every thrust wounds him terribly. I hope he will soon recover from that dreadful fever."

"He is nearly well, now," said Mrs. St. Clair. "Doctor Mosely came to vaccinate Clara, yesterday, and he told me Gurty Lansing would soon be able to ride out. The Doctor says Gurty has wound himself tightly around his heart, and he intends to advise Mr. Lansing to send him to Italy for two or three years. His health demands it, for he has overtasked his brain studying mathematics late at night, and the doctor thinks art is the vocation selected for him by nature. Oh! Blonde, the doctor asked me if you ever intended to marry, and I told him to come and ask you. He laughed, and said he hoped I would not consider him rude in asking from Miss Grayson's friend, what every marriageable gentleman in C—— was daily and anxiously enquiring about. We discussed you pleasantly for some time, and in the course of our conversation, I fancied that he intimated gently, that some friend of his was deeply interested in you, and I think he mentioned that his friend was very young. A queer idea struck me that it was Gurty Lansing."

Blonde had taken the miniature from her friend, and was intently studying it as Clara spoke. But as the last word met her ear, she looked up at Mrs. St. Clair, and said, with emphasis;

"Nonsense! he is a mere boy—what could have put that strange conceit into your head."

"Only this, Blonde, that the young gentleman whom you call a boy, and who is nearly eighteen years of age, is so exceedingly devoted to your society, that the young girls in town can never even get a peep at him. You can not be unconscious, that he is a perfect Adonis. Like that mythical beauty, he has been partly educated in the wild woods by the wood-nymphs; you have seen him often enough amid wild scenery, with his gun. And then there are other resemblances. Adonis was forced to divide his attentions; six months he tarried in the society of Venus; the other six he was forced to spend with Proserpine, the goddess of the infernal regions. Blonde, that means Gurty Lansing devotes all the time to you that he can escape from the presence of Proserpine, whom I take to be Mrs. Bounce."

Mrs. St. Clair shouted with laughter at her own conceit, and her friend was forced to laugh too, for the gossips of C—— had freely commented on the rival influences of Blonde and

Mrs. Bounce upon the young artist's disposition of his leisure hours. It was well understood in the town that the present mistress of the manor, though anxious herself to court popularity with the *people*, and on occasions to waive the dignity of her aristocratic position for the purpose of securing power, was nevertheless opposed to Gurty following her example. It was known that Judge Peyton and the deceased Mr. Grayson had both attained position and wealth from the exercise of their intellects and industry alone. They were strictly *of the people.* Hence Mrs. Bounce's opposition to her brother's frequenting the society of these two families. The fact that these families were high Churchmen rendered their intimacy with her brother still more objectionable. Mrs. Lansing's feeling of aristocracy and family pride had arisen from her very nature. Her aristocracy resembled a pure, elevated star, unapproachable, and yet universally beloved for its cheering and useful radiance. But that of Mrs. Bounce was like a miserable and frugal taper, standing in a magnificent and ancient candlestick of gold, now timidly flickering into darkness, then suddenly and unexpectedly flaring out from its untwisting and uneven wick.

When Blonde Grayson could compose her features, she said impressively,

"Don't cherish this absurd idea any longer. Gurty Lansing is a pure poetical nature. It is a lonely nature too, at times. He craves affection and congeniality. He does not find either in his sister. His father loves him to distraction, since his eldest son is lost. But the old gentleman's tastes and occupations preclude the idea of great familiarity. Gurty turns naturally elsewhere for society and sympathy. He finds it with Carl and myself. He asked me if I would not be a sister to him. I consented, so far as it lay in my power. That is the relation existing between us, and you must ascribe every action on his part towards me to that relation and to that alone. Every other construction put upon our intercourse is preposterous, and excites my mirth. I assure you that this is truth."

As she concluded, Mrs. St. Clair, who had been looking towards the street through the matted leaves of the grape arbor, exclaimed,

"Here is the Lansing carriage with the coachman in livery, driving up to this door I never knew that to occur but once before in years. What is the sensation to be now, I wonder? There is Doctor Mosely in the carriage, and some figure seated beside him whom I do not recognize. Look through this place, Blonde, you can see here, where there are fewer leaves."

The graceful figure of the mourner parted the grape leaves with her hand, in eager curiosity, and looked forth upon the street. The Lansing carriage had certainly stopped before the gate of the Grayson mansion. Doctor Mosely was giving some directions to Norman Prince, who had noticed the approach of the carriage and gone down the garden walk to meet it.

"I see who it is, Clara. Doctor Mosely has wrapped Gurty Lansing up in blanket shawls, and taken him out to ride. I see his face, and it is very pale. Poor boy! Let us go down to the carriage—they evidently do not intend to come in."

There was no chilling Mrs. Bounce in the carriage, and the two friends did not hesitate to walk down the garden path to see the invalid, with the little Clara walking between them. As Doctor Mosely saw them approaching the gate, he raised his hat, and then rising from his seat, turned to look over the back of the carriage, and beckoned with his hand to some unseen person behind. As the physician sat down again, one of the stable boys of the manor rode up to the side of the Lansing carriage, mounted on a spirited chestnut steed, which Blonde recognized instantly as the gelding on which she had won the golden cup several years before.

CHAPTER XXII.

As the two friends passed through the gate which Norman Prince opened for them, and advanced to greet the invalid, Doctor Mosely alighted and stood beside the carriage. He engaged Mrs. St. Clair in conversation while Blonde went up to Gurty's side and held a long and confidential interview with the invalid in a low tone. The young artist wore his student's cap of gray silk on the side of his head, and from under the band his wavy silken hair of light brown hue fell away almost to his shoulders. His hair inclined to curl, and its fine glossy texture was lifted by the faintest passing breeze and tossed about his cheeks and neck. His countenance was thin and wasted by the fever. But his blue eyes, the perfect copy of the wonderful eyes of the deceased Mrs. Lansing, were now two flames of fire in his happiness and interest at being once more in the presence of Blonde. He spoke feelingly of the goodness and skill of the physician who had saved his life. He was entirely ignorant, however, of the narrow escape he had made by the inhuman neglect of his sister to administer the contents of the red vial. He was smoothly shaved, wearing no indication of that feeble beard and moustache which is the pride of students of his age. His small mouth was as graceful and delicate as a woman's, and was wreathed with smiles as he listened to Blonde.

Presently the physician turned to Blonde and said,

"I imagine you have been made acquainted by this time with your beautiful present, Miss Grayson."

The graceful mourner was of course obliged to utter the ignorance she looked at these strange words:

"Certainly not—you speak in riddles, doctor! Presents to me are like angels' visits."

Gurty Lansing interrupted, speaking, however, with great effort.

"That chestnut gelding, Blonde, has been given to me by my father, and I have brought him with me to present to you, if you will accept the gift. Mrs. Bounce has taken a great dislike to the horse and had persuaded father to sell him to-day. I entreated father to give him to me to dispose of as I liked, and I succeeded. I have presented him to you, for I felt confident you would be pleased to have the horse that won the golden cup for you on my birth-day. Why that expression? Have I pained you?"

Poor Blonde! She could not conceal her agitation. She blushed, and then turned deathly pale. The carriage, the elm trees, and her companions seemed to reel and stagger around her. Mortification, wounded pride and despair struggled fiercely in her bosom. O, how could she tell them of her poverty, her inability to accept and keep the present! Ah! that magnificent gift—that high-bred steed, on which she had won her triumph over rank and beauty—that glorious beast, with which her skill had been published to the world, could not be accepted. Blonde had become too poor to incur the additional expense of keeping the gelding. That which a few months since would have caused her heart to exult, was now to be the occasion of publishing her ruin and her humiliation. She had even forgotten, in her resólute purpose to curtail her expenses, that passion which she must surrender also. Could she give up horseback riding? Worse than all, could she refuse that gift? The possession of that beautiful steed would be a triumph over Mrs. Bounce, who had maligned and persecuted her—a triumph which the whole town would hear repeated like wild fire. The *pride* of the manor stables was offered to her by the considerate hands of her friend Gurty. She knew Mrs. Bounce hated the gelding on account of her triumph at the birthday races. How bitterly, how keenly would the proud widow feel that her malice against the gelding had actually placed him in Blonde's possession, through Gurty's tact and coolness in preventing the sale. That widow had persistently and without provocation, ever since the time of Blonde's arrival in C——, persecuted and hunted her. Every mean and contemptible slander that human ingenuity could invent, Mrs. Bounce had started against her. Oh, with what exultant pride could she mount that gelding now and dash along the thoroughfares of C——, past the carriage containing Mrs. Bounce, in the sight of the whole population! The poor orphan was human, and she faltered for a moment under the violence of the temptation. Then shame came tempting her with his shrinking, half averted face. How could she tell those keen eyes about her, which already looked puzzled and astonished at her hesitation, that she was suddenly poor, barely able to find means to live, and that the gelding was not for such as her. The talent and the excellence of the town had followed in her train. Her society and her entertainments were eagerly sought after. She had been a queen of the social circle. Now she was too poor to accept a gift.

Another reflection came trailing its strange pleasure over her soul. A few years back and one word from her lips then spoken would have placed her in the sole charge of the manor as the heir's wife. When he devised the form of the golden cup, he was hoping in his secret heart that she might win it. The prize cup had been given up in generosity. Must she give up the greater glory, the ownership of the magnificent gelding? The cup would not long have attracted envious attention on her parlor mantle. But the gelding; ah! *that* would be a daily pride bounding along the broad, elm-guarded streets of C——.

"There goes the great racer that won the prize at the manor races, and there goes his successful rider and owner," and what if the lost heir should return and know of her ownership? At that thought her blue eyes took on again their look of far off, impenetrable mystery.

She faltered for a moment in her purpose; but her great soul was Christian. "Pursue the right at every sacrifice of feeling, pride, or self," whispered the Christian conscience. She had struggled once before with herself in the dreadful secret of the murder. Then had her sense of right gloriously triumphed. This was a less painful struggle, less burdened with anguish and with doubt. In this Blonde could not fail to follow out the right

Her eye grew calm, her gentle smile returned, and frankly, fully, she told all her poverty and ruin, and how it grieved her to refuse the gift. She said, "My father's creditors would suffer if I did my duty by that horse."

Gurty Lansing looked proudly and affectionately at his lily friend for a moment, studying her radiant beauty in the mourning robe. Then he said,

"When I am well enough to ride, if I will bring the gelding around to your cottage door, will you be kind enough, sometimes, to accompany me on horseback? I shall never part with this horse till my brother returns. It never shall belong to any person but you or him."

"Oh, yes, Gurty; I will do nearly everything to gratify you," she said, but studying in her mind at that moment what Doctor Mosely could be inspecting her countenance for, in that searching, professional way, habitual to him when he was contemplating a patient. Whatever the physician saw in her face unusual, he remained silent and a listener until the time had come when it was proper for the invalid to ride on. Then Doctor Mosely bade the friends farewell in his gentle way and sat down again by his patient in the carriage. The Lansing livery soon disappeared down the street, and behind the receding carriage followed the stable-boy of the manor riding the rejected gift.

As Mrs. St. Clair walked slowly up to the mansion with her friend, leading her little daughter, she said,

"Did you notice the expression of Doctor Mosely's eye? Blonde, he is in love with you, and I am really sorry. You have no pity. I know that all he said about a young friend taking such profound interest in you, is all humbug. He merely said that as a blind to conceal his own sentiment about you. I cannot be mistaken in the language of his eye at the carriage. He loves you, and he cannot conceal it. The reason I was deceived in thinking he must have been speaking to me in the interest of some young friend of his was his attentions to Mrs. Bounce. Have you heard of his horseback rides with her?"

Blonde was still thinking of her mortification at being obliged to refuse Gurty's gift. Her friend's remarks about the doctor's passion for her passed with scarcely any notice. She cared nothing for him, or his sentiments towards herself, except that she admired him as her physician, and liked to be on good terms with him as a recognized leader of the literary and musical clubs of the town. But when her friend mentioned the widow's name in connection with the physician, her curiosity was aroused. She might now be able to torment Mrs. Bounce in retaliation for her persistent persecution of herself. It was with no little interest in her tone, then, that she asked a more complete history of the physician's attentions to the widow at the manor. Mrs. St. Clair was surprised at her entire ignorance of the subject which was the present sensation of C——.

"Why, Blonde, everybody is talking about it. It commenced first by the doctor's going to the manor to attend Gurty; but since then, while Gurty has been sitting up, he goes there regularly every morning, and always stays an hour. Gurty has been sitting up several weeks. And then many afternoons, oh! I don't know how many, the doctor has invited Mrs. Bounce to ride with him, and they take right long rides, too; and once he went to her church with her, and it has made a great talk, for you know he never goes anywhere except to the Methodist church, and very seldom he goes there even. It is very strange, for he loves *you*. I saw it in his eyes just now. I tell you, Blonde, you can take him away from her without the slightest difficulty. I know you can: and, to tell the truth, I wish you would, for the fun of the thing. She thinks she can do anything as the mistress of the manor, and I wish you would encourage Doctor Mosely a little, just to *take her down*. It would do her conceit so much good."

"It is a strong temptation, Clara," she replied; "but I am so busy with my troubles and my cares now, that I cannot think of anything else. I know that she deserves a little humiliation, but I am not the one to administer it to her. She may have the doctor, for all I care. There is poor Carl just going out to conclude the contract for the lease of the cottage. He will chafe more at being poor than I will. And here is my splendid Newfoundland. I am glad *he* is going with us."

* * * * * *

It was several weeks before Blonde Grayson and her brother were finally settled in their new home. When the intelligence of their misfortune was circulated about the town, shopkeepers and other creditors lost no time in sending in their bills. The blue eyes of the orphan mistress of the little cottage were often occasioned a look of anxiety at the number and amounts of the forgotten bills which came pouring in for settlement. But finally the pulls at the cottage bell ceased altogether, and Blonde breathed freely once more that she was clear of debt. Her new house was a two-story Grecian cottage with eight comfortable rooms. She was astonished at the amount of pleasure and comfort possible in small apartments Her fine paintings looked grandly forth from the simple walls of her parlor and library. Her own tiny bed-room looked as pure and white as so many little objects covered with drifted snow. Its single window was draped in spotless muslin, drawn aside by simple blue ribbons. Her low bedstead of blue painted pine was covered also with a snowdrift-looking counterpane; and in a corner stood her oaken table, draped low in white, on which appeared her silver candlesticks and her prayer book. The small dining-room was occupied also by her brother Carl as a painter's studio. He was a finished artist, and cherished reasonable anticipations of securing the patronage of many families in C——. His portraits had ever been esteemed marvels.

The front of the cottage was graced with a narrow piazza, and from its small, round fluted columns, the white honeysuckles nodded a fragrant welcome. A small garden encircled the building, and in the rear a clear spring bubbled under the protecting shade of two young elm trees. The locality was healthful, being far from the densely packed buildings of the town; and from the windows on one side of the cottage the eye could range over the green fields which extended on either side of the highway, or continuation of the principal street leading past the retired and hidden myrtle dell.

Blonde soon discovered that from the small side window of her little parlor, where she had placed her chintz-covered rocking-chair and her work-stand, that she could rarely fail to discover when the members of the Lansing family visited the town. She could see their vehicles and their livery flashing through the fields until the highway led them past her cottage into the main street of C——. Occasionally Mrs. Bounce had seen her in her small garden and bowed to her with that cold, disapproving manner which seems to say, "I haven't character and independence enough to cut you outright, so take this nod for custom's sake." Blonde returned her bow only when she felt in particularly good humor. But she noticed that after an indifferent cut from herself, Mrs. Bounce always took particular pains on the next passing to infuse a trifle more sweetness into her bow. Tricky and malicious gossips have such a wonderful anxiety not to be cut by the victims of their slanders.

The widow happened to be passing in her carriage one afternoon, after Blonde was firmly established in her cottage, and had experienced the first feeling of home. Gurty Lansing was assisting Blonde to mount the chestnut gelding, and his own favorite saddle horse stood by. Mrs. Bounce's snaky eyes flashed fire as she bowed. Blonde did not fancy the style of her bow, and paid no attention. She did not consider it lady-like to respond to such bows. But Gurty, who witnessed the whole performance, laughed and said, "Sister puts on her Mount Sinai bow to-day. She thinks I am consorting with the Gentiles. You'll see a sweeter expression than that on her after fifteen minutes, for she is going to ride with Doctor Mosely this evening." This information did not appear to please Blonde, though she smiled faintly. The truth was that the doctor had failed to visit her as often as she had anticipated in her humble cottage. With the exception of Mrs. St. Clair, who came every day in her carriage, and Gurty Lansing who sometimes came oftener, there were few calls of civility at the cottage. The bell rang often,but they were calls generally on Carl, who was rapidly receiving orders for portraits. The rector of St. Paul's visited her frequently, notwithstanding his recollection of the scene in old Rosy's garden. He loved her unselfishly, and he had even contrived, on some plausible pretext, to have her allow him to place in her little parlor, a valuable melodeon. He had purchased it for her, but she was entirely unconscious of the gift, and imagined she was doing him a service. Her own magnificent piano-forte had gone under the auctioneer's hammer.

But Blonde had confidently counted on the physician's society. At first she ascribed his neglect to the urgency of his extensive professional business. But when she discovered that he found time to ride so often with the widow, she experienced a feeling of jealousy and rivalry for Mrs. Bounce, which was entirely new to her, and for which she could not satisfactorily account to herself. She knew well enough that the respected and favorite physician had made no impression on her heart. She enjoyed his society for his genial nature, and appreciation of music, and every intellectual or refined enjoyment which gratified herself. But he came never to the cottage, except during a slight indisposition of her brother. He lingered long with her then, it is true, and appeared reluctant to leave her.

But he never came again. Hence her disturbed expression at Gurty Lansing's remark. Mrs. St. Clair, who furnished Blonde with the current gossip of the town, informed her of the report that the doctor and the widow were engaged. But Gurty Lansing hooted at the idea, and strenuously maintained that his friend, the physician, had too much sense and liberality to form any such connection. The young artist and the doctor were fast friends. They were often seen riding together, and were known to be very intimate. Had Gurty known as much of his obligation to the doctor for saving his life as the negro coachman knew, he would have worshiped the man. But the physician had directed Norman Prince to hold his peace concerning the attempted crime, and the negro acquiesced; but his faithful eyes kept all the brighter watch on the movements of Mrs. Bounce, and his position as servant to the doctor, gave him many opportunities to study the working of her dark scheming mind. The negro, at Mr. Lansing's request, still quietly entered the old deserted manor house at night, and provided for his beloved Black Hawk. He considered himself entitled, by his birth and life on the manor, to look after the interests of his friends there. He once said to Doctor Mosely, with his chuckling laugh—"Norman Prince am the black guardian angel of that manor."

But whatever rivalry may have arisen in Blonde Grayson's mind to the widow on the doctor's account, an event soon occurred which swept away that feeling from her recollection altogether. A more serious and interesting subject of thought was destined to arise upon her retired and humble life in the little cottage.

One warm evening, early in the month of September, Blonde Grayson sat alone on the front piazza of her cottage. Her brother Carl had gone to visit some friend in the town. The efficient girl, who was both cook and maid for the little family, had obtained permission also to visit her acquaintances far up the street. Blonde was entirely alone, with the exception of the great Newfoundland dog, which lay stretched on the grass before her. The moon was struggling with the drifting clouds, now lighting every object with almost the distinctness of day, then slowly passing away into darkness again behind the cloud veil. The excited imagination might easily detect danger in the skulking shadows which slowly passed between her and the street. But when the moon appeared again, the objects of alarm revealed themselves in the well known outlines of some familiar bush or fence. Still there was an uncertain and terrifying effect produced by the fluctuating light and shadow, and the fair girl, though possessed of extraordinary nerve for her sex was not insensible to the loneliness and isolation of her home She sincerely wished her brother or the maid would return As the moon disappeared once more, she heard a step approahcing from the street. It sounded to her ear *stealthy.* Her eye dilated as she vainly endeavored to identify the approaching stranger. A protecting voice sounded near at hand. The Newfoundland dog raised his head, and uttered a low, warning growl. The unknown footstep halted. Then a voice:

"Miss Grayson, I would like to see you, but I am afraid of your dog."

Blonde called the Newfoundland to her side, and said,

"Who are you? I have heard that voice before. I do not recognize it now. Come in, sir—the dog will not molest you. I have him beside me."

The figure advanced once more, and at that instant the moon burst away from the veiling clouds and revealed the face of the intruder.

"Oh! Mr. Delaplaine, how do you do? Pardon my stupidity in not recognizing you. I am entirely alone, and have to rely upon this faithful brute for protection. Please take a seat on the piazza—it is far more agreeable out here this warm night than in the parlor. Here, sir, you will find this arm chair of my brother a more comfortable seat than the stool."

The Rev. Thomas Delaplaine advanced to the proffered chair on the piazza, and sat down beside the tall, slim figure of the mourner. He had not spoken to Blonde since the memorable day of the races on the manor, years before. They had occasionally exchanged bows on the street; nothing more had ever passed between them since their meeting on the manor. Their mutual recollections of each other were agreeable. They had been brought together on that day as the defenders of Henry Lansing, at a time of great public excitement.

After a few congratulatory remarks upon the often noticed beauty and simplicity of Blonde's cottage and garden, the clergyman proceeded to disclose the purpose of his visit. It was substantially this. He desired to learn from her, as an employer long familiar with the character of Norman Prince, the negro coachman, what reliance was to be placed in the sense and the veracity of the servant. The negro had come to the reverend gentleman, as his spiritual friend and adviser, and communicated to him in a frightened manner, but in a well-connected tale, certain mysterious manifestations of the presence of immaterial beings in the old deserted manor house of the Lansing family. In other words the negro had informed him that the quaint old tenement where he nightly attended to Black Hawk was *haunted*, and that he was afraid to go there any more to attend to his night duty. Strange noises had occurred in the deserted chambers overhead. Footsteps had been heard moving about through the hollow sounding apartments which could be traced to no human agency. The negro with his lantern had carefully searched every room in the old tenement, but found only bare walls and oaken floors devoid of furniture. The closets were examined, but were found to be perfectly empty. Not a trace of human life could be found—and the negro had concluded that the night winds had been playing tunes around the old building, and had worked upon his imagination. But on other nights the sounds had been repeated, and when the air out of doors was perfectly still. He had heard the footsteps sound overhead, and even on the same floor where he kept Black Hawk, *tramp, tramp, tramp*. Finally, one stormy night, when the moon shone distinctly notwithstanding the roaring of the wind, he had looked through a crack of a great oaken door on the first floor, and had seen distinctly the figure of a venerable old man enter the building by an outside door, and move slowly across the room to the stairs, ascend them, and disappear. The negro had hastened around the building, entered the same door with his lantern, and run up the stairs in search of the intruder, but could find nothing. On another occasion he had seen through the same wide crack, another figure, ascending slowly up the stairs, dressed in black, with a dark slouched hat and a very pale face, to whose identity he was willing to swear, for he loved him better than any created thing. It was, in his firm belief, the restless spirit of the long-lost *Henry Lansing*.

CHAPTER XXIII.

Blonde Grayson shivered as she listened. The moon veiled itself once more, and the low shrubbery seemed to sigh in the passing darkness. After a brief silence, the moon came out again, and the light fell full upon the uncovered head of the clergyman. His gaze was directed searchingly and solemnly into her countenance. Then she spoke, seriously:

"Do you believe, Mr. Delaplaine, that disembodied and restless spirits are permitted to return and visit familiar haunts of their former life?"

The clergyman answered, slowly and guardedly, but keeping his clear, hazel eyes still fixed upon her serious and lovely face:

"I know of nothing in the tenets of my church, which forbids such a belief. We take our vows in the presence of God, and His holy angels, without defining the scope of that presence, or its locality. We believe that an evil spirit goeth about to injure and decoy souls. We do not define the omnipresence of that evil spirit, nor the number of seducing evil ones sent to tempt the world. We consider such studies unnecessary and profitless, and unfathomable. As an individual speculating, in the free exercise of thought, upon the unexplored and marvelous, I can see no absurdity either in holding or rejecting the belief to which you allude. I find pleasurable emotion in the thought that my mother's spirit guards me, close at hand. I cannot reject the alternative, or rather the disagreeable proposition that the lost companions of my youth may still be allowed to tempt me to sin. I believe that the supernatural mysteries occurring by the hands of the Apostles would have induced the belief in my mind that those mysteries actually happened. I do not believe I should have questioned whether or not, by some dexterity of hand, a new and powerful medicine was communicated to the sick, who recovered beneath their touch. I believe I should now acknowledge the actuality of a mystery which showed me face to face the incorporeal dead."

The reverend gentleman paused, while Blonde was absorbed in meditations arising from his words. Then he continued:

"But my purpose, Miss Grayson, in calling, was not to study the movements of the dead. If this negro is not over excitable or imaginative, and his statements are usually clear and correct, the heir of the manor may have actually returned from his mysterious wanderings, and be desirous of concealing his return from the community. I knew him many years. He was wild, intellectual, generous. He never committed that murder, I feel assured. His motives for concealment no one can surmise. Nevertheless, it is proper that the friends of his angel mother should secretly investigate the matter, and if he is really here endeavor to convey to him the intelligence of his danger, and the cordial sympathy and affection of his friends and supporters. I fear he may be hung for murder on the singular circumstantial evidence accumulated, and which years seem not to have unraveled. I admired Henry Lansing, and I cannot see harm done to a single hair of his head."

Blonde said, warmly, awaking from her reverie: "I am so happy to meet a friend of his; and you can rely on me always for any aid to help him in this frightful affair. I know Norman Prince to be perfectly truthful, and that his highest ambition has been to see Henry Lansing once more upon the manor. But what the negro has seen there I cannot tell. Henry Lansing believed in the return of the dead sometimes to the earth. His lovely mother told me that she believed in the same startling theory. If you will allow me to show you something in a private record of Henry Lansing, which is in my possession, and which you have a sort of right to see, as his mother's trusted friend and confidential adviser, I will read it to you under the seal of confidence and silence. It matters not how it came into my possession, but it will exhibit to you his ideas of the old, deserted manor house, and its spiritual tenants."

The clergyman expressed in grateful tones his desire to see these traces of the lost heir's secret meditations, and share these glimpses of his inner life, promising the required silence. Blonde conducted him into her little parlor, and lighted her lamp. Then she disappeared in her snow white bed-room, returning in a few seconds with the long guarded and cherished Journal of Henry Lansing. Old Rosy had made her its final custodian. The clergyman drew his chair close to her little table, Blonde opened the Journal, drew the lamp nearer to her mourning figure, and, bowing her golden hair, read aloud:

"*Oct.* 12, 18–2.—*Reveries in the Ancestral Ruin.*—Strange it is that I love to linger in this deserted old place. The distant clock in the church tower tells me that evening is at hand. I can see through this open door the shadows of the trees lengthen, these venerable old trees whose arms have sheltered generations of my proud family. I have loitered here long and alone. Am I indeed alone? My question is repeated from wall to wall of this old tenement, and the answer comes back to me again in hollow tones, 'alone.' These walls are of the earth, material; their answer, therefore, cannot satisfy the spiritual. I am not alone. My mother tells me of the glorious past. My race have nobly served the cause of God and man. Shall I be worthy of the golden name I bear? I must not linger here in reverie. I must be up and doing, to win my right to glory in my family. They all, from year to year, have served a noble destiny. They have been useful, giving to the State their services, political and military, and to their fellow men professional assistance and material aid. To benefit mankind is godlike. For this service to humanity, my ancestors have won their names. I will not, I cannot permit the glory of the ancestral torch to dim. But let me tarry here a little longer. I seem always to leave this place with higher aims in life, and nobler purposes. Why is it? Ah! I am surrounded by the great and the invisible departed.—They are gathering about me now, to whisper and encourage. I am not alone. I can see yet in this fading twilight, the arrow and the bullet marks of the battle. Ah! the hurrying forms around me are the spectres of the past. The sheeted dead are coming in for shelter, women and children and strong men. Brave souls are carrying guns and muskets, and I see the bullet pouches and the powder horns. This brave, strong man with the eagle eye and the commanding mien, is a familiar face. My grandfather! How noble a countenance to be a traitor to his king. Undying, unshrinking loyalty seems written on that forehead. But the fundamental law is trampled down; constitutional rights are no longer heeded, and the strong man must strike to save his manhood and the freedom of his children. They are barricading the windows of the old manor house, and barring the stout oaken doors. My grandfather is commanding, and all obey. The loyalist and the subject has become the disloyal citizen. Why this? The king has become the usurper and defies the law. But subserviency will bring my grandfather gold and a wider manor. Ha! ha! how grimly he smiles at that, my noble old grandfather. Peace at the sacrifice of pride and precious liberty! Shall I ever be like that stern, grimly smiling patriot? By the magic of that glimpse I have now into his heroic face, I will never bow to storms of wrong. I'll rather die. See that long rifle in his hands! How firmly he clutches it as the women and the children at his command kneel low behind him to escape the tory bullets and the whistling arrows of their Indian allies. And there is a youth of only sixteen kneeling with his musket at the upper barricade. What brought him here? His father owns a wide domain; and the king offers this son a commission and a golden fee if he will only serve the king by defending his own loyal father's place from the rebels. Ask that youth why he is here if you wish to see fire flash from his eyes. He never sacrificed the right for lucre, or for ease. Thank God! that young hero was my mother's uncle. But the old tenement is alive with riflemen, and they are securing loopholes; for yonder, through the myrtle dell, come the soldiers, with glistening muskets, and the yells of the Indians are in the forest. Listen to that hissing sound! Zip—zip—zip—come the king's bullets. Surrender now, and your miserable lives will be spared! Never! never! shouts my grandfather. We will die for the right, and for the people. And the noble little band rout the king's forces, though patriots stain this floor with blood. Shall I, the grandchild, ever yield, and bow the truckling knee to wrong?

"But the sheeted dead have passed in victory. Ah! the darkness gathers faster about me. Who passes so stately in his gray, flowing hair, with the scroll in his venerable hand? My grandfather, the statesman, serving the people; and, as his shadowy form goes by, he points ahead, and beckons me then to come, following in his footsteps. Venerable and useful dead Henry Lansing, the grandson, will try.

"As I sit here in the darkness, my mother's words come to me again: 'When you were a child, your grandfather was thin, and gray, and venerable with age, and, taking you on his aged knee, he said, "Your eye is the eye of a noble race: let it never look on dishonor, or shame, or wrong, with approval. Live, fight, die, for the right, and for your fellow man."' My mother believes his spirit haunts this place, and so do I.—Hark to the venerable tramp! Nearer and nearer it comes, and now I see him, shadowy and dim, pointing the path of right and honor out to me. I am stronger, firmer in my purpose now. I will live for others.

"I believe now in the spiritual presence of the dead. I have seen him here. Even now his tramp is dying away through these hollow rooms. I, too, at last shall come to visit familiar scenes after my earth mission is ended. Through these vacant halls I shall tread, with my mother and my noble ancestry, all shadowy, dim, and slowly, passing by. Oh! may my shade likewise move some one of my race to live a virtuous, useful, noble life.

"I am writing now by the starlight in my journal. I go once more to the presence of the living. I must transcribe lines appropriate to this scene and place before their mystic beauty leaves my memory. They tell me the lines were written by the accomplished pen of the believer, *Verona Coe.*

"'THE OLD HOUSE.

"'Brown roof covered with ivy,
That trails over window and door,
Crawls through the chinks in the gables,
To sleep on the garret floor.
Cracks, where the magical sunshine
Checkers the wall with gold,
Plays at bo-peep with the shadows
That lurk in the corners old.

"'Shingles atune to the rain-drops,
That dance to the song of the breeze,
As it beats out a march on the chimney,
And whistles a waltz in the trees.
Homely old porch where the creepers
Are weaving their emerald screen,
And twining around the worn pillars
Their tremulous fingers of green.

"'Comical, old-fashioned windows,
Under the low-drooping eaves,
Peering askance at the sunshine
That glows in the shivering leaves.
Open door, propped by the footstool
That grandfather made long ago,
Ere his head grew white 'neath the harvest
Of many dim winters of snow.

'" Here's the path winding out through the clover,
To the nook where the cool shadows fall,
Over the spring and the runnel,
That sings 'neath the vine-covered wall;
Where the trembling boughs of the willow
Droop lovingly over the brink;
Where the grass grows rank, and the mosses
Creep down on the curb-stone to drink.

"'And I hear, as the bubbling waters
Fall over the smooth white stone,
A voice, as it were, welling upward
From the breast of the old time gone.
Oh! from out on life's wearisome ocean,
Old pleasures will never return;
They have floated away from their moorings,
And hopelessly drifted astern.

"'Yet they, who once peopled the homestead,
In the days of the beautiful yore,
Still come in the gray of the gloaming,
From their homes in the blest "Evermore."
From the land that lies, aye, in the sunshine,
To linger about the old home,
And their voices, like far away music,
Are awake in each shadowy room.'"

As the music of Blonde's voice died away, she slowly raised her eyes to the clergyman's face. His look froze her blood. He was staring in horror at the open window behind her. She turned quickly, and beheld the motionless, pale face of *Henry Lansing's ghost.*

She uttered one scream of terror and fell senseless to the floor. The spectre vanished.

The Rev. Thomas Delaplaine was, by nature, a courageous man, notwithstanding his medium height and his delicate frame. Had a ruffian attempted an entrance at the open window to molest Blonde, he would most assuredly have shown fight. But this pale, incorporeal face of whom they were both thinking, confirmed the negro's tale, slowly passing before the window in the lonely moonlight. When the apparition vanished, the clergyman, still nervous and excited, raised the inanimate figure of Blonde in his arms and drew her along to the parlor lounge. He placed her as comfortably as he could upon it, and adjusted the cushion under her head, his hands trembling all the while with nervous excitement. He looked at her motiorless mourning figure for a few seconds utterly ignorant of what step to take next. Fortunately for him, the maid returned from her visit, and he heard her footsteps approaching the little parlor. She seemed astonished at the strange tableau, and would have retreated from him in alarm. But he reassured her by stating his name and sacred profession, and informed her that her mistress had fallen in an unaccountable swoon. He was already sufficiently recovered from his fright to feel ashamed of acknowledging the real occasion of the trouble. Like many to whom the dead appeared at the crucifixion on Calvary, the clergyman was unwilling to acknowledge the mystery until it was found to be popular. The maid quickly flew around for restoratives for her unconscious mistress, while the reverend gentleman seized his hat and hastened after Blonde's physician. The distance to the doctor's office was a long walk, and the Rev. Thomas Delaplaine had abundance of time to collect his wits on the way. The shadows along the street grew each moment less suspicious and startling, and by the time he reached his destination he was fully alive to the fact that if the affair was made public, ridicule was very likely to attach to himself. His presence in the cottage of a high church woman like Blonde Grayson would not be calculated to increase his popularity in his own congregation. If, in addition to this, the mystery of the apparition should leak out, he would have opprobrium enough on his hands to occasion him anything but comfort in C——. Another reflection of a more generous type had its due weight in his mind as he hastened along, and decided him finally to conceal from the physician the real cause of Blonde Grayson's attack. If the ghost was no ghost but the real flesh and blood heir of the manor, to divulge the fact of the apparition would necessarily place the police upon Henry Lansing's track. To avoid this result was the very thing that occasioned his visit to the cottage. He did not wish Norman Prince's glimpse of Henry Lansing in the old manor house to be published to the police until the heir's friends were given an opportunity to have a private consultation with the wanderer. His love for the dead mother prompted his effort to aid the son.

What was the clergyman's dismay on arriving at the doctor's office weary and out of breath, to learn that the physician was out of town attending a country patient, and would not be likely to return under a half hour. Here was another difficulty. If he should summon a strange physician to Blonde's assistance, and Doctor Mosely should have a professional quarrel in consequence, he would have on his head a triple cause of malediction; a high churchwoman, a ghost, and a professional row. The reverend gentlemen was unwilling to complicate his difficulties, and so he sat down in the doctor's office to wait for him. The hands of the physician's little clock appeared to his uneasy mind to travel at an aggravated snail's pace, slower and slower. It was no satisfaction to him to think that the sweetest lady in C—— might die from his neglect to provide speedy medical assistance. His knowledge of favorable and unfavorable symptoms in ghost cases was frightfully limited. Another reflection, which he had abundance of leisure to dwell upon as he waited in the doctor's office, was that if Henry Lansing was corporeally present at the cottage window when his own eyes were dilated to such a remarkable extent, there must be in some locality near the cottage violent laughter and sideaches; that is, if Henry Lansing was still the Henry Lansing of other days. The clergyman recollected that once the wild daredevil of the manor would have deemed it a great success to occasion a hearty laugh at the expense of the high priest of any denomination. It was so like the heir to be a ghost or anything else that would occasion fun that the Rev. Thomas Delaplaine finally was forced into a smile as he awaited the doctor's arrival.

The designated half hour passed, and the physician still failed to make his appearance. The clergyman resolved to tarry still longer. When another quarter of an hour had passed, the physician's wheels rattled rapidly along the street, and finally stopped before the door of his office. The clergyman went out into the moonlight and communicated the intelligence that the mistress of the cottage had fainted unaccountably, and probably needed medical attendance. He avoided any mention, however, of the cause of the swoon.

Doctor Mosely's fervent expression of regret would have sounded to the ears of Mrs. St. Clair very like a confirmation of her opinion expressed to Blonde, that the favorite physician of C—— indulged an extravagant affection for her. He failed to pursue his usual practice of entering his office and consulting his calling slate before starting out anew. He requested the reverend gentleman to step into his buggy beside him, with a hasty, anxious manner, and immediately urged his horse ahead.

As the doctor's horse trotted along rapidly under the elms of C——, after a few minutes' silence the physician asked:

"Is Miss Grayson a friend of yours, Mr. Delaplaine?"

The clergyman stared at the interrogatory, for it was pertinent to the matter of his being alone with Blonde in the cottage on that night. He was a little confused in his manner and tone as he replied,

"No—that is to say—not exactly a friend—but you are aware that Miss Grayson was a friend of Mrs. Lansing, who died on the manor. Oh, no; that was before your time here. Well, Mrs. Lansing cherished a great fondness for Miss Grayson for the active and zealous support she gave to Henry Lansing's friends when the heir ran off and was charged with the murder of Hartwell. Mrs. Lansing never forgot that kindness, and if her daughter, Mrs. Bounce, had not been so bitterly opposed to Miss Grayson, that young lady would have been very intimate with the Lansing family."

"Ah!" exclaimed the doctor, "then Mrs. Bounce and Miss Grayson are rivals, are they."

The discreet clergyman saw breakers ahead, if he was not cautious in answering this enquiry; for he was familiar with the gossip in his congregation, to the effect that these ladies were both expecting the offer of marriage from the physician who was riding beside him. In his anxiety to explain or deceive, as to his presence alone with Miss Grayson at the time of her swoon, he was nearly at the point of circulating gossip into the ear of the identical person to whom the gossip related. It was necessary to be very guarded. So he replied—

" Not rivals, that I know of, but the real difficulty is, that Mrs. Bounce cannot tolerate high church Episcopalians ; and Miss Grayson is known to be an extremist in that way—a sort of church rivalry, you understand."

" Do you mean to say, Mr. Delaplaine," exclaimed the doctor, " that a leading member of your church, like Mrs. Bounce, who enjoys such a reputation for piety and goodness, will allow her church prejudices so far to warp her heart, that she cannot take to her bosom, so accomplished a young lady as Miss Grayson, when that young lady has so earnestly defended her own brother from the charge of murder, that Henry Lansing's mother wished to recognize that kind service by taking that young lady into the intimacy of her own family ? I trust your leading church members are not quite so dogmatic as that, sir."

The clergyman experienced the sensation, usually denominated "cornered," and he thought he could distinguish the doctor's slight chuckle in the pause which ensued. It was dangerous to defend either lady at the expense of the other, for he was ignorant to which lady the doctor was really engaged. He answered the doctor confusedly, thus :

" I trust not, sir—I sincerely hope not—but you know these jealousies of women are unaccountable, sir, very unaccountable. They are both very estimable ladies, both sir—I hear both very highly spoken of."

The doctor laughed heartily at the lame wing the clergyman extended over a leading member of his flock. Then he said, " but you were explaining to me your intimacy with Miss Grayson—you were alone with her, you mentioned, when this swoon occurred. I am really glad, sir, that you have independence enough as a Presbyterian clergyman, to be intimate with a lady whom you pronounce to be a high church extremist. I respect you for it, sir. Mrs. Talbot, of your church, who is one of my patients, assured me that you were uncompromising to the bitter end with high church people, and would consider yourself encouraging Popery by consorting with them in any way. I will undeceive her when I meet her, for your liberality should be published ; it is highly creditable to you, sir, highly."

The Rev. Thomas Delaplaine wished the doctor was at the bottom of the sea. He would now tell Mrs. Talbot, who was the clergyman's terror, of the intimate nature of the calls upon Blonde Grayson, and the elevated terms of praise he had applied to her, that he ran to the doctor as her messenger for her sick calls, and passed pleasant evenings with her. The reverend gentleman was indeed liberal at heart, but he would be tormented out of his life, if Mrs. Talbot knew it. It is the character of some minds to be tolerant, gentle, and kind, and yet to possess the greatest timidity in regard to its being generally known. The Christian impulses of such persons are like the songs of caged birds, never allowed to cheer the gardens and the meadows of God's heritage, but cramped and broken between narrow walls made by cruel hands

Before the clergyman could reply to the physician's remarks, they were at the gate leading to the cottage.

CHAPTER XXIV.

The September morning was cool. The sun shone brightly outside, promising a warm midday, but within the manor house the chill of the past night lingered yet, and a fire was burning in the great library fire-place, to cheer the breakfast party. Mrs. Bounce had ordered breakfast to be served in the library for the first time since her mother's death. Mr. Lansing had a fancy for this change, and she had finally recollected her father's request. The black marble clock on the oaken mantle over the cheerful wood fire, had struck the hour of eight, and still Mrs. Bounce and the servants awaited the coming of the venerable proprietor of the manor. The man-servant, radiant in a dark yellow jacket, with the gold livery buttons and braid of the Lansing family, and wearing white cotton gloves, stood erect near the hall door, holding his silver salver under his arm. Mrs. Bounce sat under the window curtains looking out upon the park. The widow had doffed her funereal robes, and appeared on this bright morning in a black and white plaid silk. Her dark curls were still gathered by her mourning comb, and the jet brooch containing her mother's hair, still secured her dress high in the throat. Her white, fat fingers unconsciously drummed on the window glass, and her mood was wonderfully pleasant. She was thinking of Doctor Mosely. An observer would never dream from her pleasant manner, as her dark eye roved over the park, that the young widow was capable of planning and attempting her young brother's murder. Her attempt, and its complete and mysterious failure, seemed to have left little impression upon the conscience and sensual face of Mrs. Bounce. She was ready for another attempt, whenever another as favorable occasion should arise. She believed murder or marriage attempts should be conducted exclusively on safe principles. Had she found the subtile poisons of Italy, of which she had read, within her reach, she would soon have cleared the way for her exclusive ownership of the manor. But common poisoning agents were too dangerous, and might cost her her life, as well as the manor.

But the woman was uncommonly amiable on this bright morning, for she had made great approaches to the citadel of the physician's heart. She thought so herself, and her acquaintances confirmed her impressions. She must secure him first, and then contrive to clear her way to the ownership of the beautiful estate. She had ascertained too, that Doctor Mosely did not follow in Blonde Grayson's train. His indifference to that beauty flattered her own.

At length Mr. Lansing made his appearance. He had worked late on his forthcoming political history of his native State the night before, and had overslept himself. His face and figure were those of the lost heir, with the wear and tear and changes of nearly two score years added. His step was firm, his hair frosted by age, his manner and tone genial. His eagle, Lansing eye roved with pleasure over the cheerful, comfortable arrangements made for his morning meal. The great round oaken table of the library, covered with its fine linen and glistening silver coffee urn and forks, and heavy spoons of ancient silver, stamped with the Lansing arms, the silver toast-rack, the gold washed egg-cups and the soft white breakfast napkins, all were noticed by that quick eagle eye. He ordered the servant to bring in the breakfast, and in the mean time walked to the window and thanked his daughter for her consideration in providing so carefully for his tastes. Then he smiled at her new style of dress, and complimented her on the personal attractions she had concluded to adventure once more in the matrimonial market. He listened incredulously to her assertions that she was contented with living a single life, and chatted and laughed with her pleasantly until breakfast was announced.

Then he occupied his great leather-back library chair, at the round table, and impressively said grace while the liveried servant stood behind him. When his breakfast was fairly under-way, he chanced to glance at a marble bust of the lost heir, on the top of one of the bookcases. An expression of anxiety crossed his venerable countenance, and he said,

"Where is Gurty?"

Mrs. Bounce, who was eating very lightly of the abundant dishes, in order to keep her face and figure down to the proper condition for matrimonial speculations, said with as much sweetness as she could throw into her harsh voice,

"He went very early this morning, about sunrise, with his gun to look for partridges. I am concerned for the dear boy. He is too delicate to go into the damp woods so soon after his fever. The doctor permitted him to go, but I think he is not fully aware of the dampness of the woods about the manor. Doctor Mosely has been accustomed to woods in sandy districts, and does not realize the difference in our forest."

Mr. Lansing said, with the enthusiasm of an old sportsman:

"Not a particle of danger, if he keeps moving. How many times I have ranged these woods after birds when the dew was so heavy as to wet me to the skin, and come in with a roaring appetite and not a dry rag on me. The boy knows enough—let him rove—it will do him good—a sensible doctor that. Do you know that vial he gave me has cured my rheumatism? I declare to you he has more skill than a score of these quacks and ignoramuses that have worked into practice in C——. Give me a doctor that can *cure* diseases—anybody can give doses—but give me a man who can cure in some reasonable time. Here, sir, what are you gaping at? Fly around with that rack and bring me some hot toast. Norman Prince was the boy for me. He could tell by my face what I wanted. What has become of him, Esther? By the way, have you heard the marvelous tales that boy has been circulating about the old manor being haunted? I have paid him for taking care of Black Hawk over there, but now he has abandoned the place altogether. I don't know what I shall do with the horse—no one can come near him but that negro—and I wouldn't sell him for the price of this place. He was my poor Henry's delight. Doctor Mosely says the boy is dreadfully frightened, and must have seen something wandering about there. Where does he work now, do you know?"

"Why," exclaimed the daughter, "he lives with the doctor. You are growing forgetful. I told you all about those Graysons running through their property by their extravagance. Norman worked for them as long as they would pay him. Then he went to Doctor Mosely's. I always knew Norman Prince was not to be trusted. Haunted, indeed! What sensible person believes in ghosts? The scamp expects you to pay him more for going back to take care of the horse. He has trumped up these stories about the manor for a purpose. I know him of old. Ghosts, indeed!" and the widow slapped her folded napkin and ring emphatically and contemptuously down upon the table, and looked into the old gentleman's face.

Her father answered resolutely:

"I never disliked Norman: his greatest fault was his propensity to ride my horses without permission; but then he was an admirable boy to care for horses—he could do anything with wild horses—they would follow him every place, and he could doctor them better than any man I ever knew. There is something mysterious about the old manor, I'm sure, or he would never have deserted Black Hawk."

Turning to the servant, whose interest in the conversation became apparent when the mysterious tenants of the old manor were mentioned, Mr. Lansing said:

"You may go below, sir; we shall not need you here any further until you have finished your breakfast. Go along—we wish to be alone."

The servant bowed and retired with his silver salver. The old gentleman, when he saw that they were alone, dropped his voice to a low, confidential key, and said:

"I have great confidence in Doctor Mosely's judgment. He inspires that feeling in every one, I believe. He is clear-headed and reliable, so much so, that yesterday we elected him president of our new bank. We have organized a new banking association, to be called the 'Schuyler Bank of C——.' Mr. James Emerson, one of the elders of our church, who is a large stockholder, suggested the doctor's name for president, and we elected him unanimously. There is no humbug about the man. He tells me that he has questioned Norman closely about these strange visitors at the old manor, and that some one is really prowling in that neighborhood. He advises me to be on my guard; and I shall tell Gurty to keep his guns loaded at night, and be prepared at any time for a visit from burglars. We have silver enough through the house to tempt a bold rogue, and we must be on our guard. As far as stealing Black Hawk is concerned, I would be delighted to have them try. That horse would scatter their brains at the very first attempt. He is the very devil. But this is what I desire particularly to communicate to you, relying upon your discretion and sense to keep my confidence inviolate.

"Your mother, before our marriage, and when she was only

fourteen years of age, had an uncle named Stephen Van Dam. He was young, talented, and by a certain will of a near relative, became the owner of a large property. He was excessively fond of your mother, who was remarkably beautiful, even at that early age. He promised her that some day in the future he would give her a portion of his property, as he never intended to marry, and that at his death he would will to her the residue. He was quite wild, and was frequently involved in quarrels with his comrades. Unfortunately in one of his broils he stabbed a gentleman who had struck him in the face. He fled it is supposed to Europe, fearing the consequences. Before leaving the country, however, he contrived to convert most of his property into gold, and buried it. He obtained a private interview with your mother and informed her of the unfortunate occurrence, and of the urgent necessity of his leaving the country for a time. She was in the habit of making long visits at this manor, and he informed her that he had buried his gold under the chimney of that old manor house. Her age, fourteen, and the violent excitement she and the young man were under from the fatal catastrophe, made this hurried interview appear to her like a terrible dream. Her memory retained every fact relating to the death; but such was her confusion and excitement concerning her young uncle's danger, and her anxiety that he should effect his escape, that the particulars concerning the concealment of the gold escaped her recollection. She remembered distinctly the gift of the gold to herself if he should never return, and that it was buried under the chimney of that old house. He gave her some directions as to the course to be pursued to find the treasure; but her excitement caused these important details to escape her memory. She was perfectly able to identify the chimney on the north side of the house, from a certain interview once held there with herself; but other details which proved to be vital to the discovery of the gold had slipped her mind. Stephen Van Dam has never been heard of to this day. The gentleman who was stabbed did not die, but finally was perfectly restored to health. A few years ago under your mother's direction I caused the earth to be removed from about the chimney, and continued the excavation until I reached the solid rock. The search was perfect and thorough, and utterly fruitless. No gold made its appearance. But your mother maintained until her death that her uncle's property was concealed near that chimney.

"Now my suspicion is aroused about these nocturnal visits to the old manor. Either Stephen Van Dam himself has secretly returned for his buried property, or some person to whom he communicated the secret, is searching at night for the concealed treasure. I believe that the old man seen by Norman Prince, is your mother's uncle. The young man in the dark garb may possibly be a son of Stephen Van Dam; for we can form no opinion of what may have occurred in Europe, and if so, he may resemble my own dear son Henry. But I ardently trust and hope that Stephen Van Dam has come across Henry in Europe, and persuaded him to return, and that my dear boy and heir is actually in this neighborhood. What do you think of my version of the ghosts?"

The widow had listened with the most absorbed manner to the ever exciting topic of buried treasure. She might secure the ownership of the manor, and then raze the old tenement to the ground, and dig out the entire foundation till the glittering pile of gold should reveal itself. Then her accumulated and wonderful wealth would secure her an enviable position indeed in society. The thought itself was an agreeable delirium. She leaned her fat face upon her two fists with her elbows on the breakfast table, and intently studied her father's features in the interesting recital of his theory concerning the spiritual manifestations in the old vine covered ruin. But when he suggested the bodily re-appearance of the heir, her brother, her dark crafty eyes looked down in study of the table cloth, that her sinister thought might not be revealed in her look. She guarded herself carefully, and when the affectionate old father concluded, looked up again with a smile and said—

"How wild I would be with joy if Henry had really returned. There would be great difficulty in his case, however, for he would be arrested unless we could conceal him in time. I find the undercurrent of public prejudice very strong against him yet. But after all, our wishes may be only deluding us about his really being here. Mother must have known what she was talking about, and the gold may have been hidden on the premises; but then it must have been reclaimed by the owner or his friends long before mother died. I would not devote another thought to the gold. It cannot be there *now*. But the apparition—what shall we do about that?'

The widow pondered a moment, and the thought came quickly to her that she could have a long interview, and a sentimental one at that, with Doctor Mosely by appearing to sympathize with her father in his anxiety to gain some trace of his lost son She said,

"How kind of the doctor to interest himself in your affairs. I think his caution to you, to be on your guard, was very sensible, and very kind. I am disposed to agree with him, that the ghosts are only prowlers who seek an opportunity to rob the manor. I propose this. The nights are bright moonlight, now. You take Gurty's gun and go with me early in the evening, and let us conceal ourselves, and watch. We should have another man around, too, to assist you, in case of trouble. Oh! I know an excellent plan. Suppose we invite Doctor Mosely, himself, to go with us—he might have leisure, and he is perfectly fearless—what do you think of that idea?"

The eagle-eye of the old gentleman flashed fire. It was very evident at that moment, where the absent Henry Lansing derived a share of his impetuosity and fearlessness.

"Me! call for assistance to harness a couple of skulking thieves. I'll take Gurty's gun and blow one of them over the moon. The butt of the gun is good enough for the other. Pooh! nonsense! it isn't in the Lansing blood to run for two dirty thieves."

Mrs. Bounce finally succeeded in calming the aroused old lion down into the consideration of the assistance the physician might render, in securing the persons of the burglars, if the night prowlers were really such. The old gentleman listened to her reasoning, and finally consented to ask the doctor if he was willing to participate in a ghost hunt. The widow was delighted at the prospect of a moonlight ramble with the physician, and the little breakfast party soon separated for the vocations of the day.

Just before sunset, the favorite physician made his appearance. He came whirling in his buggy over the meadow road, and soon was at the door. The stable boy was waiting for him, and took possession of his horse, and drove off to the manor stables. Mr. Lansing had dispatched a note to the doctor soon after breakfast, requesting the pleasure of his company to tea, and intimating that his assistance was required in the novel adventure of a ghost hunt. Mrs. Bounce was awaiting his arrival in the great saloon of the mansion, arrayed in her second mourning. She received the physician with her sweetest smile, and while expecting her father's arrival from his study, found time to communicate the details of the marvelous expedition in which the doctor was solicited to take a part. He expressed his willingness to participate in the effort to discover Mr. Lansing's son, but coincided with the widow in believing the search would be fruitless, so far as the finding of Henry

Lansing was concerned. He evidently inclined to the belief that the apparitions were only prowling thieves.

The elegant supper was soon over, and after Gurty Lansing had driven away towards C——, with the avowed purpose of calling on ladies, the trio found themselves at liberty to wander off over the manor walks, unnoticed in the moonlight. Mr. Lansing walked on ahead with Gurty's fowling-piece heavily loaded. The doctor, with the widow leaning decidedly and affectionately on his arm, followed slowly over the grass, pursuing the general direction of the manor brook. He carried only a formidable club cane in his hand. The widow had calculated upon the effect in the bright moonlight, of her dark graceful cloak and the white handkerchief tied loosely about her throat, and her uncovered glossy black curls. The two paced slowly along amid the fairy scenes, chatting upon the people and current gossip of C——, and soon ceased to remember the errand upon which they had started. The shadows of the great chestnuts fell upon the moon-lit grass, and the rippling manor brook glistened like molten silver. The old deserted ruin was close at hand, but the two were too absorbed in their conversation, to observe it. Presently the sound of advancing footsteps met their ears, and looking up, they beheld Mr. Lansing coming towards them; at the same instant they saw the vine-covered mansion looming up solemn and silent behind him. It was, apparently, as devoid of life as the grave. The old gentleman checked any exclamation by placing his finger on his closed lips. When they paused before him, in the shade of a large tree, he whispered:

"Some one is moving about the old house now. I have just come from the porch, where I heard distinctly the moving of feet in the room over-head. Doctor, you take a station near the door in the southern gable—you will find a large maple there which will shade you completely. I will hide under the porch again, and Esther will sit down here, under this tree, where we are now. This will give us a view of nearly all the doors and windows in the house. We will watch for a time to see if any one else enters the house. We must give both of them an opportunity to get inside before we make a noise. You know my son's appearance and style from what we have already told you. If he is here, don't you harm him, or rather don't let him have an excuse to harm you—he is quicker than a thunderbolt. We will reconnoiter, and after a time I will come around and consult with my pickets. Go cautiously—you will have no difficulty in finding the shelter I have selected for you—it is a large maple. If any one attempts to leave the manor house, pounce upon him at once. You will hear the footsteps after you are within a few feet of the door."

The widow had not calculated in the arrangements, the possibility of being separated from the doctor. But her father always assumed a peremptory tone, when he was particularly anxious to accomplish some purpose, and his manner convinced her, that remonstrance was useless; so she sat down quietly in the shadow of her tree, and commenced to study the faintly-traced outlines of the old tenement in the moonlight. The chimney where her mother had stated the gold to be buried, was visible from her point of observation. Her attention and interest became absorbed in studying the locality of the buried treasure, and she soon forgot, in the profound quiet of the lovely night, the object of her father's watch about the old manor. Her reverie was finally interrupted by a stealthy footstep approaching her from behind. It proved to be her father. He had left his gun concealed under the porch, and carried instead, a stout whip which he had cut from the wild hickory bushes growing about the old ruin. He soon ascertained that his daughter had seen nothing unusual, and heard no sound from the ruin. He whispered to her, that at intervals, he had detected the mysterious footsteps overhead, but would not effect an entrance until the other apparition should have gone into the house also. He said, "By the Lord Harry, if these are prowlers, and Henry is not here, I will warm their jackets, I declare to you," and he exhibited to her his enormous whip.

Then he left her, and soon all was silent and death-like, save the murmuring of the manor brook. The shadows of the trees slowly veered round in the moonlight, and the widow could see more distinctly the outlines of the haunted house. Not a sound arose, and the silence at length began to work upon her imagination. Might it not be possible, after all, that spirits returned to old haunts, and that the dark object which seemed slowly to move near the chimney was a creature of the other world? Her eyes dilated upon it. It certainly did move. Yes! the rays of the moon were intercepted by the figure, and now they appeared again after the dark object had passed. She shivered a trifle at the apparition. Then, as she followed it with her eye, she grew calm and self-possessed again. The widow, like all of her race, possessed nerve. Now it passed slowly out of view, noiselessly dividing the shrubbery near the front of the gloomy ruin, and disappearing. Hark! a piercing yell of mortal agony and terror rent the air, and then the bushes were torn asunder. The same mysterious, moving shadow ap peared again, plainly gliding across the moonlight, towards the manor brook. Her blood curdled at that yell, so agonized and mysterious. As she instinctively crouched lower upon the grass for concealment, another voice met her ear. It was Mr Lansing's.

"Stop there, you dirty ghost! I'll teach you to raise such a hubbub as that on my premises."

The figure of the old gentleman bounded out into the moonlight and grappled with the gliding shadow. Whack! whack! whack! sounded from the material shoulders of the ghost. The shadow fell to the earth, but still the vigorous arm of the old man rained blows upon the struggling, yelling ghost. Before the doctor or the widow could reach the scene of the strange conflict, Mr. Lansing had the ghost in his arms and was running directly for the deep manor brook. A heavy plunge in the water ensued. Then the ghost attempted to climb the bank, yelling for mercy. But the old gentleman raised it out of the water and gave it another terrific thrashing with his hickory whip till it begged for mercy in the most pitiful accents. Then he desisted, from sheer exhaustion. The ghost rose to its feet and said in the most plaintive tones,

"O my God! You have nearly destroyed me! Colonel Lansing, how *could* you abuse me so—your friend, your fast, unyielding friend."

"Eh! What? That voice sounds familiar—who in the devil are *you?*" exclaimed the old gentleman, with a sudden revulsion of feeling, and a faint idea that some blunder had been committed.

"Don't you know me, Colonel Lansing? I am the Reverend Thomas Delaplaine, your clergyman."

A violent shout of laughter ensued behind this astonished couple. The old gentleman turned with his terrible whip and beheld Doctor Mosely leaning against the maple tree, and kicking and shouting with laughter. The physician could not restrain the violence of his mirth at this remarkable denouement.

The bewildered proprietor of the manor took off his hat to the cringing, dripping figure before him, and this droll civility occasioned Doctor Mosely another immoderate fit of laughing. Colonel Lansing muttered:

"What possessed you, then, to yell in that hideous manner? I supposed you were a robber, and expected to frighten me."

"Oh!" exclaimed the unfortunate clergyman, "look at the back of my neck—see if that wouldn't make any man yell."

The widow, who had come up with a horrified expression and recognized Mr. Delaplaine, pulled back the clergyman's coat collar, while her father examined his neck.

"Frightful, frightful!" he exclaimed. "What did that, Mr. Delaplaine?"

"Black Hawk, sir, did that. I thrust my head through one of those old windows, and the brute caught me there with his teeth. I thought it was the devil, indeed I did, sir. That made me yell. He came at me with his mouth wide open."

The physician, who had been rolling over and over with laughter, when he heard that the wild steed of the manor had interfered, suddenly ceased his merriment, and came hurrying to the spot. His quick eye detected at once the severity of Black Hawk's bite upon the clergyman's neck. He said at once:

"Poor fellow! I am sorry indeed. Mr. Lansing, this wound must be attended to at once. If you will be good enough to hurry over to your stables and send my horse here, I will take this gentleman immediately to my office in town. What were you doing here at this time of night, Mr. Delaplaine?"

"Ghost-hunting," sullenly muttered the wet and shivering form of the walloped divine. "It's my last experiment in that line."

Unfortunate gentleman! He had wandered off alone to the old ruin, notwithstanding his former fright, to satisfy himself regarding the apparition of Henry Lansing. He really and earnestly desired to do Mrs. Lansing's son a service if possible, and here was the result of his night ramble, bitten, beaten and half-drowned for his ill-starred philanthropy.

There was no time to lose, for the poor clergyman was faint under his fright and sufferings. Mr. Lansing hastened after the physician's vehicle, while Mrs. Bounce and the doctor supported his shivering form. When the horse and buggy finally arrived, it was found that Colonel Lansing had brought his own heavy cloak and a bottle of wine for the clergyman. The trembling figure was lifted into the vehicle, and Doctor Mosely immediately started off with his patient for the myrtle dell.

When the two had disappeared in the distance, Mr. Lansing turned to the widow and said,

"Esther, have you nerve enough to search that old house with me before we go home?"

"Certainly," replied the daughter, "if you will let me have the gun. I don't believe in ghosts."

"Very well," said the old gentleman; "we will give it a thorough search before we leave it. The foot that I heard is in that house yet. Come on—you are a regular Lansing."

The intrepid couple entered the haunted house. The Colonel marched ahead with the doctor's club, and the widow in her black cloak and white handkerchief followed with the gun. The old tenement was silent, and nothing met their eyes but bare walls and floors checkered with moonbeams and shadows. They carefully searched every room and closet, ascended to the immense garret, groped their way through it, and then descending again, searched the old cellars. The deserted house assuredly had no corporeal tenants.

When the search proved unavailing, Colonel Lansing and his daughter started for home. The old gentleman expressed his disappointment at the utter failure of their undertaking. As they slowly followed the course of the manor brook homeward, in the clear moonlight, Mrs. Bounce chanced to look backward at the old manor house, over her shoulder. She caught a glimpse of something passing before one of the windows in the upper story which startled her, but which with the ready recollection and tact of her scheming mind, she concealed from her companion. It was in her rapidly formed opinion the *lantern* of the gold hunters.

CHAPTER XXV.

THE sensation caused by the mysterious occupants of the manor house of the Lansing family pervaded every class of society in C——. The excitement of the community never had been known to attain such height and violence since the murder of the stranger Hartwell, and the sudden disappearance of Henry Lansing years before. Norman Prince was too badly frightened and excited to confine his mysterious secret to his employer and the clergyman. He finally told it everywhere, believing his former master and friend, the heir, to be utterly beyond the reach of enemies, and existing only in a spiritual life. The physician communicated the affair to the family at Myrtle Dell, and the Reverend Thomas Delaplaine finding that the matter had leaked out, told freely the facts stated by the negro. He was silent, however, regarding his own experience at the cottage of Blonde Grayson. But the ludicrous and painful scene in which he had participated as victim under Colonel Lansing's hickory whip, could not be concealed. The widow who had witnessed it, deemed it too comical to keep from a confidential friend in the town. In this manner, the affair, which all the party concerned had promised to hush up, became the exciting topic of comment in every circle. The mysterious and startling rumors gained wonderful accessions as they traveled till it appeared to be settled upon as a fact that Henry Lansing had arisen from a sulphureous climate, and was to be found on certain nights in the vicinity of the old manor house; that the Presbyterian clergyman, the well remembered friend of the deceased mother, had been decoyed into the old ruin, and beaten by the heir under the instigation of an old man with horns, who was supposed to be his familiar spirit. This was deemed to be a particularly aggravated case, from the fact that the clergyman had always been considered one of the heir's friends and supporters at the time of the murder

Mrs. Fierygrim and a few other saints who were decidedly opposed to the heir being in any hotter climate than they were able to make for him by their long tongues, persisted in the assertion that Henry Lansing was lurking about in real flesh and blood presence. They were convinced that he should be hunted up and tried for the murder. But the conversation of a party of truant school boys, was evidence of the fact that some of the inhabitants of the manor had faithful friends in every class of society; and it was not an established certainty that every jury who might be summoned upon Henry Lansing's wished for arrest, would be happy to gratify Mrs. Fierygrim's clique, by a verdict against the heir.

This group of wandering boys preferred a ramble in the woods in the sunshine of September, to the confinement and studies of the school. They had stolen away at the morning recess, and in the course of their stroll, had found their way to the splendid woodlands which encircled the Lansing manor. They had encountered, in these pleasant woods, a boy of about eleven years of age who was a cripple. The thin-faced delicate little fellow, had a shrunken and twisted leg, and he was hobbling around through the woods on his wooden crutch. He was barefoot, but he wore a comfortable jacket of gray cloth, and a little gray cap. His pantaloons were also gray, and as he hobbled along, the cloth overlapping his helpless, shortened leg, swung back and forth with his gait. The four truant school boys were ragged and dirty, and their ages ranged from five years to fourteen. They were fearless, happy-looking little scamps, red-cheeked and stained with the mud, and berry and butternut experiences of their wanderings The cripple proved to be no stranger to some of them.

"Hurrah! Twisty," exclaimed the eldest truant, "what are you doing out here? We've all run away from school, and we've had a jolly good time. Look at my trout. Won't the master skin us to-morrow, eh!"

"It's Twisty," echoed another little voice, as the boy forced his way through the bushes; "jest look at my nosegay, ain't it pooty? Look at my pockets—butternuts, lots of 'em."

The urchin's breeches pockets were stuffed out like an alderman's paunch, and the corners of his grinning mouth were touched off freely with the crimson hue of some wild berry. Another boy made his appearance with a dozen long reeds with brown heads resembling a sky rocket, and called in truant vernacular, by the striking name of "cat-tails." He had lost one shoe in securing his prizes from the swamp, but this appeared to trouble him very little so long as the "cat-tails" were all right.

The youngest truant was the smallest specimen of juvenility ever suspected of being able to evade school, and spend the entire day roving the woods. He was obliged to walk around every large boulder that his comrades were able to leap over. But he toiled along with them, and they occasionally slackened their pace to enable the little fellow to overtake them. He trudged along, shouting at the top of his little voice for assistance when he encountered some formidable mud hole; and when he was once more on dry land, he thrust his hands into his little pockets, and marched on whistling the smallest kind of whistle imaginable He was evidently sustained in his arduous march, by a species of *esprit de corps*. This urchin had no trophies to display, except a more complete suit of mud armor than his companions. He had succeeded in the bold feat of casting himself at full length, onto his breast and face in some soft mud hole. He had sputtered the mud out of his mouth sufficiently to resume the tune to which he had been marching, and trudged on triumphantly whistling.

They all gathered about the cripple, and related their adventures "by field and by flood." Then the oldest boy, who was recognized by his comrades as a sort of leader, under the name of Mat Cowen, said to the cripple

"Twisty, where do you git such fine clothes now?"

The answer was, "Mr. Gurty Lansing gives me everything now. I work for him. You know the bridge way back of Miss Grayson's? Well, that's his barn there—that is, he rented it to keep the chestnut gelding in his father give him. I take care of his horse, and he keeps it there for Miss Grayson to ride; nobody rides him but her. Mr. Gurty had a little room built for me in one corner of the barn, and put a bed in there, and a stove, and there's where I live. Mr. Gurty's very good to me since Mrs. Bounce turned me away from the manor. He's got books for me, and I read in there nights, and I cook for myself in there, and that's the way I live."

"Crickey," exclaimed Mat Cowen, "ain't that nice? But you used to play the fiddle in the church."

"Oh," said Twisty; "I do that Sundays, and I git forty dollars a year for it from the church. Mrs. Lansing got that place for me when I lived on the manor. Mrs. Bounce drove me off when her mother died. Then Mr. Gurty come to me, and give me money, and got me a place to work in Brown's store. He's good, jest like Mrs. Lansing was. They all say that lady lives up in Heaven now, and she's an angel."

"What's that?" enquired the little truant in the mud armor; "what's angil?"

Twisty looked puzzled. All eyes were bent on him, awaiting his answer. Then he said:

"It's a sort of—of a—kind of a thing that goes flying through the sky. All good people gits to be them things. They live with God, and have everything they want."

The little urchin in mud armor was listening, with his large eyes expanding in amazement, and rolling first upon the countenance of the little cripple and then upon the beautiful manor which spread away in the sunshine, and was close at hand through the trees. When his question was answered he said,

"Do yer wanter to know what I'd do ef I was one of dem things? I'd fly right ober dem chestnut trees, and lite right in the top of dem, and git all der chestnuts I wanted, right dar on de manor."

The boys all laughed, but Twisty said contemptuously:

"Angels don't eat chestnuts, boy—they have better things nor that. Oh, Mat Cowen, did you ever hear about the ghosts over in the old house there? Mr. Henry Lansing's ghost's in there."

Mat Cowen was perfectly familiar with the town sensation, but the other boys were curious to know about it. Twisty conducted the whole party to the manor fence, which divided the forest from the meadows of the beautiful estate, and pointed out to them the old, vine-covered ruin. The boys mounted to the top of the fence to look upon the mysterious and marvel-crowned pile of buildings. Little mud armor contented himself with peeking through the openings between the fence boards.

The little cripple communicated the tale of the apparitions to the little party of listeners, embellishing the story with all the marvelous incidents which rumor had attached to the original narrative of Norman Prince. He was interrupted by many curious interrogatories, which he was unable to answer; but he succeeded in getting his young auditors into a state of horrified excitement. When his story was finished, Mat Cowen, the leader, jumped back to the ground, and picked up his string of trout. There was something on his mind, for he looked uneasy. When the cripple had slowly worked his way back to the ground, and picked up his little crutch, the boy with the trout said:

"Some people say it's Mr. Henry Lansing, and no ghost at all; and some says they'll ketch him and hang him for murder. My father says they won't hang him; not if *he's* on their jury." His lip contracted as he reflected a moment. Then he added, in his peculiarly fierce and determined way, and his black eye flashed: "I don't see how they're goin' to prove anything about that fishin' spear, nuther. Some people says it was *me* found that spear, right by that maple-tree, with the blood on it. But the boys they say was with me that day is all dead. Now jest tell me, who's goin' to swear that spear was found there, at all?—and where's their fishin' spear now, any way?"

"They'll *make* you tell!" exclaimed the little cripple, with eager interest; but looking into Mat Cowen's determined face, in the hope of finding conclusive evidence there that the compulsion would be impossible.

"I ain't got nothin' to tell," replied Mat, sullenly. "Nobody ain't got no power to make me. I don't know nothin' about the spear, and I don't know where it is, nuther—there!"

The boy leaned his back against an oak tree, with the most resolute expression that ever crossed a human countenance. His eyes were directed sidewise towards the manor. One hand hung by his side with the string of trout; the other grasped a button of his ragged jacket. His lips were clenched together like a vise. Here was an obstinate subject for a prosecuting attorney to prove an important link by in a chain of testimony calculated to bring the heir of the manor to the gallows. If the finding of the bloody fishing spear at the scene of Hartwell's murder could not be proved by the evidence of this determined schoolboy, a ray of light appeared to flash upon the case of the absent Henry Lansing. But an interested spectator and listener, unseen by the group of boys, was near at hand, and rapidly preparing to perpetuate the striking scene. He had been sitting on the trunk of a fallen tree, and half concealed by the dense undergrowth, when the group of truant boys overtook Twisty. His gun was lying against the trunk beside him, and his game bag hung from his shoulder, stuffed with partridges and gray squirrels. He was weary with his day's tramp through the forest, and had found a good seat on the decayed trunk to rest himself. He had heard the salutation of the truants on meeting the cripple, and had remained motionless and silent during the whole of their conversation. He had been a schoolboy himself, and was living over old times in listening to them. Finally, when the course of their conversation led the little party to the manor fence to have a glimpse at the haunted house, he discovered that their footsteps were approaching nearer to his place of concealment. He remained quiet, and they passed him without observing him. He now had a fine view of their interested countenances, as they listened to the wonderful ghost stories. When Mat Cowen jumped to the ground from the fence, and expressed his determination to avoid giving testimony against Henry Lansing, in case of his arrest, the half-hidden figure of the sportsman enjoyed a full and perfect view of his face and form against the oak. He noiselessly drew from the side pocket of his hunting jacket a small sketchbook and pencil, and commenced to copy the expression of Mat Cowen's face, and his determined attitude. He succeeded in obtaining the outline of the oak's trunk and lower branches, together with Mat's figure, and the cripple and the other listeners standing about him, before the little party started homewards. He then closed his sketchbook, and heard Twisty exclaim, as the boys filed off together through the bushes:

"Well! *I'm* glad you won't tell anything agin Mr. Henry, for he never did it."

Soon the footsteps of the cripple and the truant boys died away in the distance, and the hunter, shouldering his gun, stepped forth from the little thicket into the more open woods. It was Gurty Lansing. He walked slowly homeward with his game, pondering the subject of the boys' conversation. One pleasing reflection lighted his meditation regarding the combined mysteries of the murder and the haunted house. Whatever difficulties adverse fate might have in store for his beloved brother, it was clear that one material witness against Henry Lansing had determined for some unaccountable reason to hold his peace regarding his knowledge of the dreadful crime.

But Mat Cowen and his younger and less experienced followers continued on their way, accommodating their pace to the crutch of the little cripple, and the short legs of the urchin in mud armor. When they had traversed at length the woods which separated them from the town, and emerged from the shadows out upon the sunlit highway leading into C——, the owner of the string of trout whispered something to Twisty. The cripple nodded assent, and when they arrived at the fork of the road, Mat Cowen directed his followers to keep on into the town, as he was going another way with Twisty. The three younger truants obeyed, being already engaged in the discussion of the best plans to be pursued to conceal from their parents the knowledge of their evasion of school studies. Then Mat Cowen and the cripple turned down the side road and slowly made their way towards the barn where Twisty had charge of Gurty Lansing's chestnut gelding. They reached their destination, and Twisty, drawing the stable key from his pocket, opened the door for his companion to go in. The cripple closed and locked the door behind them, while the other boy, after a careful examination of the barn, to see that they were alone and unobserved, made for a corner of the stable, and raising one of the heavy floor plank, crawled down through the aperture and disappeared. In a few minutes he re-appeared with an old rusty fishing-spear in his hands. It was the weapon which had broken through the skull of the murdered Hartwell. Twisty's eyes expanded with horror when the fatal weapon was actually before him, but the poor boy's memory of his kind rescuer and friend, Mrs. Lansing, was too acute to allow him any protracted legal scruples in regard to suppressing testimony. He conducted Mat Cowen into his little bed-room in the barn, and there the two made a fire in his stove and burned up the wooden handle of the fishing-spear, shoving it slowly into the fire as fast as the end was consumed. At length naught remained but the iron trident or spear at the end. When this rusty piece of iron was sufficiently cooled by pouring water on it, Mat Cowen put it in his pocket, and said, "Now come, and I'll show you the very place."

Once more the two boys went out of the stable into the September sunshine, and leaving the road near the little bridge, took to the green fields, following up the banks of the brook until they arrived at a large mill pond. The boy with the iron in his pocket now eagerly led the way, skirting the sheet of water and forcing his way through the brushes until he reached an old stump where he paused. When the cripple had come up with him, Mat Cowen took the iron from his pocket and hurled it forty feet out into the deep water. The fragment of the fishing-spear disappeared forever. Then he turned to the cripple and said, with his serious black eyes sparkling with tears:

"It seems to me a good while ago—but there's the very place, seven years ago, where Mr. Henry Lansing, when I broke through the ice and floated away under it, drowning, dove in after me and saved my life. It was under the strong ice, and he most drowned a doin' it. Twisty, I guess I've a right to keep mum—don't you?"

The boy gulped down something which arose in his throat, and brushing his dirty coat sleeve across his eyes, started homeward in silence, followed by the sympathetic cripple. Some truants who never draw prizes carry great hearts.

CHAPTER XXVI.

"Clara, it seem to me as if my dress was growing too large for me—does it look so to you? Why certainly! See there how much I can gather at the waist with my hand. I believe I am really growing thin."

Mrs. St. Clair laughed heartily. "Why Blonde, is it any wonder that you are thin, when you haven't eaten a mouthful for four days? Not a particle of nourishment has passed your lips until this morning. Do you realize, sweetheart, how long you have been sick?"

"Why no!" replied the pale-faced beauty, standing erect before the mirror in her little parlor, and shaking out the skirt of her mourning dress. "I had an attack of dizziness last night, and you came and sat with me. What do you say?" she answered again, as she turned away from the mirror with a bewildered look; "four days? What are you talking about, Clara? I don't understand you."

Mrs. St. Clair looked up from her sewing, and repeated, "four days, and not an hour less. Oh, I have been so concerned about you, Blonde; the first and second nights the doctor sat up with you all night, he was so alarmed. He said your symptoms foreshadowed insanity. About two o'clock the second night he seemed to lose all control of himself. I was bathing your head with ice water, and he was consulting a large book, some French medical work. An expression of the most acute anguish passed over his face. He laid the book down suddenly, and his usual calmness appeared to desert him altogether. He came and sat down on the foot of your bed, and putting his hands to his face he moaned and sobbed bitterly. When he discovered that his grief started me off crying, he ceased suddenly, and said calmly again, 'Mrs. St. Clair, it is unbecoming a physician to exhibit any emotion but hope in a sick room. But she is too lovely to pass her life in a lunatic asylum. The Great Physician is her only hope now.' Then he walked away to your little prayer-book table, and sat for a long time with his head bent down upon your prayer-book. I believe he was praying all the time. I thought before he loved you—now I *know* it."

The pale, graceful mourner had been utterly unconscious of the crisis which had determined her fate. So great had been the shock to her system, that memory, thought, consciousness, had all reeled away and fallen into oblivion. She knew not the passing hours, or friends, or pain. Four long days of her existence had been crushed in silent darkness by the finger of the Omnipotent, and she had arisen at last from her bed as from a single night's indisposition. When Mrs. St. Clair mentioned her long days of unconsciousness, her mind assented as a child does to the stories told of its earliest infancy. There were no means or inclination to dispute her friend's assertion. She could only curiously sit and enquire. She had forgotten the visit of the Reverend Thomas Delaplaine, and reckoned all that Clara told her of his presence as a part of her unconscious experience. She learned that old Rosy had called upon her and left the beautiful flowers which graced her little parlor mantel; that the basket of luscious grapes which Mrs. St. Clair produced from the little closet in Carl's studio had been brought to her by Gurty Lansing, and that five hundred dollars in gold which she had placed in her brother's rosewood dressing-case to meet the rent of her cottage and her household expenses for the year had been stolen by a prowling thief who entered the window during the hour when all were watching at her bedside. When this robbery filled her with anguish, her friend quickly relieved her by detailing the manner in which the negro Norman Prince, sitting at the door in the doctor's buggy, had watched the scamp, and pounced upon him before he could leave the premises with his booty. Her brother Carl had offered the negro twenty dollars of the gold, which the coachman had refused, saying, "Norman Prince owes Miss Grayson a heap more money than that."

In the course of the day, as Mrs. St. Clair communicated to her the occurrences and matters of town interest and gossip, the subject of the wonderful visions at the old manor house arose. Blonde appeared to be intensely interested, avowing her belief in the possibility of occasional apparitions being sent from the spiritual world for some wise purpose, and even hinting at the doctrine that the spiritual myriads of another world are ever present to the scenes and occurrences of this. Her blue eyes studied mysteriously after these communications of her friend, and secretly she acknowledged to herself that if the lost heir was lurking about the manor in material life, the long buried and thrilling secret of the murder must soon come knocking at the inner door of her conscience for release. If Henry Lansing was still alive, and the law should grapple him in strong embrace, the compass needle of her duty knew no diverting agent. It pointed steadily at the name of the real murderer of Hartwell. And as she studied the details of the prevailing excitement of C——, the advance sighs of the grief storm began to whisper over her soul. Two sounds of woe were now to haunt her silent hours. "Alas! he may be here alive." "Alas! he may be here and dead." The solemn clock of God in the high heaven tolled mournfully the warning and reproachful words, "My child;" and the fair girl, raising her blue eyes to the great white throne, softly replied, "Thy holy will be done."

In the evening, after Mrs. St. Clair had returned home, Doctor Mosely drove up to the cottage gate. He appeared weary and care-worn, for his patients were numerous and widely scattered over the adjoining country. The month proved to be unusually unhealthy. Blonde was sitting by her parlor table, in the lamp-light, meditating on the doctor's devotion during her illness, when suddenly her maid announced the physician's presence. A faint blush stole to her pale face as she sat more erect in her chair to receive him. Doctor Mosely advanced quickly and took her proffered hand, saying, "I am so very happy to see you sitting up once more—this is the first time you have known me since your attack."

He drew a chair to her side and looked searchingly into her countenance. After a few trivial remarks concerning her condition and diet, he said:

"Miss Grayson, I have been unable to ascertain what exciting cause of grief or joy has occasioned this sudden illness—Mr. Delaplaine, who was with you, says you turned partly away from him, and immediately fell insensible to the floor. I would like to know, as a matter of science, to relieve the mystery of your sickness, if your conversation with the clergyman was calculated to induce a violent excitement or irritation of your mind. Of course your conversation is none of my business, I only desire to be informed if it was of a nature to suddenly or violently excite your nerves. I have heard of two remarkable instances in your experience, where you exhibited unparalleled coolness and self-possession in the most fearfully exciting scenes. Had I not heard of the wonderful control you possess over your nerves, it would be less difficult for me to understand your case. Thank God! you are well now; but during your temporary alienation of mind, you raved to me of a neck-tie, to recover which, your whole soul was aroused and eager. Everything depended upon that neck-tie, and you raved to me of the intense interest you had in the gentleman who owned it."

The physician noticed Blonde's sudden start, and the gleam of terror which came to her face. He added, soothingly:

"Don't be alarmed, Miss Grayson, you are my patient. Secrets obtained during illness, by me, are buried and forgotten in an honorable heart. I will press this subject no further, only I will say, that you mentioned no gentleman's name during your raving. Your natural start confirms my impression, that some overpowering previous mental excitement occasioned your sudden illness. As a physician I am now satisfied; but as a man, susceptible of appreciating your rare loveliness of person and character, I must not even comment on the good fortune of the mysterious owner of the neck-tie. That subject dies on my lips now and forever."

The kind physician's countenance was for a single instant convulsed with his mental struggle. It passed, and his sad, quiet smile returned as he continued:

"You will require no further medical attendance, Miss Grayson, and to-morrow you must not fail to take the air—you know winter will stalk in upon us in a very few weeks, and you need all the exercise you can take before that dreaded time. I would be so happy if you would permit me to call for you to-morrow afternoon with my fast horse. The lake and its surroundings, are so beautiful now, and I would feel so honored to have you ride with me."

Then the bright side of his nature came out as he added with a laugh, "You will not refuse my offer—I must have an afternoon to myself—I am worn out and need relaxation. You have never seen me when I was really unrestrained in the open country, and the wild woods, and I want to make you laugh. I will describe to you the most comical and absurd scene you ever heard of. It is all betrayed to the town now, and you have probably heard of it. But I was a spectator, and I must describe to you the thrashing that the estimable and Reverend Thomas Delaplaine received one night on the manor by the mistake of his beloved parishioner, Colonel Lansing; my sides are sore yet, laughing. Say that you will honor me to-morrow, and I will drive around for you at two o'clock."

Blonde Grayson had listened with terrified, and then annoyed, and then pleased reflections, to her physician's words. She felt relieved that he had misunderstood her ravings concerning the neck-tie; but his conclusion that she cherished a secret affection for its owner was provoking. But he had forced his conclusion, and she did not feel called upon to explain it away. If the physician cherished any idea of offering himself to her, she determined that he must approach her openly and not under cover of hints obtained during her alienation of mind. It appeared to her that he had nearly offered, and then rejected himself. She looked composedly into his intellectual eye as he concluded, and said:

"Doctor Mosely, strange as it may appear, I do not recollect one thing that occurred on the evening when I was taken ill. Whatever I raved about is equally unknown to me, and must pass as all other coinage of a disordered brain, into oblivion. You are very kind to invite me, and I shall be exceedingly happy to accompany you. But answer me this one enquiry to-night. Was there to your personal knowledge, a *mysterious* occurrence at the old manor on the night to which you allude?"

The doctor's expression changed as he replied guardedly:

"I heard footsteps moving for a time inside of the old ruin, what they were occasioned by I cannot say. They sounded distinctly and mysteriously, but I could not probe the matter, inasmuch as Colonel Lansing was the superior officer and leader. I awaited his orders. He confirmed my sense of hearing by stating that he also detected footsteps in the empty rooms above."

Blonde Grayson looked serious again. She said:

"I understood there was a mysterious phase as well as a comical one; but I must wait patiently, I suppose, until our ride to-morrow."

"I am so happy at your acceptance, Miss Grayson, of my offer Remember, at two o'clock to-morrow. Good night,"—and the faithful doctor bowed himself out of her presence.

Two motives had prompted her acceptance of the doctor's invitation to ride. One was, that Mrs. Bounce would be deprived of the exclusive claim to his attentions, which she paraded to the town as her especial property. Blonde knew the widow would be annoyed, and she rather enjoyed the idea. The other motive was, that she was touched by the respectful and profound interest Doctor Mosely had manifested towards herself during her helpless condition. She began to give credence to Mrs. St. Clair's statements regarding his affection for her. But why then had he devoted himself so closely to the widow before Blonde's illness? The whole matter was an enigma. She determined to study it.

She was soon summoned to the little tea-table in her brother's studio. Carl was delighted to see her sweet face presiding once more at his evening meal. He informed her of the great success he was meeting with in receiving orders for his portraits, and chatted and laughed with her for an hour. Then he went off to have a cigar with his friends in the town, and Blonde was left alone with her maid.

For a long time she sat in her parlor window looking out upon the beautiful evening. The air was warm, and from her open window she watched the moonlit hedges and the occasional trees scattered through the fields in groups. The curving line of the highway looked white in the full moonlight, and she could distinguish the dark forms of the pedestrians moving along it in relief. She was vexing her brain with all manner of conjectures as to the apparitions in the old ruin, and the part she would be called upon to play in the event of the heir really "turning up." She was just in that condition of mind to be prepared for either a material or a spiritual solution of the mystery. If Henry Lansing had returned in the body, would he still remember her? Had he found another fair girl to be the repository of his heart? Or was he already married? If his feelings in regard to herself remained undimmed by years, and by some chance he should witness her drive with

Doctor Mosely, what would be the effect upon his ardent and impetuous temperament? Would the last gleam vanish from his long consuming taper of hope? Had he not written in his journal that the love of woman would never be his? This latter reflection induced her to read once more, from the treasured journal, the article on the language of the locust tree. She took her lamp from the parlor table and went to her bed-room to find the journal. With the instinct of regularity and order she went to its accustomed resting place. *It was gone.* She placed her hand over her eyes, as was her wont when studying deeply. In vain she tried to recall when last she read from the journal. Her mental attack had wiped out entirely the memory of her last interview with the Rev. Thomas Delaplaine. She had ceased to remember Henry Lansing's ideas of the spiritual tenants of the old manor as embodied in the article, "Reveries in the Ancestral Ruin." She had forgotten the pale visage of the apparition listening to the reading of his own secret journal. A kind Providence had obliterated the memory of that ghastly face that the fair Blonde might recover and live with reason unimpaired. The more she reflected the more confused and annoyed did she become. She carefully searched her private room. It was not there. She looked through the parlor. It was not there. She felt confident that these two rooms were the only ones in the cottage where she had ever read in the journal. But to satisfy herself she searched the entire house, carrying her lamp with her. Alas! it was gone. The journal had really fallen to the floor with her when she swooned. But she remembered nothing of that occurrence. Her unworthiness, as a trusted custodian, overwhelmed her. At length she resolved to await Mrs. St. Clair's coming on the ensuing day, and seek information from her regarding the lost record. The matter, however, terribly annoyed her, and finally she walked out on the little piazza to forget it temporarily. The exceeding loveliness of the moonlight tempted her. She recollected how ill she had been, and entered the cottage for her large black shawl and her hood. Then she went out again into the moonlight, looking like a tall, graceful shadow. She called to her Newfoundland, and the dog came to her, stately and solemn in the moonlight. He received her caresses with dignified pleasure, and assented to her proposition for a stroll with a graceful wave of his tail. She walked slowly to the front gate and looked towards the town. The heavy, drooping branches of the elms looked too sombre in that direction. She turned and looked in the opposite direction towards the open fields which bordered the highway leading towards Myrtle Dell. That view was more agreeable, and she opened the gate, and followed by her faithful body-guard, wandered slowly along the highway, enjoying the soft moonlight. Every object was distinctly visible along the road. She experienced no fear, as the pedestrians were apparently housed at last. It was a benefit night of the moon, and Blonde had it all to herself. She was amazed at her strength, after all Mrs. St. Clair had told her of her sickness, and she unconsciously walked on a long distance. Several little brooks crossed the highway, and she would pause upon the bridges and study the white pebbles shining under the water. Then she walked on past a dense hedge fence of English blackthorn. Its fantastic effect in the clear moonlight pleased her eye, and she left the beaten road and went up to it to examine it. She stood a few moments in the shadow of the hedge looking over it at the gentle swells of the meadows stretching away under the moon. The Newfoundland walked up to her side, and then stretched himself at full length under the hedge to enjoy a brief rest while his fair mistress indulged her sentimental reverie. Blonde was recalled to recollection of her loneliness by a distant sound away off in the direction of Myrtle Dell. It was faint, but it seemed to increase. At that moment the town clock broke the silence. She counted *twelve.* She started at the unexpected lateness of her ramble. Before adventuring herself once more on the beaten road on her return, she listened for the strange, distant sound in the direction of the manor. Now she recognized the familiar sound of a horse's hoofs rapidly approaching. She felt timid, and crouched down under the hedge, placing her white hand on the head of her prostrate dog. The horse seemed to come at a fearful speed. He was near at hand. Blonde crouched lower in the shadow of the hedge to escape observation. A turn in the road brought the horse into view. He had a dark object for a rider. The steed himself was as black as the raven's wing. He bounded along the highway in frantic strides, guided by a fearless rider. An interfering fragment of rock flung a shower of sparks into the air, and then the black whirlwind swept by. Glorious and erect in conscious power over the black demon, with glittering black eyes, roving and beautiful flashed by the lost heir of the manor. His soft black hat was rolled up from his forehead, his strangely pointed chin and the aristocratic outline of his dark face distinctly traced in the clear moonlight. The crouching girl knew him, and back to her memory flashed the *cottage spectre*. She grasped a branch of the blackthorn hedge, and leaning her shadowy figure forward, peered out after him. Her hand trembled, and her heart beat quick, and the music of the past came booming along the aisles of her memory, for she *loved* him. In the silent hours of the night watch, in the morning prayer, and in the dim aisles of the chapel she had whispered to God his name. She had learned to love the far-off heart that was exiled for her. The unselfish love which had roved the earth like a lost bird had won her own. Would the rejected heart return again? Would the spurned and wounded pride crawl once more to the author of its agony? It mattered not. She loved him. Death was before him. She alone could save him. Did he know of his danger? Why else would he hover about the scenes of his childhood like a spectre and a shadow? The sound of the flying hoofs grew fainter. She could see the rider no longer. Yes; he ascended a rise in the highway at the same wild speed, and once more his dark figure appeared shadowy and dim in the moonlight. A few seconds longer he appeared; then he vanished in the distance.

The apparition, then, which had agitated the town of C——, was a reality. Henry Lansing had appeared in truth, at her parlor window, and in the confusion attendant upon her swoon, had glided in unnoticed, and recovered his secret journal. Would he be offended to find it in such keeping? Would he condemn old Rosy's confiding it to the girl who had rejected him? Was he conscious of the danger regarding the murder, and was this midnight flight on his favorite Black Hawk one of his fearless acts of defiance, to tempt the officers of the law to follow him, only to have the satisfaction of evading them? Or was he really flying in earnest, and was this the last glimpse of his manly form which would ever greet her eyes on earth? Was the love which had grown and secretly nourished itself for years in her heart, to prove now, at the moment its intensity was revealed to herself, only a mockery? Was her dream of happiness on earth, to be only a dream? At this thought of his final departure without seeing her who so longed to confess to him, that she regretted the answer she had written to his passionate offer, her heart was ready to cease its pulsations from agony and despair. She could have called after him, but her maiden modesty caused her to blush at the mere thought. She eagerly returned to the beaten road, and walked rapidly homeward. Occasionally she paused, and listened for the sound of hoofs on the silent and lonely road. He might return soon to the old manor house, and discover her on her way. All was quiet now, and she continued on. The bold rider had gone on into the heart of the town. But that might be the shortest and safest route of escape. The hour was so late there appeared slight hazard of his being met on the elm-shadowed streets of the town. Oh ! if he was really alarmed and flying once more, what would she not give to tell him that she possessed the evidence to clear him of any complicity with the crime of murder--that under the protecting wing of her testimony, he had nothing to fear. Where had he tarried so many long years, and where now was he going again ? And who was the old man seen with him stealing into the old ruin ? She listened often, standing tall and shadowy in the highway ; but no evidence of his return met her anxious ear and her throbbing heart. He was gone, then, never to return. She shivered and whispered to herself, "lost, lost to me forever." "But these sad locust leaves are ever whispering to me, 'the love of woman will never come to thee—*never*, oh ! *never*.' "

She pressed her white hand to her forehead, and struggled mournfully on. Now she realized the agony of his rejected heart long years before. Ah ! was not that the sound of his returning steed ? Her palpitating heart stood still. No ! it was a cruel cheat of the imagination. Poor, trembling lily ! the web of destiny was woven for you in mourning colors. He did not return.

On the ensuing morning, the proprietor of the manor went early to the vine-covered ruin. He had fancied on his bed at midnight, that the sound of flying hoofs passed his window, and a well-known voice shouted with the clear, ringing sound of a trumpet, till it was lost in the distant meadows towards the myrtle dell : " Farewell, dear old home, farewell."

The old gray-haired sire searched the deserted tenement in vain. *Black Hawk was gone.* The alarm was sounded over the county, and many a vigorous rider scoured the vallies and plains in search of the lost steed. He could not be tracked. When the search was finally abandoned, it was noticed that the old gentleman stooped a trifle in his walk, and his eagle eyes looked weary, as if the scenes and occupations of the earth had lost their golden interest, and were draped in gloom

---

CHAPTER XXVII.

Doctor Mosely was punctual to his appointment with the fair mistress of the cottage. As his buggy drove up to her gate, Blonde noticed that the wheels and the box had received an extra polish at the hands of Norman Prince, and that the fast horse was resplendent in an entirely new harness, whose silver ornaments flashed in the sunlight. The doctor had laid aside his solemn beaver hat, and appeared in a black velvet cap, which gave him a younger appearance by at least five years. He did not look a day over forty. His dark brown hair, with its occasional streaks of gray, fell from beneath his velvet cap in heavy masses of curls upon his neck, and reaching even to his shoulders. But the doctor's glory was his magnificent and massive beard of brown mixed with gray, extending low upon his breast. It was the frequent subject of remark among the girls of C——, and together with the thick moustache concealed the physician's mouth almost from sight. His nose was thin and straight, and his large dark eyes seemed ever in deep study when in repose. But when unusual excitement aroused them, they were brilliant and startling. Exposure to the sun and rain had darkened his complexion, but he was nevertheless styled a handsome man. He was a trifle under six feet, and powerfully framed. There were several young ladies resident in C—— who imagined it would be an exceedingly fine thing to have the dignified and intellectual-looking physician for a beau. But his female fancies evidently did not extend to very young ladies, so that the old maids and the widows entertained more reasonable hopes of some day ensnaring the heart of the favorite and successful practitioner, who had superseded his friend Doctor Cramer.

Blonde came to the door of her cottage to meet him, arrayed in her fall mourning cloak, whose sombre hue was only relieved by the flash of the jet buttons on the loose sleeves and front. Her white, dimpled face looked modestly forth from her crape bonnet, and her small, slender hands were displayed in accurately fitting gloves of black kid. As the physician assisted her to the seat of his vehicle, he wondered that the graceful lily should ever fancy light colors in her toilet. The dark chestnut steed, with his long black tail sweeping the earth, was impatient and eager, and the instant Doctor Mosely sprang to Blonde's side, the fiery beast was off.

Many curious eyes followed them as they passed along the principal street of C——, and some ladies who were promenading under the elms smiled at the idea that there was now to be a diversion of the doctor's attentions in favor of a member of the other church. Mrs. Bounce was far from being a favorite even in her own church. Her manner and tone were too dictatorial, and she was courted by many out of sheer terror of her slanderous tongue. It was a secret satisfaction, therefore, to many observers along the street, to realize that the intolerant widow was to have her claim on the favorite physician disputed. But the flying couple in the buggy were soon far beyond the reach of inquisitive eyes, and traversing the broad green fields on their route to the blue lake which was adjacent to the town, but hidden from view by an encircling belt of dense woods.

Blonde's pale face still bore traces of the anxiety and grief which had occasioned her a sleepless night. Long after she was safe again in her little home, had she watched by her parlor window in the faint hope that Henry Lansing and Black Hawk would yet reappear on the moonlit highway on their return to the manor. When she was too exhausted to watch longer, she had retired to her snow-white bed to weep that her hopes for life were so cruelly dashed to the earth and dissipated. She believed fate had sundered forever two hearts which only needed to understand each other to be united and happy. But her companion would not allow her thoughts to rove over such hopeless and desolate fields. He kept up such a running commentary of sense and wit upon everything and everybody in C——, that she was forced to laugh, and presently, under the exhilarating influence of the fresh air which whistled so swiftly past them, and the doctor's amusing conversation, she forgot for the hour the painful meditations of the past night. Nothing of interest in the country through which they were passing escaped the doctor's quick eye. To his poetic suggestions as to objects in the beautiful landscape, he added occasional hints as to the geological formations of the hills and valleys and the outcropping rocks. This subject was entirely new to Blonde, and with the quick appreciation of her clear intellect, she discovered that in the familiar scenery of her every day life, were to be found new and engrossing subjects of thought. She listened eagerly to the physician's enthusiastic discourse upon the ever new formations of the earth's surface, and their undoubted cause, for he spoke as one to whom the subject had long been one of close investigation, and profound interest. The moments sped rapidly in discussing this new theme, and Blonde became so absorbed, that when the buggy rattled upon the pebbles on the lake shore, she started in surprise at the rapidity with which their journey had been accomplished.

The beautiful sheet of water was indeed before them, stretching away to the northward, with no apparent boundary at that point of the compass. They were standing upon its southern border, which was covered with dense thickets of low bushes. The eastern boundary was a dense forest of oaks and pines, whose roots were level with the surface of the lake. But the western boundary of the lake was remarkably wild and beautiful. There the perpindicular rocks arose from the water's edge to a height of three hundred feet, exhibiting an irregular wall or boundary stretching along the lake shore for many miles to the northward. The face of this rocky wall was full of cavities, and to it clung the tangled roots of young pine trees and bushes and long mosses. Occasionally the strata of the rocks assumed the form of irregular stairs ascending from the lake shore to the very top of this gigantic wall. The eastern and the southern boundaries were low and tame; but this western wall of towering rocks was gloomy, unaccountable and grand.

It required little persuasion on the part of the agreeable doctor to induce his companion to leave the buggy and enjoy an hour's row upon the silent sheet of water. The horse was secured to a strong bush on the shore, and the little boat which was drawn up on the beach, was speedily entered by the doctor and the fearless Blonde. A few powerful strokes of the oar sufficed to carry the little party beyond the glare of the sun's rays, and into the shadow of the western wall of rocks, Now in the clear depths of the lake were seen the darting fish plainly revealed against the white pebbles on the bottom. As they glided by the wall of rocks, small caves were discovered in its face, but only extending a few feet back. Many of these openings were sufficient to shelter a score of men against the rain. Blonde peered into these occasional hollows in the towering wall, and finally expressed her disappointment that nothing worthy of the name of cavern could be seen. All were too shallow, and their distinctly-revealed interiors possessed no darkness or mysterious windings to attract the passing fancy of the imaginative and the romantic.

"All my life," she said, "I have been hoping to have a glimpse at a real *bona fide* cave. I have never seen one yet deeper than those holes. How much I would give to see a genuine, deep, mysterious cave, where one could hide from the world, and enjoy all sorts of wonderful adventures, such as we read of. It seems to me, Doctor Mosely, that with all your insight into the earth's formation, and your knowledge of the various strata of the rocks, you should be able to gratify my romantic curiosity by discovering a real cave for me."

The doctor rested on his oars in the shadow of the cliff, and looked steadily into the fair mourner's countenance. Blonde fancied she discovered an expression of uneasiness or anxiety in his dark eyes. Whatever may have been the cause of that expression, he quickly recovered his composure, and said, smilingly:

"You must not expect us to perform impossibilities, Miss Grayson. I have several times, since I became settled in C——, rowed past this wall of rock, and closely and carefully inspected its face. But I have failed to find in it any cavity larger or more important than these trivial fractures or openings between the strata. But I imagine you have little conception of the difficulties and dangers of penetrating the recesses of great caves. In many of them are pitfalls where one false step in the darkness would precipitate you instantly into eternity. Sometimes they are damp, and dripping with moisture; and other are filled with noxious gases which destroy life. Do you believe you would possess nerve sufficient to attempt the exploration of a cave where these difficulties were to be encountered?"

"The very danger and uncertainty of the thing is what would delight me most in a cavern," she answered, with spirit. "I know I shouldn't enjoy a tame cave any more than I do these trifling holes we are passing: but give me a mysterious opening in the rocks, where there is uncertainty enough to put me on my guard, and caution enough required to keep me from breaking my neck, and I would be willing to undertake its exploration."

She was watching the cliff as she replied, for she fancied a figure of animated life was just passing behind some bushes which clung high against the lofty rocks above her. She felt convinced, at another glance upward, that it was only imagination; for the bushes were absolutely inaccessible, being at a point at least two hundred feet above the level of the lake. No one could reach this clinging shrubbery, from the summit of the rocky wall, without leaping down a perpendicular face of rock a distance of one hundred dizzy feet. The physician observed that upturned look, however, and followed the direction of her eyes, but discovered nothing unusual against the side of the cliff. He was gazing in his companion's blue eyes again by the time she had concluded; and when Blonde glanced at his countenance she detected in that gaze such admiration and interest as Mrs. St. Clair had assured her possessed the physician's heart in her regard. The fair mourner pretended not to observe anything unusual in the doctor's expression, but looked steadily down again into the clear depths of the lake, at the darting movements of the fish. Dr. Mosely soon recovered his calm control over the secret sentiment which he had determined to suppress, and said, gaily:

"Your manner indicates resolution enough for any hazardous undertaking; but I have had some experience in caves, and I fear your courage would be tested severely in some of them."

"Try me," was the prompt and resolute reply to this remark; and then she continued the study of the lake's depths.

At this sententious challenge, her companion looked as if he was about to communicate some intensely interesting fact, but he changed his mind, and said, as he drew a small ivory flute from the inside breast pocket of his coat,

"You speak with the firmness of a Spartan, Miss Grayson, and the first genuine cave I come across, shall be made known to you. But there is a peculiar echo returned from these rocks which you must hear. I brought my flute with me thinking it possible we might have use for it. This flute was presented to me by a medical friend who took a desperate fancy to me while I was pursuing my professional studies. The instrument has a remarkable history—but never mind that now. Notice that point where the cliff deviates from its regular northward direction. You see that deflection which almost makes an angle in the uniform line of the rocky wall, well, that is the point to which I shall run. There a singular effect is produced by any loud noise, or even a slight sound. I first noticed it in the echo occasioned by my oar grating on the row-lock."

The doctor placed the ivory flute, with silver keys, across his lap, and grasping his oars once more, pulled away for the point indicated. As the boat reached the obtuse angle in the cliff, Blonde could hear the sounds from the row-locks repeated faintly as if the echo was directly over her head, high in air.

The illusion was that another boat was passing in the air above her. Her companion rested a moment on his oars. Then he raised the small ivory instrument to his lips, and played softly, "Home, sweet home." Then he paused and enquired if she detected anything unusual. Her surprised answer was, "No, nothing, except that you play remarkably well."

Then he directed her when he commenced again on the flute to look directly upward to a large white cloud which appeared to rest motionless in the blue sky. She raised her beautiful face to the cloud, and listened intently. The low, silvery melody of the flute trembled gently upon the air and floated away in dying cadences over the silent lake. Ah! She heard it faintly then. Some winged seraph hidden in the snowy veil of the motionless cloud took up the melting cadences and adapted them to the more perfect flutes of Heaven The angel who looked in the face of God was playing softly too of "Home, sweet home." A gentle, pure and eternal home, where love was nurtured, sighs hushed into melody, and fruition full. Again and again the hidden angel softly wooed her weary spirit *home.* The celestial tempter would not leave her, but still breathed on the alluring notes which soothed the human yearnings of her lonely heart and drew it closely to the side of God, her Father. Home, dear, dear home, with its outstretched angel arms, its beaming eyes, its low, sweet, never-ending music was unfolding its golden portals in the snowy cloud to tempt her far from earth and human love. The hidden angel slowly left her, closing the golden portals of his home with his passing wings as he gently whispered himself away into the majestic presence of God.

Then she heard once more the low plash of the blue lake upon its rocky barrier, and looking down beheld the doctor with his ivory magic flute quietly regarding her. Tears were in her gentle, mysterious eyes as she silently extended her gloved hand to her companion in gratitude. He took it, pressed it kindly, and immediately relinquished it with a smile, saying:

"I know that I have been entirely alone for a moment in this boat. Would to God we were both with that echo music in Heaven."

Then Doctor Mosely reluctantly turned the prow of his boat homeward, and pulled away slowly down the lake. When the blue-eyed dreamer after a few moments broke the silence, she said:

"To whom did you first communicate this mystery of the echo?"

The doctor answered as he rowed, "To Miss Blonde Grayson."

She said with warmth, "You have made this one of the loveliest days of my life. Not content with watching over me and rescuing my life from disease, you have sought to beautify that life by giving me one golden day of pleasure. You have artfully converted your patient into a grateful friend."

Her companion was strongly tempted to enquire if she could ever experience a still more tender sentiment than friendship. But he feared to offend her now and dispel the powerful impression he had made. He therefore only said:

"I am honored by the friendship of the lily of C——. My life too has its golden hours and words, and you are now contributing to them. But if you are not weary, I would be happy to make you a joint owner of another mystery. Will you keep a secret?"

Blonde looked at him in surprise.

"Why certainly, if it does not trespass on the claims of God. Does it concern this lake?"

Her companion reflected an instant before he replied. Then he spoke from sudden impulse:

"It does concern this lake and its surroundings. I know of a real cave, dark and mysterious enough to satisfy your vein of romance entirely. Will you promise to conceal its existence if I will disclose to you the entrance? A question of property is involved in the secret existence of the cave, and I am reluctant to hazard my material interests in the gratification of your romance. I should be happy to share the secret with you."

The required promise was instantly and eagerly given. The physician then glanced carefully over the lake to detect the presence of human life. The two appeared to be alone upon the calm sheet of water. He then glanced at the western sun. There would plainly be more than an hour remaining of bright sunlight. That glance decided him, and bending to his oars with renewed vigor, he forced the sharp bows of the boat through the calm, sleeping waters of the lake. He was heading directly for the point where he had secured his horse at starting. The dividing waters at the prow of the gliding boat rippled musically away, and for a few moments were the only sounds to break the silence of the evening scene, save the regular jarring noise of the oars on the row-locks. Blonde's eye was roving over the contrasting colors of the dark green pines and oaks on the low eastern shore, the dark brown rocks of the cliff whose shadows were lengthening over the lake from the west, and the apparently limitless sheet of blue stretching away to the northward. She was wondering where the entrance to this mysterious cave would be reached. But her companion's occasional glances at the rocky western shore gave her no clue to his secret, and soon the barrier of rocks was passed entirely, and the tamer view of the low shrubbery on the semi-circular beach at the south was discovered. The terminus of the lofty range of rocks gradually receded until it resembled an adamantine mountain rising from the lake and the bushy swamps.

At length her wandering eyes caught a glimpse of the ivory flute resting against the gunwale of the boat. She reached forward for it, saying, "May I examine it?"

"Certainly," was the reply; "there is no mystery about *that*, except the Arabic characters in gold at the small end. I do not understand that Eastern dialect, but I have been informed the motto interpreted signifies literally 'the charmer of serpents.' You are probably aware of the strange tales told of the powers of Oriental snake-tamers. The physician who presented me with the flute taught me several tunes which he declared he had known personally to quiet and subdue serpents when writhing in the most fearful excitement and rage. I intend to try its influence upon the very first reptile I meet Do you believe it is superstition, Miss Grayson?"

Blonde looked at the doctor as if she fancied he was quizzing her. But his dark eyes looked so calm and earnest under his graceful velvet cap, and his flowing splendid beard made him resemble so accurately engravings of savants and scientific discoverers which she had in her portfolio at the cottage, that she checked the dart of satire which flashed to her lips. She answered doubtfully:

"It is hazardous to designate anything as superstition in these scientific days. If I understand the results of scientific discovery, as many superstitions have been confirmed to be facts as have been swept away from human credulity and acceptance. I know, Doctor Mosely, of men with beastly natures and lives being subdued by the power of music. But I must confess there are persons in C—— with *snaky* natures, whom no earthly strains of melody will ever subdue or improve. I fear both they and their serpent prototypes are beyond the salutary influences of music."

She laughed, for the physician was aware of several instances in point, and she knew his attention had been called to the subject in the course of even his brief practice in C——. He laughed too, but he shook his heavy beard and said:

"Don't surrender all hope of poor human nature. No doubt there is some gentle influence powerful enough to tame even these—but here we are at our starting point. Fortunately the lake shore is remarkably deserted and lonely this evening. We can all the better conceal our movements in approaching the entrance to the cave. It is perfectly splendid to have a secret to share with *you*. In our wanderings to-day I have been thinking of 'Beauty and the Beast.' I am the Beast, and you are the other interesting personage of that remarkable tale. If Gurty Lansing had been present to-day, you may rely upon it we and our boat would have figured in a painting."

The doctor was interrupted by the grating of the boat's bottom upon the pebbles. He sprang to the beach with his Arabian flute, and drew the skiff high upon the strand. Then he assisted the dark, graceful figure of the orphan to alight upon the pebbly shore. He informed her, as he did so, that they were to have another short ride in the buggy around the bushy swamp to the rear of the lake's western adamantine boundary.

The horse was found secure and undisturbed, fastened to the bush. They were soon whirling along the road which curved among the bushes of the morass, and after a few rods turned into a half broken and unused road which entered the dark and dense wood which encircled the lake. Finally a point was attained where the further progress of their vehicle became impracticable from the fallen trees and bushes in the road. The physician remarked, upon assisting his companion to alight, that their walk would be short, and the sun was still an hour high in the West. Then he secured his horse and advanced slowly before Blonde, selecting the dry and hard places for her to walk through the bushes. She succeeded, with his assistance, in passing through the woods comfortably, and presently the two emerged from the shadows of the trees on to slightly rising and firm ground covered densely with low shrubbery. In the midst of this entangling thicket of undergrowth, from which the great oaks and pines had been cleared away, Doctor Mosely paused, and kneeling down, parted with his arms the closely standing bushes, and disclosed to his companion a dark opening in the ragged and disordered rocks. The aperture was large enough to receive his figure by crawling on his hands and knees. He informed his friend that she must stoop sometimes to conquer, and she fearlessly and laughingly gathered her dark skirts together and prepared to crawl down into the frightful hole on her hands and knees after her conductor. The thick bushes closed together after them, and they disappeared in the profound darkness of the cave.

CHAPTER XXVIII.

BEFORE Blonde had crawled twenty feet in the profound darkness, she heard the calm voice of her guide warn her of an abrupt angle in the low tunnel. She put out her hand, and touched at one side the dry rocky wall of the cave. Then she crawled on a few feet further and put out her hand again, till finally she groped her tedious way to the designated angle which changed her course to the right. The bottom of the tunnel was soft, dry sand, and the only painful part of her gloomy journey was bending her head so low to avoid striking it against the jagged corners of the rock above her. She had never experienced before the horror of being in total darkness, where the sun's rays had never penetrated since the creation. She was in a low tunnel on her hands and knees, with her head bent nearly to the ground, and utterly ignorant of one foot of the frightful way. She was entirely in the power of a man whom she had known only for a few months, and in darkness which was fast becoming oppressive. She could only hear his voice ahead of her, and once her hand touched his foot. But he was her physician, and his brief acquaintance had inspired unbounded confidence. Had she known the arduous and gloomy nature of the undertaking, she would never have left the buggy. But it would appear weak and childish now to recede, particularly after the favor the physician had extended to her in making her the sole partner of his secret. She braced her nerves, which had never failed her but once, for whatever might occur in this intensely dark hole. Finally the guide said;

"Here is my hand extended to you, Miss Grayson; find it, if you can; crawl a few feet further, and you will reach me."

She obeyed his instructions, and her outstretched hand finally came in contact with his leg. He grasped her gloved hand firmly in his muscular palm, and raised her to her feet. He said,

"Now the rock is two feet above your head. This is my reception room we are in now. Wait one minute, and we will have a light."

He left her standing erect in the impenetrable gloom, and groped about for his torch. In a few seconds a pale blue flame was visible in a thin wreath of smoke. It revealed the shadowy outline of the doctor's form. Then the increasing flame of the sulphur match was applied to the birch bark of the torch in his hand. The combustible bark lighted into a glorious blaze, and the cavern was distinctly revealed. It was an apartment twenty feet square, and nearly eight feet in height. Blonde saw on one side the low, dark tunnel through which she had crawled, and opposite to it was another tunnel at least four feet wide, much higher than her head, and which appeared to indicate further wonders when their journey should be continued. The doctor's reception room was roofed with ragged rocks. The walls were mingled rocks and dark earth, and the floor carpeted with soft, dry sand. A pile of birch bark had been placed at one side to replenish the torch. The physician filled his pockets with the bark, and after enjoying her surprise at the first apartment of his subterranean mansion, proposed that their journey should be continued. His tall, graceful companion assented, and he led the way with his blazing torch. Entering the new tunnel, they proceeded cautiously but easily along for two or three rods till the narrow way suddenly widened into another cavern extending at least one hundred feet in every direction. The guide held his torch high in air, and Blonde could see overhead in the dim distance the tangled roots of immense size, which the doctor stated belonged to the great oaks on the surface of the earth. They were fantastically woven about the overhanging rocks, and Blonde fancied she could see some of them moving and swaying back and forth in mid air. What was her horror when the guide explained the twisted roots which seemed to move. They were immense snakes, and this was one of their favorite dens. She turned instinctively at a soft, gentle sound near her on the rocks, and beheld two brilliant eyes moving directly towards her on a level with her head. There was an undulatory motion of the creature's head as it approached her, and she darted, shivering with terror, behind the guide for protection. It was an enormous *rattle snake*. Doctor Mosely calmly presented his blazing torch close to the eyes of the deadly reptile, and the snake glided away down the side of the cave with a writhing motion, sounding his dreadful rattle. At the same instant Blonde felt another serpent glide swiftly across her foot. She sprang backward, and detected it coiling itself, and darting its head, watching for an opportunity to spring. Cold chills ran down her back, and she retreated with terrified bounds into the tunnel. Oh! horror—the crevices of the tunnel were full of them, and a dozen rattles commenced to sound at her cry of alarm, on every side. She sprang back again to the doctor's side. She was just in time. He swung his blazing torch around her, as she clung to his arm, and held the writhing, gliding devils at bay. He said quickly to her,

"Take some pieces of the birch bark from my pockets, and while I swing the torch, light them and fling them about."

Blonde obeyed nervously. She drew a handful of the pieces from his coat pocket. But it was very difficult to ignite them, while the torch was circling about her. One by one they blazed forth at the touch of the whirling flame and she flung them with the accurate aim of despair into the eyes of the enraged and gathering serpents. A circle of blazing fire was gradually established about the two, and the calm, self-possessed doctor found time to sound his ivory flute. Placing his torch in Blonde's hands, he raised his Arabian charmer to his lips, and played a wild, strange melody. Suddenly the angry rattles ceased. The serpents glided softly around the ring of protecting fire, and their ire appeared gradually to subside. The burning and scattered fragments of bark illumined the whole cavern, and Blonde shuddered at the animated and tangled clusters of the reptiles which swung from the roof and sides of the rattlesnake den. The wild, soothing strains of the ivory flute echoed strangely through the subterranean aisles, and the serpents exhibited their pleasure in the softened expression of their lustrous eyes and their gentle, playful motions. The physician slowly commenced to advance, still sounding his flute, while Blonde clung to his side, swinging her torch. Their route lay across the centre of the den, and they carefully picked their steps, so as to avoid trampling on the charmed reptiles.

At the opposite side of the cavern was another broad tunnel which fortunately was untenanted. Slowly the guide marched to the sound of the snake-charmer, and slowly followed the shadowy figure of his companion, with the blazing torch. One by one the snakes were left behind. At the mouth of the new tunnel Blonde dropped three lighted pieces of the bark to prevent pursuit. But the danger was already over, for the serpents were soothed and dreamy, and heeded only the softly-stealing strains of melody.

Slowly moving and softly playing, the guide continued on through the tunnel, which was gently rising to another cavern of enormous proportions. Not until the two had entered this new cavern did Doctor Mosely discontinue his flute melody. Then taking the torch from Blonde, he said :

"Your first alarm was natural, but you recovered yourself with wonderful quickness. There was a more extensive gathering of the infernal family than I ever witnessed. But your beauty, Miss Grayson, always gathers a crowd of admiring eyes. Thank God! you are safe. Here is a seat made on purpose for you, ages ago. You are pale, and a brief rest will benefit you.

He pointed the torch at a snow-white stalagmite on the floor of the cavern, fashioned in rude imitation of a chair with a sloping back. Blonde sank gratefully into the seat, and immediately the doctor said :

"Look upward, Miss Grayson, this is my palace."

The fair girl was utterly bewildered. She had just passed through a scene in which many girls would have fainted and fallen, and thus jeopardized both her own life and the guide's. Her efficiency at the critical moment when the fire circle was required to give the doctor's flute time to produce its soothing effect, had probably saved them. But she fancied yet that she heard the sound of their dreadful rattles, and saw the baleful glitter of their approaching eyes. At first she could only discover the calm eyes of the physician regarding her, his heavy flowing beard, his velvet cap, and his blazing torch held high in air. As she discerned in his pleased look, at last, that all danger was really over, the realization of the guide's last word suddenly burst upon her astonished vision. *Palace!* the word was tame. The snow-white pinnacles, and minarets, the well-defined mausoleums with their attendant angels, the bride in her orange blossoms and veil, the maiden with her first love-letter unopened in her trembling hand, the procession of nuns with the mitred bishop following with his crosier, the foaming cataract, the bridal chamber with its flowing drapery, the firmament with its clusters of stars, all, all were revealed in that wonderful cavern, fashioned and draped entirely in snowy white. The blazing torch of the guide revealed them all buried as they had been for centuries from human sight, to serve some inscrutible purpose of their Divine Architect. The figure of the mourner in her white stone chair, and her guide with his torch, were the only dark objects in the glorious stalactite chamber of the earth.

Blonde sprang to her feet with a thrill of pleasure in every vein. Placing her dark-gloved hand on the arm of the guide, she asked :

"Is this the real fairy-land of my childhood, or am I dreaming?"

The doctor enjoyed her delight for a moment; then he said gaily:

"Take my torch, Miss Grayson, for one moment, till I wake up the ancient and enchanted sleepers who have never realized the importance of two citizens of C——. We shall soon have all these venerable white heads recognizing the charms of our music, and taking their lessons from us."

The doctor shouted at the snowy bride—"Who made your dress?"

A few seconds silence ensued, and then the immense assembly of white heads seemed to answer—" dress, dress, dress."

The guide shouted again at the procession of white nuns.

"You're a nice party of religious characters to be mixed up with brides and sinners, and talking so much about dress."

After a short silence the white assembly, nuns and all, reiterated, "dress, dress, dress."

Blonde and the guide roared with laughter at this reply. And then the whole assembly joined in the laugh. The doctor shouted once more—

"You 're in such a laughing mood, I'll play for you all to dance."

The whole incongruous assembly soon echoed back their assent, "dance, dance, dance."

The physician said again, "Well, bishop, take one of the nuns and lead off."

The assembly assented again, "off, off, off."

The Arabian flute trilled forth a waltz, and immediately a thousand unseen flutes joined in. Every snowy statue appeared to own a flute, and the cavern was filled with the melody of the grand orchestra. The physician ceased his playing, and said:

"We shall get no dancing out of the dead."

Again the great white assembly solemnly replied, "dead, dead, dead."

When Blonde appeared sufficiently satiated with the marvelously beautiful formation of the stalactites, and was willing to proceed, the guide looked quizzically at her and asked:

"Are you willing to return through the beautiful chamber of serpents?"

"Oh! mercy, no," exclaimed his companion, with a look of genuine terror, "I wouldn't have one of those things *touch* me, let alone their fangs. Oh! is there no other outlet to this cave?"

The great white assembly answered vaguely, "cave, cave, cave."

The physician said with marked earnestness of tone:

"I would not take you through that den again for worlds—you are too dear to me—I would not have come that way at all, only that our time was short, and then I have never seen anything like as many snakes in that cave. I have traversed it several times before. And then you recollect your challenge to me in the boat. That decided me. And now I am both sorry and glad. You are the kind of woman to rely on in times of trouble, and I have found it out now—come this way, and we can find a way out."

The guide started ahead with his torch, and the tall, graceful mourner gladly followed, bearing the Arabian charmer of serpents in her gloved hand, the whole assembly in white repeating rudely to their visitors, "out, out, out."

The flame of the torch flashed wildly ahead through another lofty tunnel, resplendent with the grotesque and ever-varying shapes of the stalactites. Then they emerged into a small cave with a perfectly-formed dome of pure transparent crystal, which flashed in the light like so many enormous diamonds of the first water. The guide remarked in passing, "here is the repository of my crown jewels." Then he hastened on expressing his anxiety to reach the outlet and emerge into the practical world again, before total darkness should have settled upon the earth. He informed Blonde that their expected point of egress from the cave would be a long distance from the wood where his horse was secured, and that when they were once more safe among the haunts of men she would have to sit down alone and wait for him until he could return to the distant wood and drive his horse around for her. She quickened her pace at these words, for she recollected that the sun was only an hour high when she first crawled down into the darkness of the physician's reception cave.

The scene was ever changing in marvelous beauty and wildness. Now a clear stream was crossed on the dry stepping-stones; now a small waterfall sounded with singular echoes through the extensive caverns. The guide would not allow his companion to tarry a single moment to inspect and discuss the novelties on their route, informing her from his own experience in the cave that hours were thus unconsciously consumed in passing. At another and more favorable opportunity he would enter the secret cave with her again. On, on they passed with rapid step, the torch-light flaring back over the doctor's head, and the long avenues and successive caves appearing to be interminable. Sometimes the echoes of their conversation boomed away into side avenues and caverns and rolled away in the unknown distance like sullen thunder. Occasionally they skirted the edges of yawning pits, whose mysterious blackness and uncertainty caused Blonde to shudder. But the physician proceeded ahead with such an air of confidence and familiarity with every locality, that her alarm was speedily hushed, and she followed in his footsteps at last devoid of fear, and striving only to keep closely behind him. The air of the subterranean passages was remarkably pure and invigorating, and she experienced no anxiety except as to the late hour at which she felt confident she would reach her home. Her guide several times paused to adjust a fresh piece of the birch bark to the end of his torch, and when it was fairly ignited started on again at his steady pace. He informed her constantly of some strange novelty ahead in the caves and passages, and she was thus enabled to have a glimpse at all the prominent curiosities of the underground journey without losing any of the precious time.

Finally, when Blonde commenced to experience decided symptoms of fatigue, the guide suddenly halted at a dark side tunnel. He then informed the astounded girl that she had passed a distance of two long miles under ground. She could scarcely credit the assertion, so absorbing had been the beauties and wonders of the subterranean journey. Then he pointed to the dark side tunnel, and said:

"This is our route now, Miss Grayson. The distance to the surface of the earth through this side tunnel is very short. But extraordinary caution is required in passing not to come in contact with its sides, for they are merely composed of sand. A slight jar might suffice to bring down upon us a thousand tons of sand and destroy us."

Before the words had fairly left the physician's lips, a heavy sound like the fall of ten thousand sods upon ten thousand coffins met their startled ears. At the same instant the torch, which was extended into the side tunnel, was extinguished, and they were in total darkness. The dreadful sound could have but one appalling meaning—the side tunnel *was closed up for ever.*

Blonde's eyes dilated with horror in the darkness, and her brave heart was clutched as by an iron hand. Two long miles of caverns to be retraced, and then a battle with the slimy rattlesnakes in their den. This was their only hope of escape. The voice of the physician in the utter darkness called her. His tones were despairing.

"Miss Grayson, I trust to Almighty God you are unhurt!"

"No! I am standing here alone and safe, doctor," she answered.

Then the dreadful interrogatory ensued: "Miss Grayson, have you a friction match about you? Mine are all gone."

The poor girl fell on her knees in agony, and raised her clasped hands to God. Two miles of diverging caverns, with a thousand pitfalls to eternity, *and no light!* Buried alive in the bowels of the earth, they were never to look upon the bright sun again. Two miles of darkness and pitfalls, and then a den of venomous reptiles, tangled, deadly serpents, buried in the gloom and impenetrable darkness of the grave. Hope was the mockery of their despair.

And yet God reigns, and no sparrow falls to the ground unnoticed.

"Miss Grayson, I have found one match and only one—if that fails us, are you prepared to die here?"

"Doctor Mosely," answered a low, sweet voice, "God is here, and I shall pray, long after the match fails us. His power is unfettered by the success or failure of that puny source of light. Try the match, while I pray to Him who has promised to hear the cry of the despairing."

A faint blue light arose in the doctor's hand. The match feebly burned, and then *went out.* The faithful physician moaned in agony, and murmured half reproachfully, "I fear God is not here."

"Doctor Mosely, my God is everywhere," softly answered the lost, doomed girl.

"Amen!" was solemnly uttered along the cavern aisles by a strange voice, which seemed to issue from a pit. "The God whom I adore is your God too, strange girl."

> "In vain do you seek to behold Him;
> He dwells in no temple apart:
> The height of the heavens cannot hold Him,
> And yet He is here in my heart."

The strange and mysterious solemnity of the voice echoed along the blackness of the cavern, and then all was silence again. Suddenly the stalactites of the cavern glistened, the crystals flashed from the walls, and the glorious glare of a light poured along the course of a side tunnel. They were saved.

An old man slowly came into view with a great torch in one hand and a *steel hammer* in the other.

Blonde Grayson anxiously studied the face of the approaching stranger; then exclaimed as she saw his lion eyes, "Thank God! it is old Hugo."

The delighted old geologist knew her, and warmly shook her proffered hand. Then she informed him that the tunnel which was now filled with sand had been their expected route of egress from the cave. She carefully avoided betraying Doctor Mosely's secret entrance, hoping old Hugo knew of some other outlet to the cave. She said, "This gentleman with me is Doctor Mosely, a new physician in C——. He loves the study of geology as well as you."

The physician advanced with his extinguished torch and shook the hand of the old man. Then he expressed the hope that old Hugo would pilot them out of the cave by whatever route he had penetrated to this point of meeting. The old geologist replied in his hoarse, stern tones, that since their own tunnel was now closed against them, he believed he had a fair right to insist upon certain terms in effecting their release. He finally told them that if they would consent to be blindfolded until they were both conducted to Blonde Grayson's cottage door, so that his secret entrance might remain his secret still, he would willingly conduct them into the open air. There was no reason why they should not assent. The old geologist was known to be honest and reliable. With light hearts they suffered folded handkerchiefs to be bound over their eyes. Then taking hold of each other's hands, and securing a firm grip also of their guide's belt, they contrived to follow his steady, moderate pace, relieving the tedious nature of their long journey by conversations and jests with their conductor.

After an hour's march this queerly linked trio felt the soft grass yielding under their feet, and old Hugo informed them that the stars were brightly shining above them in the September evening. After a long walk through the fields and along the roads, the old guide paused and requested them to remove the bandages from their eyes. They required no second invitation, and looking out in bewilderment, saw Blonde Grayson's cottage gate before them in the clear starlight.

CHAPTER XXIX.

WHILE Blonde Grayson and her physician were wandering in the subterranean chambers of the secret cave, the widow at the manor was maturing her plans to solve the mystery of the lantern passing across the window of the deserted manor house. Her skeptical nature at once rejected the prevailing theory that the old tenement was *haunted*. She firmly held to the belief of her dead mother that the uncle's gold was concealed in the neighborhood of the old-fashioned chimney, and that the apparitions were only persons familiar with her mother's tradition, who were searching to recover the lost treasure. She resolved on the very night of the ludicrous thrashing of her clergyman, the Reverend Thomas Delaplaine, that she would secretly and alone maintain a watch every night upon the old ruin. Her father had become so thoroughly disgusted with the subject of supernatural visitations since the sufferings of his friend were caused by his own hand, that he studiously avoided the subject, and the old manor house itself, after the strange disappearance of Black Hawk. Thus the fearless widow found little difficulty in stealing away an hour or two every night unnoticed, to keep an eye upon the silent old tenement of her ancestors. Finally her patience and perseverance were one night rewarded when she had watched unusually late, hidden in the shrubbery, by seeing her lost brother, Henry Lansing, emerge from the old ruin, mounted on the back of his favorite steed. He reined in Black Hawk near the manor brook, and remained motionless for several minutes, apparently studying deeply. The moon shone brightly in his face, and to her eyes he appeared to be little changed physically by the flight of four years. He looked the same elegant, fearless gentleman he was when the murder of Hartwell occurred. She saw him at length move off at his swift pace, as of old, directly across the moonlit fields towards the colonnade of the new manor house. She saw him ride swiftly by his home, and heard his clear shout ringing over the meadows as he dashed off towards the myrtle dell. She felt confident he could not long remain hidden, and must soon fall into the clutches of the law. It was evident to her mind that he must know something of the hidden gold of his mother's uncle, for he had evidently entered the old ruin itself in some mysterious way, and she hoped the gold was in this hidden passage, and might yet fall into her own hands. She deemed it highly probable that the apparition of the old man might be the uncle, who had also fled the country to avoid the consequences of his crime. The two were apparently in communication with each other, and no doubt shared the secret of the gold.

The evening following the heir's departure on Black Hawk, the widow went out before the moon had arisen, and concealed herself again in the shrubbery on another side of the vine-covered ruin, in order to have a better view of whatever figure might come out, and to endeavor to see from what particular room the apparition issued. The stars were softly beaming in the sky, and she hoped to be able to see and identify the figure of the strange old man by their faint light, in case he should appear before the rising of the moon. She waited long and patiently, sitting under the bushes, entirely concealed, and with her dark eyes fixed attentively upon the open door in the southern gable of the haunted house. The evening was chilly, and she crouched low under the shrubbery, drawing her cloak closely about her throat, and leaving her dark hood open only sufficiently far to give her snaky, glittering eyes a fair view of the gable door. The stars yielded a feeble light, serving to render her position a perfect cover from unwelcome eyes, but occasioning the watcher sensations of loneliness and gloom which were new to her. Her conscience, sere and hardened as it was, was nevertheless busy; for the wicked really enjoy no rest, even when their plans and purposes seem fairly and successfully under way. Employing religion and her church only as a cloak to the evil passions of her nature, and fully conscious of the immunity a woman enjoys from opprobrium if she can only succeed in passing herself off for a zealous communicant of a religious denomination, Mrs. Bounce was nevertheless to a certain extent susceptible to the influences of that God and that Bible in which she firmly believed. When her hand held up to the light the red vial which was to cost Gurty his life, so far as she could effect that result, the words of that Bible, familiar to her from childhood, came to her recollection with all their serious meaning and warning.

She did not disbelieve God at that moment; she only defied Him for the sake of the manor. She believed firmly that her punishment would some day come, and yet she was willing for the sake of the brief enjoyment of the present, to await the long and bitter chastisement of the future. When she persecuted the "lily of C——" on account of her church principles, and sought to injure her for that moderate exercise of her privilege of dancing and gayety which her church tolerated; she knew, that in the sight of God she was seeking to destroy the character of one whom she believed to be actuated by principle and by a sense of duty. She knew that in refusing to her neighbor charity and consideration on account of professing a different creed, she directly violated the command of God. And yet for the sake of parading her own dogmatism, and exhibiting to the town how many severe and satirical remarks she could make, she was willing to defy God, by her intolerance. And thus while her moral sense was as perfect and clear as in her girlhood, she advanced steadily from intolerance to slander, from slander to covetousness, and from covetousness to murder. She had failed in destroying Gurty's life; she now was planning the death of the returned heir, whom she believed to be innocent. She was scheming to secure his arrest, his condemnation and his execution. And strangely clear and solemn through all these criminal efforts did her conscience declare to her, "Esther Bounce, no woman knows better than yourself, the well-defined boundaries between right and wrong. Your intellect is cultivated and clear—no one can appreciate the holiness of your dead mother better than yourself—you know what she was—you know what you ought to be—you know that you meditate and plan sin with the clearest sense of its atrocity in the sight of a holy God, that any cultivated intellect is incapable of—your punishment in perdition will surpass in intensity the pains of most souls, because you realize so clearly the distinctions between right and wrong. You are concealed here now to find materials for compassing the death of your brother; you are here too, to appropriate entirely to yourself that gold which, if your mother's uncle is really dead, is the inheritance, not of one, but of many, and *you know* that fact. I shall cease my voice now, for a footstep approaches—but in the name of God who loves your soul—beware."

She listened intently, for the sound of footsteps was behind her, and near. She turned her eyes away from the door in the gable, moving her dark figure slowly and carefully around that no leaf might rustle and no twig break. She detected in the star-light, the muffled figure of a woman. She expected some one from that direction, but remained perfectly still that no mistake might occur. The figure advanced slowly and cautiously, peering into every shadow. Then it paused in uncertainty. In a few seconds, it advanced very near to the widow's place of concealment, and said in a low tone,

"Mrs. Bounce, are you here?"

She replied in the same guarded tone, "Yes, Mary—crawl under these bushes as noiselessly as you can."

The accomplice carefully followed this direction. and finally sat beside the widow in a little area formed by the encircling shrubbery.

"What success have you had, Mary?"

The servant replied by producing a miniature from her bosom, and handing it to her employer. The starlight was too feeble for any identification of the small picture. Then the widow enquired again:

"What are the eyes? what color? and the hair?"

The maid replied, "They're black, staring eyes, and his beard is black as ink, and so is his hair. The case it's in is all covered with little tiny doves—I tried awful hard to get hold of a letter, but there wa'nt none from him."

Mrs. Bounce reflected a moment, and then asked:

"Will you be perfectly willing to go into court and swear that she showed this to you as being one of her lovers?—will you swear that she permitted you to keep it for her with her other valuables?"

"Of course I will," replied the servant, "if I get the gold you promised me."

The widow handed the servant a little paper package containing ten pieces of gold.

The accomplice opened the paper and poured the money into the palm of her hand. She could not detect, in the star-light, the denomination of the coin, but she said—

"Thank you, Mrs. Bounce, you're a fine lady—and I s'pose it's all right—it feels right, in my hand, but I can't see whether it's silver or gold."

Her companion deigned no reply to this dubious remark, and for a moment was silent. Before she could think of other instructions to give the servant, the girl suddenly recollected that she had other information to communicate.

"Oh! Mrs. Bounce, I most forgot one thing—when I was a-rummaging in her drawers, I came across a letter of your brother, Mr. Henry. It was a love-letter to her. I read it all through, and I declare to you, he laid it on thick—would that be any use to you? fur if it is, I can get it easy. He wanted her to marry him awful bad."

The widow could not avoid a sudden start—she said quickly, "Why! Mary, that letter is everything—it's worth more than this miniature—the vile hussy! how dared she to lead him on so? the unscrupulous intriguing parvenu. If you'll get that letter of Mr. Henry's for me, I'll give you fifty more dollars in gold. I wonder the hussy did not marry him—she probably was waiting to get some agreement from him to settle property on her."

The avaricious servant said;

"I'll bring that very letter to you the first chance I git—it was lucky my gittin' away to-night; but she's bin gone so long, I thought I'd steal out and make some excuse or other."

"Where had she gone, Mary?"

"I don't know exactly where," replied the girl, "but I heard her tell Mister Carl one place was the lake. Dr. Mosely cum in his buggy, and all fixed up in fine clothes, and a new harness on his horse, and tuk her away. They've bin gone ever since two o'clock, and Mister Carl had to eat his tea all alone, to-night."

Here was information with a vengeance. The widow was ready to yell with rage. It was by a powerful effort she succeeded in preventing her jealousy from attracting the attention of the servant. She controlled herself sufficiently to say with a nonchalant tone of voice:

"Doctor Mosely must be a beau of your mistress. I suppose it is no strange matter for him to ride with her."

"Oh! indeed it *is* strange, Mrs. Bounce," replied the girl. "He never comes to see her unless when she's sick. He never came except on a sick call before—and to be gone so long, too. I tell you, Mr. Carl is worried about it. He said some accident must have happened. I'll have to hurry back, Mrs. Bounce; it won't do at all for me to be gone long—they may be back already."

The widow said slowly:

"I don't want to keep you, Mary—but—but—well! this is what I want to say to you. If you will keep a close watch on your mistress, and tell me once in a while what she is about—that is, whom she receives letters from, and who comes to see her, and all that sort of thing, I'll be the making of you. This whole business, I'm so anxious about, concerns me very closely. There's a regular mint of money to be made out of it for me, and I'll pay you handsomely if you'll hold your tongue, and help me. I want to confide the whole thing to you; I have unbounded faith in your prudence and good sense. Now if you will promise to keep everything secret that passes between you and me, and faithfully to report everything to me about your house, I will confide in you, and whenever you want fifty or a hundred dollars, or any nice dress, you ask me, and you shall have them. Will you promise ?"

"Certain, Mrs. Bounce," replied the unscrupulous hireling, "I'll be as mum as old Croft the dumb tinker—you jest try me. I knows what's what as well as some other people. I'll keep anything still what I gets pay for."

The widow was satisfied, for she knew that the girl was compromising her own character and chances for life by intermeddling with her mistress' secret papers and drawers ; and then the girl would have little opportunity to be bribed by others as liberally as the mistress of the manor could do it. She therefore communicated her plan in these words :

"I knew you could be trusted, Mary. Now listen carefully to me. It may be necessary some day to prove in court that my brother, Henry Lansing, who ran away several years ago, was in love with your mistress, and offered himself to her, and that she refused him on account of this man whose picture you have brought me. I am trying to collect all the evidence I can of that refusal of my brother's marriage offer, and that he left the presence of your mistress in a great rage, and the same day left town. You know you told me once before how excited and furious he was when he rode up to the garden at your other house, and wouldn't come in, but paused in the garden and seemed to change his mind, and then turned back and rode off."

The maid interrupted her. "I didn't say he looked mad—only pale and sorrowful-like that morning. He acted just like his heart was broken—that's what I said, Mrs. Bounce."

"Well, well, Mary," exclaimed the widow impatiently, "that will not answer my purpose. I want you to remember that he was in a perfect rage, gnashing his teeth and cursing and shaking his head as if he intended to have vengeance on somebody. Don't you remember how it was ?"

"O yes !" said the instructed witness, "I remember now he was so mad I was afraid of him. He had his hand clenched, too. He was dreadful to look upon, so he was. I remember now all about it."

The widow continued her instructions. "You know, Mary, how a man would feel when his lady love rejected him, by showing him this other man's picture, and telling him *that* was the one she was going to marry—you know he would feel like tearing that other man to pieces with jealousy and rage, don't you ?"

The servant assented to this conclusion—but some sudden light appeared to break in upon her, for she said, in surprise :

"Why! Mrs. Bounce—you don't believe *he* did it, do you ? You don't believe your own flesh and blood, your own brother, murdered that man what was found dead out by old Rosy's garden. I didn't guess that was what you was comin' at. I'd rather hate to git mixed up in that thing, I would indeed. Why! jest think of it—your own brother might get hung on what I said."

The widow saw her platform sliding from under her. If this unexpected specimen of mingled wickedness and scrupulousness was to be secured at all as her tool, it must be by a bribe ample and tempting enough to overwhelm the slight germ of virtue remaining in the faithless servant. Mrs. Bounce possessed in abundance one prominent characteristic of the Lansing family, namely, the penetration and decision requisite to seize upon a sudden and difficult obstacle and overwhelm it by vigorous action. She at once caught hold of the servant's hand and said emphatically,

"Mary, nobody has a right to conceal a murderer from justice, no matter what relation or kindred they are. Henry Lansing murdered that man, just as sure as those stars are shining in that sky. Why, girl, there's evidence that he did it with his own fishing-spear, and then hid it It was found all covered with blood. Do you think any other murderer would have hidden that spear ? Why no ! he would have left it laying around, so as to throw suspicion on the owner of it. Don't you see how it stands ? Come, none of that nonsense, Mary—my object is not to particularly bring my brother into trouble, but something of mine own, my own plan. I tell you what I'll do for you if you consent to swear just as I direct. I'll give you one thousand dollars in gold—just think of that—pure gold. I'll give you half of it to-morrow night, and the other half when the court is over, and I'll never let you want for a thing while you live. Speak quick—there's another girl I know would jump at the chance, but I like you, and I want you to have it. What do you say ?"

One thousand dollars in gold appeared as tempting to the servant as the whole manor did to Mrs. Bounce. Neither had the moral power to reject the bait. The faithless servant consented to follow the widow's directions and swear away a human life. The maid however was not as sanguine as Mrs.

Bounce in regard to the heir's return, and fancied she might secure half of her bribe without being called upon to testify at all. She had heard of the apparitions, but her credulity did not run in that line—otherwise she would not have approached the haunted house alone after dark. When the bargain had been satisfactorily determined upon, the widow inquired:

"Mary, do you know where Squire Bramlet lives, just below your cottage?"

"O yes, Mrs. Bounce—I goes by there every morning to market."

"Well, Mary, I want you to take this note and hand it to him quietly when you go by there. Don't you let any one see you deliver it to him—in his own hands, remember—you must give it to him just as soon as you can."

Mrs. Bounce drew a letter from her bosom and gave it to her accomplice as she spoke. The servant took it and concealed it in her own dress, promising to deliver it to the magistrate promptly and secretly. After a brief recapitulation to the servant of the several duties she was expected to perform from day to day, the widow sent her back to the town. The maid was anxious to arrive at the cottage before her mistress should return, and lost no time in crawling out from the shelter of the bushes and hastening away over the starlit fields of the manor.

The treacherous sister resumed her watchful attitude, fixing her dark eyes once more upon the gable door of the haunted house. While she waited for the apparitions to appear from the old ruin, some singular and shadowy formation, either of the spiritual or material world, was gliding across the starlit fields after the retreating figure of Blonde Grayson's maid. It could not be the girl's shadow, cast upon the grass by the intercepted light of the evening stars, or else it would have followed her from the instant she left the concealed widow and came out into the starlight. No! the mysterious shape only appeared when she was at least forty rods away from the widow on her return home. Then the dense shadow first made its appearance, slowly moving out from the trunk of an enormous chestnut tree, and commenced to follow her. The girl would have screamed had she turned a backward look and observed it. But she was too anxious to think of any other subject just then except the rapidity with which she could reach the cottage, which she had left without permission. The maid quickened her pace, and the shadow followed faster. Over the fields, through the myrtle dell, and even as far as the brown gate leading into the highway, hurried the treacherous servant and her attendant blackness. It might have been the foul fiend, if an aggravated shade of soot is the peculiar and exclusive type of that dreadful majesty of the eternal pit. The probabilities were strongly in favor of this latter solution of the shadow, inasmuch as the Prince of Darkness is currently believed to cherish a violent penchant for the transaction of such bargains as had just been consummated under the shrubbery adjacent to the haunted manor house. However this may be, it is certain that when the maid issued from the myrtle dell out upon the highway, the black shadow ceased to follow directly in her footsteps, but kept to the inside of the manor fence, following along its length, and keeping near enough to the servant to tempt her again, if perchance her good angel should contrive to make himself heard once more in her guilty ears. When the maid at length reached the gate of Blonde Grayson's cottage, and found the house as dark and gloomy as when she had left it, she concluded to sit down upon the low steps of the piazza and wait for her mistress' return from her remarkably long ride. She cherished the delusion that she was entirely alone. But no ! on the opposite side of the road, and behind the dark boundary fence of the open field lurked the attendant dense shadow which had followed her from the manor. What would have been the terror of the treacherous maid had she known that this same shadow had started out with her when she left the cottage, had followed her to within a few rods of the haunted house, and while she was transacting her infernal business under the shrubbery, was waiting for her behind the great chestnut? And yet such was the startling fact.

After waiting on the piazza until she was chilled by the night air, the servant entered the cottage. When the door had closed upon her muffled figure, the shadow crawled over the fence and glided across the road to the cottage gate. There it comfortably seated itself upon the horse-block to wait for Doctor Mosely's return. The Lansing manor might be utterly destitute of the society of white ghosts, but it is an unquestionable matter of history that it possessed a veritable "black guardian angel" in the person of Norman Prince, whose discretion always enabled him to keep away from ghosts at the traditionary distance of forty rods.

CHAPTER XXX.

Norman Prince sat motionless upon the horse-block, awaiting his employer's return. He could not conceive what detained Doctor Mosely so long, particularly at a season of such pressing demand for his professional services. But the mystery of the maid's movements puzzled him still more. He had followed her to the manor and approached as near to the haunted house as his superstitious fears of the ghosts would allow. He imagined from his hiding-place behind the chestnut that she had actually entered the building. What business could she have in that ill-omened neighborhood? He had studied the girl's character for several years, and his conclusions were that she was devoid of principle. His faithful heart told him she was out that night on some errand of wickedness connected with Gurty's safety. The doctor had warned him to watch the widow, that no further attempt upon the young artist's life might be made, and the negro had willingly obeyed when he found leisure from his work. He had ascertained that Gurty's visits at the cottage dreadfully offended the widow. He had seen Mrs. Bounce talking confidentially with Blonde Grayson's maid on the streets, and he had rapidly made up his conclusion that some deviltry was afoot. But what was the meaning of this clandestine night visit to the haunted house? As he in vain endeavored to unravel the proceeding in his mind, he heard the door of the cottage open again. With the instinctive quickness and quiet of a cat, he slid down to the ground and crouched behind the horse-block. The maid came to the front gate and looked up and down the street. After listening attentively for the sound of wheels and hearing nothing, she opened the gate and walked towards the town. The negro peered out from his hiding-place after her. When she was far enough away, he arose and followed her in the starlight. He tracked her to the residence of Squire Bramlet. saw her ascend the steps, and heard the door-bell faintly ring, Presently the hall lamp shone out through the open door. He saw that she did not enter the house. In a few seconds the servant who had answered the bell returned with the master of the house to the street door. The negro crept nearer to the scene, hiding behind an elm, and peering curiously at the open door. He saw that Squire Bramlet sent his own servant back into the house and stood alone with the maid. He could not hear the conversation of the two, but he saw that the maid handed something white to the Squire. The lamp-light shone full upon it, but he could not see what the object was, only that it was white. The maid then descended the steps and the door was closed again. The negro slowly and with cat-like tread followed the maid back to the cottage gate. She paused at the gate, and listened again for the sound of carriage wheels. Her mistress was not yet coming, and the girl entered the cottage once more. The negro thought she might come out again, so he crossed over into the opposite field and hid behind the fence, where he could watch the cottage gate He had now possession of two facts—her visit to the haunted house, and her almost immediate delivery of something white to Squire Bramlet. He suspected it was a letter and that it might be from Mrs. Bounce. He studied the mystery over in his brain, and finally chuckled low to himself and thought, "Norman Prince mustn't sleep much these nights." While he lay behind the fence waiting for the doctor and watching the gate, he heard the tramp of footsteps along the road. What was his amazement to see three persons approaching, one walking ahead and the other two following so closely that they appeared to be tied to the leader. He saw that they were two men and one woman. They came close up to his lurking-place, and then at the direction of the leader, separated and removed bandages from their eyes. The leader bade them good night and walked away towards the town. He recognized the other two, who passed through the gate and entered the cottage, as his employer, Doctor Mosely, and the young lady with whom he had started on the ride at least seven hours before. He was puzzled indeed at this strange termination of the physician's ride. He waited until the cottage door closed behind them, and then returned once more to the horse-block before the gate. The doctor soon came out again, and finding his servant seated on the horse-block, informed him that the moon would be up in half an hour, and that he must walk out towards the lake and find the horse and buggy. The negro had been left with the horse once before in that identical wood by the doctor, and he assured his master that he could find the place again. Norman Prince started off on his long tramp in wonder at the whole performance, while Doctor Mosely made his way to his office in the town.

While Norman Prince had been watching the strange unlinking of old Hugo and his followers, Squire Bramlet, in the private office of his residence, was silently engaged in the perusal of the widow's note. The magistrate was a short, coarse, fat-looking person, with curly, red hair, and a nose almost flattened against his face. His eyes were a sickly light blue, and his mouth wide and ugly in expression. He was a fair sample of the legal scum who owe their elevation to office to their cultivation of the friendship of pot-house politicians. He was ready for any transaction that would pay, without regard to the principles of law or justice. He held the note close to his small oil lamp and studied very carefully its contents. The communication read as follows:

"Myrtle Dell, 5 o'clock, P. M

"Squire Bramlet: Dear Sir—This communication will be delivered to you before ten o'clock this evening. The bearer is trustworthy, and anything sent by her will be perfectly safe at all times. I have negotiated the matter of your loan with my father. He was rather doubtful as to the value you put upon your farm, but I have finally obtained from him the promise that you shall have the money upon giving him the proposed security. I made it a point to do you this favor on account of the position you hold in the church of God. It becomes us all to love and assist our brethren. You must hasten to close up the matter early to-morrow morning, and secure the money at once. The reasons for this dispatch of your business will suggest themselves to you as you read on.

"I am addressing you, not only as an upright supporter of the law, but also as a Christian brother in the church, who will be able fully to appreciate the struggle in my mind between my natural affection for my own flesh and blood, and the greater love and duty I owe my God and my Saviour. The Old Testament informs us of that sublime spectacle of the man of God offering up his own son, raising the knife to shed the blood of his offspring at the command of Heaven. Shall I expect to win eternal life, if I hesitate to sacrifice my natural affections at the same holy command? My duty is plain, but not the less terrible and revolting. I owe it to society, to the violated law, to my Heavenly Father, to expose a murderer. With tears and agony and prayers, have I arrived at this conclusion, and I write to you before the tempter regains his power over my poor, weak human nature, to tell you that Henry Lansing is really lurking about the town at night, and that you must take measures to have a watch placed that he may be detected and secured. I saw him myself, near the hour of twelve last night, riding Black Hawk into the myrtle dell, and disappear from the manor. I have not the slightest idea that he has left the town. It is his dare-devil nature unrestrained by grace, to linger where danger is known to be, merely for the sake of defying and baffling it. I shall take measures myself to have the manor watched. It rests with you, in your magisterial capacity, and your character as a professing Christian, to have other places watched where he would be likely to pass at night. We both owe it to God and to society, to see that righteousness, and justice, and law prevail. You know me too well in the church, to doubt what the violence of my grief, and temptation, and agony has been. I have done my duty in informing you, and now look to that divine source of all consolation, from which we have a right to expect peace when we have performed a frightful and disagreeable duty. My struggle has been stern, but truth has triumphed, and I shall, I fear, be miserable for the residue of my life. Your own sense of consideration for my woe, will suggest the propriety of your concealing this note from every human being. Please burn it when you have finished reading it. Every line has been watered by a sister's tears.

"Your Christian sister,

"ESTHER BOUNCE."

When the magistrate had finished the perusal of the note, he laid it beside his lamp, and reflected upon the matter. Then a sardonic chuckle escaped his ugly mouth as he exclaimed:

"A very exemplary woman, no doubt. By George! my faith is unable to come up with hers. I fancy there's a technical objection for her conscience, too, but the poor woman don't see it; no, she don't see it: and then, let's see, the next heir will be Gurty Lansing—but he's sickly. Well, well, it's none of my business. I've only to see that a criminal is overhauled. The law is no respecter of persons. But that note, ha! ha! that strikes me as a cash article. I'll jest quietly sequester that. She may be anxious to purchase that note some day. Of course she's my Christian sister, and a cash one at that. But I'll put out a watch to-night, and see if we can nab the young scapegrace. The old man may be willing to fork over something to have the heir break jail. There's gold laying around loose on several sides. Keep your eye peeled, Squire, and you may be able to pick up some of the filthy lucre. Well, well, the widow has played her cards shrewdly, to get me the loan on my farm. Of course she knows nothing of the first mortgage. No doubt her mental anxiety, ahem! regarding her *beloved* brother, ahem! has made her overlook the necessity of searching the records in the County Clerk's office. But it's very kind of the widow to accommodate me with the money: I mustn't be ungrateful, oh, no!—that is to say, *at present*, ahem!"

And the zealous upholder of the sword of justice proceeded to make out a warrant for the arrest of Henry Lansing. When he had completed the document, he appeared to recollect another paper of interest, for he went to his desk, and hunted for several minutes, till he drew out a large printed poster, covered with dust. He shook out the notice, and, bringing it to the light, read the amount of money which had been offered years before for the heir's apprehension. He smiled one of his ugly smiles as he said, "Rob Graves and Jim Sumner and me will divide that amount amicably." These worthies were two of his friends in the police department, whom he intended to put upon the track of Henry Lansing.

Then Squire Bramlet pocketed his papers, and, taking his ivory headed cane and his beaver hat, walked forth into the night to execute the widow's request in regard to her brother's apprehension. The rising moon promised a brilliant midnight, and he determined to post two separate guards on the highways leading into C—— to intercept the heir, if he should dare to attempt another night ride. He was aware that Colonel Lansing's riders had been gone all day in search of the missing Black Hawk. But he inclined to the widow's belief, as expressed in her note, that the heir was lurking nearer the town. He found no difficulty in hunting out the policemen, and sending them, heavily armed, to the places he deemed most likely the heir would pass. By the time they were at their designated points of concealment, the squire was safely snoozing in his bed, dreaming of three streams of gold, flowing in upon him from three points of the compass, and falling into the depths of his capacious pockets with a musical clink, clink, clink

Mrs. Bounce had maintained a patient watch near the gable door of the manor house after her accomplice had returned to the town. She congratulated herself upon the smoothness with which her schemes had thus far moved forward to their accomplishment. Her greatest concern was in regard to Dr. Mosely's ride with Blonde Grayson. What could be his motives, in the midst of his devoted and marked attentions to herself, to be wasting an entire afternoon of his precious time upon that girl? She was painfully conscious that, with all the physician's interest in herself, he had never hinted even at offering her his hand in marriage. It was evident, from his attentions, that he regarded her very highly. But why did he so worry her impatient heart by his delay in proposing? She was exceedingly anxious about this strange ride with Blonde. She knew the fair girl's powers of fascination whenever she chose to exert them; and she feared "the lily of C——" might have concluded that the time had arrived when she must make her arrangements for life. The widow was aware that many in the town regarded the talented and successful physician as an eminently eligible match.

While these furious and galling doubts possessed her, and destroyed the serenity of her starlight watch, her attention was suddenly attracted by a strange noise issuing from the upper chambers of the lonely and dim-looking haunted house. She was all eagerness and curiosity, and with her hand she pressed aside the shrubbery, that a full and more perfect range for her eye could be secured. She certainly heard the heavy tramp in the upper room which had been described to her by her father and Dr. Mosely on their former memorable watch. She strained her eyes at the building, but could see nothing resembling human life. Ah! something was certainly approaching the upper window, over the gable door. The vines were closely matted over the unglazed casement; but she could see them slowly and carefully parted, till a face with glowing eyes was pressed against them, looking out. The face looked cautiously in every direction, as if reconnoitering the shadows and shrubbery around the old ruin. Then it disappeared from the window. She congratulated herself that her patient watch was at length to be rewarded. For long, long hours had she crouched under that low shrubbery, watching to find some clue to the old man and his hidden gold. Regardless of the lateness and loneliness of the night she had remained, and in the depths of her heart defied God. Now she whispered to herself: "I shall win, I shall win: no power of light or of darkness shall wrest from me the manor, the gold, or the power." What was her horror to see the pale face with the glowing eyes approach the upper window again, and solemnly pronounce her name in the silent starlight: "Esther Lansing, Esther Lansing, in the name of God, *beware.*" A shudder passed over her frame, but it was only the dampness of the place where she was concealed. She felt confident her figure could not be seen under the shrubbery, and so remained silent. But what was the strange significance of the warning from this solemn and unknown voice? The moon, which had been struggling with the eastern clouds, suddenly burst forth and flooded the old ruin with light. The glowing eyes at the window were fixed unmistakeably upon her pale face. Another shudder passed over her frame, but it was again only the dampness of the place. The pale face with the glowing eyes pronounced solemnly again, "Esther Lansing, *beware.*" She sprang to her feet as another shudder passed over her, and exclaimed, as an undefined terror thrilled her every vein, "Who dares to haunt my family estate, and lecture me?" Again the pale face with glowing eyes solemnly pronounced the warning: "*Beware, beware, beware.*" And then the distant clock of the town of C—— chimed in the startling hour of twelve. Her frame shook like the aspen leaf, but not with terror. The dreadful clang of the distant bell seemed fraught with meaning. Under its solemn strokes she had entered the assembly of the worshipers, and God had entreated her there to live a holy life. Under its mournful clang her holy mother had moved slowly off to her peaceful grave. At its startling sound of *two* God had warned her to spare the sleeping Gurty from the angel of death. But she had defied the God of her mother, and now the solemn bell tolled the full midnight of her soul. The face disappeared from the window, and she smiled her bitter, sneering, God-defying smile. "A ghostly warning, uttered by a mortal voice, to frighten Esther Lansing." But why that shudder again? She looked around her in the flooding moonlight, and started with real terror. Strange she should have forgotten until this minute the only sensible superstition of her family. She stood in the center of the *fever marsh* of the manor. No wonder she shuddered, when so many of her race had in this very spot of swampy soil inhaled the fatal fever. She shivered again, and hastened away in terror homeward. But a shadow closely followed her guilty footsteps. It was the grim and relentless and fatal spectre of the *Shadow of Death.*

Before daylight came, Doctor Mosely was summoned from his bed, to attend at the manor. The servant who waited at the door with the fleet steeds of the manor stables, seemed to be much excited. In their hurried drive out to the great estate, he informed the physician that the whole household had been aroused about the hour of three o'clock, by the most fearful screams from the room of the mistress of the mansion. Hastening to the room, Colonel Lansing and Gurty had found the widow sitting upright in her bed, with her eyes inflamed and glaring, and striving to avert with her hand some invisible persons whom she declared to be the Saviour of the World, with her own dead mother leaning sweetly on his bosom. She screamed for them to be taken away, as they were only sent to mock her despair by the sight of holiness, and peace and joy, to which she might never come.

When the physician reached her, he found his patient, the Reverend Thomas Delaplaine, with his neck closely bandaged from his injuries, sitting beside her, and using every argument and soothing word of his religion, to comfort her. All was in vain, for the mind was equally disordered with the body. The doctor administered to her some powder, which finally composed her excited nerves to sleep. At daylight, when she awoke, the apparitions of her brain were seen by her no more. Only the wasting, fitful, hopeless fever remained.

Through the days and nights of the long fever Doctor Mosely was at her side every hour that he could spare from his extensive practice. His anxiety and his devotion confirmed the reports which had been current of his attachment to the widow And Gurty Lansing softened (in his resentment for the coldness and heartlessness which had been his portion), by the sight of such long continued suffering, sought by every means in his power to cheer the weariness of the sick room. But the irrevocable decree had been issued. One stormy night in October, as the wind howled across the manor and the rain rattled dismally against the great windows, the dark angel swept by. With his dart he parted the mysterious link which binds the soul to the body, and the flickering life of the scheming and intolerant woman passed forever. She who loved the rich and hated the poor, with the name of Christian stamped plainly on her forehead and the name of slanderer and bigot showing clearer on her heart, departed to her final account before the sovereign Ruler of all things No word of hope came from her dying lips. She seemed to harden in heart as the last gasp approached and asked only to live that she might secure rank and wealth and power. Just before the final struggle came, she realized how near was the dark shadow, and then the agonized glance of despair came to her face, and death froze it there. Old aunt Roby, the negro woman, slowly descended the stairs with a solemn face, to the kitchen of the manor. "Well, folks, she's gone, and the manor hain't no mistress. She's dreadful to look on—dreadful hopeless. But I tell all you white folks, if Mrs. Lansin' kin look on her frozen face now, she's prayin' to God for her. You may all dispute and argufy, and aunt Roby's no way equal to you all—but aunt Roby knows how she loved her God—and I jest tell all you white folks she's prayin' this minit. But jest tell me, what's goin' to turn up for our mistress? This fine place hain't got no mistress. Jest answer me that."

CHAPTER XXXI.

The rising moon was just visible through the low branches of the dark pines. As yet it diffused no silver radiance, but seemed to linger near the surface of the earth, a huge and perfect ball of gold. It was the eye of evening looking calmly through the mournful pines at a still more mournful scene beyond. For it could see imperfectly beyond the dark fringe of the pines the willows drooping and the maples bare of leaves, and the funereal branches of the cedars, all clustered about the marble white memorials of the dead. It was the sleeping-place of the departed citizens of C——. Here slumbered the proud, ambitious father, the gentle mother, the faithful wife, the lily child. They whose loving eyes and warm hearts had so often brightened the pathway of life, were resting here neglected in their frozen sleep. Of all the hundreds who had been nurtured by their labors and their gentleness, not one was here to watch beside them. That solitary golden eye, the huge rising moon, was their only watcher and friend. No sound disturbed the sleeping dead, and that watchful moon slowly ascended to the tops of the pines till their velvet fringe glistened in the increasing silver light. Then the great gate of the lonely cemetery slowly grated on its hinges, and two dark figures intruded upon the precincts of the dead. They were females, and as the heavy iron gate swung back with a startling *clash* behind them, their carriage which had brought them slowly departed along the highway, only to pass and repass the gate, awaiting their return from the graves. The moonlight was increasing, and afforded them a sombre view of the avenues and narrow paths which passed between the orderly rows of the sleepers.

"Blonde," said the shorter of the two, as they passed slowly along, arm in arm, "it is no doubt superstitious for me to dwell so much upon my dream of last night. But my mother's words haunt me. I cannot shake them off, and hence my request that you would come with me this lovely night to my mother's grave. I know I should have come here oftener—she loved me so fondly. And when they buried her away from me, in this place forever, I thought I should often visit her in her death-sleep. But it has seemed as if something would always arise to prevent me, and I have failed since my marriage to visit this place once every month, as used to be my habit. But last night—Oh! that strange dream, I cannot forget it. She appeared so distinctly before me in her old touching beauty, and said to me, 'Oh! my Clara, my darling child, I have suffered so much in my life, and you have never known it—but you must know it soon—it must be exposed now—the cause of this exposure often passes thoughtfully beside my grave at night—there you will see that cause.'"

Blonde passed her arm around Mrs. St. Clair's waist and pressed her closely to her side. She replied mournfully and slowly:

"My sweet Clara, everything looks sad to me now. I am prepared to expect every ill to me and to my friends. Oh! life is so dreary to me now—you always looked to me for support and consolation, but now I must look to you. Oh! Clara, I am deserted, and it is my own fault. I have unburdened my weary heart to you, and I feel all the while like talking over my loneliness to you for sympathy's sake. But your dream—Oh! your dream is stranger to me than to you. If your dream were to be realized beside your mother's grave, its consequences might be to change the whole tenor of my own life. But I have no right to speak to you in enigmas. I should not have said this much to you, for its meaning cannot be unraveled for you without violating the seal of confidence and holy promise before God. Forget what I have said. Here, turn this way—I want to go past my father's grave."

Her friend turned away with her down the avenue of drooping willows, which yet remained untouched by the October frosts, though all the other leaves had fallen. She was distressed to hear Blonde speak so despairingly of life. She knew her secret love for Henry Lansing, and that he had fled again without approaching the lily of C——. But what connection could the dream have with Blonde's hopes or fears? She saw that the unguarded words and mystery had fallen from her friend's lips in the bitterness of her loneliness and desolation of heart, and she would not under these circumstances press her for an explanation. But she puzzled her brain over the matter, nevertheless, as they paced along through the lonely moonlit streets of the dead. What possible connection could Henry Lansing have with the dream concerning the departed mother?

Blonde lingered beside her father's grave, but the air was chill, and she turned away at length with Mrs. St. Clair and followed her under the dark cedars till they reached the spot where Judge Peyton's wife was buried. The gloomy trees excluded the moonbeams, and the two friends leaned over the iron fence of the lot, holding each other's hands. Blonde looked at the grave, but her thoughts were with the portrait of Clara's beautiful mother which hung against the walls of Mrs. St. Clair's bed-room in Judge Peyton's residence. Though her eyes had never looked on the original, she knew the significance of Clara's dream, and the awful sufferings which had brought the beautiful idol of the home circle to an untimely grave. She could not, she would not reveal the secret cause to the daughter; but this hidden tenderness for the feelings of her friend made her love her all the better, and she passed her arm around Clara's neck and pressed her head to her bosom, as she watched her mother's gloomy grave. This movement diverted Mrs. St. Clair's eyes for one minute from the grave, and at that instant she detected a figure rapidly approaching the shade of the cedar trees in which they were partially concealed. She seized Blonde with a frantic, startled grip by the arm, and whispered, "Merciful God! there comes Henry Lansing!"

Why they crouched to the earth and clung fast to the iron fence, neither could afterwards satisfactorily explain. It was an instinct of delicacy at being found alone and unprotected. It was a sudden thought, that one whom they esteemed was in danger of arrest, and imagined he was safe and alone, and they must not interfere with him in the sacred errand upon which he had come. It may have been the two impulses combined. But whatever the motive, they shrunk out of sight behind the iron paling, and he passed them at his well-remembered rapid pace without seeing them. The moonlight had become brilliant, and there was no mistaking that princely bearing and that impetuous movement. As when he dashed by Blonde on his raven-colored steed, at midnight, his dark hat was rolled up from his forehead, and his aristocratic profile was visible in the moonlight. His dark eyes, roving and beautiful, glanced cautiously about him. But the dense shadows of the cedars proved an effectual cover to the startled friends. They held their breath, as he glanced into the profound shade of the cedars; but his brilliant eyes failed to discover them. In full view of their hiding-place, and distinct in the moonlight, stood the monuments of the ancient Lansing family. He placed his hands upon the granite fence of the family enclosure, and with one leap cleared the barrier and stood among the graves. A short Spanish cloak fell gracefully from his shoulders, and his features were plainly revealed as he looked about in uncertainty. Then he stooped to read a name upon a white shaft erected over some member of his family. It was his mother's grave, and with a piercing cry of agony he flung himself upon it and pressed his lips to the cold sod.

"Oh! my mother—my mother!—the sun shall rise and set, the stars glisten coldly in the evening sky, and the lonely midnight mark the passing days of my lonely life, and you will never, never come again. The blue eye which loved the wandering boy is closed forever. The lips that breathed the prayer for me are hushed and cold. When I roamed the earth, unconscious of the bitter dart of slander, unknowing even of the crime which had written my name with characters of blood, you in the sweet confidence of a mother's heart defended me. You have gone while I dreamed fondly of placing my acquisitions at your feet, and knowing the pride of my mother's heart. Oh! is there no hope that your winged spirit may yet embrace me and whisper to me the holy counsels of a pure and protecting God. Oh! mother, your resting place is cold; but colder still my heart. My God, my God, I could bear and suffer all but this. We cannot die and perish—we must live again, and in a purer life clasp once more the idols to our hearts. Oh! mother, dearest mother, remember me in Heaven."

He sat erect upon the grave, and raising his cloak to his eyes, sobbed bitterly. The solemn clock of C—— recalled him once more to life and its troubles. He arose and looked around upon the graves. The freshly broken sods of a new grave whose marble headstone looked new and white in the moonbeams, attracted his attention. He bent above the stone to read the inscription. It was the grave of the widowed sister. The victim of the *marsh fever* slept beside her holy mother. He looked uneasy, and then said thoughtfully, raising his eyes to God, as if to fathom the length and the breadth and the depth of the words, "And their works do follow them."

He breathed a heavy sigh, and then turned a parting glance

at his mother's grave. Then he looked cautiously around him on every side, peering into all the shadows stretched over the cemetery by the moonlight. His scrutiny was unrewarded by any sign of human life. He placed his hands again upon the granite fence, and leaped over it. Turning towards a point opposite to the great gate of the cemetery, he walked away, wrapping his Spanish cloak tightly about him. The silent spectators of all his movements heard him clamber to the top of the great wall which bounded the property devoted to the dead, and then spring with a crash into the shrubbery beyond. In a few seconds they heard the beat of flying hoofs in the adjacent field.

As Mrs. St. Clair stood erect once more, she saw that her companion was agitated, for she placed her hands upon Clara's shoulder, trembling violently. Then Blonde broke the silence.

"He has returned, God knows why. I fear it is not to see me. If I was still remembered, he would have seen me before when he returned the first time. If he is fully aware of his danger, I cannot comprehend why he should come. He can only know that the feeling against him is bitter, and the evidence exceedingly hazardous for him to controvert. I do know this, my sweetest friend, that I would sacrifice every hope, but Heaven, to save him. I once had almost called to him to speak a kind and cheering word as he stood by the grave. But something seemed to bind me down with you. I never felt so helpless to do right before. Oh! let us go, I feel so sad and weary."

The chilly air warned them of the hazard of the night exposure, and they walked away, with their arms twined in the clear moonlight, and leaning on each other. After a deep reflection, Mrs. St. Clair startled her companion from her sadness by the serious remark:

"*He*, then is the cause for which my mother's suffering in life must be made known. How unaccountable my dream."

A shudder passed across Blonde's frame, and her friend perceived it but ascribed it to her thoughts of Henry Lansing. No reply being made, Clara continued:

"I wonder if my dear mother did really suffer. Father has often spoken to me of her beauty and loveliness of character during her life, and never mentioned then that she had been a sufferer beyond the ordinary ills of all mortals. But I have often wondered that he does not seem disposed to talk often of her, since she has been dead now several years. After all, it is only a dream—and yet an irresistible impulse led me here to-night to see if anything strange passed near my mother's grave. He certainly did pass very near us."

Blonde still remained silent. Every word that her friend was speaking bordered on dangerous ground, and she concluded at length, to divert Mrs. St. Clair's attention entirely to herself. As they passed through the cemetery and entered the carriage of Judge Peyton, she spoke of the faint hope which lighted her heart that this unexpected appearance of the heir of the manor, might, after all, be the result of a desire on his part to have an interview with herself. But her efforts proved unavailing. For as the carriage rolled away in the moonlight, Mrs. St. Clair relapsed into a reverie upon her own dream and a foreboding of evil took possession of her, which could not be shaken off The friends parted at the gate of the cottage in tears. A cloud seemed to hover over them, and Blonde whispered, "Your trouble is a dream, but I have seen a reality; pray for me this night as earnestly as I shall pray for you, dear Clara."

The carriage rolled on, and Blonde entered the cottage. What was her surprise to find old Rosy waiting in her little parlor to see her. She had arrived soon after Blonde went out, and had determined not to leave the town without seeing her, for the honest old soul found few opportunities of visiting her friends in C——. The neighboring farmer who had given the old woman a ride into town, was engaged as a witness in some reference suit, and would call for her again when his testimony should have been concluded. The mistress of the cottage produced a plate loaded with grapes from her little garden for old Rosy's entertainment, and the discussion of their mutual friends and experiences served to divert Blonde's thoughts from the exciting vision among the graves. Finally, the old woman produced from her handkerchief, which she carried in a black silk bag, a flower, and handed it to her entertainer, informing her that a gentleman, who had been purchasing flowers at her garden that day, requested her to give it to Miss Grayson, without divulging his name.

Blonde took the flower carelessly, and endeavored to recollect its language, but it had slipped her memory. Such tokens were often sent to her through the medium of old Rosy, and she thought nothing further about it after old Rosy had persisted in refusing to communicate any information regarding the gentleman who sent it.

When old Rosy had gone, however, the fair girl, before retiring for the night, chanced to see the flower again lying on her table in the lamp light. Curiosity prompted her to hunt up its meaning in her book of flowers. She saw that the token was the most delicate shade of the purple heliotrope. Her book informed her of its language thus:

"HELIOTROPE.

DEVOTION.

"Still the loved object the fond leaves pursue,
Still move their root, the morning sun to view."

Who could have sent it? Could it be possible the rector of St. Paul's chapel still cherished the hope of winning her hand. Or might it not be a sudden impulse of her physician? It must be Doctor Mosely. She had discovered how vainly he was striving to suppress and control his passion for her. It was like one of his unguarded moves. She esteemed him very highly. Their experiences on the lake and in the cavern, had elevated his character and his attractions in her appreciative soul.

But the wild, wandering, gifted young heir of the manor was the being who had touched the silver bell of her pure heart, and its musical vibrations engrossed her thoughts to the exclusion of all other love. And yet there was something so respectful and touching in the love which had prompted the doctor to send the purple heliotrope. "Poor fellow," she whispered to herself, with her blue eyes regarding the flower, "his love could make any woman happy." Then came the golden thought which imprinted the bright red rose on her fair dimpled cheek. What if it came from Henry Lansing? She shook her head sadly at this bright thought. The heir was too proud to come again. And yet if he took the fancy into his head to send her the flower, old Rosy, his friend, would be the very person he would be likely to select for his agent. Her tall, slight mourning figure stood thoughtfully in the lamp light of the little parlor. Her lily hand, on which appeared her brother's pearl ring, held up to the light the purple flower in study of its mystic meaning. It was useless to spend the whole night puzzling herself about the source from which the flower might have come. She placed the heliotrope in a glass of water on her parlor mantel, and retired to her snow white bed for the night. As she knelt before her prayer-book on the oaken table between the silver candlesticks, she remembered the impetuous "pride of the manor" at the throne of God.

Then with a heavy sigh she invoked the tenderest favor of Heaven upon her violet-eyed friend, and all who were dear to her.

As her misty, waving golden hair fell, unrestrained, over her white pillow, and her pearl ring pressed the dimples of her sleeping face, the dream angel passed his sceptre fitfully above her. She saw again the murdered Hartwell, and concealed the fragment of the neck-tie in her bosom. The heir of the manor swept by, on his beautiful steed, and his cheek was pale with despair. The glance he gave her seemed to freeze her blood. The scene changed to the wonderful cavern, and the stalactite chamber was filled with the gliding serpents. The Reverend Marcus Seymour and Henry Lansing, in their efforts to save her, were stricken to the earth by the countless rattlesnakes. Then she was moving in the boat over the unruffled lake of C——, alone with Doctor Mosely, who, in his velvet cap and flowing beard, played softly on the Arabian flute to the serpents swimming harmlessly in the wake of the enchanted boat. Then the dream angel with his sceptre touched her lips, and she was singing with the flute in Heaven.

CHAPTER XXXII.

The window curtains of the little parlor had been carefully drawn together and pinned to exclude the wind which whistled dismally without. The night promised to be a stormy one, for at sunset the wind had veered around to the north-west, and the ground was rapidly freezing. The sound of the flying autumn leaves came occasionally from the side-walks as they danced along on tiptoe before the increasing gale. The bare arms of the trees rattled against each other, and low ominous moans came at intervals from the hollow chimneys. It was dreary enough without, for the stars of heaven were shrouded by masses of dark, flying clouds. But the closely-fastened, long crimson curtains of the parlor windows bade defiance to the chill breeze which struggled for admittance. Within the little room, warmth and cheerfulness and mellow lamp light held sway. An open chimney fire of crackling wood gave forth a broad glare of light, and mingling with the steady rays of the centre table lamp illumined the apartment, chasing out all gloomy shadows, and giving to the little parlor an air of indescribable comfort and luxury. The large andirons on the hearth were ornamented with huge lions' heads of brass, and the encircling fender was of the same bright metal, and both polished to a brightness which told of a careful and tidy mistress of the cottage. Before the blazing fire was spread a large rug woven into figures of gorgeous tropical flowers and plants, in the centre of which was stretched a living figure enjoying the warmth. It was the great Newfoundland dog, admitted for the evening to the parlor in consideration of the freezing cold without. His great nose was jammed close against the brass fender, and his dreamy eyes were calmly studying the glowing mass of coals, and blinking occasionally at the sharp crackling of the burning wood. The black marble centre table with its shaded lamp was drawn up near to the fire place, and on it were seen books in costly bindings of scarlet and brown colors. On one corner rested the inevitable lady's work-basket, small and tasty in its new lining of mazarine blue silk. In it glistened the ivory-headed bodkin, the steel scissors, the small round cake of white wax, the blue pin-cushion full of needles, and the scattered tiny buttons of pearl playing disorder with the white spools of thread.

The dark mantel over the fire sustained two bronzes facing each other from its ends. They were grayhounds couchant. Between them and suspended from the wall was the emblem of salvation, a cross of purple violets pressed against white paper and all enclosed in a narrow gilt frame and protected by a glass. The simple wall paper of the room was adorned at intervals with elegant paintings in heavy gilt frames; and in one corner of the apartment a fluted pedestal of black marble sustained a snowy bust of Dante with his poet's wreath. No sofa graced the room, but in its stead a lounge with heavy pillows and covered with crimson cloth like the window curtains, invited the weary. A few dark chairs rested against the walls. Opposite to the long luxurious mirror stood the melodeon, left as a secret gift by the elegant rector of St. Paul's. Over the musical instrument a red cloth was spread, on which stood a solitary glass of water nourishing a recently plucked heliotrope of a delicate purple hue. It was the token of the mysterious and unknown friend.

In the midst of this comfort and warmth and light sat "the lily of C——," busily plying her needle. She was alone with her dog. Her ear caught the occasional sound of the sweeping wind without, and she thanked God in her heart, that though her fall from wealth and influence had been a long one, she had not been forced into that sad condition where the poor shiver with cold, and look anxiously for their daily bread. Her little quiet home was cheerful on this lonely night, and she was thinking how happy she would be even in this cottage, if her heart could only win that aliment which it at length had learned to crave. It would have been a cold heart, an unappreciative nature that could have looked into that silent room during that stormy night upon her loveliness, and not have yearned to own her and her gentle love for life. The graceful outline of her figure revealed through the closely fitting waist and arms of her mourning dress, the little jet buttons flashing from her white throat to her slender waist, the fair dimpled cheek, the mysterious gentle eye of blue, the refined thin lips, moist with kisses yet to be stolen, the long eyelashes, the white forehead with the misty, wavy golden hair sweeping backward from it, the lily hand with its pearl ring, and the gentle bosom rising and falling with every breath and emotion, all, all constituted a picture to melt the heart of man with that fire which refines and beautifies a noble being true to himself and his God. She was one to charm by her person, to cheer by her silvery laugh and song, to refine by her thoughts in the realm of intellectual culture, and to soothe by the earnest, loving character of her religious faith. It was a dream to clasp that soft cheek to one's bosom, and hear those lips pronounce softly words of affection and trust for life. And yet her own true heart had learned its own secret yearning, and the idol came not. The gifted and the affluent had worshiped at that shrine, but her heart whispered and sighed, "one, only one."

The wind howled at last in fury; the windows shook, the chimney moaned, the branches fell to the earth with a crash, and the night demons went shrieking past. The dog raised his startled ears to listen, and the brute seemed conscious of the passing anger of God. He came slowly to the side of his mistress, and poked his shaggy head into her lap for a caress and a human voice to cheer him amid the terrible voices of the wild storm. It was so like a human instinct she laid her work aside and circled her arms lovingly about the neck of the shaggy brute. She too experienced the sense of terror at the shrieks and moans and yells of tortured nature, and the faithful dog was her only friend in the room. Again the fierce storm lulled, and the moaning ceased. It was only for an instant. The scattered forces of darkness and of terror were only gathering for a fresh assault upon the trembling elms and shrubbery of the place. They came once more from another point, stealing around the gables and the chimneys in piercing cries, shrieks, moans and howls, and then the full force of the hurricane roared on. The very building shook to its foundation, and an elm branch torn from its mangled trunk was borne on the blast and crashed with frightful force against the shutters of the window. The demons of the storm seemed to yell with mocking laughter at their havoc, and hastened on upon the rushing blast for more. Once more the lull came, and the solitary girl started at a loud, mysterious knock upon her parlor door. Her brother had retired early to bed in a remote corner of the house, and she felt nervous. The strange discord made by the chill winds was well calculated to work upon the imagination and the nerves of the lonely. A robber or a spectre might well be expected on such a night. None but prowlers and vagrants would be abroad in such a freezing storm. Who could have entered her hall unnoticed, and now stand separated from her by only her parlor door? How thoughtless in her to leave the street door unbolted on such a night and in so remote a locality. The heavy knock sounded again, and the dog sullenly uttered his warning growl to the intruder. Blonde stood behind her marble table on the defensive, with her great dog by her side. She recovered her courage quickly, as she always did, and said calmly, "Come in."

The parlor door swung quickly open, and the muffled figure of a man stood upon the threshold. Who could it be? He removed his hat and the small shawl which was wound around his throat, and advanced with an apology for entering the hall unannounced. He had repeatedly knocked at the front door, but the noise and fury of the gale had drowned the sound of his knuckles. He had seen the bright light through the front windows, and felt confident his knock had not been heard. So he had the presumption to come further. It was the intellectual face of Dr. Mosely. He said:

"Your brother told me on the street an hour ago that he was weary and would retire to his bed early. I thought you would be alone and might like company for an hour. I have really been so busy for a week that I could not find time to fulfill my promise to come and see you."

Blonde drew an arm chair to the fire while the doctor was removing his muffler and gloves and placing them on the lounge.

"Here, take this chair, doctor—you will find it more comfortable. I am so glad to see you. I am half frightened tonight at the strange sounds outside, and when I heard that knock in such an unusual place, I was startled. I consider it a great compliment to be visited such a night. Are you not half frozen ?"

The physician replied as he drew his chair nearer to the table, where Blonde had resumed her sewing:

"You have little idea of this storm inside the house. The north-west wind cuts like a razor. The elms will suffer to-night. The sidewalks are strewn with branches. But I do not mind the gale much—there is a sort of exhilaration to me in the spirit with which the storm dashes on. Oh ! you should be in that cave such a night as this. Once I was there during a storm. In some parts I could hear it rushing along, and the walls of the cavern trembled. The echoes under ground reminded me of a great artillery battle, only more mysterious."

"Oh that cave—that cave !" said Blonde. "It has been a fruitful source of dreams to me since. I feel quite proud to share your secret. But how have you arranged with old Hugo ? You told me, if I recollect aright, that the secret was important to you in a pecuniary point of view. You will have to buy his silence. How queer that each of you should have known the existence of the secret cave, and yet been ignorant of each other's mode of access to it. I am afraid, doctor, that it was indelicate in me to wander off so with you till that hour of night. I could not allow such a thing to happen again Why all C—— would be delighted to have such material for gossip. But tell me about old Hugo. Have you ascertained how long he has known of the existence of that cave ?"

The physician did not reply, and the fair girl looked up from her work. He was in a reverie over a miniature which he had carelessly taken up from her table. He was studying it intently in the lamp-light. What could absorb the gallant doctor in such a wonderful manner that he neglected to respond to a lady's question ?

Blonde studied his features with the puzzled air of one who sees again a face once long, long ago familiar, but to which it is impossible to connect the name. She felt confident that the physician's face was one she had seen long before her arrival in C——. She said suddenly :

"Doctor Mosely, I do not wonder at your absorbed manner. That face is the sweetest in expression that I have ever known. Do you know who it is ?"

He looked up from the miniature as one awaking from a dream. He answered slowly, fixing his clear, dark eyes upon the blazing fire,

"You must excuse my abstraction, Miss Grayson; but this beautiful woman recalls incidents and associations of my past life which I can never remember without a thrill of emotion. Who painted this miniature? I have certainly seen that face before. Is she a friend of yours? Does she live in this State? It certainly resembles strongly a woman who was considered a marvel of beauty."

He continued that earnest gaze into the fire on the hearth, studying deeply.

"That is a lady whom you have probably never seen," replied Blonde, her wonder increasing at his strange manner "It was copied by your friend Gurty Lansing from a miniature of his mother. It is Mrs. Lansing, of the manor, who died several years ago. She was surpassingly lovely, and is now in heaven."

The doctor asked abruptly, looking up at her,

"Did she ever live in Hudson?"

"Not that I ever knew of. But you must know, doctor, that I have lived in C—— only a few years, and I knew nothing of the Lansings until my arrival in this town. Were you acquainted in Hudson?"

He answered again, in his singularly abstracted tone,

"Slightly."

This, then, was the place she had seen that physician's face; for Hudson had been Blonde's residence for years. In vain she endeavored to recall when she had seen him. But her reverie was now interrupted by Doctor Mosely, who placed the miniature on her table, and said, with a sigh,

"Well! I am acting strangely to you, no doubt, Miss Grayson; but the resemblance is remarkable. Let it pass, however. It is a subject which now can only bring me regret."

He looked into the glowing fire again, and seemed to hesitate in uttering something which burdened his mind. Then he turned towards Blonde's sweet face in the lamplight and said, with an impressiveness which instantly recalled her to the present:

"Would you like to know, Miss Grayson, who sent you that purple heliotrope which I see yonder in that glass of water on the melodeon?"

The question was abrupt and startling. She had forgotten the flower. Quicker than the fall of the thunder-bolt flashed to her mind a speculation of her friend Mrs. St. Clair weeks before. The doctor was acting in behalf of a young friend Her heart stood still at the thought that the young friend might be Henry Lansing. She endeavored to speak calmly, but her voice trembled.

"Can you believe in the curiosity which your sex attribute to woman, and yet ask me such a question? I would indeed like to know—that is, if it is the gift of a gentleman.

"And do you know its language, Miss Grayson?"

"Yes," she replied. "It signifies devotion, a quality in a man as rare as it is beautiful."

Her cynical tone rather discouraged the physician, for he reflected a moment before he replied. Some bitter remark was nearly uttered. But he suppressed it, and said, with a steady, searching look into the lovely face which was bent over her sewing,

"The one who sent you that flower sincerely trusts that the world regards him as a gentleman. *I* had the presumption to send you that flower, Miss Grayson. Do not be offended at me."

Her pleasant illusion vanished. The dreaded offer of a hand which she had made every kind and considerate effort to avert, was about to be made. She felt conscious that she had done nothing to encourage the doctor. The solitary instance of accepting his offer to ride to the lake was the only encouragement she could recall. She respected him so highly, admired his intellect, his tastes, and desired his friendship to such an extent that it was not in her heart to wound him. Why would he place himself in a position to be mortified by her refusal of his hand? Her voice, however, was gentle as she answered,

'I esteem you too highly to be offended at anything you may do, Doctor Mosely. I feel flattered at receiving this beautiful flower at your hands. It shall be the pledge that our new friendship possesses the attributes of constancy, fervor, devotion."

She looked at him with the smile and manner of a sincere friend, but that single glance revealed to her a sullen fire gleaming in his dark eyes. He shook his head mournfully as she concluded. Then a change passed over his face, and he compressed his lips with a determined purpose. The words which followed seemed to be wrung from his heart in its despair.

"I have sent you that token, Miss Grayson, for another purpose. I am not your friend—but I love you, oh God! I love you. Do not turn away. I love you with a passion that will watch and wait for years. If you will only say that after years and years of devotion you may possibly learn to love me, I will be happy. I will try to be happy in the very torture of waiting."

The lily of C—— was bending her golden-crowned beauty lower and lower over her needle-work. Did she waver? What were her thoughts? They ran thus in her confusion. I am sending away a noble heart. That man can render any woman happy. I am rejecting him for what? A mere illusion that Henry Lansing still loves me, after the lapse of years. Why, the pride of that family is proverbial. He will never come near me again—never, never. My age justifies the conclusion that this may be my last offer for life. But if I marry for any other consideration than love, I am false to my word, false to my character, and I believe strongly it would be sin. Live the sweet and the holy illusion of love. Perish wealth, position, comfort.

The fair girl averted her face; she could not look upon the misery of his noble nature. She said, firmly but kindly, looking at the glowing coals in the far corner of the hearth:

"Listen to me, Doctor Mosely. I am not cruel. You would not barter the feeling you have towards me for any other woman's love. I feel confident no consideration would induce you to forget me for another through all the limit of your life. Would it, candidly?"

"No—never!" he answered, vehemently. "My love for you will go down only with the sunset of my life."

She continued, with averted face,

"Then do not refuse to me the credit of a like constancy. I love with my soul. Many, many nights have my tearful eyes watched the holy stars while my heart prayed to God to take me before I began to murmur at His holy will in denying me a return of the secret love which possessed me. Oh! I will trust you, Doctor, because you are so noble, so good. A bright young heart loved me. An eagle eye grew gentle when I was near. A proud heart kneeled to me. But I, confused, bewildered, and surprised as I was, refused him, and he fled a wanderer through the earth. And I love him. Oh! the love of a woman's heart is his. I love him next to God."

She raised her lily hands to her face, then bowing her forehead to the marble table, wept as if her heart would break. The fervor and the bitterness of her confession passed, she dried her eyes and looked slowly up. Doctor Mosely was violently agitated. He clutched at his throat with his muscular hand as if he struggled for breath. He sprang to his feet and struck his hand against his temples violently. The terrified girl started towards him, but before she could reach him the deed was done. The heavy beard and the curling locks tinged with gray fell to the floor, and the eagle-eyed idol of her soul, *Henry Lansing, stood before her.* Beardless, but with the matured beauty of four added years, he bounded to her side, and wound her in his lion's grasp to his bosom, while his lips pressed the lips of the woman who loved him.

The heir of the manor was the gifted and loved physician of C——.

CHAPTER XXXIII.

The slender, mourning figure of the orphan stood on the piazza of the cottage, gazing after his retreating footsteps. The violent rush of the wind nearly took away her breath. A fresh gust from the northwest tore another branch from the tree, and flung it at her feet. Then she went shivering into the cottage, a happy, but an anxious girl. The little, cheerful parlor looked like a paradise, in contrast with the howling storm without. She closed the door, and went to her long mirror to arrange her disordered hair. She blushed, as she looked at herself:

"The scamp has put my hair in a pretty fix," she said, with her mouth full of hair pins. "And my lips, too—he has kissed them right red. Oh, I am so happy! I wish Clara was here. Hark, to that dreadful storm! I hope nothing will happen to him this night."

She shook out her skirts, as she gave a backward glance into the mirror, and then walked to the fire and stood gazing into it thoughtfully, with her hands clasped before her.

"How dearly he has loved me all this time. What a perfect actor he has been. These wretches! will they dare to arrest him? He said he would never have put on disguise, only that he hoped to win me. He would have delivered himself up, and demanded a trial when he heard of it, if old Hugo had not prevented him. What a strange old man! What makes him take such an interest in Henry? How they deceived me in the cave. They knew each other the whole time, and had traversed every part of it together. He is the very old man that was seen in the haunted house, I verily believe

They must have some secret passage into the old manor house through the floor: that explains the whole thing. How Henry must have enjoyed that scene, disguised as Doctor Mosely, when the Reverend Mr. Delaplaine received the thrashing in hunting for Henry Lansing's ghost. And then Mrs. Bounce, poor woman, she was really in love with the doctor, who was attending his own brother. Gurty will be almost as happy as I am. And Colonel Lansing, poor old gentleman, he will die from joy. And I am to be his daughter; so soon, too. Dear, dear fellow! he is right; he will be imprisoned a long time, at the best, and I must be his wife, so that I can go to him in prison."

A shade passed across her sweet face: "Oh, if it would only turn out in such a way that I would not have to expose *him!* That is too dreadful to think of."

The mourner sank into her chair before the fire, and studied long and deeply the whole mystery of the murder with the fire-light dancing upon her serious face. The scales of justice held two lives in suspense. Blonde could rescue either one, but not both. She had no shade of doubt as to which one she would choose to save. Her glorious betrothed young husband of twenty-five years would be saved. But the *other*, oh! the *other*, how could she testify against *his* life. She prayed inwardly and earnestly, as she sat late before the fire in her profound reverie.

While Blonae pondered the subject before the fire of the little parlor, with her Newfoundland sleeping beside her, her lover was rapidly hastening along the highway against the storm, and towards his father's estate, Myrtle Dell. He had adjusted his disguise again to his face and head before leaving the parlor of the cottage, and no one could now imagine that the favorite Doctor Mosely, who had won the hearts of hundreds of patients, was the well remembered daredevil and heir of the Lansing manor. In pursuing his medical studies in Europe, he had come across this admirable disguise, and had already, in the space of a few months, by its use, secured an enviable medical reputation among many of the families of C—— who were actually hunting for him to try him for his life. His purpose in assuming his disguise was merely to secure Blonde's heart. But old Hugo, his mother's friend, had, at an early day, met him in the cave, and advised him to wear the mask until the whole testimony against him could be sifted by his friends. Henry Lansing was astonished to hear of the murder and still more bewildered by the evidence which had accumulated against himself. How little did the faithful servant, Norman Prince, dream that his master, the doctor, who had climbed the vines of the piazza to Gurty's room, was actuated by eagerness to save his own cherished brother's life.

Dr. Mosely hurried along towards the brown gate of the manor, with the fierce, chilling wind beating against him, and at times causing him to pause in the road from its exhausting violence. The darkness was now impenetrable to the eye, and he was obliged to pick his way carefully along to avoid falling off the bridges which spanned the little streams. When he had at length toiled on as far as the manor gate, and passed into the myrtle dell, it seemed as if the quintessence of darkness and of gloom had enshrouded him. He groped along, however, through the long and difficult avenue, and where it terminated he caught a glimpse of a light shining from a window of the manor house. He felt confident it came from the private study of his father, Colonel Lansing. But that was not at present his destination, so he left the light at his right hand and wandered off through the meadows in search of the old and deserted manor house. His familiarity with the localities proved of little service to him now, but after a tedious groping and an occasional collision with a chestnut tree he succeeded in reaching the haunted house.

He placed his hand upon the wall of the old ruin and felt his way around the gables and doors of the house till he reached the open door in the southern gable, opposite to which his sister, Mrs. Bounce, had maintained her watch in the fever marsh. He groped up the stairs till he reached the enormous old Dutch chimney in a room of the second story. At the angle made by the chimney and the wall of the room he placed his hands against the bricks, and pushed gently against the chimney. A portion of the brick wall yielded, and swung inward noiselessly on hidden hinges. It was a small brick door, barely large enough to allow his body to pass into the inside of the chimney. His foot struck upon the topmost stone of a narrow flight of stone steps leading down the huge chimney into the very foundation of the building. He closed the secret brick door behind him, and reached his hand up over his head till it met a lantern on a little shelf above him. Beside the lantern he found matches. His lantern soon was shedding its rays on the narrow stone steps on which he stood. Its light revealed an iron ring upon the brick door, by which it could be pulled open from the inside of the chimney. He saw that the small door was accurately pushed back to its place before he descended the steps. This secret passage had been adroitly constructed by his ancestor when the chimney and the manor house were built. The original proprietor of the manor being aware of the narrow opening in the rock under the foundation, which admitted one person at a time to the great cavern below, had no doubt constructed this passage for the secret conveyance of valuables, or even his family, to the cavern in the troublesome times of Indian warfare and outrage. Colonel Lansing was unaware of its existence. It had been forgotten by the successive families of the manor in the lapse of years; and Henry Lansing had discovered it in his boyhood, when he loved to prowl so much alone in the ruins of the deserted old house. It was the secret cause of his youthful and prolonged visits to the old ruin, and his adventurous disposition had made him familiar with every tunnel and pitfall of the subterranean wonder. In one of its outlets in the mountain above the town of C——, he had evaded the two horsemen who were unaccountably following his flight, and when his pursuers were baffled, he emerged again on the side of the mountain and turned Black Hawk loose. Then he made his way at his leisure to the seaboard, and crossed the ocean to bury his disappointment at his refusal by Blonde Grayson in an intense pursuit of his professional studies in Germany. When he encountered old Hugo in the cavern upon his return, he supposed the old man had discovered its existence in the course of his geological researches in the neighborhood of C——. It was in one of the outlets of this cavern in the mountain, that Black Hawk was now concealed. Fearing that his night ride on his favorite steed would be prevented by the watch that might be kept up at the old ruin, he had ridden the horse off to the mountain to secure him for his own use.

Doctor Mosely descended the narrow stone steps till he reached the solid rock on which the massive foundations of the old manor rested. Here a short and abrupt turn in the steps which were cut in the rock, brought him to the narrow cavity in the roof of the cavern. He descended the small iron ladder, which was now revealed, a distance of twenty feet, till he stood on the solid floor of the cave. It was only a small chamber, leading to a more extensive cavern beyond. Swinging his lantern ahead to avoid a mysterious looking pit in the centre of this chamber, he passed slowly along till he reached a great crack in the rocky wall, through which his body was just able to pass. This fracture at a distance of forty feet, brought him to one of the great stalactite chambers of the cave It was a lofty and extensive cavern, but full of dangerous chasms in the floor which required his constant attention to avoid. It opened into a safer chamber, still deeper under the earth. He had been descending every foot of his way until he reached the level rocky floor of this safer cave. A great light now attracted his attention. It arose from a dozen flaming torches thrust into the fissures of the rocky wall. In the midst of them, and seated on the floor, was old Hugo. The doctor gave him a saluting yell, which echoed along the cavern, and moaned away through the distant caves like sullen thunder. The old geologist looked up and recognized him with his lantern. Then he went on again, beating with his steel hammer, the fragments of the rock before him, until the physician came up to his side. He desisted from his work, and said, with his harsh, stern voice:

"Well, boy, what luck?"

The physician sat down beside him with his lantern, and said,

"Splendid!—we are to be married to-morrow night, sir."

"Ho! ho!" growled the old man; "you're Lansing all over—impetuous, hasty. The girl was thinking of you—waiting for you, likely."

"You're right," replied the doctor, deeming it best to accept old Hugo's brief English statement of the lady's condition of mind. He said no more, but sat watching the geologist, who commenced work again with his hammer. He knew the old man liked to carry on conversation in his own style. Presently old Hugo ceased examining his fossils, and asked,

"Was the girl troubled about the charge against you?"

"Not on my account. She says if they try me for my life, she can swear to the person of the real murderer. She won't tell me who it is, but she says positively she can testify clearly against the man on the trial. She is mysterious about the matter, and says she prays God that she will not have to testify at all. She declares her testimony cannot be controverted. Strange, is it not? But she is a determined character—clear and true of intellect, and I believe her implicitly. She will be my wife to-morrow night—I certainly ought to trust her."

"Why didn't she testify, then, before the coroner's jury?" growled the old man.

The physician replied,

"I'm sure I cannot surmise. Why, for the same reason,

I suppose, that she does not wish to testify now, except to save my life. She has some object in shielding him as long as she can. She is firm as this rock about the matter. She is concealing the affair out of principle, and I admire her for it. I would not press her further about it for the world."

"She's a pious girl, I'll vouch for that," said the stern voice. "She was tried sorely in this cave. She knew where her God was. Well, well, I'm glad your case looks so much better And so the girl is independent enough to marry you without a fine bridal dress—she can't make one by to-morrow night, I'll venture. Many girls think the dress is the chief part of the wedding. I congratulate you, young man—you've done well."

The old man remained silent examining his broken fragments of the rock, and occasionally pointing out to his companion the well defined wings and heads of his fossil insects. The keener eyes of the physician detected formations which escaped the geologist's eye, and the old man laid them aside for inspection by daylight.

Then Dr. Mosely said—

"I have fulfilled my part of the contract. The young lady is engaged to be my wife—now, what is your secret?"

Old Hugo reflected a few minutes. Then he drew from his bosom an old leather money-pouch, and took from it a queerly fashioned miniature of a young girl, and handed it to the doctor.

"Why, that resembles my own dear mother's face—but it is so young; where did you get that?" said Dr. Mosely, in astonishment.

"She gave it to me—your mother—she was only fourteen years old, then—don't it resemble your brother Gurty?"

The old man looked anxiously at the physician's face for his reply.

"Most assuredly it does—it's the perfect picture of Gurty; but where in creation did you obtain possession of it. The case looks ancient—it's brass, I believe."

Old Hugo looked delighted at this reply. Then he said,

"Your mother gave that to me when she was only fourteen—she was very fond of me in those days."

The doctor replied,

"I know she visited you when you were sick before I went abroad. But I never knew she was so intimate with you as that. I wonder she never showed that picture to me."

"Boy, your thoughts are rambling. Your mother gave that

picture to me when she was fourteen years of age. She did not know who I was when you were here on the manor. Henry Lansing, I am your mother's uncle, Stephen Van Dam. Did you never hear of her uncle who ran away when she was a girl, on account of wounding a comrade and leaving him for dead? I am that uncle Your mother loved me dearly. When I returned long years afterwards, she did not know me, and I never revealed my real name to her. But she came to me when I was suffering, for pure humanity's sake, and she made me love God. No one in this town of C—— knows who I am. I charge you to reveal my real name to no one. I am your mother's uncle; for her kindness to me I intend to divide a large pile of gold between you and Gurty. It is concealed in this cave, and I intend to show you the place presently. Gurty is just like her—the same blue eyes, the same expression. I will give him the larger portion of my money. You will be the heir of the manor, and I shall give you less. But you shall have enough. I trust so firmly in your honor that though I give you the smaller portion, I shall make you the guardian of the remainder, to preserve for your brother until he is of legal age. You and your brother are to be the sole keepers of my secret and of my gold. Will you promise to keep inviolate my confidence while this poor old body lasts?"

Doctor Mosely was astounded, but he found words at last:

"My mother's favorite uncle, Stephen Van Dam! This then explains your interest in me. Give me both hands, old man. God bless your old soul! I don't know what to say. Yes! I'll guard your secret, and you too when that aged body is too feeble to travel under the earth. But why in the name of all that is marvelous did you keep this from mother? She clung to your memory with more tenacity than any friend she had ever known. But she believed that you were dead."

The old man answered sorrowfully,

"I was bitter then towards the world. Every one seemed determined to persecute and torment me with their religious cant and ignorance. I felt like shunning the society of my species. Your mother made a Christian of me by her holy example. Stand by her standard, boy. It was love—pure love of God the Creator. I never could reveal myself to your mother. It would have entailed on me habits of life and society for which my wandering life had unfitted me. It is better as it is. But my old heart warms towards her boys. Come with me. Life is uncertain I will give you something to buy your wedding gift with. I shall feel anxious, boy, until you are safely out of this murder business. Come along—it will relieve my mind when the money is in your keeping."

He placed his hand on the doctor's shoulder and raised himself to his feet. Then extinguishing all the torches but one, he seized that and led the way towards the stone steps in the chimney of the old manor house. His companion followed with the lantern, bewildered at the destiny which offered him in a single night a wife and a fortune.

Old Hugo steadily tramped on with his torch in one hand and his steel hammer in the other. The intervening caves and passages were soon passed, and the old man led the way up the iron ladder again. Standing at length on the rock upon which the foundation of the house stood, he removed one of the stone steps and exposed a cavity which was crammed entirely full of yellow gold coins of the dates of his boyhood, mingled with silver coin and diamonds. It was the proceeds of the sale of an immense estate, and he had accepted in payment everything of the nature of coin and portable jewels that he could get for his lands. The treasure looked dazzling as the glare of the torch flashed upon the incongruous heaps of valuables in the large cavity under the stairs. The astonished physician exclaimed,

"There must be half a million of dollars in that pile, at east."

"Plenty more than that, boy, when you come to fish to the bottom of that hole. There is considerably over a million. Remember, one-third of it belongs to you—the remainder you must guard for your young brother. I have already removed enough of the money to keep me comfortable for the few remaining years of my life. It is invested in stocks, and the interest is all that I require. The stocks I have provided for by my will. They will go to some one else whom you have no concern with. Come, slide the stone back again—your young sinews are better able than mine. If you stare in that way at the coin, you will forget to lay up treasures in Heaven. Come! on with the stone. My part of the contract is now fulfilled. If you intend to enjoy real happiness from that treasure, you must imitate your holy mother. Stand by God's poor, my boy. Then you will be investing your funds where God will pay you the interest. Send me over, by Norman Prince, tomorrow morning, some of your fluid preparation for my back. The ulcer is running again—it will kill me after a while. How the storm rages up above there. It seems like leaving a comfortable home to go out from this cave on such a wild night.

One thing more, boy—don't forget to get me a picture of your mother, just as she looked before her death."

"I will try, Uncle Stephen," replied the delighted doctor; "if I don't succeed, Miss Grayson has one now which I will persuade her to give me."

He had replaced the stone step and commenced to follow old Hugo up the secret passage in the old chimney. The torch was extinguished and left on the rock for future use. Before they reached the iron ring of the brick door, the physician informed his uncle that he was about to reveal himself to his father, Colonel Lansing, and invite him to his wedding on the following night. As old Hugo desired to remain unknown, he could not be expected to attend.

Extinguishing the lantern and replacing it upon the little shelf, the doctor opened the small brick door and entered the darkness of the upper room, closely followed by the old man. The old tenement was shaken to its foundation by the violence of the storm. The wind roared through the unglazed casements, and the leafless vines which clung to the gables flapped against the window casings in the fury of the rushing blast. With difficulty the two groped their way out of the ruin and faced the storm. When they arrived at the manor brook they separated, the old man heading for the myrtle dell, and the physician directing his steps towards the new manor house.

The aged proprietor of the manor was seated at the desk of his private study, engaged in writing, when his visitor was announced. The lamp-light which illumined his venerable and aristocratic features, revealed at once the change effected in his appearance by his recent disappointment in regard to his son Henry. The wrinkles were deeper, his frame less erect, and his eagle eyes were sunken farther back in his head. The doctor's heart was touched. He advanced to the old man's side and shook him warmly by the hand. He drew a chair close beside Colonel Lansing, and removing the shawl from his neck, placed it with his hat on the floor beside his seat. He replied to the old gentleman's surprised salutation thus:

"You may readily believe that nothing but pressing business would have brought me here on such a night. You have often expressed confidence and esteem for me. I have something to communicate to you which will certainly startle you. It is not sad or unfortunate—far otherwise. Will you be perfectly prepared to receive intelligence which is full of happiness for you, I must believe? No! you must not start in that way, and grow excited. I must feel assured that you will be perfectly calm and self-possessed. There is one whom you earnestly desire to see—is there not?"

"Yes, yes—Henry, my beloved son—my lost boy. What about him—tell me!" exclaimed the trembling old father.

The physician folded his arms calmly, and leaning back in his chair, said resolutely:

"I cannot tell you to-night, Colonel Lansing. You are growing excited—too much so. Calm yourself, sir. You believe me to be your friend. I have some rights then in the matter. You must wait patiently therefore until I tell you in my own way what has become of your son. All is right with him, I assure you."

"You know then," said the eager old gentleman, rising to his feet in excitement. "where my boy is!"

The physician made no reply, but pointed quietly to the Colonel's chair. The old father detected the expression of unconquerable determination in the doctor's eye, and resumed his seat.

"Colonel Lansing, your son Henry is not many miles off. He is coming to see you, all in good time. Will you wait patiently a few days for him to make his appearance on the manor?"

"What can I do, Doctor Mosely? I am helpless—I *must* wait—but do, for God's sake, tell me at once where my boy is. Yes, yes, I will wait patiently. Did he tell you that he would return to me—to me, his old father, who has never enjoyed a peaceful day since he left?"

"Yes," replied the doctor calmly, "he did say those very words—and he is now hidden in the town of C——. He is so disguised, however, that you never would recognize him on the face of the earth. Colonel Lansing, will you excuse me for asking you for a glass of wine? I am chilled to the bone—you have little idea how cold it is out."

"Wine!" exclaimed the old gentleman. "Certainly, all the wine in my cellar is at your disposal. But you will not be cruel enough to make an old father wait till that wine comes?"

"Indeed I will," responded the imperturbable doctor, rising from his seat and walking to the window to look out upon the storm. He remained there silently until the bell was rung and the servant had returned with a bottle of red wine. It was full fifteen minutes before the wine and glasses were placed on the table before Colonel Lansing, the old gentleman meanwhile sitting in his chair and wondering what made the doctor so mysterious. Then the physician insisted upon the Colonel taking a glass of wine with him. When the empty glasses were finally placed upon the table, the physician said coolly,

"Your son is hidden on the manor this very night—but he is perfectly comfortable—rest assured. Please send for Gurty. I wish him to be present when I communicate to you the identical place where your son is concealed."

It was evident his visitor was not to be hurried, so the Colonel directed the servant, who again answered the bell, to summon Gurty Lansing. The younger brother, after a few minutes' time, made his appearance, arrayed in a blue velvet smoking cap and dressing-gown of the same color. After a brief conversation, the physician drew from his mouth a thin plate of gold, curiously twisted, which had been fitted to his teeth, and handed it to Gurty, saying,

"Do you recognize my voice now, Gurty?"

The youth exclaimed in amazement, "It is my brother Henry's voice—but who are you?"

A familiar laugh met their ears, and the old gentleman, who was staring at the physician's countenance, said with a bewildered air, "The eyes are like Henry's, too—what does all this mean? Who in the devil are you, any way?"

The same familiar laugh ensued, and the doctor said,

"I am Henry Lansing—at least, I am so much like him that you all can't tell the difference. What would you say if my beard should fall off? Come now, father, is it impossible for your keen eyes to recognize your own son? I give you all fair notice, now, that my beard is going to drop to the floor. Why, Gurty, can't you tell your own brother's voice?"

"It is Henry Lansing," exclaimed the astonished brother, "with his hair turned brown, and his beard, too. What is all this?"

The beard and wig fell suddenly to the floor at the doctor's touch upon the hidden springs, and the laughing, brilliant countenance of the lost heir was revealed.

"Eh! What, my boy! my lost Henry! Thanks to the adorable name of Almighty God!" exclaimed the proprietor of the manor, as he took his long lost son in his arms, and wept with joy.

But Gurty, the dreamer, the artist, what was he doing all the while?

Standing with his soft white hands clasped before him, and listening to the familiar music of that dear voice, which told him of a recovered brother's love, and a dream of life fulfilled. He could not realize his happiness, till Henry left the father and clasped the brother in his arms. The windows shook with the rushing fury of the night storm, but within the lamp-lit study Peace spread her happy wings.

CHAPTER XXXIV.

Again the long crimson window curtains of the little parlor were drawn together, and pinned closely against the night air. The parlor door was locked, and three anxious figures were collected in front of the long mirror.

"Now, my darling angelic old maid," said one with violet eyes and dark curls, arrayed in a white silk dress low enough in the neck to reveal whiteness and plumpness, and with a wreath of white roses about her temples, "now you look ready for your flight to the happy land. Superb!—no, that word won't do—it is not ethereal enough. I have heard you called 'the lily of C——.' Now you look like the lily of heaven.—Kiss me before all the sweetness of those lips is stolen by *him*. Ha! ha! that brings out the color among the dimples—does it? Look here, Kitty—see this new style of white lily with a red flush in it."

This last remark was addressed to a young girl of fifteen summers on the opposite side of the bride, who was stooping to arrange a long wreath of natural white lilies which circled downwards almost to the hem of the snowy muslin bridal dress which trailed on the floor. The young bridemaid, who wore white muslin also, and a slender fillet of tiny white rose-buds about her remarkably heavy braids of dark brown hair, turned and glanced her brown eyes at the face of the bride in the glass. She smiled, and said, as she resumed her attentions to the lilies on the skirt,

"Mrs. St. Clair, wouldn't that be sweet if it would only last? But you'll see nothing but snow, I'll venture, when the ceremony commences—there, my wreath is done at last. Wouldn't that veil appear better," she timidly suggested, passing behind the bride, "if it was drawn a trifle farther this way? Such hair is seldom seen as that shade of gold. It seems a pity to hide so much of it—don't you think so?"

Mrs. St. Clair glanced at Blonde a few seconds before she replied,

"We can try it your way, at least—it is easy enough to change it."

When the position of the bridal veil was changed, the taste of the young school-girl was acquiesced in. She had just donned long dresses, and rejoiced in the pet name of Kitty Van Vorst. She was not tall, but slight and graceful, her large brown eyes full of pathos and sweetness, her small lips curling like two red rose leaves, and her fair face brightly tinted with the flush of health and excitement. The exuberant growth of her brown hair was wonderful, so much so that it was a puzzle always at the toilet to decide upon its arrangement. She was the sister of the Miss Van Vorst who rode with Blonde Grayson for the golden cup at the manor races. She was Gurty Lansing's "*flame.*" This accounted for her being selected to attend the bride at the secret wedding. She belonged to a wealthy old family of the neighborhood, and her easy carriage and manner, for one so young, had quickly attracted the admiration of the Adonis of the manor. She was Gurty's dream. Her own sentiment was expressed in the brighter flush of her cheek and the drooping timidity of her young brown eyelashes when the blue-eyed and flaxen-haired youth approached. The young artist's room at the manor was full of studies of the various styles and profiles of her sweet young face. All the lilies and roses which appeared on the dresses and about the little parlor, had come from her father's conservatory. In complicity with the gardener she had secretly stripped the greenhouse of its choicest white flowers for the private night wedding. She had stolen into the cottage after dark, lugging an enormous basket of them, to the surprise of Blonde and her friends, saying fearlessly,

"I have been robbing father's green-house, but what on earth are flowers made for but weddings? Look at those white lilies. I cut every one in the conservatory that I could lay my eyes on. Don't be concerned that the wedding will be exposed. I left the door on the street unlocked, and they will think some burglar or other dreadful thing has been in there stealing."

When Mrs. St. Clair and the young girl had arranged the bride's dress and hair to their satisfaction, they stood aside, and directed Blonde to inspect herself in the glass, and see if everything was consonant with her own ideas of propriety and taste. The desire of the disguised groom that the marriage ceremony should occur so soon after their engagement, had prevented any other bridal preparations than such as Mrs. St.

Clair and Blonde could hasten in a day. A formal bridal dress was out of the question. But the wardrobe of the once affluent bride furnished costly party dresses enough to select from. The mystery and uncertainty attending the whole affair, the serious question as to what would be the result of Henry Lansing's trial for murder, and the secret wedding at night, rendered the three occupants of the little parlor nervous and excited to the highest pitch.

But there she stood at length before the mirror, dressed, thoughtful, and waiting for the coming of the bridegroom.

Twenty-eight summers had passed over the head of that fair girl, and still were her charms as fascinating as at twenty. Care and experience had not dimmed her beauty. Her caution and distrust of life's alliances had not soiled the purity and purposes of her heart. And there at last she stood in her ripe loveliness, possessed of a yearning fondness and passion for a young man of twenty-five, whose wife she expected to be in less than an hour. In one hour she would be subject to the will of another for a lifetime. She had no misgivings for the future. Years had confirmed his first love for her, and now she longed to make him happy. But he was charged with the foul crime of murder, and at any moment he might be torn from her arms by the officers of the law. She knew that a legal gentleman of the highest reputation in his profession had commenced that very afternoon to search for all the testimony which it was alleged was ready to be established against Henry Lansing, with a view of advising him whether or not it would be dangerous for him to announce himself in his true character and name at once; and yet she felt conscious that when the trial came on, her own evidence would save him beyond all question, should it prove to be necessary for her to step forward in his defense. It was this anxiety that her own testimony might be requisite, which gave a shade of seriousness to her fair face as she stood before the mirror. Could it be possible that a Christian maiden, mindful of God's law, could hesitate to enter a court of justice and swear away the life of one who had mercilessly flung a strong man, murdered and bleeding, to the earth? Did not the blood of a fellow-being call to Heaven for vengeance? Could she, the graceful lily of C——, a light of a Christian church, refuse to do so plain and manifest a duty to society? Strange hesitancy for one who loved God's law and the well being of society. But the girl had a will and a conscience of her own. Had Henry Lansing never returned, or even now if it should be possible for him to escape without her assistance, her lips would be sealed with the reserve of the cold grave. She firmly believed the law would hang that murderer between earth and heaven. But she, in the clearness and purity of her heart, would take counsel of none in this trying state of the case except of God in prayer. To save Henry Lansing's life she would testify ; not otherwise. Torture could not otherwise wring from her the confession of what she knew. Principle, a firm conviction of duty, held its warning iron finger pressed to her lips, and she was silent. She was no masculine woman with a remarkable forehead and strong, hard lips that could knit themselves into a resolute, compressed firmness to carry out a stern duty. No ! She stood before the mirror in her trailing bridal dress a fair, gentle woman, with soft, sweet lips, a loving, but mysterious eye of blue, and a gentle heart that intended to follow Henry Lansing lovingly through life, palliating his faults as they might manifest themselves, and leading him by her goodness to love her God and her church, that they might live and reign together at last in Heaven.

But the mystery of her silence is not yet.

There she stood, a waiting bride. The sombre drapery which she had worn for the dead had fallen to the floor. Hereafter all mourning for her father would be hidden in her heart. Another duty was glimmering before the daughter ; the holy duty of a wife.

The low-necked, misty-looking muslin revealed her white throat and her gently rounded, gently sloping shoulders and timidly her rising and falling bust. Her round, white arms were bare. At the wrist white lava bracelets were clasped, and her tapering fingers, yet ungloved, wore the pearl and diamond ring of her engagement, the brother's pearl ring, and the chased gold ring of her dead mother. From her slender waist the snowy muslin swept to the floor, wreathed and festooned with the beautiful lilies presented by the young bridemaid, Kitty Van Vorst. The fresh lilies formed a fringe for the short sleeves of her dress, and a wreath of the same flowers was twined through her rippling golden hair. From this lily wreath flowed away the bridal veil ; and Mrs. St. Clair's gift, pearl and diamond ear-rings, fashioned in the form of lilies, were pendant from her ears. White slippers, slender and dainty, occasionally peeped out from the misty hem of her muslin dress as she turned before the mirror to satisfy herself that all was right at last

Happy dreams are in that moment of a woman's existence.

God grant her for all the after disappointment and grief the greater glory beyond the stars.

Mrs. St. Clair, with her quick, flying footstep, gathered up the mourning robe and the scattered articles of the toilet, and conveyed them away to the snow-white bedroom which she had craved the privilege of adorning and arranging for the bridal chamber without interference or inspection from Blonde.

While the bride and the young Kitty Van Vorst saw that the little parlor was arranged, and the flower-wreathed cake and the glistening decanters placed on the side table for the expected guests, it occurred to Blonde to examine her floral interpreter to learn the language of the flowers in their wreaths of white. She said, suddenly:

"Do you know the language of any of these beautiful white flowers, Kitty? It has just occurred to me that we ought to find out, for the curiosity of the thing. Our wreaths are different. Here is my book of flowers. Come here, on the lounge with me, and read the symbolical meaning of them. We have some time to wait yet. Wasn't it fortunate my sending away my maid to visit her sister at the time I did? She is becoming too prying in her disposition, and I would not have her in the house to-night on any consideration. Her sister lives somewhere near old Rosy's garden. Come now; what is the language of my wreath?"

Kitty Van Vorst sat down beside the bride, and found "lily" in the interpreter.

"It's very appropriate for a bride," she said. "White lily signifies *purity* and *beauty*. Now what is mine? Something frightfully flattering, I've no doubt, and consequently very inappropriate. Here it is. White rose-bud; that's my wreath. It signifies 'Too young to love.' Indeed I'm not," she exclaimed.

Blonde laughed and said,

"That's candid of you, Kitty, to say the least—that is, if my eyes have not deceived me."

"Oh! mercy!" exclaimed the young girl, blushing up to her very eyes; "I didn't mean *that*; indeed, I didn't mean anybody in particular. I assure you I didn't. Who do you mean? I only said I was capable of loving. You never saw anything. What can you mean?"

Her confusion increased at every word she uttered. Blonde laughed heartily and said,

"Your eyelashes droop sometimes when somebody comes—that is all—you know, you sweet little witch; but I won't tease you. Find what Clara's wreath signifies; it must be something like yours, for they are full white roses."

Kitty Van Vorst, still blushing deeply, turned over the leaves of the book and read:

"Rose, white—why! I declare, its language is 'sadness.' Is not that strange? Why do you start so?"

The bride looked uneasy, but she regained her calmness and said,

"Read on. What is the verse connected with it?"

Kitty read:

> "We have long dreamed of happiness, long known
> Joys which were more than mortal, long have felt
> The bliss of mingled hearts and blended souls;
> And long have thought the vision was eternal:
> It vanishes, and now I am a wretch,
> And what will be thy sorrows none can tell."

"What can that all mean?—it is gloomy enough, why do you shudder so? You are pale—I hope you don't place any faith in these books. I'm sure I don't, after what is said of *my* wreath."

The agitated bride made no response. Inexpressibly sad and dejected, she looked down, with her hands clasped before her. Before she could make any reply, the tramping of feet sounded on the piazza, and then a knock at the front door. She whispered to Kitty,

"I charge you to mention nothing of this to Mrs. St. Clair. She is a little given to superstition—indeed we all are, for that matter—but don't say a word to her about the wreaths or their language. You go to the door, and see if it is any one proper to be admitted—you know whom to admit."

Kitty Van Vorst looked puzzled at all this. But then she knew nothing of Clara's dream about her mother's grave, and Henry Lansing's unexpected appearance in the cemetery. She carefully approached the front door of the cottage, and opened it slowly till she recognized her family physician. It was Dr. Mosely. The physician enquired for Blonde, but Kitty informed him that the mistress of the cottage was engaged, and could see no visitor that evening. The bride recognized the voice, and went herself to the door.

"Why, Kitty, have you forgotten?—come in, doctor."

Henry Lansing entered the hall, and the door was immediately locked behind him. The young girl was astounded when he entered the parlor, and sitting beside the bride on the lounge, removed his wig and beard, and appeared as the long-lost and hunted heir of the manor.

Mrs. St. Clair was informed of his presence, and coming out of the little bed room, was warmly greeted by the handsome groom, who had been so attentive to herself and child during their illness, in his disguise. She was an impulsive, ardent soul, and the heir had always been a favorite of hers, so that her brief welcome and conversation could be but charming. But she soon returned to her secret work in the bridal chamber, and her friend observed a troubled expression cross her lovely face as she went out. Mrs. St. Clair was evidently worrying herself about Henry Lansing being the cause of her mother's unknown sufferings being exposed. She could not shake off the superstitious influence of her dream. But the few guests who were to witness the secret marriage, soon came in, and everything but the ceremony was temporarily forgotten.

The rector of St. Paul's, who was to officiate on the occasion, soon entered the parlor, and was introduced to his successful rival. Then followed the Reverend Thomas Delaplaine, who took the son of his holy friend in his arms, and wept the tears of a warm and generous nature. Then came Colonel Lansing, Gurty, and Carl Grayson. Old Rosy stole in, at last. She was the first person to whom Henry Lansing had revealed himself upon his return. The ceremony was soon arranged, for all were conscious of the necessity of hurrying through with the matter, as secretly and expeditiously as possible. It was pretty generally known that the officers of the law were hunting diligently for the suspected murderer of Hartwell. Carl Grayson stood up with Mrs. St. Clair, and Gurty Lansing with the young and blushing Kitty Van Vorst. The lily of C—— was soon declared to be the wife of the dashing and gifted heir of the manor. The cake and the wine circulated freely, and for a few happy moments all forgot the hazard of Henry Lansing's position. The bride was the only one who felt no concern for his safety; secretly conscious of the real criminal and secure in the evidence which she could bring to the trial, she gave way to the happiness of the hour, and the consciousness of being now united for life to the idol of her dreams. When all were gone but her brother and Mrs. St. Clair, she sat in her arm chair before the blazing fire on the hearth, holding the hand of her husband on one side and that of Clara on the other. The days that were passed, and the hopes of the future, were cheerfully discussed, till the great clock of C—— warned Mrs. St. Clair and all of the lateness of the hour. Then Blonde and her friend retired to the bridal chamber, which had been ornamented with flowers, literally from top to bottom, and Mrs. St. Clair continued with her for a long time, in the earnest intercourse of friends whose intimacy and confidence had become cemented by the experience of years, and of trials shared together. Then Clara left her, and announced to Henry Lansing that his bride awaited his coming. The heir lingered with the violet eyed beauty for a moment, before the parlor fire, which flashed upon his happy eyes, roving and beautiful, to say,

"God bless you for the love and constancy which have brightened the pathway of my darling Blonde. When this unfortunate affair is all cleared up, we shall have glorious times on the old manor, and I expect you to rank there with your family as the nearest and dearest friends we have in the world." He bowed, gallantly kissing the soft white hand which he held in his own. Then the door of the bridal chamber closed upon him for the night.

CHAPTER XXXV.

The gentle breath of May whispered over the meadows of Myrtle Dell. The cheering sun glanced from the rippling manor brook, and warmed the hearts of the delicate young leaves upon the branches. The brilliant green of the fields stretched away in the distance over valley and rise of ground, and above the great expanse of the emerald carpet, the early spring birds were flitting their musical flights from tree to tree, bearing the slender materials for their tiny nests in the branches. The great gardens of the manor were alive with workmen. The flower beds were rapidly assuming shape and neatness; the walks were being cleared of the accumulated winter rubbish, and the glass roofs of the conservatories were opened for a few hours each day to the genial influence of the midday air and sun. On every side were evidences of the industry which would soon have the great estate in order and comfort for the summer. The old manor house yet remained cheerless in the landscape, covered with its net of bare, leafless vines. But the new manor house, with its lofty colonnade, was alive with enjoyment and visitors.

The warm spring sun had tempted a party from C—— to ride out for a call upon the venerable Colonel Lansing. Judge Peyton's dashing equipage had brought out the visitors.

Mrs. Doctor Mosely (for by that title she was still known to the citizens of the town,) was seated beside the gray-haired proprietor on the great piazza of the manor house, in her winter velvet bonnet, and her brown cloth mantle, with her gloved hand resting confidentially on the old gentleman's arm. She was communicating to him the happy intelligence that she expected soon to be a mother. Seated on the steps of the piazza, was a little girl in a scarlet cloak and with a white velvet flat pressed upon her dancing curls. She had a long whip, cut from the shrubbery of the garden, in her little hand, with which she was beating the columns of the colonnade, and shouting, " Whoa— horsey " to her imaginary steed. Occasionally a lady on horseback, in a dark green riding habit with silver buttons, and a black feather in her green cap, would dash past the piazza, and the little girl would rise to her feet and shout,

"Don't go fast, pretty mamma; let 'ittle Clara ride now."

But Mrs. St. Clair would only nod her dark curls, and wave her riding whip as she kept on over the green fields. Kitty Van Vorst, the other visitor, was standing in the distance, and learning to fire Gurty Lansing's rifle at a target which the young artist had placed for her against a chestnut tree. Half a dozen sporting dogs, fox hounds and bird pointers, were sunning themselves on the lawn in front of the colonnade or chasing one another in circles about the place. Occasionally an ambitious hound with long black ears drooping from his brown head, would attempt to attain the level of the piazza, but the little girl who stood on guard with her long whip, drove him back to the lawn with her brandished threats, and her emphatic "git out."

The coachman of Judge Peyton had driven his carriage near the manor stable in the distance, and could be seen lolling on his high seat, and flourishing his long whip lazily, as he chatted with the grooms of the stables. It was a luxury to be out in the warm sun after the tedious cold of the long winter, and all appeared to be enjoying the scene and themselves. Presently the old negro cook, Aunt Roby, waddled her fat figure from under the piazza, out onto the lawn for a comfortable sunning of herself. She chuckled with delight to see the company, and the old manor once more animated. Her eye fell upon little Clara with her long whip, and she coaxed her slowly down to the foot of the steps. Then she caught her up in her arms, whip and all, and carried her down to the manor brook to show her the speckled trout flashing their sides in the sunlight. The old servant was wondering to herself what made

Colonel Lansing so interested in Doctor Mosely's beautiful wife. As the faithful old soul held the little girl over the brook so that she could see the darting fish, her keen old eyes detected some one just emerging from the myrtle dell.

"Gorry!" she exclaimed; "Aunt Roby 'spects dat's the werry identical Norman Prince. Law! what a drefful shame to turn dat boy off. Dare's no life, no fun, no nuffin on dis place eber since he leff. Norman's real superior nigger. Lor, hab mercy on us, how de boy cums."

Other eyes had seen the phyician's horse and buggy rapidly hurrying over the meadow road.

The negro servant was sparing no horse flesh. Mrs. Mosely saw him, and stood up with anxiety to learn the cause of the unexpected coming. Mrs. St. Clair saw that something had gone wrong, and dashed up to the piazza on her steed to learn what had happened. When Norman Prince at length whirled up in front of the piazza, he was surrounded by an excited group. The poor boy was trembling with excitement as he shouted out,

"The doctor has been arrested and sent to jail. They pulled off his wig and his beard, and it's my own Mr. Henry Lansing. They put him in irons, too!"

A scene of wild confusion ensued. The carriage was ordered, and words of sorrow and anxiety uttered on every side. Colonel Lansing was dreadfully aroused. The old man trembled and muttered to himself, and seemed utterly at a loss what to do. Mrs. Mosely was the only self-possessed person in the crowd. She calmly drew from Norman Prince all the particulars of the arrest of her husband, and learned that her maid, whom she had discharged from her service, had been the means of putting the police upon Henry Lansing's track. She was conscious of the necessity of remaining calm and unexcited in her delicate position, and waited with remarkable composure for the arrival of Judge Peyton's carriage from the stables. But before the horses drove up before the piazza, another messenger appeared in the direction of the myrtle dell. It was a horseman, whose anxiety could not be held under either by his experience or his usual self-possession. It was the dignified and learned criminal lawyer, Stephen Lansing, who had been instructed during the past winter to fathom and report upon all the testimony and difficulties of his young relative's case. He now came flying up to the manor house on his gray steed, with trouble written in every line of his fine countenance. He was a powerfully built old gentleman, with a clear gray eye and mobile features, ever restless and nervous, but clear-headed and quick in his discernment of the law and the facts of cases entrusted to his learned and legal care. His hair was completely gray, showing thinly under his soft brown hat. He dismounted nervously, and made directly for Mrs. Mosely, who yet stood with her gloved hand against one of the pillars, waiting for the carriage. The lawyer's blue coat was buttoned tightly across his breast, the gilt buttons flashing in the sunlight. He jerked off his buckskin glove as he approached her, and extended his hand.

"You are wonderfully calm for this bad news. I take it for granted you are Henry Lansing's wife. He told me to hunt you out here. I never knew you were married to him until an hour ago. He said, 'Find my wife—she can furnish you further testimony in my favor.' I sincerely hope you can put me on the track of witnesses who will aid his case—it looks bad for him—very. Your maid who worked for you has produced a miniature of the murdered man found in your possession. She is going to testify that he was one of your lovers. That, my dear madam may go a great way in showing a motive for the murder—jealousy—you understand. If you have any witnesses to whom you can refer me, please do so at once, as there is a secret matter to which I must see to-day—time is precious just now."

Mrs. Mosely turned to Colonel Lansing and asked:

"Does this gentleman enjoy your full confidence in everything relating to your son?"

"Certainly—perfect confidence. He is my lawyer and kinsman," replied her husband's father.

She addressed the lawyer quietly:

"*I* am the witness in this case, sir—you will have to call me. I can point out the real murderer."

"My dearest madam," exclaimed the lawyer, but lowering his tone, for the remainder of the party were not far off, "you do not mean to say that you married Henry Lansing, and yet knew yourself to be a material witness in his favor?—you cannot mean this?"

"Why not?" she asked, with an undefined terror creeping over her.

"Why not, madam? *Because the law will not permit a wife to testify either for or against her husband in a trial for his life.* If *you* are the witness, you can be of no more service to your husband than that stone.'

She raised her delicate gloved hand to her temples, as if a

sudden dizziness overcame her, stared wildly at the lawyer in vague terror, and placed her other hand on his arm to detain him until she could speak. Her white lips struggled to whisper something, but her strength failed her and she reeled away into Colonel Lansing's arms, her hands clutching at the air, then falling helpless beside her. She had fainted at the shock. She had married to cheer and comfort him in his danger, and that one act had cost Henry Lansing his life. Her evidence was utterly powerless to save him. The court would not allow her to testify, in strict compliance with the principle of law, that husband and wife are so far deemed to be one person that the testimony of either for or against the other would not be considered free and impartial testimony.

They carried her helpless form to a bed of the manor house, and dispatched Norman Prince for a physician. Mrs. Lansing before the ensuing morning was considered in a fair way to recover; but the hopes of Colonel Lansing that he was to be a grandfather were blasted.

CHAPTER XXXVI.

THE whole county was aroused. The excitement pervaded every class of society. From an early hour in the morning a stream of vehicles of every size and description had been pouring into the little county town, bringing curious persons of both sexes to attend the criminal court. From the town of C—— the drive was short to the court house, consequently every conveyance that could be mounted on wheels was in requisition for the occasion. The father of the suspected criminal was emphatically the *first man* of the county. From his wealth, from his ancient family, from the prominent positions he and his ancestors had occupied in the State, he was styled appropriately the *first*. His broad lands supported an extensive tenantry; his public charities were visible to every eye in stately edifices for the suffering and the ignorant. The wealthy descendants of the old Dutch settlers of the State were numerous in this county, and most of them, in one branch or another of their houses, were connections of the venerable Colonel Lansing of the manor.

The mysterious circumstances attending the arrest of the

murderer were unusual. He was the most successful and devoted medical practitioner that had ever set foot in the county. In less than a year's practice he had won a wide reputation for professional skill, and had gathered a circle of powerful and earnest friends about him, who fairly wept at the idea of his arrest. This reputation and popularity had been secured under a mask which even his own family had failed to detect. The gray beard of the physician of forty-five, and his curling wig, had been torn off, and there stood the closely shaven face of the brilliant young genius of twenty-five, the most fearless horseman and the most agile and perfectly formed young man in the county. Hundreds of families of the intellectual and the opulent citizens would not exchange him as a medical adviser for the best professional name in the State. He was remembered as a wild young man, emerging from the smoke and dissipation of college life, but above meanness, unselfish and liberal. His reputation since his return from his suspicious flight, years ago, and while he was practicing under a mask, had been irreproachable. But his flight on the day of the murder, and his return years after under a mask, appeared like conscious guilt. It had leaked out, too, that under the same mask he had married "the lily of C——," a lady of whom the murdered Hartwell had been the lover. It was known that Blonde Grayson's maid had revenged herself for being discharged, by producing to the prosecuting attorney of the county her mistress' miniature of Hartwell, and by intimating to the police her suspicions that Doctor Mosely was a disguised criminal.

The suspected murderer had moreover been deemed worthy and efficient enough to preside over the affairs of a new bank of C——, with a large capital. He was the president of several literary and scientific clubs in the county, and had established himself in various ways in the highest confidence and affection of the community.

It was rumored extensively at the time of the first excitement over the body of Hartwell, that a boy named Mat Cowen had informed his schoolmates that he found near the scene of the murder Henry Lansing's fishing-spear, concealed and covered with blood. When this clue was attempted to be followed up, Mat Cowen disappeared for several weeks, and now the district attorney was unable to track him again. The boy was gone, no one knew where. His testimony was unavailable—that was certain; and the fishing-spear, which every one had counted on, was not to be found.

The prejudice against the heir of the manor was very strong.

A very large party were convinced of his guilt. His friends, however, were strengthened by accessions from the ranks of his old enemies. The kindness and skill of the physician in their own families had overturned their judgments formed at the time of his flight. Such are the selfish mutations of human nature. Self moulds and reverses the judgment.

The favor which Doctor Mosely had secured among many of the laboring class will be illustrated by the language of a poor woman to her husband a few days before the trial came on:

"Daniel, just look at my baby—don't you see my little sweet, precious child has had those spasms three times now, since that doctor was put in jail. I wouldn't give the snap of my finger for that other doctor. I won't have him in my house. Daniel, just you listen to me. It's sheer wickedness locking that gentleman up and trying him for murder, and I want you to remember one thing. You may be put on that jury. Don't you dare to offer any excuse. You go, and mind what I tell you. I never threatened you much, and then I meant it. If you don't make that jury disagree, I'll watch for a night when you are sound asleep, and I'll take that kettle of boiling hot water and scald your wicked head till the hair comes off. Now you just remember—you *shall* go if you're summoned, and you *shall* kick up a rumpus if you see it's going against that most excellent doctor. Disagree or scald—that's your choice; I swear it before my baby's God."

That juryman would have a dreadful sense of his responsibility if he should be sworn in.

As the hours of the bright June morning wore away, the scene outside of the court-house was exciting. A crowd of men and women were jammed against the side of the old stone building and the jail which adjoined it; some looking up to the inmates of the prison cells whose iron-barred windows showed on the street, and others endeavoring in vain to learn from their neighbors in front who were crowded into the hall of the building, how the trial was progressing within. Vehicles of every description were standing near the fences in long rows, and among them appeared many of the elegant private carriages of C——. Many ladies had arrived very early, and secured seats in the gallery of the court-room, nearly all of whom were partisans on the side of the heir or against him.

One stylish equipage was drawn up under the shade of a group of beech trees, and the party who had come in it from C——, still remained in the carriage. The confined and stifling air of the court-room was too exhausting for the pale, beautiful woman who sat on one of the luxurious seats, supported in the arms of a lady who had borne the name of Mary Livingston at the manor races, and to whom Blonde Grayson had presented the golden cup. The other inmate of the carriage was an elderly physician, in attendance upon the helpless invalid, Mrs. Henry Lansing. Weak and exhausted as she was, Blonde had nevertheless insisted upon being as near her husband as possible on this dreadful occasion. Her weary eyes wandered over the excited throng with a pitiful and anxious expression, and then reverted again to the crowded entrance of the court-house, as if she expected every instant to see some one announce to the crowd her husband's condemnation. The unborn child in which her heart had been centred, had been lost in her agony, and now, emaciated and hopeless, she watched for the messenger from the court-room who should convey to her Henry Lansing's and her own fate, *death.* The lawyer had informed her that the moonlight scene at the fatal maple witnessed by Norman Prince afforded no point sufficiently strong to divert attention from her husband. The mysterious citizen may have been out that night for any innocent purpose, and since the testimony in regard to the fishing spear had failed to be produced, all the suspicious night search in the hollow of the tree for the weapon, amounted to mere conjecture on the part of the negro. Alas! her hope, her life, her heaven depended on the expression of countenance of those men who stood crowded in the doors, or were clinging to the outside of the court-house windows. She recognized many faces of his friends, and the physician in her carriage pointed out the anxious faces of Henry Lansing's enemies or opponents in the matter of the murder. Her attention was chiefly directed to the face of the Reverend Thomas Delaplaine. The clergyman had secured a foothold on the water table of the building, and clung by his hands to the window shutter looking into the court-room. His face looked so cold, so hopeless, so riveted upon whatever was transpiring within. Ah! they all must be swearing away his dear life in there. Even her bosom friend, Mrs. St. Clair, was a witness, and could do nothing in the young doctor's favor, only describe the scene of the murder as it appeared to her senses from old Rosy's garden. The old flower woman herself could only add the weight of her evidence to that of the red-faced girl of the neighborhood, that Henry Lansing was somewhere near to the locality of the murderer's blow as it fell upon the head of the victim.

But the faithless maid, and the miniature must be rapidly fixing a motive upon him for the crime.

But the scene within :

Encircling the narrow box where the heir would be guarded by the officers of the court, were crowded the friends of Henry Lansing. They were many, influential, rich, poor, gathered from all grades of society, and wrought up to the highest pitch of excitement. Against them were gathered a considerable majority of the densely-packed court-room. A sensation in one corner arose. A way was being cleared. Hark! to that clank of cold iron—how dismally the sound fell upon the ears of all, "He is coming."

Amid the slowly parting crowd a face was approaching. The head was erect, firm, fearless. Short black hair curled away from his temples, and glittering black eyes, roving and beautiful, greeted the throng. A singularly pointed chin was seen, and thin lips, on which played a calm, conscious smile of innocence. A murmur of admiration ran around the room. Enemies and friends joined in it. "There is no sign of guilt in that face—look! look!"

The face of the criminal had gained a point.

But hark! to that cold sound again of iron, "clank—clank." He is fettered, for his strength and daring are well remembered by the neighbors. But the sound is dismal. Why is it? The iron of a sabre and of spurs rings with melody for the chivalrous, and the iron of the blacksmith tinkles away in the distance with the cheer of industry and life. But the same iron on a criminal! Alas! God's image fettered for whom Christ died.

Another sound and excitement was coming in another corner of the room. *Tramp, tramp, tramp*, came the ominous tread of the jurymen. The twelve men owned a human life, and a calm, earnest face was reading their countenances and their characters as they slowly filed along to their place. This gentleman sat with his legal opponent before the judge's bench. It was Stephen Lansing. His white hair circled a large bare spot on the crown of his head. His blue coat with brass buttons was, as usual, closely buttoned over his broad chest. His mobile features were in repose. But that wonderful gray eye, deep set under gray, bushy eyebrows, twinkled with brightness as he fixed its penetrating power upon the jury. He was studying physiognomy, and at the same time taxing his memory to know who of them had young men for sons of Henry Lansing's age, and who had brothers starting in the race of life.

He intended to speak to their very souls at the proper time. Finally his eye glanced at the last one of the marching twelve. Here was a study. It was *Daniel.* If clear words were ever written on a human face, they were traced distinctly there. "Disagree or scald." The poor juryman at times involuntarily raised his hand to his scalp. "It is certainly there yet, thank God!" was the covert thought. Stephen Lansing detected the unwilling juryman at once. If every other scheme should fail in summing up the evidence, he determined to address himself to that reluctant mind with all the force of his great will and reason till he wrung from him a disagreement of the jury

Squire Bramlet sat among the spectators. His wishes led him to expect the condemnation of the heir. He had secured the money on his worthless mortgage, and now desired an opportunity to secure more. If Henry Lansing should be found guilty, then he might arrange with Colonel Lansing for his escape from prison for a large bribe of gold. He felt confident that the keeper of the prison belonged to him.

While Henry Lansing was surrounded by his relations and friends, and the witnesses were sworn and proceeded to give their testimony before the Court, his pale, lovely wife in Colonel Lansing's carriage awaited the result in anguish of soul and weakness of body. Many times she raised her head of soft, wavy, golden hair from the lady's bosom, as the hours slowly passed, and whispered, "Oh! is it going on yet?" At length she closed her eyes from exhaustion and weariness, and they thought she slept. But when the physician whispered his relief at the thought of her now receiving soothing rest for her poor, suffering body, she said, "Oh, no!—there is no rest for me but the grave."

After a brief silence she whispered:

'Mary, please raise my head again, that I may see the court house, for I have a strange consciousness of something going on in there. I have an instinct that I have not utterly been deceived in the words and the promises of men. Oh! there must be nobility of character towards me and mine when I have sacrificed and suffered so much for love of them."

These strange words conveyed no meaning to her listeners, and they looked at each other as if they imagined her mind was unsettled from her illness and her troubles. They raised her, however, to a more erect position, that she might see the doors and windows of the court house. As her blue eyes rested once more on the window where the Rev. Thomas Delaplaine was clinging and looking in, she exclaimed,

"Look! look! Something has excited him."

As her companions looked away from the carriage they saw the clergyman spring into the air with a yell and land in the prison yard. At the same instant a strange sound of many voices came from the court room in unaccountable confusion. The noise grew wilder, and the intelligence of what was transpiring within reached the vast crowd without. Hark! to the wild music of joy. Cheer after cheer rolled away over the heads of the vast assembly, and the adjacent hills rang with the echoes. The Rev. Thomas Delaplaine broke from the crowd and came tearing towards the carriage in most unclerical bounds. He was too excited to wait until he reached the carriage, but shouted out,

"Glory be to God; he's acquitted."

Blonde folded her weak arms about the neck of her friend, and sobbed in her bosom. But the cheers grew wilder and louder, and from the excited crowd broke away another figure. He did not run, but flung himself on his hands and turned summer-sets, rolling over the ground like a wheel. When he reached the highway he came to his feet erect and laughed a crazy laugh, half choked with tears. Then as his feet touched the board sidewalk he broke into a regular Virginia shuffle, bringing his shoes down upon the boards with a will which started a crowd of men after him. Then he whistled a snatch of a tune, thrust his tongue into his cheek, and broke into a chuckling laugh. As the crowd gathered around him he removed his hat and bowed with inimitable grace, then ran away suddenly down the street, laughing and crying from pure joy. It was Norman Prince. But the scene within the court house was the solution of the mystery.

The prosecuting attorney on behalf of the people, had stated a strong case against Henry Lansing, which he declared himself prepared to prove. It was substantially this: That the heir of the manor was known to have been devoted to the society of Miss Grayson, of C——, and ardently seeking to obtain her hand in marriage. Under the influence of this passion, he had been known to offer himself to her. She had refused his offer, at the same time exhibiting to him the miniature of her lover, Benjamin Hartwell. Of hasty and ungovernable temper, the young man had left her house in a violent rage, and mounting his horse, had ridden off in search of his successful rival, who his charmer had informed him was just arrived in C——. Failing to discover his whereabouts, he had left his horse, and seizing his fishing spear, started off in search of his rival, who had been seen to walk off in the direction of the woods near old Rosy's garden. His first search proving unsuccessful, he had left his fishing spear in the old woman's garden, and made her a brief and excited call. Then with the same symptoms of ungovernable rage, he had left her presence, and, passing through the garden, taken his spear, and entered the woods for a still further search for Benjamin Hartwell. Meeting his rival and victim under the maples, and recognizing him from the miniature, he had a hot altercation with him, and then murdered him in cold blood, and fled the country. For years he had remained away, and returned at last only in fear and a complete disguise.

Upon this statement of his case, the district attorney had produced his witnesses, who substantially confirmed it. He failed to produce a witness as to the finding of a fishing spear, but stated that such a witness was known to the community of C—— to be in existence, and had been privately put out of the way by the friends of the prisoner, to defeat the ends of justice. The maid who had lived long with Miss Grayson, swore positively to everything necessary to prove a motive for the commission of the crime, and produced the miniature of the murdered Hartwell.

The evidence was producing a marked effect upon the jury and the audience, when suddenly a loud voice pronounced the words: "In the name of God, *stop!* this trial has gone far enough." The presiding judge looked around in surprise to the startling voice beside him. It was the Chief Justice of the Supreme Court of the State who spoke. His distinguished judicial position had secured him an invitation to sit beside the judge who was trying the case.

The proceedings were at once discontinued, and the Chief Justice requested permission to address the Court. This being granted, he descended the steps amid the most profound silence, till he stood between the jury and Henry Lansing. A thrill of horror flashed to every heart of the great throng, as the beloved Judge Peyton raised his eyes and his hand to God, and said: "As certainly as the Eternal Ruler of all things is my Judge, I declare to you that *I killed Benjamin Hartwell.* Listen to me, and credit my words for the sake of the years I have devoted to the public service, and for the name of judge I have worn untarnished among you. With Henry Lansing's fishing spear I murdered this man, and when I sought the weapon again to bury it, that this innocent young man might not suffer suspicion, it was gone from the hollow of the tree where I had first concealed it. I am here beside the innocent, that you may vindicate in my trial and person the majesty of the law. I destroyed Hartwell's life, and this was my motive.

"I had the sweetest and loveliest wife that ever fell to mortal lot, and this man outraged her. In a distant town he enticed her, under the name of my personal friend, to a lonely spot, and, in spite of her screams and yells of agony, ruined her. She came at once to my home, and died from her physical and mental distress. On her dying bed she put up her soft pure lips to mine, and, with her white arms about my neck, said, 'Husband, avenge me.'

"When I met this wretch for the first time, the weapon was in my hand. I heard again my poor wife's prayers and screams for mercy, as he dragged her to shame, and I slew him. Gentlemen, try me for the murder. I have confessed to save this boy's life."

He dropped into a chair, trembling with emotion, and a great shout went up from the audience: "Acquit Henry Lansing, and let the judge pass out, unmolested, to his home. No jury shall harm a hair of Judge Peyton's head in this county, for he did right."

A scream which chilled the blood arose upon the agitated crowd, and the form of the proud Mrs. St. Clair sank away insensible to the floor.

CHAPTER XXXVII.

"Clara, do take this child for a few minutes, till I can give Norman his instructions—there, my hair is hopelessly down now—oh! you rogue." The mother who uttered these words was seated on the great piazza of the manor house with her lap full of party invitations folded, directed and ready for delivery. Her negro servant in livery stood before her with a basket on one arm and his hat under the other. His raven-black steed stood at the foot of the steps impatiently pawing the graveled walk. The lady was giving explicit directions to the servant in regard to many of the invitations as she put them into his basket. Her little boy in petticoats, dark haired and brown eyed, looking as if he might be nearly three years of age, was climbing the back of her chair and amusing himself at pulling out her hair pins and letting down her golden hair while her attention was occupied with the servant. As Mrs. Lansing spoke he had succeeded in removing the last fastening from her wavy mass of rippling hair, and down came the whole golden flood, covering the mother like a mantle. Mrs. St. Clair caught little Henry, and ran down the steps with him towards the green lawn, laughing heartily at his mischief. At the foot of the lawn she found a young lady leaning over the railing of the little bridge and gazing sentimentally into the manor brook.

"Come, dreamer," she shouted, "let's go over to the studio and find out why he neglected his dinner, and his *especial* company to-day—I know what you are looking so solemn about—he did n't come—I think he is right, too—inspiration does n't come every day in the year—we will go over and teaze him—I wonder what he is painting now ?"

The young lady seemed reluctant to follow up this suggestion: "When he cares to see us he will come for us, I reckon."

"Nonsense, child—don't go into the sulks about such a trifle—he will come to see you after a while, and I imagine from what I have seen before, he will devote himself to you till after midnight—come along."

Mrs. St. Clair caught the young lady's arm, and started her off with her for the studio, nolens volens. She did not require a wonderful amount of urging, and forgot her vexation before they were half way to the myrtle dell. She walked along through the meadow grass holding one of little Henry's hands and Mrs. St. Clair the other. The young lady wore a light blue summer lace over white, and her uncovered head revealed a remarkable mass of heavy brown braids.

The first rise of ground after entering the Lansing manor from the myrtle dell was crowned by a small, new building of brick, standing between two great chesnut trees and built for an artist's studio. It was a one story affair, constructed in the Gothic style, and the ivy was already climbing to its eaves. It boasted of only two rooms, the southern one for a library, and the other, with its great Northern window for steady and uniform light, was the sanctum sanctorum of the artist.

At the door of the library they found the cripple Twisty seated on the single stone step busily engaged in cleaning Gurty Lansing's gun. He seemed doubtful concerning the reception they would meet. He said the artist had given him orders to admit no visitors that day. Mrs. St. Clair said she would assume all responsibility in the matter, and entrusting little Henry Lansing to Twisty's care, quietly entered the library, followed by the more timid young lady. They passed across the room to the door of the studio, which was closed. Mrs. St. Clair made a sign to her companion for silence, and cautiously pushed open the door a little way, and looked in. Then she motioned the young lady to take a secret glimpse, also. They were unnoticed by the artist, and quietly studied the scene within.

Gurty was seated at a table with his arms resting upon the cloth. His easel stood behind the table, and on its pegs rested the painting which he was contemplating with the most absorbing interest. He wore a dressing gown of orange colored silk with the border embroidered with silver leaves of the ivy form. A smoking cap of the same colored silk, with a long silver tassel, clung on one side of his wavy, flaxen hair. His exquisite blue eyes were fixed upon his finished painting. It was nearly six feet square. The scene was a cavern, illumined only by two great torches on either side of a natural white tomb of stalagmite formation. A pile of broken rocks had been raised behind the tomb, and on it sat an old man with shaggy hair and long beard and lion-like eyes leaning forward over this white table in profound study of the word of God, which was spread open before him.

The leaves of the book were held down by a small steel hammer. Above his head the pointed white stalactites were glistening in the torch lights, like thousands of angels' fingers pointing at the book. At one side of the old geologist, a few feet away, sat the figure of a boy, looking emaciated and half starved, but engaged ravenously in devouring the old man's dinner in a little basket. It was the truant, Mat Cowen. Old Hugo had found the boy wandering in the forest, and nearly dead from his exposure and hunger in the self denying effort of his young grateful heart to escape the trial of Henry Lansing for murder.

The face of the old man was striking. The artist had contrived to blend the two expressions, faith and doubt, in the intellectual countenance. He was struggling to reconcile revelation with the discoveries of geology. The subterranean silence of death was around him; the fossil creatures of the voiceless Past, suggesting an eternity of matter stretching backward, were scattered on his snow-white table; and one of them, held between his thumb and finger, had recently been the object of his study. The elements of unbelief were about him, and God was in his heart.

The dreaming artist started at a soft hand placed upon the shoulder of the orange dressing-gown, and, looking up, beheld the loving eyes of his betrothed, Kitty Van Vorst.

THE END.

www.ingramcontent.com/pod-product-compliance
Lightning Source LLC
LaVergne TN
LVHW020221110826
845151LV00003B/781
* 9 7 8 1 4 2 5 5 3 2 3 7 6 *